Sublime Economy

Over the last two centuries, artists, critics, philosophers, and theorists have contributed significantly to representations of "the economy" as sublime. It might even be said that much of the emergence of a distinctly "modern" art in the West is inextricably linked to the perception of art's own autonomy and, therefore, its privileged, mostly critical, gaze at the terrible mixture of wonder and horror of capitalist economic practices and institutions. The premise of this collection is that, despite this perceptual sharing, "sublime economy" has yet to be investigated in a purely cross-disciplinary way. *Sublime Economy* seeks to map this critical territory by exploring the ways diverse concepts of economy and economic value have been culturally constituted and disseminated through modern art and cultural practice.

Comprising 14 individual essays along with an editors' introduction, *Sublime Economy* draws together work from some of the leading scholars in the several fields currently exploring the intersection of economic and aesthetic practices and discourses. A pressing issue of this cross-disciplinary conversation is to discern how artists', writers', and cultural scholars' constructions of distinct conceptions of economic value, as pertains to aesthetic objects as well as to more "everyday" objects and relations of mass consumption, have contributed to the ways "value" functions in and across disparate discourses. Thus this book looks at how cultural critics and theorists have put forward working notions of economic value that have regularities and effects similar to those of the "expert" conceptions and discourses about value that have been the preserve of professional economists.

This book will be of great interest to students and researchers engaged with economics of art and culture, aesthetic criticism, and cultural studies, as well as those with an interest in art, entrepreneurship, and marketing.

Jack Amariglio is Professor of Economics at Merrimack College. **Joseph W. Childers** is Professor of English at the University of California, Riverside. **Stephen E. Cullenberg** is Professor of Economics at the University of California, Riverside.

Routledge frontiers of political economy

1 Equilibrium Versus Understanding
Towards the rehumanization of economics
within social theory
Mark Addleson

2 Evolution, Order and Complexity
*Edited by Elias L. Khalil and Kenneth E.
Boulding*

3 Interactions in Political Economy
Malvern after ten years
Edited by Steven Pressman

4 The End of Economics
Michael Perelman

5 Probability in Economics
Omar F. Hamouda and Robin Rowley

**6 Capital Controversy, Post Keynesian
Economics and the History of Economics**
Essays in honour of Geoff Harcourt,
volume one
*Edited by Philip Arestis, Gabriel Palma and
Malcolm Sawyer*

**7 Markets, Unemployment and Economic
Policy**
Essays in honour of Geoff Harcourt,
volume two
*Edited by Philip Arestis, Gabriel Palma and
Malcolm Sawyer*

8 Social Economy
The logic of capitalist development
Clark Everling

**9 New Keynesian Economics/Post
Keynesian Alternatives**
Edited by Roy J. Rotheim

**10 The Representative Agent in
Macroeconomics**
James E. Hartley

11 Borderlands of Economics
Essays in honour of Daniel R. Fusfeld
*Edited by Nahid Aslanbeigui and Young
Back Choi*

12 Value, Distribution and Capital
Essays in honour of Pierangelo Garegnani
Edited by Gary Mongiovi and Fabio Petri

13 The Economics of Science
Methodology and epistemology as if
economics really mattered
James R. Wible

**14 Competitiveness, Localised Learning and
Regional Development**
Specialisation and prosperity in small open
economies
*Peter Maskell, Heikki Eskelinen, Ingjaldur
Hannibalsson, Anders Malmberg and
Eirik Vatne*

15 Labour Market Theory
A constructive reassessment
Ben J. Fine

16 Women and European Employment
*Jill Rubery, Mark Smith, Colette Fagan and
Damian Grimshaw*

17 Explorations in Economic Methodology
From Lakatos to empirical philosophy
of science
Roger Backhouse

18 Subjectivity in Political Economy
Essays on wanting and choosing
David P. Levine

19 The Political Economy of Middle East Peace
The impact of competing trade agendas
Edited by J. W. Wright, Jnr

20 The Active Consumer
Novelty and surprise in consumer choice
Edited by Marina Bianchi

21 Subjectivism and Economic Analysis
Essays in memory of Ludwig Lachmann
Edited by Roger Koppl and Gary Mongiovi

22 Themes in Post-Keynesian Economics
Essays in honour of Geoff Harcourt,
volume three
Edited by Claudio Sardoni and Peter Kriesler

23 The Dynamics of Technological Knowledge
Cristiano Antonelli

24 The Political Economy of Diet, Health and Food Policy
Ben J. Fine

25 The End of Finance
Capital market inflation, financial
derivatives and pension fund capitalism
Jan Toporowski

26 Political Economy and the New Capitalism
Edited by Jan Toporowski

27 Growth Theory
A philosophical perspective
Patricia Northover

28 The Political Economy of the Small Firm
Edited by Charlie Dannreuther

29 Hahn and Economic Methodology
Edited by Thomas Boylan and Paschal F. O'Gorman

30 Gender, Growth and Trade
The miracle economies of the postwar years
David Kucera

31 Normative Political Economy
Subjective freedom, the market and the state
David Levine

32 Economist with a Public Purpose
Essays in honour of John Kenneth Galbraith
Edited by Michael Keaney

33 Involuntary Unemployment
The elusive quest for a theory
Michel De Vroey

34 The Fundamental Institutions of Capitalism
Ernesto Screpanti

35 Transcending Transaction
The search for self-generating markets
Alan Shipman

36 Power in Business and the State
An historical analysis of its concentration
Frank Bealey

37 Editing Economics
Essays in honour of Mark Perlman
Hank Lim, Ungsuh K. Park and Geoff Harcourt

38 Money, Macroeconomics and Keynes
Essays in honour of Victoria Chick,
volume one
Philip Arestis, Meghnad Desai and Sheila Dow

39 Methodology, Microeconomics and Keynes
Essays in honour of Victoria Chick,
volume two
Philip Arestis, Meghnad Desai and Sheila Dow

40 Market Drive and Governance
Reexamining the rules for economic and
commercial contest
Ralf Boscheck

41 The Value of Marx
Political economy for contemporary
capitalism
Alfredo Saad-Filho

42 Issues in Positive Political Economy
S. Mansoob Murshed

43 The Enigma of Globalisation
A journey to a new stage of capitalism
Robert Went

44 The Market
Equilibrium, stability, mythology
S. N. Afriat

45 The Political Economy of Rule Evasion and Policy Reform
Jim Leitzel

46 Unpaid Work and the Economy
Edited by Antonella Picchio

47 Distributional Justice
Theory and measurement
Hilde Bojer

48 Cognitive Developments in Economics
Edited by Salvatore Rizzello

49 Social Foundations of Markets, Money and Credit
Costas Lapavitsas

50 Rethinking Capitalist Development
Essays on the economics of Josef Steindl
Edited by Tracy Mott and Nina Shapiro

51 An Evolutionary Approach to Social Welfare
Christian Sartorius

52 Kalecki's Economics Today
Edited by Zdzislaw L. Sadowski and Adam Szeworski

53 Fiscal Policy from Reagan to Blair
The left veers right
Ravi K. Roy and Arthur T. Denzau

54 The Cognitive Mechanics of Economic Development and Institutional Change
Bertin Martens

55 Individualism and the Social Order
The social element in liberal thought
Charles R. McCann Jnr.

56 Affirmative Action in the United States and India
A comparative perspective
Thomas E. Weisskopf

57 Global Political Economy and the Wealth of Nations
Performance, institutions, problems and policies
Edited by Phillip Anthony O'Hara

58 Structural Economics
Thijs ten Raa

59 Macroeconomic Theory and Economic Policy
Essays in honour of Jean-Paul Fitoussi
Edited by K. Vela Velupillai

60 The Struggle Over Work
The "end of work" and employment alternatives in post-industrial societies
Shaun Wilson

61 The Political Economy of Global Sporting Organisations
John Forster and Nigel Pope

62 The Flawed Foundations of General Equilibrium Theory
Critical essays on economic theory
Frank Ackerman and Alejandro Nadal

63 Uncertainty in Economic Theory
Essays in honor of David Schmeidler's 65th birthday
Edited by Itzhak Gilboa

64 The New Institutional Economics of Corruption
Edited by Johann Graf Lambsdorff, Markus Taube and Matthias Schramm

65 The Price Index and its Extension
A chapter in economic measurement
S. N. Afriat

66 Reduction, Rationality & Game Theory in Marxian Economics
Bruce Philp

67 Culture and Politics in Economic Development
Volker Bornschier

68 Modern Applications of Austrian Thought
Edited by Jürgen G. Backhaus

69 Ordinary Choices
Individuals, incommensurability, and democracy
Robert Urquhart

70 Labour Theory of Value
Peter C. Dooley

71 Capitalism
Victor D. Lippit

72 Macroeconomic Foundations of Macroeconomics
Alvaro Cencini

73 Marx for the 21st Century
Edited by Hiroshi Uchida

74 Growth and Development in the Global Political Economy
Social structures of accumulation and modes of regulation
Phillip Anthony O'Hara

75 The New Economy and Macroeconomic Stability
A neo-modern perspective drawing on the complexity approach and Keynesian economics
Teodoro Dario Togati

76 The Future of Social Security Policy
Women, work and a citizen's basic income
Ailsa McKay

77 Clinton and Blair
The political economy of the third way
Flavio Romano

78 Marxian Reproduction Schema
Money and aggregate demand in a capitalist economy
A. B. Trigg

79 The Core Theory in Economics
Problems and solutions
Lester G. Telser

80 Economics, Ethics and the Market
Introduction and applications
Johan J. Graafland

81 Social Costs and Public Action in Modern Capitalism
Essays inspired by Karl William Kapp's theory of social costs
Edited by Wolfram Elsner, Pietro Frigato and Paolo Ramazzotti

82 Globalization and the Myths of Free Trade
History, theory and empirical evidence
Edited by Anwar Shaikh

83 Equilibrium in Economics: Scope and Limits
Edited by Valeria Mosini

84 Globalization
State of the art and perspectives
Edited by Stefan A. Schirm

85 Neoliberalism
National and regional experiments with global ideas
Edited by Ravi K. Roy, Arthur T. Denzau and Thomas D. Willett

86 Post-Keynesian Macroeconomics Economics
Essays in honour of Ingrid Rima
Edited by Mathew Forstater, Gary Mongiovi and Steven Pressman

87 Consumer Capitalism
Anastasios S. Korkotsides

88 Remapping Gender in the New Global Order
Edited by Marjorie Griffin Cohen and Janine Brodie

89 Hayek and Natural Law
Eric Angner

90 Race and Economic Opportunity in the Twenty-First Century
Edited by Marlene Kim

91 Renaissance in Behavioural Economics
Harvey Leibenstein's impact on contemporary economic analysis
Edited by Roger Frantz

92 Human Ecology Economics
A new framework for global sustainability
Edited by Roy E. Allen

93 Imagining Economics Otherwise
Encounters with identity/difference
Nitasha Kaul

94 Reigniting the Labor Movement
Restoring means to ends in a democratic labor movement
Gerald Friedman

95 The Spatial Model of Politics
Norman Schofield

96 The Economics of American Judaism
Carmel Ullman Chiswick

97 Critical Political Economy
Christian Arnsperger

98 Culture and Economic Explanation
Economics in the US and Japan
Donald W. Katzner

99 Feminism, Economics and Utopia
Time travelling through paradigms
Karin Schönpflug

100 Risk in International Finance
Vikash Yadav

101 Economic Policy and Performance in Industrial Democracies
Party governments, central banks and the fiscal-monetary policy mix
Takayuki Sakamoto

102 Advances on Income Inequality and Concentration Measures
Edited by Gianni Betti and Achille Lemmi

103 Economic Representations
Academic and everyday
Edited by David F. Ruccio

104 Mathematical Economics and the Dynamics of Capitalism
Goodwin's legacy continued
Edited by Peter Flaschel and Michael Landesmann

105 The Keynesian Multiplier
Edited by Claude Gnos and Louis-Philippe Rochon

106 Money, Enterprise and Income Distribution
Towards a macroeconomic theory of capitalism
John Smithin

107 Fiscal Decentralization and Local Public Finance in Japan
Nobuki Mochida

108 The 'Uncertain' Foundations of Post-Keynesian Economics
Essays in exploration
Stephen P. Dunn

109 Karl Marx's Grundrisse
Foundations of the critique of political economy 150 years later
Edited by Marcello Musto

110 Economics and the Price Index
S. N. Afriat and Carlo Milana

111 Sublime Economy
On the intersection of art and economics
Edited by Jack Amariglio, Joseph W. Childers and Stephen E. Cullenberg

Sublime Economy
On the intersection of art and economics

**Edited by
Jack Amariglio,
Joseph W. Childers and
Stephen E. Cullenberg**

LONDON AND NEW YORK

Transferred to digital printing 2010

First published 2009
by Routledge
2 Park Square, Milton Park, Abingdon, Oxon OX14 4RN

Simultaneously published in the USA and Canada
by Routledge
270 Madison Avenue, New York, NY 10016

Routledge is an imprint of the Taylor & Francis Group,
an informa business

© 2009 selection and editorial matter, Jack Amariglio, Joseph W. Childers
and Stephen E. Cullenberg; individual chapters, the contributors

Typeset in Times New Roman by Keyword Group Ltd

All rights reserved. No part of this book may be reprinted or reproduced or
utilised in any form or by any electronic, mechanical, or other means, now
known or hereafter invented, including photocopying and recording, or in
any information storage or retrieval system, without permission in writing
from the publishers.

British Library Cataloguing in Publication Data
A catalogue record for this book is available
from the British Library

Library of Congress Cataloging in Publication Data

Sublime economy : on the intersection of art and economics / edited by
Jack Amariglio, Joseph W. Childers and Stephen E. Cullenberg.
    p. cm. – (Routledge frontiers of political economy ; 111)
   Includes bibliographical references and index.
   1. Economics–Philosophy. 2. Art and society–Economic aspects.
   3. Value. I. Amariglio, Jack. II. Childers, Joseph W. III. Cullenberg,
   Stephen.
   HB72.S83 2008
   330.01–dc22   2008012957

ISBN 10: 0-415-77191-9 (hbk)
ISBN 10: 0-415-78121-3(pbk)
ISBN 10: 0-203-89057-4 (ebk)

ISBN 13: 978-0-415-77191-7 (hbk)
ISBN 13: 978-0-415-78121-3(pbk)
ISBN 13: 978-0-203-89057-8 (ebk)

Contents

List of figures, illustrations, and tables	xiii
Contributors	xv
Acknowlegments	xix

INTRODUCTION
Sublime economy: on the intersection of art and economics   1
JACK AMARIGLIO, JOSEPH W. CHILDERS, AND STEPHEN E.
CULLENBERG

PART I
"Tokens of eccentricity": value and the aesthetic
representation of economy   27

1   Tracing the economic: modern art's construction
    of economic value   29
    JACK AMARIGLIO

2   Meaning to say ...   65
    JUDITH MEHTA

3   Use, value, aesthetics: gambling with difference/speculating
    with value   82
    JOSEPH W. CHILDERS AND STEPHEN E. CULLENBERG

x *Contents*

PART II
Sublime intercourse: economics meets aesthetics
(and vice versa)   93

  4 Reluctant partners: aesthetic and market value, 1708–1871   95
     NEIL DE MARCHI

  5 On the contemporaneousness of Roger de Piles' *Balance des*
     Peintres   112
     VICTOR GINSBURGH AND SHEILA WEYERS

  6 How aesthetics and economics met in voc ed   124
     EVAN WATKINS

  7 Economics meets esthetics in the Bloomsbury Group   137
     CRAUFURD D. GOODWIN

  8 Individualism, civilization, and national character in market
     democracies   152
     REGENIA GAGNIER

  9 Art, fleeing from capitalism: a slightly disputatious
     interview/conversation   172
     DEIRDRE McCLOSKEY (AND JACK AMARIGLIO)

PART III
Name your price   201

10 Imaginary currencies: contemporary art on the market—critique
    confirmation, or play   203
    OLAV VELTHUIS

11 The sociology of the new art gallery scene in
    Chelsea, Manhattan   220
    DAVID HALLE AND ELISABETH TISO

12 The lives of cultural goods   250
    ARJO KLAMER

PART IV
Moral economies and the romance of money 273

13 The rhetoric of prostitution 275
JENNIFER DOYLE

14 A heap of worthless fragments: the nineteenth-century literary
revaluation of the classical statue 291
YOTA BATSAKI

Index 312

List of figures, illustrations, and tables

Figures and Illustrations

Chapter 1

Image 1	Kasimir Malevich, *Red Square: Painterly Realism of a Peasant Woman in Two Dimensions*.	29
Image 2	Henry Wallis, *The Stonebreaker*.	32
Image 3	Carel Willink, *The Bank of Philadelphia*.	35
Image 4	Jenny Holzer, *Protect Me From What I Want*, 1984–85 or 1985–86.	37
Image 5	John R. Hicks, Graph.	42
Image 6	Marcel Duchamp, *Tzanck Check*.	44
Image 7	Barnett Newman, *Vir Heroicus Sublimis*, 1950–51.	45
Image 8	Kurt Schwitters, *Mz 1926, 7. Slagen*.	47
Image 9	Kurt Schwitters, *The Big-I Painting*.	48

Chapter 4

Figure 1	Portion of De Piles's 'Catalogue of the Names of the most noted Painters, and their Degrees of Perfection, in the Four principal Parts of *Painting*; supposing absolute Perfection to be divided into twenty Degrees or Parts.'	99
Figure 2	Richardson's modified de Piles table, with added column for portrait.	99
Figure 3	Jevons's experiment no. 2: useful effect from lifting weights (observations and fitted curve).	107
Figure 4	Jevons's graph of diminishing "intensity of effect" as quantity consumed increases.	107

Chapter 5

Figure 1	Three cases of adjustment by regression analysis.	114

Chapter 11

Figure 1	Growth of galleries in Chelsea, 1997–2008.	221
Figure 2	Art gallery areas, Manhattan and Brooklyn, 1978–2008.	221
Photo 1	Matthew Marks Gallery, Chelsea.	225
Photo 2	Gagosian Gallery, Chelsea.	225

xiv *List of figures, illustrations, and tables*

Photo 3	Gagosian Gallery, Interior (section).	226
Figure 3	Trends in direct asking rents and new construction completions in Manhattan, 1980–2001.	227
Photo 4	High Line railroad.	231
Figure 4	West Chelsea rezoning, 2005.	232
Photo 5	**Nigel Cooke** *Silva Morosa*.	240
Photo 6	**Mary Ellen Mark** Putla with a Gold Necklace, Bombay, India.	244
Photo 7	**Mary Ellen Mark** A New Girl Being Made-up for the First Time, Bombay, India.	245

Chapter 14

Figure 1	Etruscan-shaped vase. Antoine Béranger (1785–1867), "Entry into Paris of the artworks destined for the Napoleon Museum." 1813. Sèvres, National Museum of Ceramics. Photo RMN/© Christian Jean/Jacques L'hoir.	292
Figure 2	Fiorelli plastercast, Pompeii. By permission of the Italian Ministry for Cultural Heritage and Activities, Archeological Surintendance of Pompeii.	304
Figure 3	The Dying Gaul, Capitoline Museum, Rome. Photographic Archive of the Capitoline Museum.	305

Tables

Chapter 5

Table 1	Estimation results	118
Appendix Table		119

Chapter 11

Table 1	Subject matter of the art shows in the sixteen most important ("star") Chelsea galleries	239

Contributors

Jack Amariglio teaches Economics at Merrimack College. He is the founding Editor of the journal *Rethinking Marxism*. His writings include the co-authored book, with David Ruccio, *Postmodern Moments in Modern Economics* (Princeton, 2003). He is currently the editor of the "art/iculations" section of *Rethinking Marxism*, which is dedicated to the political economy of art, aesthetics, and culture.

Yota Batsaki has a Ph.D. in Comparative Literature from Harvard University. She is a Fellow in English at St John's College, Cambridge, and a Newton Trust Lecturer in the Cambridge English Faculty. Her research focuses on the Enlightenment philosophical and fictional career of the concept of self-interest; the relationship between literature and sculpture; and exile and translation.

Joseph W. Childers is Professor of English at the University of California, Riverside. Most recently he co-edited *Victorian Prism: Refractions of the Crystal Palace* (Virginia, 2007). He is currently completing a book on representations of the colonial "other" in Victorian England. He also serves on the editorial board of *Rethinking Marxism*.

Stephen E. Cullenberg is Dean of the College of Humanities, Arts and Social Sciences at the University of California, Riverside, where he is also a Professor of Economics. He is the co-author (with Anjan Chakrabarti) of Transition *and Development in India* (Routledge, 2004).

Neil De Marchi teaches a course on the art market at Duke University and one, with Marina Bianchi, on the economics of creative goods, at Venice International University. For many years he has collaborated and written with Duke art historian Hans Van Miegroet, on the emergence and functioning of early modern art markets in Europe, with a focus on dealer strategies. Out of this has also come an ongoing interest in unscrupulous dealing in the Australian Aboriginal desert paintings market. Current research explores the changing role of art in business, as successfully competing firms find they must attend more to non-material value added.

xvi *Contributors*

Jennifer Doyle is an Associate Professor of English at the University of California, Riverside. She is the author of *Sex Objects: Art and the Dialectics of Desire* (University of Minnesota Press, 2006). She is currently writing a book about difficulty and the cultural politics of visual art.

Regenia Gagnier is Professor in the School of English at the University of Exeter. Her highly influential books include Idylls *of the Marketplace: Oscar Wilde and the Victorian Public* (Stanford, 1986), Subjectivities: *A History of Self-Representation in Britain 1832–1920* (Oxford, 1991), and The *Insatiability of Human Wants: Economics and Aesthetics in Market Society* (Chicago, 2000). She has just completed a study of individualism, ethics, and the nineteenth-century roots of globalization, and her current research is on the global circulation of the literatures of liberalism.

Victor Ginsburgh is honorary Professor of Economics at the University of Brussels. He has written and edited a dozen books and is the author of over 160 papers in applied and theoretical economics. His recent work includes writing on economics of the arts, wines and languages. He has published over 50 papers on these topics, some of which have appeared in *American Economic Review, Journal of Political Economy, Games and Economic Behavior, Journal of Economic Perspectives, Economic Journal, Journal of the European Economic Association, Empirical Studies of the Arts,* and the *Journal of Cultural Economics.* He is coeditor (with David Throsby) of the *Handbook of the Economics of Art and Culture* (Elsevier, Amsterdam, 2006).

Craufurd D. Goodwin is James B. Duke Professor of Economics at Duke University where he has served as department chair, vice provost, and dean of the Graduate School. He was director of the European and International Affairs Program at the Ford Foundation (1971–1976). He has received a Guggenheim fellowship and a Smuts fellowship at Cambridge University. He is editor of the journal *History of Political Economy* (Duke University Press) and of the book series *Historical Perspectives on Modern Economics* (Cambridge University Press). He is the author of 77 articles and book chapters, author of eleven books and editor of nine more.

David Halle is Professor of Sociology at the University of California, Los Angeles. He is writing a book, with Elisabeth Tiso, titled *The Structure of Contemporary Art: A Global and Local Perspective via Chelsea, New York's Newest Dominant Gallery District* (forthcoming, University of Chicago Press). His previous books include *New York & Los Angeles: Politics, Society and Culture* (University of Chicago Press, 2003), *Inside Culture: Art and Class in The American Home* (University of Chicago Press, 1994) and *America's Working Man: Work, Home and Politics Among Blue-Collar Property Owners* (University of Chicago Press, 1984). He is also the author, with Louise Mirrer, of "Prints of Power: A Sociological Study of the Artist, LeRoy Neiman, and 1000 Neiman Collectors"

Contributors xvii

in *The Prints of LeRoy Neiman 1980–1991*, by LeRoy Neiman (Knoedler Publications, 1991).

Arjo Klamer is Professor of the Economics of Art and Culture at Erasmus University in Rotterdam, The Netherlands, and holds the world's only chair in the field of cultural economics. In 1984, he attracted a great deal of attention with his *Conversations with Economists*. In his latest book, *Speaking of Economics* (Routledge, 2007), he pursues themes that emerged from that book. He has collaborated with Deirdre McCloskey to promote the rhetorical perspective on economics. *The Economic Conversation*, a textbook forthcoming in early 2008 (Palgrave) and co-authored with McCloskey and Stephen Ziliak employs a groundbreaking "open-method" approach to teaching first-year micro- and macroeconomics. His current research focuses on the cultural dimension of economic life and the values of art. He is actively involved in public debates in the Netherlands and is founding director of a new university, Academia Vitae in Deventer.

Deirdre McCloskey teaches economics, history, English, and communication at the University of Illinois at Chicago. Well known for her books on rhetoric, on statistical significance, and now the ethics of capitalism, she describes herself as a "postmodern, quantitative, literary, free-market, ex-Marxist economist, historian, rhetorician, Midwestern progressive Episcopalian woman who was once a man."

Judith Mehta is Research Coordinator for the ESRC Centre for Competition Policy, and she convenes the MA program in the Economics of the Mass Media, at the University of East Anglia, Norwich, England. She is a pluralist with respect to theory, methodology, policy and teaching. Her research interests include behavioral approaches to decision-making, and the implications for economic analysis of recent developments in Continental philosophy, and she has published numerous journal articles and essays in these areas. She is on the Committee of the Association for Heterodox Economics.

Elisabeth Tiso is an art historian living in NYC and Paris. She studied art history at Sarah Lawrence College and the Graduate Center at the City University of New York. She has taught art history at Parsons, City College of New York, Univ. of Delaware, and UCLA in New York.

Olav Velthuis is an Assistant Professor in the Department of Sociology of the University of Amsterdam. He is the author of *Imaginary Economics* (Nai Publishers, 2005) and *Talking Prices: Symbolic Meanings of Prices on the Contemporary Art Market in Amsterdam and New York* (Princeton University Press, 2005). He also writes free lance journalism for a number of Dutch media.

Evan Watkins is Professor of English and Cultural Studies at the University of California, Davis. He has published widely in cultural studies, education, and

xviii   *Contributors*

composition theory. His most recent book is *Class Degrees: Smart Work, Managed Choice, and the Transformation of Higher Education*, Fordham University Press, 2008.

Sheila Weyers has a degree in philosophy, and is interested in aesthetics and its relations with art history. She has published on movies, including remakes, on the art historian de Piles, and is now working on canons. Her papers have appeared in *Artibus et Historiae*, the *Journal of Cultural Economics*, *Annales d'Histoire de l'Art et d'Archéologie, Poetics* and *Empirical Studies in the Arts*.

Acknowledgments

Sublime Economy is the culmination of several years' work and even more years' worth of patience on the parts of many people. Not least of, of course, are its contributors, who bore with the editors at a time when personal circumstances cast a doubt as to whether this project would ever come to fruition. Having its genesis in a conference held at the University of California Riverside, this book owes a debt of gratitude to that campus's Center for Ideas and Society, especially the director Emory Elliott and staff, Laura Lozon, Antonette Toney, and Marilyn Davis. We also wish to acknowledge the financial assistance the conference received from the University of California Humanities Research Institute. Thanks to David Ruccio, Amitava Kumar, Shelly Errington, Anna Scott, John Ganim, Josh Kun, Susan Jahoda, Marc Shell, and Hans Abbing, Carole-Anne Tyler, Ryan Mason, and the late Philip Brett for participating so productively in our initial conversations over aesthetics, economics, and value. Rory Moore was invaluable in helping us to acquire permissions for several of the images reproduced in this volume. Thomas Sutton and Rasika Mathur were paragons of professionalism and good humor during the editing process. Portions of "Individualism, Civilization, and National Character in Market Democracies" by Regenia Gagnier appeared in *Partial Answers* (Jerusalem) I,I (Jan. 2003): 103–128. An early version of Jennifer Doyle's essay, "The Rhetoric of Prostitution" appeared in *Pop Out* (Durham: Duke University Press, 1996) pp. 191–209. We also wish to thank a number of individuals and institutions for the permission to reproduce the images that appear in this volume: Carel Willink's *Bank of Philadelphia* © Mrs. Sylvia Willink. *Red Square* by Kasimir Malevich courtesy of the Russian State Museum, St. Petersburg, and image resolution © Erich Lessing/Art Resource, NY. *Vir Heroicus Sublimis*, by Barnett Newman © 2008 The Barnett Newman Foundation, New York/Artists Rights Society (ARS), New York and courtesy of The Museum of Modern Art, New York, NY, U.S.A., image resolution © Digital Image © The Museum of Modern Art/Licensed by SCALA/Art Resource, NY. Marcel Duchamp, *Tzanck Check* © Artists Rights Society (ARS), New York/ADAGP/ Paris/Succession Marcel Duchamp. Jenny Holzer, *Protect me from What I Want* © 2008 Jenny Holzer, member, Artists Rights Society (ARS), New York. Henry Wallis, *The Stonebreaker* courtesy of Birmingham Museums and Art Gallery, Birmingham, UK. Kurt Schwitters, *The Big-I Painting (Merzbild 9b: Das grosse*

xx   *Acknowledgments*

Ichbild) and *Mz 1926, 7. Slagen* © 2008 Artists Rights Society (ARS) New York/ VG Bild Kunst, Bonn. John R. Hicks, "Value and Capital," (1972), Figure 11, page 39, by permission of Oxford University Press. Nigel Cooke, *Silva Morosa* courtesy of Andrea Rosen Gallery, NY. Mary Ellen Mark, "Putla with a Gold Necklace, Bombay, India" and "A New Girl Being Made-up for the First Time, Bombay, India" courtesy of Mary Ellen Mark Library/Studio. "Vase de forme étrusque à rouleaux" courtesy Agence Photographique de la Réunion des Musées Nationaux; Fiorelli Plastercast, Pompeii courtesy of the Italian Ministry of Culture, Soprintendenza Archeologica di Pompei. Photograph of "The Dying Gaul" courtesy of Archivio Fotografico dei Musei Capitolini, Rome.

Introduction

Sublime economy: on the intersection of art and economics

Jack Amariglio, Joseph W. Childers, and Stephen E. Cullenberg

"Economics is Everywhere." This is the title of a recent svelte primer by the prolific labor economist, Daniel Hamermesh (2004), intended for undergraduate students in introductory microeconomics. The user-friendly title is reminiscent of the familiarity and jovial warmth of popular how-to books in car mechanics or cooking. True to form, Hamermesh's book is a series of poppy, perky vignettes, of "everyday" problems and circumstances that can be seen (after so long remaining "unseen") to have underlying "economic" content, and, therefore, as worthy of economic theoretical solutions. The vignettes take the form of proposed or actual "real world" experiences, or at least, as Hamermesh acknowledges, his own experiences and those of his students.[1]

Yet, there is also something edgy and even overbearing about this title (not surprising, of course, for a professional economist, even one as well meaning as Hamermesh). A drop—maybe even a flood—of awe infuses the ubiquity and omnipresence of economics: that is, the discourses, theories, and concepts of economics, the discipline.[2] Economics, the discipline, is everywhere, but this is because "the economy"—Hamermesh's "real world experiences"—everywhere precedes it.

Everywhere. A colossal, inchoate space. Certainly—if even thinkable—one that summons up limitlessness, saturation, the overcoming and futility of boundaries, the infinite. It conjures, as well, an attitude, a disposition, or a "propensity"— to attach a Keynesian inflection—to wonder: an awe perhaps even verging on terror. A vast and worrisome source of ambivalent pleasure. The possibility of delight beyond the assimilable, of being overtaken, rendered dumbstruck, flattened by surprise, all rendered palpable by an intermingling of indefinable fear. This admixture of the uplifting and the overwhelming is the stuff, of course, of the (Western) aesthetic sublime, at least those notions of the sublime that can be traced back to the Enlightenment writings of such diverse thinkers as Joseph Addison, Frances Hutcheson, Edmund Burke, and, of course, Immanuel Kant.[3]

2 *Jack Amariglio, Joseph W. Childers, and Stephen E. Cullenberg*

Paul Mattick (2003) suggests a material context for the general rise of aesthetic theory in the eighteenth century and the specific elaboration of the concept of the sublime:

> Edmund Burke's essay on the sublime directly influenced the thinking of such different writers as Denis Diderot, Gotthold Lessing, and Immanuel Kant. The international character of the discussion reflected the scale of the changes—the growth of market economies, urbanization, nation-state formation, and the rise of new social classes—that produced modern society. During the later eighteenth century, people experienced the accelerating emergence of capitalism as a continuous series of upheavals in social, political, economic, and cultural relations, which provided a desire for principles, practical and theoretical, in terms of which order could be imposed on this alternatively or even simultaneously exhilarating and terrifying experience. As the reconfiguring of the arts was an element of this general social transformation, classically based definitions of art as the pursuit of beauty no longer seemed adequate. New times called for new concepts. (47)

In his "History of Astronomy" (1980a)—probably composed in the 1750s—Adam Smith implicitly participated in these new aesthetic discussions through his conceptualization of the contours of what Burke and others would contemporaneously label "the sublime."[4] Smith's contribution takes the form of his attempt to sort out the differences, but also the complementarities, between Surprise, Wonder, and Admiration. The essay—concerned as it is with the magnificence of the cosmos and the sublime discoveries of centuries of astronomers—employs mostly the first two of this triumvirate of "sentiments." Indeed, Smith's thoughts on the intertwining of Surprise and Wonder act as a kind of addendum to Burke's writings on the sublime.[5] Focused as usual on the affects or sentiments that give agents and their forms of knowledge their primary and subsidiary motivations, Smith attributes the initial apprehensions associated with Surprise and Wonder to scientific star-gazers from the Greeks to Copernicus to Newton. More importantly for Smith, the most talented among the astronomers made connections and linguistically captured the sublime—or at least that aspect of it he calls Wonder—*in* or *as* a textual, literary effect: an inscribed exemplification of the ultimate extension and limitations of "the imagination." Smith waxes eloquent regarding Newton's capacity to place into the language of system, and therefore to make available for human imagination, "the greatest discovery ever made by man, the discovery of an immense chain of the most important and sublime truths" (1980a, 105).

Smith's conception of Wonder is occasioned in the main because of an *aporia*, a gap or interval that emerges in the imagination. For Smith, when a chain of unexpected events following upon one another provokes the repetition of Surprise, then Wonder will be stimulated: "The stop which is thereby given to the career of the imagination, the difficulty which it finds in passing along such disjointed objects, and the feeling of something like a gap or interval betwixt them, constitute the whole essence of the emotion" (1980a, 42).[6] The emotion to

Introduction 3

which Smith alludes, however, is *precisely* that "feeling of something like a gap or interval," the sensation of having the imagination at that moment stopped dead in its tracks:

> The imagination and memory exert themselves to no purpose, and in vain look around all their classes of ideas in order to find one under which it may be arranged. They fluctuate to no purpose from thought to thought, and we remain still uncertain and undetermined where to place it, or what to think of it. It is this fluctuation and vain recollection, together with the emotion or movement of the spirits that they excite, which constitute the sentiment properly called Wonder, and which occasion that staring, and sometimes that rolling of the eyes, that suspension of the breath, and that swelling of the heart, which we all may observe, both in ourselves and others, when wondering at some new object, and which are the natural symptoms of uncertain and undetermined thought. (1980a, 39)[7]

The prevalent objects of Wonder for Smith reside almost entirely in the realm of nature. In the privileging of novel or unique natural objects or events, Smith's Wonder shares much in common with the specific examples given by both Burke and Kant[8] for their discursive explorations into the sentiments or aesthetic judgments that they name "the sublime."[9] Likewise, the stoppage of reason or understanding in the face of Smith's "Wonder" links him to other attempts in aesthetics and the estimation of art to account for a disposition that is simultaneously mute and overflowing. What remains to be said, however, is that the shift over the course of the nineteenth and twentieth centuries from the natural to the social in the examples of "the sublime" has surely included in its wake Smith's own naturalistic, but nonetheless "social," description of the capitalist economy, that remarkable chain of Newtonian-like, seemingly unconnected and, initially, undetermined events and actions that comprise a network of efficient markets and the extensive and harmonious capitalist social division of labor.

If an affective or conceptual divide obtains between contemporary academically trained economists and cultural critics regarding the "sublimity" of modern, market capitalism (by no means a foregone conclusion), it may hinge on the sense of boundedness or finitude (or not) of such an economy. An economist titling a book *Economics is Everywhere*, of course, can conjure up this sense of the sublime. But it equally can bespeak an attitude of supreme self-confidence in the ability of the understanding or reason exemplified in economic theory to comprehend, to the point of modeling, the totality of such an economy, thus rendering it sensible and capable of mastery. Hence, the possibility that an economy—even a "global" one—will be sensed and experienced as "sublime" is not the stock-in-trade reaction of a large segment of professional economists.[10] That the imagination is incapable of grasping an object's whole, and that reason stands, for a time, blocked by this incapacity and can only apprehend its own limits (as we have seen in Smith's formulation above), has been, for many philosophers of aesthetics, one of the defining qualities of the aesthetic judgment that Kant categorized as

4   *Jack Amariglio, Joseph W. Childers, and Stephen E. Cullenberg*

"the sublime."[11] At least in our experience, there is a more pronounced tendency within the communities of cultural theorists than those of mainstream professional economists to perceive the capitalist economy as such an object, one whose borders are constantly overflowing to the point of boundlessness, and whose characteristic temporal quality is that of unceasing turmoil and often riotous upheaval.[12] In the view of some cultural critics, the imagination simply cannot grasp this capitalist whole. Although typically qualified as "a system," capitalism is portrayed in many "cultural" texts as one whose unlimited open-endedness and spatial sprawl render it sensually overwhelming and perhaps formless, at least in the retrospect of critical reason.[13] In the very attempts to comprehend its scope and effects, a distinct *apprehension* also arises that underscores the simultaneous workings of excess (of capitalism as an "object" to be known) and lack (of our ability—either imaginatively or through reason to know it). Thought of in this way, it follows that the global capitalist economy informs a particularly modern (some may argue postmodern) instance of the sublime.

One historical point of departure for this apperception may be the rise and spread of capitalist metropolises and international imperialism in the late nineteenth century. Paul Crowther, notable for his work calling attention to the place of the capitalist and/or market economy in examples of the sublime since the nineteenth century, makes just such an argument. He notes that nineteenth- and then twentieth-century literature and art point to the shift in focus in the location and occasion of the sublime. Working meticulously through Kant, Crowther attempts to categorize and sort out the different senses and objects upon which rest that German philosopher's own elaborate investigation of the aesthetic sublime. Crowther reads Kant against his frequent admonitions that art in general, indeed any object or event "where the human end determines the form as well as the magnitude" (Kant quoted in Crowther, 152) of that thing or action, cannot be the site of the sublime. While Kant remains adamant in restricting the sublime to "things of nature," he does indicate that—in the end—it is the magnitude, the monstrosity of size, the magnificent, the horrible, that makes those things pass into the realm of the sublime (or at least susceptible to the subjective disposition that is the primary form of their "apprehension").[14]

As Crowther asserts, however, Kant's occasional examples from architecture, sculpture, and poetry to help his readers envision the sublime also enable a reading of Kant in which artifice and artistic human activity are likewise stimuli for sublime "judgment" even if they are not, in and of themselves, examples of the sublime. Crowther notes that, for Kant, "a work of artifice can be so perceptually overwhelming as to transcend our sense of its human origin" (Crowther, 153). But while Kant frequently denies this effect in most works of representational art, Crowther finds sufficient evidence of Kant at least implicitly concurring that "representational artworks *can* have a content or subject-matter which *in itself* is somewhat sublime" (154). Crowther pushes this a bit further to argue that, "given that art can have such subject-matter, there is no intrinsic reason why, if one is sensitive (or, less charitably, fanciful) enough, one should not be totally carried away by the artist's vision" (155). In the same vein, Crowther contends that, although Kant "has a

Introduction 5

tendency, when expressing himself in terms that point to a link between art and sublimity, to emphasize sublimity as a feature of content rather than sublimity of expression" (160), it is possible, once again, to reread Kant's notion of the sublime to include, for example, Van Gogh's painting of peasant shoes. As Crowther writes, those shoes may be "as unsublime a subject-matter as one could hope for" (160); nevertheless, Martin Heidegger, for one, calls attention to Van Gogh's "sheer style of expression," one that can "open out a sense of the immense possibilities of toil and the passage of the seasons across the earth" (160–1).[15]

Crowther's hermeneutical reading of Kant's rendition of the sublime beckons him toward a general definition that includes not only things of nature as the only and proper objects which may be apprehended in this "disinterested" way, but "the domain of human artifice and contrivance" as well (163), what Crowther calls the "artefactual sublime" (162). At such a juncture the "economy," or more pointedly (and perhaps narrowly) "capital," inserts itself into the discussion.

Emile Zola's *Germinal* serves as Crowther's exemplum. The passage he quotes has the coal miners imagining a terrifying "hidden power," a "god" somewhere removed, but also immanent in the very conditions of the mine operations and in the veiled and explicit threats and pleas of the coal mine manager. For Crowther, that god is Capital. Nor is this deification (not to say, reification) of Capital historically accidental or casual. Crowther explains:

> In the late nineteenth century, the experience of society becomes fundamentally an urban one organized around the capitalist economy. This organization implies at once order and disorder. Order in so far as capitalism is a force for cohesion; disorder in so far as it involves crisis, and oppression, and breeds revolt. In the society which grows around this structure of order/disorder, we can see a displacement of the sublime from nature to the urban experience. In this experience there is a fascination with Capital as a mighty power or god ... and with the direct products of Capital; yet at the same time there is an equal fascination with its epiphenomena and with patterns of resistance to it. Vast urban landscapes, violent mobs and crowds, the prospect of revolutionary violence. (163–4)[16]

Resistance to capitalism, its structures, and the conflict it engenders provides "immediate and inescapable images that overwhelm our perceptual or imaginative powers, yet make the scope of rational comprehension or human artifice and contrivance all the more vivid. The spectacle fascinates us in itself, and irrespective of its broader practical significance for us" (164–5).[17] Although, as Crowther argues, in the twentieth century the sublime takes on a more technological bent (that is, awe at technology and its powers of supposed earthly transcendence and planetary destruction), its continuing connection to economic forces, and particularly those of capital, maintains a dominant aesthetic largely oriented toward wondrous apprehensions (in all senses of the word) of "the economy."[18]

Instrumental to considerations of contemporary avant-garde art's confrontation with "presenting the unpresentable," and the place of the sublime in modern

6 *Jack Amariglio, Joseph W. Childers, and Stephen E. Cullenberg*

and postmodern art and society, has been the work of Jean-François Lyotard, especially as he comments on the connections of sublimity to market economies, capitalism in particular, and the role of new technologies. In "The Sublime and the Avant-Garde" (1993), Lyotard emphasizes the form of the sublime in which privation—the moment when "nothing happens"—figures as a primary determination in the feeling that simultaneously overwhelms and inspires avant-garde artists and their audiences. The anxious, fearful waiting for the "now" to happen—indeed the threat to avant-garde artists that "it may not happen"—often in response to the initial shock of encountering an object, an empty canvas, say, which is the stimulus for the feeling of being overcome, terrorized, and so forth: all of this, in Lyotard's words, today "proceeds 'directly' out of market societies" (254). On the one hand, the avant-garde's artistic passage to the sublime may be cut short, obstructed, or attenuated through its sublation into the discursive and artistic forms that are believed to be hallmarks of modern market culture.[19] On the other hand, however, Lyotard sees in the capitalist economy itself a moment of "the sublime," and he asserts that, in this regard, avant-garde artists find themselves in "collusion" with capital. That is, the creative force of capitalism's unceasing destructiveness and spread may provide the push necessary for the avant-garde to "experiment with means of expression, with styles, with ever-new materials" (255). This is a roundabout—even inverse—way of making the triumphalist claim that capitalism is the economic system, bar none, that promotes creative genius and artistic experimentation.

Lyotard is less invested in such claims, however, than in attempting to find the moments in which the experience of the sublime are both possible and developed as a source of renewal for contemporary art and culture, even as they must take shape in the face of capitalism's global extension and its fetishism of technological dynamism. "There is something of the sublime in capitalist economy," declares Lyotard:

> It is not academic, it is not physiocratic, it admits of no nature. It is, in a sense, an economy regulated by an Idea—infinite wealth or power. It does not manage to present any example from reality to verify this Idea. In making science subordinate to itself through technologies, especially those of language, it only succeeds, on the contrary, in making reality increasingly ungraspable, subject to doubt, unsteady. (254)

Capitalism, as an economy that is met by a subject's sense of its "infinitude," is thus conceivable in the form of a metaphysical "Idea," but, as Lyotard, Fredric Jameson, and others have insisted, this totality as the occasion for sublime feeling cannot be expressed or (re)presented.[20] The totality ("infinite wealth or power") is not intuited by a subject, nor does it appear to the subject's imagination other than through the moment of inexpressibility, or the privation of the imagination. This image of capitalism as a total system that is experienced as "unpresentable" and, therefore, for some, intuited *only* as a infinite magnitude, with concomitant (and perhaps horrifying) reach, remains on the familiar terrain of "the sublime."

Introduction 7

The size, the intensity, the extension, and the sheer power of the modern capitalist (or, if you like, postmodern, late capitalist) economy is, of course, right in the sights of many contemporary cultural critics, regardless of whether or not they are followers of Lyotard. In our view, it is not an exaggeration to say that, sublime or not, "the economy" is a favorite object of critical, and perhaps even practical, reflections and representations in the arts.[21] For instance, as a corrective to any tendency toward seeing contemporary informational technologies as providing the new occasion for aesthetic stimulations of terror and the colossal—the "too much"—Fredric Jameson in his famous 1984 essay on the postmodern as "cultural dominant" warns against relativizing, compartmentalizing, and/or detaching technology, at any stage in the history of capitalism, from the immeasurable reach of global capitalism. His discussion of the "postmodern sublime" is built upon the idea that there are few, if any, adequate aesthetic figurations available to represent that which has overcome representation itself: "the whole new decentered global network of the third stage of capital itself" (Jameson 1991, 38).

As George Hartley (2003) points out, Jameson transfigures the "sublime reaction" as described in Burke and Kant within an early phase of capitalism from one of fear and then respect (or "negative pleasure") to a different one, within "postmodern late capitalism," of "'hallucinatory splendor,' marked by euphoria and oxymoronic 'intensities'; the postmodern subject finds the bleakest and most horrendous spectacles—such as urban decay or auto wrecks—as objects of exhilaration" (224).[22] While the characteristic aesthetic response to a crisis of representation in Western capitalist society has been "the sublime" (in Hartley's view, what has changed is only the object of the sublime—from Nature as the unrepresentable Other to global capital as the unrepresentable Other—but not the dominance of the sublime itself), for Jameson that response has mutated into the "hysterical sublime." And, again, this hysterical sublime corresponds to (but does not apprehend) a new stage in the historical evolution of capitalism. Paradoxically, this stage, late capitalism, comes closest to its figuration in the digitalized world of computers and their global, technological constellation even as it simultaneously smashes through the boundaries of aesthetic representations, narratives, and depictions of that very same hyper-technological global matrix. Even the most daring, insightful narratives and images achieve only a privileged distortion of "a representational shorthand for grasping a network of power and control even more difficult for our minds and imaginations to grasp," that is, "present-day multinational capitalism" (1991, 38).[23]

Globalization, of course, is just the latest signifier of the shock and awe attendant upon the ubiquity and inexorability of capitalism's unceasing spread and steady growth in this supposed late capitalist phase.[24] In the history of twentieth-century art and in the art of the new millennium, as well as in the social sciences (economics included), countless examples abound portraying capitalism as the great insatiable devourer of all pre- or non-capitalist spaces.[25] Sometimes this voracious spread of global capitalism—often labeled "imperialism"—is presented as heinous and monstrous,[26] as we can see in the contemporary paintings of Sue Coe and of many other artists and writers. For others, in contrast, this same

8   *Jack Amariglio, Joseph W. Childers, and Stephen E. Cullenberg*

process is hailed as the standard-bearer of "economic reform," the inevitable and benevolent completion of modernization and even "democratization" of a stubbornly recalcitrant "third world" characterized by tradition, cultural stagnation, and economic underdevelopment. Despite the differences in outlook about the costs and benefits of this global extension of capitalist economies, however, both the art and social commentary engaged in these issues express similar sensibilities: we live in an era of "engulfment" by economic forces that make the effectiveness— whether as collaboration or resistance—of individuals and even of nations nearly inconsequential in comparison to the juggernaut of global capitalism.[27] The size and scope of global capitalism, thus, often achieves the representational status of the sublime even if the lingering reaction to it is disgust rather than ultimate pleasure.[28] Or, rather, in line with Kantian notions of the sublime, there is a perverse pleasure that often adheres to the resignation that anti-global activists and others register when complaining that international economic forces are, unfortunately, mostly beyond local control. As other writers have noted about the persistence of "ressentiment" as a primary affect for oppositional forces to capitalist power and extension, the aesthetics of (arguably pleasurable) disgust is partly constituted by the fear and loathing and despair that occur in reaction to perceiving, in horror, the all-encompassing features of a globalized economy.[29]

This is to say that one does not require an economist to reflect upon the implications of the "everywhereness" of economy, and the aesthetic implications of them trying to grasp, imaginatively and figuratively, this potentially horrifying, but always "awful," omnipresence. Among many cultural critics and artists, the monstrosity of what they take to be global capitalism and market economic forces matches perfectly the more "benign" acknowledgment that these super-natural entities are now indeed everywhere. The economy, in such writings and depictions, is an unbound Prometheus, a terrible beauty (if at all "beautiful"), existing beyond all attempts to represent it.[30]

So, in a sense, the idea that "economics is everywhere" has functioned—in some discussions, for at least the past century and a half—in the arts and the broader sphere of "culture." This premise, without the negative affect that accompanies many of the current cultural reactions to the "everywhereness" of economics, was one of the guiding imperatives that gave rise to the collection of essays contained here. The initial occasion for the presentation of these essays was a conference on the "aesthetics of value," by which we meant largely the ways in which representations and constructions of economic value have been rendered within the arts and literature, and, alternatively, the ways in which aesthetic values and experiences have themselves influenced, and have been influenced by, the economy, all-pervasive or not. Additionally, the conference was an attempt, once again, to bring together in conversation economists and cultural critics and practitioners to reflect upon the intricate intersections of the arts and economics.[31] To distinguish it from some other noteworthy undertakings at cross-disciplinary and transdiscursive convocations, the conference and the present collection is not intended to provide a perspective, from one side of a divide, about what is presumed to exist on the other. So, we did not start from the notion that the conference

Introduction   9

would emphasize economists' various "engagements" with art, though of course we welcomed such work as a part of the program. Nor did we focus our efforts primarily on the crucial and emerging field of the culture and economics of art markets, that is, how art and culture "enter" the realm of the economy.

We did wish to highlight what we believed to be a mostly underrepresented idea, however. And that is the premise that if economics is everywhere—and if, in the strictest sense, this means that economic discourse is itself unbounded in regard to when and where it appears—then the arts constitute a legitimate and consequential location not only for the representation, but also for the production and distribution of economic concepts and theories, including that of "economic value." To put this otherwise, the conference commenced with the presupposition that, over the span of at least the past 150 years, artists and critics have been key players in the spawning and disseminating of modern (Western) economic ideas. "If everywhere," then, economic ideas may arise in the works of artists, writers, sculptors, architects, musicians, and so forth, in ways unfamiliar or unrecognizable even to professional economists. As David Ruccio and Jack Amariglio argue in their book *Postmodern Moments in Modern Economics* (2003), the production of economic knowledge is not the exclusive preserve of academic economists, and, in fact, the "everyday economics" of cultural practitioners may, at times, be more influential than the officially sanctioned theories of professional economists in determining popular discourses regarding how and why economic activities occur.[32]

Yet, the analysis of cultural productions for the ways they "represent" or "construct" economic values, concepts, and theories is still in its infancy, at least among those trained in professional economics.[33] While there have been innumerable attempts from the mid-nineteenth century forward by cultural practitioners and critics to elucidate the perceived economic "content" of painting, sculpture, film, dance, literature, etc., this activity has not been matched by economists who, perhaps paradoxically, are trained to "see" the economy in virtually every living and non-living thing.[34] While this unevenness is curious, to say the least, it is also part of the broader modern division of labor in which economists are trained less in reading aesthetic objects and experiences for their representational value than in overcoding all human activities with the representational precepts of their preferred theories of human economic action. So, again, this book was born in the difficult circumstances of attempting to take seriously for economic discourse, official and otherwise, the representations and constructions that have been bequeathed by artists and other cultural producers or that can be "read" by those willing to consider the possibility that art and culture can "mean," if not convey, important and innovative economic ideas and images.

Bringing economists, literary and art critics, artists, philosophers, sociologists, and others together in this book has fostered the emergence of a rich set of concerns about the intersections of art, aesthetics, and economics that has overflowed our earlier, more restricted focus of textual readings of aesthetic objects for economic content. Nevertheless, the essays in this volume are more in the line of a still inaugural set of "encounters" between economists and cultural theorists

10 *Jack Amariglio, Joseph W. Childers, and Stephen E. Cullenberg*

and practitioners. Along with contributing to our recognition of the places and practices in which economics, art, and culture touch significantly upon each other, such cross-disciplinary encounters also help to forge new strategies for the interrogation of those disciplines' shared concerns. In this sense, the present collection participates in the continuing emergence of a distinct field of inquiry, one in which the "everywhereness" of economics is modified, and equaled, by the "everywhereness" of culture and aesthetics. In such an undertaking, the "sublime" character of the economy is, itself, sublimated into a project of understanding, one in which the limitations of the attendant disciplines and points of view are conjoined with an appreciation of their transgressions and excesses, terrifying or not.

The specific topics of the fourteen essays in this collection are far ranging—from prostitution to classical statues, from vocational education to "bourgeois virtues," from Bloomsbury to Pompeii. Yet, in considering how these chapters speak to each other and engage in new ways of thinking the connections between aesthetics and economics, we discovered that they fall "naturally" into four distinct, though by no means numerically symmetrical, groups. The first part, "Tokens of Eccentricity: Value and the Aesthetic Representation of Economy" serves as a kind of theoretical overview and introduction, outlining—sometimes provocatively—many of the issues that shape the investigations of the book's contributors. In Chapter 1, "Tracing the Economic: Modern Art's Construction of Economic Value," Jack Amariglio investigates the dynamic that emerges when art, such as Kasimir Malevich's *Red Square*, refuses conventional realistic representation even as it claims a foundation in "the economic principle," what Malevich views as the organic principle of all material life. For Amariglio, the problem of such a position raises issues that often are elided (or avoided) in considering "how can we connect in a meaningful way this revel into abstraction with the materiality of everyday life" (Amariglio, Chapter 1). In a theoretical turnabout, Amariglio is less interested in following the example of most art critics, from John Ruskin forward, who have delved into the "political economy of art." Rather, he posits an important proposition that forces us to reconsider the relationship between art and economic discourse. As Amariglio puts it, "the question [is] of how works of modern art may be read as constructive of economic discourses, and particularly discourses that presume notions of economic value, that is, the determination and effects of the economic 'worth' of objects. My premise is that 'the economy,' 'the economic,' and 'economic value' are represented, figured, and disseminated as images within modern art—or more to the point, they can be read as that which is gestured toward in such art" (Chapter 1). Ultimately, for Amariglio, the question of how it is possible to value something that purportedly "doesn't mean" is answered by the excessive play of meaning that such works of art produce, a play that he characterizes in the theoretical (and "economic") terms of the "gift." Yet, as he points out, even as an "oblique economic referent emerges," the historical conversation that abides in "modern," "non-representational" art, though dialectical, resists synthesis into "one or another of the well-known value theories and well-worn referents for 'the economy.' "

Introduction 11

The fusions, and sometimes con/fusions, of discourses of representation and their failures inform the challenging and experimental piece, "Meaning to Say ..." by Judith Mehta. Beginning with the concept of the *parergon*, that part of a text separating "that which is integral to, or a part of, the work, and that which is extraneous to it, while having no part in determining the meaning and value of the work" (Mehta, Chapter 2), Mehta elaborates on Derrida's difficulties with limiting a text and its meaning, of "deciding" what is inside and outside, what is "fundamental" and what is "supplement." For her, as for Derrida, the parergon is particular and separable *as well as* nonparticular and nondetachable; more even than a "frame" it speaks to a *lack* in the text, and in so doing creates the possibility for that text's articulation. Mehta sees this theoretical construct as descriptive of the tensions between "culture" and "economics" as the latter, disciplinarily, typically constructs itself. Whatever subsidiary role "culture" may have in the discourse of the dismal science, there is no speaking or knowing "economics" outside of culture. As she says, "if every thing can be conceived as a cultural construct, the economic domain must surely collapse into the cultural domain and *il n'y a pas de hors-culture.* By the same token, as the cultural field itself admits concepts and ideas appropriated from economics, so, too, *il n'y a pas de hors-economie.* Each term has reproduced itself to the point at which all meaning has been evacuated" (Mehta, Chapter 2). Mehta's "Meaning to Say ..." is a *tour de force* in its challenging of the boundaries and boundedness that constrict our discourses. There is no separating the content from the presentation of this essay, and indeed the presentation draws considerable attention to itself as boundary testing, not only through its sparkling prose, but also through the very typography and layout of the piece. Mehta asks her readers to consider how we might identify the parergon, what it may be, what it may do. In experiencing her essay (or more precisely the *performance* of her essay), the reader sees the conventional connections between "culture" and "economics" exposed in their simulacral functions, and the limits of the discourses of "art" and "critique" defied.

Rounding out the first part of this volume is "Use, Value, Aesthetics: Gambling with Difference/Speculating with Value" by Joseph W. Childers and Stephen Cullenberg. This piece takes up Gayatri Spivak's discussion of the "textualization" of value as it runs the "continuist" signifying gamut from labor to value to money to capital and how in so doing the place of "use value" remains untheorized. Childers and Cullenberg find in this critique an opening for a rethinking of the connections of labor to value. Like Spivak, they wish to retain those connections as part of the "textualization" of value. Unlike her, however, they do not see textualization as necessarily a nostalgic move to "keep randomness at bay"; instead they argue for a more open, overdetermined, model of value theory that adduces labor as an important contributor to value, but does not rely so completely on an essentialized conception of labor for value's representation. In arguing for a more aleatory theory of value, they note the similarity between such an approach and the assumptions that operate in discussions of aesthetics and value. Further, they stress the importance of including conventionally "unremarked" labor and

12 *Jack Amariglio, Joseph W. Childers, and Stephen E. Cullenberg*

of beginning to theorize more fully the place of use value in the labor/value matrix.

"Sublime Intercourse: Economics Meets Aesthetics," the second part of this volume, comprises five essays and one interview, with Deirdre McCloskey, which speak directly to dialogs between economics and aesthetics, and the assumptions of each that bedevil the other. Neil De Marchi's essay, "Reluctant Partners: Aesthetic and Market Value, 1708–1871," demonstrates how important it was to Enlightenment economists and aestheticians alike to establish a system for valuing the aesthetic in a way that is removed—at least partially—from emotional, metaphysical, or otherwise non-quantifiable influences. Tracking the history of attempts to create systems of valuation for aesthetic products, he reveals the significance of the aesthetic to economic deliberations, the difficulties economics had with quantifying or "scientizing" the aesthetic experience, and the resulting effects such endeavors had on each discourse. From attempts to schematize the aesthetic effectiveness of art by early eighteenth-century art critics Jonathan Richardson and Roger de Piles to the mid-nineteenth-century insistence of William Stanley Jevons that an economic analysis of pleasure be confined to necessities, an increasing number of barriers have been erected for the integrating artistic and market value rankings into a single framework.

In Chapter 5, "On the Contemporaneousness of Roger de Piles' *Balance des Peintres*," Victor Ginsburgh and Sheila Weyers closely investigate de Piles' 1708 attempt at decomposing the value of a painting into several basic properties (composition, drawing, color, and expression) which can be quantitatively rated. Through their use of regression analysis they determine the weight each of these various properties would carry in de Piles' system of "quantifying" the "value" of the several paintings (and the "talent" of the painters) he includes in his *Balance*. Surprisingly, their articulation of de Piles' method shows that his eighteenth-century quantitative evaluations are strikingly similar to the market reception of those same artists and artworks today.

Evan Watkins' "How Aesthetics and Economics Met in Voc Ed" departs significantly from the problem of quantifying the aesthetic and market values of great (or near great) works of art. Approaching the juncture of the economic and aesthetic spheres from a much different direction, Watkins begins by considering the phenomenon of "working-class" aesthetic, especially as it is reproduced through vocational educational classes in cosmetology. For him this intersection between the aesthetic and the specifically working class body helps us to see more clearly those class processes that "are now difficult if not impossible to discern in an economic order where accelerated shifts of social positioning seem the norm rather than an anomaly" (Chapter 6). Yet rather than accede to an inevitable "middle-classing" of America, Watkins proclaims that when these class processes do become harder to recognize we "must learn to look into those motors of acceleration rather than continuing to peer behind them in order to locate some hidden, stable, hierarchical indices of inclusion and exclusion" (Watkins, Chapter 6). As he cogently, and without compunction, polemically, contends, "Class processes ... can no longer be imagined as if a kind of hidden, stubborn

Introduction 13

reality behind the appearance of a continually shifting, unstable social order. The motility implied by an emphasis on class *processes* must be understood at least literally enough to recognize, again, the inherence of an exploitative devaluing within the constitutive conditions of a 21st century production of labor power" (Watkins, Chapter 6).

From the aesthetic as a class process we move to Craufurd D. Goodwin's "Economics Meets Esthetics in the Bloomsbury Group," which focuses on the early twentieth-century, high modernist London cohort that included Virginia and Leonard Woolf, Clive and Vanessa Bell, E. M. Forster, Roger Fry, and John Maynard Keynes. Goodwin's interest is primarily in the work of Roger Fry, the art critic, his attempts at a "science" of aesthetics that could forward many of the shared beliefs of these artists and thinkers, and the effects of his work on thinking about the connections between aesthetics and the market, or the "economic." Goodwin observes that for the Bloomsbury circle that which mattered most was what took place in the "imaginary life" rather than in the "practical life." For them, it was in this register that things like music, art, literature, and science took place; it was in the imaginative life that "civilization" established and reproduced itself. Yet, how to "value" these achievements? For Fry it meant a distinction must be made between valuation in the imaginative and practical lives—each producing its own standards of worth. And while Fry's speculations on these matters had considerable purchase among academics and aestheticians for years (consider, for instance, the resilience of formalism), Goodwin contends that to pursue Fry's theories, especially his speculations over the "creation and transmission of an esthetic emotion, threatened the notion of utility maximization and would have required close collaboration of economics with psychology, a dangerous heresy then and now" (Goodwin, Chapter 7).

In many ways the high modernist aesthetic bequeathed to the late twentieth and early twenty-first centuries by the Bloomsbury Group can be (and has been) described as the articulation of a particular, *classed*, version of the English national identity that emerged in opposition to the strictures of Victorian and Edwardian England. In Craufurd Goodwin's essay, the Bloomsburys' attempts at thinking through an economics of the aesthetic—the "imaginative life"—gets pride of place, and upon reflection we see the effect that such efforts have on Englishness itself between (and after) the two world wars. In her essay, "Individualism, Civilization, and National Character in Market Democracies," Regenia Gagnier takes up these issues, but in a rather different way. Rather than working outward *toward* the economic, she suggests that the ways we understand national character, our notions of what it means to be "civilized," and, of course, our investment in "individualism" are inseparable from the operations of market democracies. Put another way, that is to say, in Gagnier's own words, "the political system of 'social democracy' and the economic system of the 'market' have collapsed into one, so that whether our choices are 'free' or the product of multiple constraints, what we buy reveals all the preferences we are allowed to express" (Gagnier, Chapter 8). For Gagnier, then, the very aesthetics of existence is shaped by a market that we cannot avoid. In her essay she selects three national stereotypes of individualism for her

14   *Jack Amariglio, Joseph W. Childers, and Stephen E. Cullenberg*

analysis: "the recombinant consumer-citizen pursuing happiness and maximizing self-interest, the fascist individual in service to the state, and the reflective, often female, subject of Arnoldian liberalism" (Gagnier, Chapter 8). In each of these, she finds that the market democracies so reliant on these (and other formations of) individualism reproduces the *phantasm* of the notion of the individual even as they undercut its operation as a reality. As the last bastion of individualism—the gene—is increasingly co-opted by market democracies, we will find ourselves continually rethinking the "politics of labor and the economics of scarcity."

The final contribution to this second part of *Sublime Economy* is a "slightly disputatious" and wide-ranging "conversation" between Deirdre McCloskey and her interlocutor, Jack Amariglio. Moving from Plato to Charlie Parker, from the Dutch masters to the "Ashcan school of art," from nineteenth-century novels to contemporary economic theory, McCloskey offers her insights on the relationships between aesthetic production and value and economic discourses and practice. Ever the defender of capitalism and the middle classes, McCloskey argues for the ethical responsibility of the artist. Situating herself as an anarchist with liberal (perhaps one should say "ironic-liberal" in the Rortian sense) tendencies, McCloskey maintains the importance and salutary effect of what she identifies as "bourgeois values," and sees them operating productively and positively in aesthetic and economic realms alike.

Olav Velthuis' essay, "Imaginary Currencies: Contemporary Art on the Market—Critique, Confirmation, or Play" maintains the serious playfulness of the McCloskey interview in opening "Name Your Price," the third part of this collection. In his piece, Velthuis looks at the issues that arise when artists, particularly contemporary artists, strategically—sometimes disruptively—and always "imaginatively" take up the very economics of art as their subject matter. As Velthuis points out, such incursions are not unique to late twentieth- or early twenty-first-century artists; nevertheless, he focuses on recent attempts by contemporary artists to draw attention to the ways in which the "economic" is inextricably connected to the production of art. From the work of Swiss installation artists Christoph Büchel and Gianni Motti, whose exhibition "Capital Affair" at Zurich's Helmhaus was to present an entirely empty museum space in which was hidden a "certificate" redeemable for 50,000 Swiss francs for the first visitor to find it—but who decided against opening their exhibition when the Swiss government insisted they reduce their "reward" to 20,000 Francs—to American artist J. S. G. Boggs' use of hand-drawn versions of U.S. currency (with blank backs and mottos such as "Red Gold We Trust" and "Please Give Me a Fair Trial") to purchase everything from Harleys to Big Macs (with change), and which because vendors accepted his "currency" landed him in court facing charges of counterfeiting, Velthuis examines the multiple ways such acts unsettle and challenge the assumptions underlying economics and aesthetics, and their imbrication.

The second contribution to this part is "The Sociology of the New Art Gallery Scene in Chelsea, Manhattan" by David Halle and Elisabeth Tiso. They studied the phenomenal growth of art galleries in Chelsea in the early twenty-first

Introduction 15

century, whereby Chelsea has now dwarfed other art districts in the United States and supplanted SoHo, once the most dynamic gallery neighborhood in New York City. They did a five-year study that investigated the relative role of markets and commercialization versus patronage as the major way in which art is produced. In their detailed case study of the Chelsea gallery scene, they find that theories stressing the commodification of art "are consistent with some features of Chelsea such as the agglomeration of commercial galleries, the rise of the global gallery, and the threat that the commercial real estate market may replace galleries with residential condominiums and/or stores selling more profitable merchandise" (Chapter 11). On the other hand, some of Chelsea's more vibrant artistic productions cannot be reduced to commodification and commercialization. Chelsea provides a giant free art show for people who are not consumers of art and an "open structure of opportunity for artists that far surpasses the opportunities offered by museums, and the fact that the vast majority of galleries are not global or star but small, boutique-like operations selling unique products each one of which proclaims its individuality and the creativity of the artist who produced it" (Chapter 11). They conclude that a commodification theory does not fully capture the nuanced manner in which art often creates meaning and has significance for the lives of its viewers.

The final contribution to this part is by Arjo Klamer, who states his conclusion "up front: cultural goods are exceptional and therefore easier to distinguish from other goods" (Chapter 12). For Klamer, they are exceptional not because of some intrinsic difference, but because, as cultural and discursive constructs, they take place in conversations that set them apart from other goods. In this Klamer separates himself from other economists, by insisting that the "value" a thing has is, in large degree, attributable to the kinds of "conversations" that surround it and in which it may participate. These conversations are, typically, multiple, and changing. And while Klamer is not arguing that cultural goods are *essentially* different from other goods, and thus that economists are fundamentally mistaken in the way they talk about commodities, he does believe that in order to understand the operations of the "art world" it is necessary to realize that "economic arguments play a subordinate role" in the deliberations in which the value of cultural goods are realized. In his essay "The Lives of Cultural Goods," Klamer attempts, through his heuristic of the "conversation," to mediate between the "culturalist" and "economistic" discourses of valuation, and in the process to re-evaluate notions of value, culture, and valorization.

The last part of this volume, "Moral Economies and the Romance of Money," is comprised of two powerful essays that discuss how money, language, culture, and economy intersect in various methods to construct nation-states, bodies, and diverse forms of representation. In "The Rhetoric of Prostitution," Jennifer Doyle takes the figure of the prostitute in late nineteenth- and early twentieth-century art and literature as the cultural site that contains, and reconstrues, issues of modernity, commodification, aesthetics, industrialization, sexuality, and the "economic." Pointing out that—for so many critics—"the observation of the link between the prostitute and modernity is almost *de rigeur* ... as if the connection

16   *Jack Amariglio, Joseph W. Childers, and Stephen E. Cullenberg*

between the prostitute and modernity were obvious," she goes on to note that, even when the "prostitute is invoked to attempt to identify the specific concerns of modernism and realism," with few exceptions there is little focus on what "this association between prostitution and art means, where it comes from, or what its legacy might be" (Doyle, Chapter 13). Even when critics like Sander Gilman or Charles Bernheimer do venture to address these issues, says Doyle, they disappoint in their lack of attention to the "textual flavor" of such representations and they fail to address the reasons for the "staying power" of the prostitute as cultural/aesthetic figure. In her analysis, Doyle carefully reads works by William Dean Howells and Frank Norris as she works through what she describes as a "somewhat different configuration of desire and the 'real'—the puzzle that grows out of trying to imagine, characterize, or inhabit the space between people and the art objects they consume" (Doyle, Chapter 11). For Doyle, "the prostitute works in art and criticism as an index of the truth about the work of art. It is not the sociality of sex that she represents in these texts, but the aesthetic" (Chapter 13). And, one might add, the economic as well—as it is imbricated in the bourgeois aesthetic–that—*contra* McCloskey—is so reliant on and invested in realism.

In the final essay of this collection, "A Heap of Worthless Fragments: The Nineteenth-Century Literary Revaluation of the Classical Statue," Yota Batsaki offers a fitting conclusion to the volume. Her reading of three nineteenth-century texts, Prosper Mérimée's "The Venus of Ille" (1837), Nathaniel Hawthorne's *The Marble Faun* (1860), and Henry James' "The Last of the Valerii" (1874), considers the ways in which a modern aesthetic mode—prose fictional narrative— passes aesthetic as well as economic judgment on the artifacts of the past. In her analysis, Batsaki considers the ways in which these works elevate the aesthetic value of classical statues as emblems of a bygone, somehow "superior" era, even as they dismiss the possible use values of these artifacts as emblematic of the "pagan, sensuous, unselfconscious," and thus in direct conflict with the pragmatic, moralistic, responsible self-consciousness of modernity. As Batsaki states, "In contrast to the endurance of the classical statue as aesthetic object, the function of the literary statue is to be ultimately and unsympathetically dismissed by modernity" (Batsaki, Chapter 14). In many ways, Batsaki's argument highlights the issues that continue to arise and bedevil the discussions that take place throughout this book. It is possible to identify desires—often leavened with more than a hint of nostalgia—to celebrate the aesthetic, to attempt to figure the value of art outside a "simple" exchange matrix, even while denying (or certainly having difficulty with) the use values that obtain in those objects. Similarly, we see endeavors at figuring the links between the aesthetic and the economic in ways that insist upon dialogue or "conversation," allowing new tropes of signification to emerge. We see economists attempt to write about aesthetics and humanists struggle to write about economics in order to move across disciplinary and conceptual boundaries to a place where that conversation—in a shared and agreed-upon vocabulary—can take place. In these attempts, we see clearly where the difficulties lie, but we also become aware of the possibilities. If sublimity is a goal, we must remember that it is also, always, more than a little unsettling and it must be able to cause us to consider the

Introduction 17

foundations from which we move, speak, act. The voices raised in this collection are willing to take that risk; consequently what we hear in *Sublime Economy* is a chorus that is sometimes discordant, sometimes contrapuntal, sometimes at odds about the very melody it is trying to carry, but it is always engaging and never cacophonic.

Notes

1 This is by no means a new strategy by economists of various stripes. In *Illustrations of Political Economy* (9 vols., 1832–34), Harriet Martineau used similar tactics to educate the English on the importance and ubiquity of what, at that time, was called "political economy."

2 Consider, for example, one paradigmatic expression of the supposed overarching imperialism of economic—and here by "economic" is meant "neoclassical"—theories and ideas in the imagination of the professional economist, if no-one else. David Throsby, who is by no means a gung-ho mainstream economist, unaware of the larger culture within which neoclassical economics and its many offshoots have thrived, is still able in his fine 2001 book *Economics and Culture* to state categorically that "the apparent universality of the economic model of individual behaviour and of the transactional relationships which that behaviour engenders has pushed economics into center stage among the social sciences. The paradigm of the rational utility-maximizing individual is thought to be so comprehensive in its coverage of human motivation and action that there remain few if any phenomena that cannot be caught within its ambit" (154).

3 Before we begin our discussion of the figure of "the sublime," we wish to note the exhaustion that some have felt with the revival over the past 25 or more years of the idea of the sublime. Feminist art critics, in particular, have been vocal in deriding the new central emphasis—exemplified in the writings of Jean-François Lyotard—that has been accorded to "the sublime" in "postmodern" art and literature. As Margaret Iversen (1991) expresses in her insistence that "the sublime was then" (by which she means the 40s and 50s), the reappearance of "the sublime" among mostly male and Euro-American critics and aestheticians since the 1980s is seen by some feminist critics as a reactionary reactivation of individual (male) creativity (as Jane Flax has noted) in a heroic struggle against the persistent and now global "banalities of mass culture." For a related and more extended critique of the "masculine tradition of the sublime," see Joanna Zylinska, (2001). Zylinska imagines and substitutes a "feminine sublime" that is focused more on the excesses—concerned primarily with the experiences of alterity, difference, and uncertainty—that characterize or are condensed in an economy of (feminine-inflected) gift-giving. Such a feminine sublime and its consequent ethics of incalculable generosity and/or respect would then stand as a critique of the masculine sublime that, instead, revels or wallows, in critique or celebration, in the gains and losses of capitalist economic modernity. Our own interest in the sublime is born more out of our perceptions of current aesthetic reactions to and representations of the purported everywhereness of capitalist economy—indeed, of economy itself—and less out of a desire to reinstate the project of fetishizing creativity, radical individuality, and the commercial, "hyperreal" excesses of contemporary capitalism. In our discussion of "the sublime," we are more concerned with taking note of the place "economy" has come to occupy in its aesthetic apprehensions and representations than we are in the dubitable and politically regressive premise that "the sublime" has displaced all other modes of aesthetic experience in the present historical conjuncture.

4 Smith's reflections on aesthetics were not limited to the passages on surprise, wonder, and admiration in the "History of Astronomy." Among his other writings on literary

18 *Jack Amariglio, Joseph W. Childers, and Stephen E. Cullenberg*

and cultural texts and trends, Smith's most extended discussion of the aesthetics of art and culture is his essay "On the Nature of that Imitation which takes place in what are called The Imitative Arts" (1980b).

5 Burke was a friend and correspondent of Smith's; in a letter from David Hume to Smith from 1759, Hume describes Burke as "an Irish gentleman, who wrote lately a very pretty Treatise on the Sublime" (Smith, 1987, 33).

6 In the academic discipline of economics, G. L. S. Shackle stands out as one of the few theorists who has seized upon the notion of Surprise as a central organizing theme for economic behavior. Shackle's "surprise" is not reduced to a sub-category of calculable risk and domesticable uncertainty. Nor is surprise, for him, solely a narrative device and/or an aesthetically loaded metaphor, but, rather, is an analytical category of utmost importance in determining how and why economic agents might behave as they do when they experience the "counter-expected" or "unexpected." Shackle was able to retain a good deal of Smith's "wonder" about the experience of surprise, but he also indicated that imagination and ingenuity are activated in strategic decisionmaking in the face of genuine surprise. Indeed, such imaginative and ingenious decisionmaking explained the ability of some to economically prosper, while others would be unable or unwilling to take equally imaginative or brilliant actions, and would thus suffer their fortunes accordingly. For one example of his views, see Shackle's discussion of what he perceived as the exclusion of "tactical surprise" from contemporary game theory, and his critique of this exclusion, in *Epistemics and Economics: A Critique of Economic Discourses* (1992).

7 Olivier Asselin (1996) summarizes Kant's sublime in similar language. For Kant, "the imagination is incapable of comprehending the entire series simultaneously, of grasping its totality instantaneously in an aesthetic evaluation or synthesis" (248).

8 There is a good deal of disagreement among aestheticians and philosophers about the limitation of "the sublime" in Kant to "nature." Jacques Derrida (1987), among others, notes Kant's reluctance to extend the sublime to anything "man-made," such as "the productions of art," since, in Kant's view, what is made by "man" is, in Derrida's words, "on the scale of man, who determines their form and dimensions. The mastery of the human artist here operates with a view to an end, determining, defining, giving form. In deciding on contours, giving boundaries to the form and the cise, this mastery measures and dominates. But the sublime, if there is any sublime, exists only by overspilling. ... It is no longer proportioned according to man and his determinations. There is thus no good example, no 'suitable' example of the sublime in the products of human art" (122). Soon after, though, Derrida argues that, for Kant, "nature" has to be amended to exclude "the things of nature ... [whose] concept already contains a determinate end" (122). Only in "raw nature" can one find objects that are candidates for the experience of conceptual indeterminacy that comprises the sublime. But, Derrida insists, as have others, that it is not the objects of raw nature themselves that are sublime. The sublime "cannot inhabit any sensible form" and cannot reside anywhere "but in the mind and on the side of the subject" (131). The Kantian "subjectivist" sublime, then, is due to a lack "in us": "So, although the sublime is better presented by raw nature than by art, it is not in nature but in ourselves, projected by us because of the inadequation in us of several powers, of several faculties" (132). Of course, other theorists argue that if "the sublime" properly "relates to the ideas of reason" (Derrida, 1987, 131) and the "unpresentable," then whatever event or object sets off the perception or idea of the indeterminate and infinite can be regarded as potentially productive of sublime reflection.

9 Regenia Gagnier (2000) argues, though, that "social and psychological as well as physical landscapes—genders, crowds, leaders, and appropriate forms of response to them—were embedded in Edmund Burke's classic distinction between the Sublime and the Beautiful of 1757" (37). As such, Gagnier includes Burke's thoughts on this

Introduction 19

distinction within the more general observation that "political economy informed both philosophical and literary aesthetics" (38) in the late eighteenth and nineteenth century.

10 The twentieth-century introduction of the theme, and sense, of "uncertainty" in economic matters may represent one limiting factor of this belief that economic models can grasp the totality of capitalist extension in space and time. There is a huge literature in which uncertainty, in a variety of understandings, has been conceptualized and mathematically operationalized within modern economics. In some versions, uncertainty takes the form of statistical/probabilistic outcomes and, therefore, falls "within" the models (that is, serves as an explanatory variable, even when it also encompasses catch-all residuals or random error terms). In these models, the "whole," which includes uncertainty, is safely theorized within the confines of economic reason. Yet, there have been other attempts at introducing uncertainty (perhaps most famously the "fundamental uncertainty" that can be gleaned in the writings of Keynes and Shackle, among others) that may indeed keep alive the sense that reason and even imagination are halted by an untranscendable limit comprised of a type of uncertainty that eludes systemic totalization. It is here, and in these traditions, that the sense of the "sublime economy" may rear its disturbing (though "pleasurable") head.

11 This point is highlighted in Kirk Pillow's *Sublime Understanding* (2000). Pillow, though, reworks the Kantian categories to suggest not only that formal and bounded works of art and culture can "represent" the sublime in their content and effects (thus countering the idea that, for Kant, only formless objects are capable of inducing the aesthetic reaction called "the sublime"), but also that it is within the realm of understanding and even through reason that sublime sensibility is conducted and transmitted. He posits this view in contrast to many contemporary theorists of the sublime, and certainly as a riposte to Lyotard's influential formulation of the "postmodern sublime." For Pillow, the sublime is not merely, or not even, an "aesthetic judgment," à la Kant, but, rather, is a form of understanding about aesthetic ideas. Thus, in Pillow's analysis, sublime understanding "helps invent our indeterminate worlds; it also violates the limits of current comprehension without pretending that its product is complete or that it now captures some given reality" (303). He continues: "Contrary to Lyotard, the postmodern sublime not only disturbs and dehabituates our secure categorical sense of reality; it also contributes to the ongoing projection of the historically sedimented, multiple, and ambiguous networks of 'irreality'" (303).

12 This tendency is captured by Marshal Berman (1982) in the reiteration of Marx and Engels's poetic claim that, with the rise of capitalism, "all that is solid melts into air."

13 Though there are strong differences among aesthetic theorists on this point, Lyotard (1994) reads Kant to emphasize "formlessness" in the sublime experience. That is, the initial perceptions of objects that create the subjective sublime feeling have no form—they defy form in their unboundedness. Lyotard states: "In the sublime ... form plays no role at all. In fact form conflicts with the purity of sublime delight. If one is permitted to speak of 'nature' in this feeling, one can speak only in terms of a 'rude nature' ... 'merely as involving magnitude.' This magnitude is rude and arouses sublime feeling precisely because it escapes form, because it is completely 'wanting in form or figure.' It is this formlessness ... that Kant evokes to begin the analysis of the sublime by quantity" (78).

14 It is important to note that the Kantian tradition includes "the sublime" as a form of aesthetic pleasure. That is, there is a form of pleasure that comes, perhaps in the moments following the immediate apprehension of the sublime spectacle, from experiencing objects and experiences that terrify. Christine Battersby (1991) explains that, in addition to or in accordance with the mostly pristine aesthetic pleasure occasioned by apprehension of "the beautiful," "Kant also registers that there are other less pure forms of aesthetic pleasure. His key example is that of the 'sublime,' which involves a

20 Jack Amariglio, Joseph W. Childers, and Stephen E. Cullenberg

response to the terrifying (to gaunt mountains, thunder, storm-ridden seas, earthquakes, etc.). Here the pleasure comes from the overcoming of threat and pain: of registering that the world is constructed by the imagination as an unknowable infinity which, at any moment, threatens to overwhelm the ego and reveal to the self its limits. But since the sublime involves registering this threat and transcending this threat, the enjoyment of the sublime is itself also an enjoyment of power over nature" (36–7). In Edmund Burke's discursus on the sublime, as Olivier Asselin (1996) recounts it, "the sublime feeling is not all made of terror. According to Burke, when the observer is at a certain distance (spatial or temporal) from what seems menacing, when she or he is safe, that is 'hors-scene', terror is then mixed with a kind of pleasure which comes from this suspension of danger or its *mise en représentation*. This is what Burke calls 'delight' in opposition to 'pleasure'" (Asselin, 247).

15 Heidegger is only one commentator among many on this topic (and, indeed, these very shoes). For instance, both Jacques Derrida and Fredric Jameson have affirmed the overwhelming vista created by the intersection of the natural and the social as revealed in Van Gogh's painting.

16 The growth of nineteenth-century European cities and urban planning on a massive scale is seen, by Iain Boyd White, to have inspired what he calls "the Expressionist Sublime," instilled in post-WWI Expressionist architecture, primarily in Germany. Marking the sublime's shifting terrain from Nature to human creation, Boyd White explains, "just as the chaotic forces of nature exceed our powers of comprehension and threaten us with destruction, so the great urban centers of the late nineteenth century were invested with entropic qualities. Like an overheated boiler, these massive concentrations of energy carried in their very fabric the potential for self-destruction" (125). Boyd White sees in the abandonment of Expressionist projects around 1920 the rejection of the sublime—"the elements of fear, uncertainty, and self-overcoming were willfully abandoned in favor of the mechanical and physical certainties on which functionalist modernism was grounded" (135). Thus, the rise of the "International Style" and its "comprehensibility" was, in Boyd White's view, "the antithesis of the Expressionist sublime."

17 Margaret Iversen (1991) informs us that the conscious appropriation of the notion of "the sublime" by 1940s and 50s abstract artists, such as Barnett Newman, was part and parcel of their general embrace of forms of resistance to "totalitarian" and "capitalist" systems of conventional social and artistic life. Since, "the fallen social sphere is bound by convention, the artist operates outside history and artistic conventions" (83). The "sublime" in all of this consists of acts and experiences of spontaneity and immediacy that, presumably, allowed abstract artists to have, in Newman's words, a "relation to the absolute emotions" (83). Iversen notes that the art historian David Craven insightfully links abstract artists' recourse to the rhetoric of the sublime to an ethos of "romantic anti-capitalism."

18 The artist and critic Jeremy Gilbert-Rolfe (2001) sees the contemporary sublime as a "techno-sublime." He argues that, "while driven by electricity rather than hydrogen and oxygen in combination, the techno-sublime is sublime in the way that nature used to be: It is ungraspable because of its uncontrollable immensity" (84).

19 See, for example, Lyotard's references to "matter-of-fact positivism and calculated realism" (Lyotard 1993, 254).

20 Jameson asserts that the concept and history of capitalism, indeed, can be thought: "what is affirmed is not that we cannot know the world and its totality in some abstract or 'scientific' way. Marxian 'science' provides just such a way of knowing and conceptualizing the world abstractly, in the sense in which, for example, [Ernest] Mandel's great book offers a rich and elaborated knowledge of that global world system, of which it has never been said here that it was unknowable but, merely, that it was unrepresentable, which is a very different matter" (Jameson 1991, 53).

Introduction 21

21 Richard Brettell (1999) reminds us that the impact of Arnold Hauser's *Social History of Art* may have been to constitute the entirety of modern art (and its apperception by critics since the 1950s) as primarily a structured critique of capitalist economy.

22 Jameson's strategic use of "the sublime" in works preceding his famous postmodernism essay, and in that essay itself, is scrutinized carefully in Steven Helming's 2001 book (see especially pages 103–25). Helming contrasts the earlier Jameson identification of the sublime with forms of contemporary horror, occasioned by entrapment within a spreading, omnipresent capitalism and its "logic," to the somewhat later postmodernism essay, with its mention of moments of libidinal resistance to such entrapment in the form of new (postmodern) cultural "intensities." All the same, Helming finds that, in the postmodernism essay, Jameson joins forces with those who see, in modernity, a shift in the locus of the sublime from Nature to that which is historically "man-made." Specifically, in Helming's reading of Jameson's postmodernism essay, "it is the world system of technology and finance that now exceeds our power to grasp, to represent to ourselves. In 'the cultural logic of late capitalism,' what uniquely defeats our understanding is … precisely what 'we' have made. This 'postmodern or technological sublime' necessarily generates 'high-tech paranoia' or 'conspiracy theory' as the mind's 'degraded attempt[s]' to figure what cannot be figured, to represent what cannot be represented, 'to think the impossible totality of the contemporary world system'" (Helming 2001, 113).

23 Jameson's claim that late capitalist globalization contains within it a "vertiginous new dynamic" (for Jameson, this pertains to "international banking and the stock exchanges") is seized upon by Alix Ohlin (2002) as an apt descriptor for the overall subject matter of the photographer, Andreas Gursky. Gursky's super-panoramic "99 Cent" is, by now, the iconic artistic representation of the global supermarket. And Ohlin asserts that in this work, and in others, in order to produce a representation of the new global sublime, Gursky combines the sense of globalization's "vertiginous dynamic" with a version of Burke's "artificial infinite"—through which the eye is manipulated by art or architecture to sense its own failure to "see" all, and the imagination is thereby unable to grasp the totality or bounds of a structure's or artifact's parts. Ohlin is certain that Gursky is a premier painter of today's sublime, and Gursky has become so by substituting the vastness, greatness, and infinitude of globalization (and the subsequent smallness his representations of globalization produce in viewers) for the God of Burke's day.

24 It is uncanny the degree to which both defenders and opponents (or at least would-be reformers) of globalization perform the unceasingly repetitive narrative ritual of pronouncing capitalist globalization as "inexorable" and any attempt to "reverse" it as "futile." This is particularly marked among professional economists, whose proclamations about the inevitability of global capitalist dispersion are, of course, part of its cultural dispersion. Even thoughtful and reform-minded economists, such as Joseph Stiglitz (2003), or the cultural economist, David Throsby (2001), put forward the shared view that "managing" the process of globalization to provide for "fairer" outcomes in the distribution of economic rewards and preventing the worst of capital-flight and/or international meddling in the affairs of independent nations is the most—and best—that can or should be done.

25 In many cultural histories of aesthetics "under" capitalism, the inner boundaries that may have characterized an earlier stage of capitalism—such as the supposed "relative autonomy" of art and economy in the mid-nineteenth century, an autonomy that often worked to marginalize, but also made possible the "resistance" of, artists—have long been surpassed. So the trajectory of capitalist economy has not only been seen as the widening of its realm of operation, but also in its "internal" deepening, one moment of which is thought to be the nearly complete subsumption of art, architecture, etc. to commodification and the recomposition of all aesthetic practices into the structure

22   *Jack Amariglio, Joseph W. Childers, and Stephen E. Cullenberg*

of "industries": art becomes (commercial) design. Hal Foster alludes to this pervasive theme in his *Design and Crime* (2003) when he avers that "today, when the aesthetic and utilitarian are not only conflated but all but subsumed to the commercial ... everything— not only architectural projects and art exhibitions but everything from jeans to genes— seems to be regarded as so much design" (17).

26 The "ugliness" of imperialism is what bell hooks (1995) finds partly represented in the work of Jean-Michel Basquiat. For hooks, Basquiat "struggled to utter the unspeakable. ... In his work, colonization of the black body and mind is marked by the anguish of abandonment, estrangement, dismemberment, and death" (38). In one of Basquiat's untitled paintings of a black female, hooks reads a "critique of Western imperialism, and, then, the critique of the way in which imperialism makes itself heard, the way it is reproduced in culture and art. This image is ugly and grotesque. That is exactly how it should be. For what Basquiat unmasks is the ugliness of those traditions. He takes the Eurocentric valuation of the great and beautiful and demands that we acknowledge the brutal reality it masks" (38). On the idea that the sublime in art has, at times, been historically distinguished from the beautiful by the "code value" of "ugliness" see Luhmann (2000, 190).

27 There are innumerable examples of this narrative of engulfment. The economic geographer David Harvey (2001) presents it succinctly and powerfully when he says, "The drive for capital accumulation is the central motif in the narrative of historical-geographical transformation of the western world in recent times and seems set to engulf the whole world into the twenty-first century" (121). To be clear, Harvey is less than sanguine about this state of affairs.

28 While the artist/critic Jeremy Gilbert-Rolfe believes "techno-capitalism" is experienced by many subjects as "indispensable and irresistible," his description of its sublime pull is characterized much more by disgust than pleasure. He states that "we like techno-capitalism while knowing it to be terrifying: We know how preposterously cruel the market is, what bullshit the arguments for it are. ... We experience ourselves as powerless before it, not because we're seduced, but because it is uncontrollable. What irritates us about the interpolation of an image of the placeless sublime into the sublime which is associated with a specific place (or vista) is that we should like to have both and we can't. One should be able to choose, but the one thing about which capitalism allows no choice is whether to have capitalism. One can only have it and only it all the time" (Gilbert-Rolfe 2001, 89).

29 For a superb presentation of the resentment and immobility that are the theoretical and political consequences of the stifling constraints of discourses of "capitalocentrism" and of the all-pervasiveness of "the economy," see Gibson-Graham (1996).

30 The expression "terrible beauty" may capture the moment of pleasure that Burke and others found possible in experiences of the sublime. In strict terms, though, the beautiful and the sublime have been seen as distinct, even if their commonalities can sometimes warrant their conflation. Derrida (1987) explains that, for Kant, the beautiful and the sublime could not be regarded as opposites: "An opposition could only arise between two determinate objects, having their contours, their edges, their finitude. But if the difference between the beautiful and the sublime does not amount to an opposition, it is precisely because the presence of a limit is what gives form to the beautiful. The sublime is to be found, for its part, in an 'object without form' and the 'without-limit' is 'represented' in it or on the occasion of it, and yet gives the totality of the without-limit to be *thought*. Thus the beautiful seems to present an indeterminate concept of the understanding, the sublime an indeterminate concept of reason" (127).

31 Other collections that have sought to bridge the disciplinary gap in discussions of economics, art, literature, and culture include De Marchi and Goodwin (1999), Klamer (1996), and Woodmansee and Osteen (1999). The catalogue (2002) accompanying the Hamburg exhibition "Art & Economy" is another excellent introduction to the

Introduction 23

evolving interdisciplinary field of art and economics, though economists are certainly underrepresented in the essays included.

32 See Klamer and Meehan (1999) for a related argument.

33 While there are exceedingly few academic departments or a well-established field dedicated to the investigation of the intersection of economics and art (though there are, of course, burgeoning programs in cultural entrepreneurship and other "business"-oriented courses and degrees), this does not mean that there are no classics already in this field-in-the-making. Marc Shell's *Art and Money* (1995) is a touchstone in present and future considerations on how economic "content" is complexly represented in art (and vice versa). Shell's focus is on money, and not "economy" more broadly conceived, but his implicit dialectic, in which he shows the instability and consequent intricate transpositions of art, aesthetics, money, and economic value, is instructive and serves as a model for research in this area.

34 In addition to being relatively scarce, those few endeavors by academically trained economists to "read" economic practices and ideas "in" art/cultural objects often have been clumsy and reductionist, sometimes in the extreme (the economists among the editors of this volume do not exempt themselves from such a criticism). Such a lack of "success" may, unfortunately, contribute to the self-conscious hesitation of professional economists to refrain from interpretive analysis of works of art. Indeed, even when economists try their hands at cultural analysis, such as texts on famous painters or paintings, the tendency is to gravitate toward the economic conditions surrounding the production, consumption, and distribution of the art objects, and much less to the production of textual readings whereby economic representations would be illuminated. For example, John Michael Montias, the noted Yale economist, has written a finely detailed (perhaps obsessively so) "social history" of Johannes Vermeer (1987). Yet, in this meaty tome, there is very little attempt at reading the paintings, and in the few places in which Montias provides such interpretations, they are extremely brief, provisional, and conventional (and, also, have little to do with "economic" themes, perhaps appropriately). Montias's text can be compared with art historian T. J. Clark's *The Painting of Modern Life* (1984), which focuses on Impressionism and its emergence in the changing Paris of the 1860s and 70s. Clark's volume is marked, from page one, by an effort to connect the forms and contents of Impressionist painting to a thoroughgoing Marxian-inspired economic and class analysis. While readers may not subscribe to his Marxist materialism (which is fairly deft and non-reductionist in the main), still, it establishes a standard for interpretive readings in which economic "realities" and ideas show up, in Clark's view, on the canvases of the Impressionists. One notable exception amongst those formally trained in economics is the writings of the economic sociologist Olav Velthuis (see Chapter 10 in this volume). Velthuis's recent book *Imaginary Economics* (2005) includes wonderfully insightful and novel readings of "contemporary art as a source of knowledge pertaining to the economy" (12).

References

Asselin, Olivier. 1996. "The Sublime: The Limits of Vision and the Inflation of Commentary." In *Theory Rules: Art as Theory/Theory and Art*, edited by Jody Berland, Will Straw, and David Tomas, 243–56. Toronto: XYZ Books.

Battersby, Christine. 1991. "Situating the Aesthetic: A Feminist Defense." In *Thinking Art: Beyond Traditional Aesthetics*, edited by Andrew Benjamin and Peter Osborne, 81–93. London: Institute of Contemporary Arts.

Berman, Marshall. 1982. *All That Is Solid Melts into Air: The Experience of Modernity*. New York: Simon and Schuster.

24   *Jack Amariglio, Joseph W. Childers, and Stephen E. Cullenberg*

Brettell, Richard R. 1999. *Modern Art 1851–1929: Capitalism and Representation*. Oxford: Oxford University Press.

Clark, T. J. 1984. *The Painting of Modern Life: Paris in the Age of Manet and His Followers*. Princeton: Princeton University Press.

Crowther, Paul. 1989. *The Kantian Sublime: From Morality to Art*. Oxford: Oxford University Press.

De Marchi, Neil and Crawford D. W. Goodwin, eds. 1999. *Economic Engagements with Art*. Durham: Duke University Press.

Derrida, Jacques. 1987. *The Truth in Painting*, translated by Geoff Bennington and Ian McLeod. Chicago: University of Chicago Press.

Felix, Zdanek, Beate Hentschel, and Dirk Luckow, eds. 2002. *Art & Economy*. Ostfildern-Ruit: Hatje Cantz.

Foster, Hal. 2002. *Design and Crime (and Other Diatribes)*. London: Verso.

Gagnier, Regenia. 2000. *The Insatiability of Human Wants: Economics and Aesthetics in Market Society*. Chicago: University of Chicago Press.

Gibson-Graham, J. K. 1996. *The End of Capitalism (As We Knew It): A Feminist Critique of Political Economy*. Oxford: Blackwell.

Gilbert-Rolfe, Jeremy. 2001. "I'm Not Sure It Is Sticky." In *Sticky Sublime*, edited by Bill Beckley, 84–93. New York: Allworth Press.

Hamermesh, Daniel S. 2004. *Economics Is Everywhere*. New York: McGraw Hill/Irwin.

Hartley, George. 2003. *The Abyss of Representation: Marxism and the Postmodern Sublime*. Durham: Duke University Press.

Harvey, David. 2001. *Spaces of Capital: Towards a Critical Geography*. New York: Routledge.

Hauser, Arnold. 1999. *The Social History of Art, Volume IV: Naturalism, Impressionism, the Film Age*. London: Routledge.

Helming, Steven. 2001. *The Success and Failure of Fredric Jameson: Writing, the Sublime, and the Dialectic of Critique*. Albany: State University of New York Press.

hooks, bell. 1995. *Art on My Mind: Visual Politics*. New York: The New Press.

Iversen, Margaret. 1991. "The Deflationary Impulse: Postmodernism, Feminism, and the Anti-Aesthetic." In *Thinking Art: Beyond Traditional Aesthetics*, edited by Andrew Benjamin and Peter Osborne, 81–93. London: Institute of Contemporary Arts.

Jameson, Fredric. 1991. *Postmodernism, or, The Cultural Logic of Late Capitalism*. Durham: Duke University Press.

Kant, Immanuel. 1987 (1790). *Critique of Judgment*, translated by Werner S. Pluhar. Indianapolis: Hackett Publishing Company.

Klamer, Arjo, ed. 1996. *The Value of Culture: On the Relationship between Economics and the Arts*. Amsterdam: Amsterdam University Press.

Klamer, Arjo, and Jeniifer Meehan. 1999. "The Crowding-Out of Academic Economics: The Case of NAFTA." In *What Do Economists Know? New Economics of Knowledge*, edited by Robert F. Garnett, Jr. New York: Routledge.

Luhmann, Niklas. 2000. *Art as a Social System*, translated by Eva M. Knodt. Stanford: Stanford University Press.

Lyotard, Jean-François. 1993. "The Sublime and the Avant-Garde." In *Postmodernism: A Reader*, edited by Thomas Docherty, 244–56. New York: Columbia University Press.

Lyotard, Jean-François. 1994. *Lessons on the Analytic of the Sublime*, translated by Elizabeth Rottenberg. Stanford: Stanford University Press.

Mattick, Paul. 2003. *Art in Its Time: Theories and Practices of Modern Aesthetics*. London: Routledge.

Montias, John Michael. 1989. *Vermeer and his Milieu: A Web of Social History*. Princeton: Princeton University Press.

Ohlin, Alix. 2002. "Andreas Gursky and the Contemporary Sublime." *Art Journal* 61(4), 22–35.

Pillow, Kirk. 2000. *Sublime Understanding: Aesthetic Reflection in Kant and Hegel*. Cambridge: The MIT Press.

Ruccio, David, and Jack Amariglio. 2003. *Postmodern Moments in Modern Economics*. Princeton: Princeton University Press.

Shackle, G. L. S. 1992. *Epistemics and Economics: A Critique of Economic Doctrines*. New Brunswick, NJ: Transaction Publishers.

Shell, Marc. 1995. *Art and Money*. Chicago: University of Chicago Press.

Sheppard, Anne. 1987. *Aesthetics: An Introduction to the Philosophy of Art*. Oxford: Oxford University Press.

Smith, Adam. 1980a. "The History of Astronomy." In *Essays on Philosophical Subjects*, edited by W. P. D. Wightman and J. C. Bryce, 31–105. Indianapolis: Liberty Classics.

Smith, Adam. 1980b. "On the Nature of that Imitation which takes place in what are called The Imitative Arts." In *Essays on Philosophical Subjects*, edited by W. P. D. Wightman and J. C. Bryce, 176–213. Indianapolis: Liberty Classics.

Smith, Adam. 1987. *Correspondence of Adam Smith*, edited by E. G. Mossner and J. S. Ross. Indianapolis: Liberty Classics.

Stiglitz, Joseph. 2003. *Globalization and its Discontents*. New York: W. W. Norton & Co.

Throsby, David. 2001. *Economics and Culture*. Cambridge: Cambridge University Press.

Velthuis, Olav. 2005. *Imaginary Economics: Contemporary Artists and the World of Big Money*. Rotterdam: NAI Publishers.

White, Iain Boyd. 2001. "The Expressionist Sublime." In *Expressionist Utopias: Paradise, Metropolis, Architectural Fantasy*, edited by Timothy G. Benson, 118–37. Berkeley: University of California Press.

Woodmansee, Martha, and Mark Osteen, eds. 1999. *The New Economic Criticism: Studies at the Intersection of Literature and Economics*. New York: Routledge.

Zylinska, Joanna. 2001. "Sublime Speculations: The Economy of the Gift in Feminist Ethics." *j_spot: Journal of Social and Political Thought* (1)3, June.

Part I

"Tokens of eccentricity"

Value and the aesthetic representation of economy

1 Tracing the economic
Modern art's construction of economic value

Jack Amariglio

Image 1 Kasimir Malevich, *Red Square: Painterly Realism of a Peasant Woman in Two Dimensions.*

Let us begin in Red Square. Well, at least somewhere in proximity to a red square. The red square I have in mind was painted in 1915 by the Russian Suprematist artist, Kasimir Malevich. The painting, entitled *Red Square: Painterly Realism of a Peasant Woman in Two Dimensions*, was one in a series of works by Malevich in the midst of the turmoil and incredible burst of creative energy during and after the Bolshevik Revolution.[1]

In the view of the art historian Richard Brettell, "there is no more important social/aesthetic/political experiment in the history of modern art than Malevich's Suprematism and its general offshoot, Constructivism" (1999, 40). As Brettell explains, Malevich was one of the originators of non-figurative and non-representational abstract art. But, if this is so, and if Malevich's art stands somewhere relatively early in establishing the claim that art no longer has a connection to representation of an ostensibly material world, then in what sense

30   *Jack Amariglio*

can it be said that his work marks a social and political (and further, an economic) experiment? How can we connect in a meaningful way this revel into abstraction with the materiality of everyday life?[2]

Malevich was a superb polemicist. His work with a collective of other vanguard artists led him to construct, in words as well as image, what Brettell terms "a theory of autonomous, non-representational art" (39) that linked in a powerful way such seeming visual "self-referentiality" with social and economic forces that were thought, at the time, to replace an exhausted and discredited capitalism.[3] In search of explanations for the vitality and revolutionary purpose— even the meaning inscribed—in such work, Malevich turned to what he called "the economic principle" (1992, 292–7). Malevich had little doubt that this economic principle constituted a "measure of our contemporary life," and that therefore "we should apply this measure absolutely, to all forms of our expression, in order to be in accordance with the general plan for the contemporary development of an organism" (1992, 293). That this "economic principle" was defined both in terms of utilitarian ideals as well as Marxist or at least communist precepts may seem quite odd to the historian of economics, if not to aestheticians.

Malevich's peculiar notion of the economic principle as the life force and that which is "represented" by his own squares and diagonals is a kind of excessive hybrid, a position in relation to notions of economic value that are quite often separated rather than combined in the official discipline of economics. In my view, to the extent that modern art—and here I simply use the convention of referring to art produced mostly in the West from the 1850s until at least the 1960s and 70s—can be read as contributing to economic discourse, one strong tendency within it has been the hybridization and then ultimate overflowing— codifying excess—of distinct notions of economic value.[4] And, if there is a loose heading under which I would like to group all the forms of excess and intermixing that can be read as inscribing or tracing concepts of economic value within much modern art, and particularly that which is considered non-objective and abstract, it is the gift.[5] I return to this point below. But, first, I foreground my discussion with a more general overview of the problem of art and economics.

Economic value and its representation in modern art

Art and economics. The connections, potential and actual, are numerous and substantial. The connections are ones that show up even in the realm of what is "represented," that is, in what artworks depict as well as what they could possibly mean. For I have little doubt that the economic conditions surrounding the production, distribution, and consumption of artworks can be "read" in or into the works themselves.[6] These conditions include everything from the facts that many artworks pass through art markets; that a subset is displayed in institutions that have been increasingly dependent on direct subvention by the state or by viewers; that they exist as luxury items in a world governed by commodity production and

Tracing the economic 31

exchange; that they have rarely existed in the past 150 years completely "outside" market relations; and much else. One strong component of any approach to the intersection of artworks and the sphere of the economic is that art today is most often bought and sold and that, perhaps dripping from every pore, exudes all of the glitz, glitter, and gore that are presumed to come along with capitalist commodification.[7]

Yet, this essay has a different focus from what is termed (from John Ruskin forward) the "political economy of art." While influenced by discussions of the social and economic conditions that have been part of artistic practice since the mid-nineteenth century, I focus instead on a different part of the problem: the question of how works of modern art may be read as constructive of economic discourses, and particularly discourses that presume notions of economic value, that is, the determination and effects of the economic "worth" of objects. My premise is that "the economy," "the economic," and "economic value" are represented, figured, and disseminated as images within modern art—or more to the point, they can be read as that which is gestured toward in such art.

This premise suggests two additional propositions. The first is that artists have been extremely important in generating and affecting the ways in which others understand economic ideas—ideas about what is and has economic value, how various economic activities work, how they can be known and measured, and much else. The second is that the constructions of economic value that can be read in much modern art diverge in important ways from—but also have a relationship to—the dominant modes of economic thought that have existed in the West since the mid-nineteenth century. "Modern art" is largely productive of an alternative or at least "altered" set of images, concepts, and discursive moments from those that comprise the core of the neoclassical, Keynesian, and sometimes even Marxian notions of economic value that have prevailed among late nineteenth and twentieth century academic economists.

On the first proposition, while I do not present here empirical evidence, such as that offered by Pierre Bourdieu (1984, 1993, 1995), David Halle (1996), Mihaly Csikszentmihalyi and Eugene Rochberg-Halton (1981), and others, about the ways in which artworks and cultural practices are popularly received, read, and/or used by audiences/consumers, this essay is guided by a point David Ruccio and I made in previously published work (2003) on economic discourses that are largely outside those that are found among academic economists. Ruccio and I argued that there is an integrity to these "everyday" or "ersatz" economics, and that, to some degree, the economic ideas of the "man in the streets" is derided by many academic economists because these ersatz practitioners hold views that are often critical or at least alternative to the most cherished theories held by those trained in universities.[8]

One place where people may be confronted with such alternative ideas about economics and value is in the realm of cultural practices and artifacts—and in artworks. Economic ideas do not originate or spread out purely from a center within the academy, but, rather, they are produced and learned in multiple sites, including the artworld, and as images and figures that are interpreted and/or read by

Image 2 Henry Wallis, *The Stonebreaker*.

anyone exposed to art. To settle this matter empirically, of course, would require an exploration into the actual reception of works of art in order to catalogue the determinate effects of art on economic ideas. For the purpose of this paper, though, I seek to establish a prior claim: the claim that modernist artworks can plausibly be read as "representing" economic ideas.

The Stonebreaker and the value of labor

The issue of representation or reading for economic ideas or content is not hard, of course, when one is viewing a figurative painting like *The Stonebreaker*, rather than Malevich's abstract "peasant woman," even though the titles link these works in a very direct way.

In 2000, *The Stonebreaker*—painted in 1857 by Henry Wallis—was part of an exhibition at the old Tate Gallery. The exhibition, entitled "Ruskin, Turner, and the Pre-Raphaelites," was organized around the collection of the great art critic and social thinker, John Ruskin. As I mention above, Ruskin is considered, along with William Morris, to have initiated an economic approach to modern artwork, or a political economy of art. In her superb text on economics and aesthetics in Victorian England, the literary critic Regenia Gagnier (2000) credits Ruskin, and then Morris after him, with focusing critical attention "not on the spectator or consumer but on the producer of the work and the conditions of production" (128). Gagnier claims that such a focus was not merely concerned with the conditions of

Tracing the economic 33

a work's emergence into the field of the artistic, but was also the aesthetic content itself, inscribed within valuable art. That is, one might say that Ruskin's emphasis on the artist and the material conditions of the work as well as a work's impact on the body were themselves interiorized as represented "within" and "through" a work of art.

The Stonebreaker, then, can be read as such an interiorizing work, since in it the work of the artist, Wallis, and the scene depicted do double duty in referring to the vicissitudes, pleasures, and difficulties of valuable labor. Yet, of course, there is a wonderful irony in the painting. First, the stonebreaker appears either asleep (and therefore at the end of a day's work, as the sun sets) or worse (at the end of an occupation, threatened, of course, by industrial practices and machines that will, one day, replace this labor-intensive activity—relegated, later on, to the most onerous and degrading forms of doing penance, as on chain-gangs).[9] That is, labor is not only implied in the worn, ragged body and clothes of the expended stonebreaker, but also in the simple tools and especially the stone shards that are strewn about the poor man as a nearly demented dispersion of wasted (but still noble) labor. It foretells of a time when the value of this once-skilled labor will stand in exact inversion to the difficulty and toil the task depicts (that is, it foreshadows the cheapening of such exhausted but knowing labor).[10]

It is a scene that emphasizes the solitariness of so much craft labor soon to pass out of existence, or to be collected and organized within workhouses and factories. The peace of this pastoral scene belies the tragedy of a world changing forever, and the stonebreaker seems poised, even if asleep, to haunt this brave new world with a reminder of what must, it is hoped, remain valuable within the new regime of labor discipline. In a way that will be repeated many times in modern art (even where there is no iconic reference to labor—that is, no "direct" representation of labor being performed), *The Stonebreaker* is one relatively early romantic attempt to come to grips with the fate of labor and labor value (here, identified largely with craft labor) in the wake of capitalism's supposedly inexorable spread. The painting thus can be seen in a long line of work within modernism that constitutes an immanent critique of capitalist production and its destruction of the worker's body if not the dignity and integrity of labor itself. And it raises the question of the valuing of labor's product, and if there is, in fact, any virtue to be granted to an age in which cheapness due to mass production under conditions of alienated and exploited labor is the norm.

Gagnier's take on Ruskin's political economy of art connects Ruskin and Morris to the Marxist tradition of labor as the source and measure of economic value. While Ruskin more than Morris diverged in important ways from Marxian value theory, their writings, and the art of the Pre-Raphaelites, like Henry Wallis, promulgated an iconic view of labor value. William Morris, of course, is seen in this light as the great defender of the idea that the quality of artwork, and its ability to be perceived as aesthetically pleasing, is directly correlated with the conditions of the laboring artist and craftspeople more generally. In his 1883 lecture, "Art, Wealth, and Riches" (in Morris, 1993), Morris makes clear that it

34   *Jack Amariglio*

is the system of "competitive commerce" and its degradation of the worker and the worker's craft—and here artists are accorded no exception—that is signified on the face of every ugly and vulgar object, including contemporary artwork. So, Morris implicitly endorses the idea that degraded labor, a consequence of competitive capitalism, can be transparently read as the submerged but still visible representation of art produced and consumed under that system. Morris's view, then, sets up a simple hermeneutical strategy, one that sees in every surface of an artwork the inscribed conditions of production—which is why, when he turns to discuss what would lead to a marked improvement in aesthetic sensibility and output, he once again specifies transformed conditions of production—closer to craft socialism—as the determinants, but also the "meaning" that can be read in more aesthetically pleasing artifacts.[11]

I return to the question of the inscription of the conditions of production of artwork and labor's value as signified in modern art when I consider the issue of so-called non-representational art. To preview one aspect of this discussion, the question becomes pertinent, assuming one shares Morris's interpretive leanings, if modernist abstract art likewise can ever be read as a mirror of its own production. That is, can we read non-objective art as representing the quality and quantity of the labor that went into its production, as well as the degree to which the modern artist conceives and materially produces in degraded circumstances due to the immersion of art practice in a hyper-individualist commercial capitalism?[12] And is there an equivalent aesthetic judgment implied if the answer is, like Morris's, that such art must de facto be inferior in comparison to other work produced under a regime of cooperative and unalienated labor?

Much continues to be made to this day of the conditions of production and consumption in contemporary capitalism as an underlying referent—even if unintentionally—for all works of modern art. In cultural circles, despite or perhaps because of the supposedly deep penetration of commodification into all aspects of art's continued existence, there remains a strong anti-bourgeois and anti-market sentiment pertaining to the idea that art under the yoke of the market is always compromised and degraded.

This degradation can be read more or less directly in the content and form—including the banal celebration of the commodity—of much modern art. Such a tradition gives rise to vigorous readings in the "social history of art," which was led by the Marxist art historian, Arnold Hauser.[13] Brettell (1999) credits Hauser with stressing "two major aspects of capitalist modernism that are seen as essential to modern representation: speed and dislocation. The modernist ideas of alienation, dislocation, rapid transformation, and anonymity are essential to these views of artistic representation in capitalist society" (60). Thus, as Brettell concludes, "this view of modern art as a structural critique of capitalism has worked so well for certain objects of art that it has created a whole idea of modern art as *essentially* critical of capitalism" (60). Thus, artworks can be read either as examples of the economic degradation of labor's value or as the means to reveal this degradation, but in either case the representation is read as "depicted" in an artwork's surface.

Image 3 Carel Willink, *The Bank of Philadelphia*.

The Bank of Philadelphia: the critique of finance capital

It is relatively straightforward to produce this kind of reading with *The Bank of Philadelphia* by the Dutch artist Carel Willink. This painting continues the theme of modern art as an implicit, if not explicit, critique of capitalism. The representational strategies in this painting are redolent of notions of disvalue and alienated labor—and of modern life in general—that are inversely related to the pomp and self-importance of bourgeois economic institutions, like the Greek Revival bank. Willink painted this "magic realist" canvas in 1928, the year before the stock market crash and the disaccumulation that sent shock waves through all western—and global—financial institutions. Willink's painting is ominous with not-so-fantastic signs of the impending disaster.

Here are some of the portentous elements in Willink's painting:

- A ravaged tree with a broken branch ("When the bough breaks ...")
- Paper trash (Does a newspaper in 1928 now suggest not just any news, but financial news in particular?)
- A spotted dog (Finance as a matter of black and white? Just the facts, ma'am!) ...
- ... looking away from his bone (Whose? What species?)
- Threatening clouds (So, does capitalism always presage cataclysmic thunderwaves of what Joseph Schumpeter called "creative destruction"? And, in Willink's painting, is there a hint of "creativity" other than its own surrealist self-reference?)

36   *Jack Amariglio*

- A school of birds (Heading toward what refuge?)
- An object that transmutes between paper and/or a strange piece of bleached cartilage (So, stock quotes or bank notes transmogrified into the remains of a visit from the grim reaper?)
- Streets empty of human life (as though an economic holocaust has swept Philadelphia's urban landscape), and so forth.

The climb-up in stock prices, and the speculative fever that banks were part of fueling, is once again inversely related to the disvalue created, as human labor is effaced—wiped away—in this eerie representation of finance capital, antediluvian.

Protect Me From What I Want: the (problematic) representation of utility and desire

I have yet to address in a direct manner the prevailing value theory within economics associated with the neoclassical revolution of the late nineteenth century. Put bluntly, at least until the 1930s, the "subjective" theory of value, as it has been called, enshrined the satisfaction of desire in the form of "utility" as the motivating principle behind the determination of market prices. That utility was and for some economists still is seen as the only reasonable premise upon which to base economic and even aesthetic value is apparent in this painful assertion of disciplinary imperialism by the economist William Grampp in his *Pricing the Priceless: Art, Artists and Economics* (1989).

> Economic value, strictly speaking, is the general form of all value, including that which is aesthetic and that which is not aesthetic but is the value of another kind. An object ... has economic value if it yields utility. If it is a work of art, the utility is aesthetic. If it is something else, it yields another kind of utility and that utility is economic value. To say that aesthetic value is "consistent" with economic value is to say no more than that the particular comes with the general, or that aesthetic value is a form of economic value just as every other form of value is (20–1).

There are countless examples of modern art that have been and can be read as inscribing desire and utility. And yet, there is something sometimes just a little "off" in these inscriptions, to the extent that the representation of desire (or at least our reading of it) is in some way made to double-back on itself. Such works raise the question of desire's primacy, its consistency, and most importantly its sociality and embeddedness in relations of production and culture. Far from being depictions of desire as a first principle and increasing function in the determination of value (economic or aesthetic), some work treats desire ironically and deconstructively and shows that desire can lead to devaluation and ultimately to the destruction of value. What is left, in its place, is the "problem" of desire in relation to value, rather than its visual coronation.

Tracing the economic 37

Image 4 Jenny Holzer, *Protect Me From What I Want*, 1984–85 or 1985–86.

Jenny Holzer's *Protect Me From What I Want*, at first blush, is a prototypical statement of the overwhelming power and also the ubiquitousness of desire. The outward display of desire unbound is evidenced here by an unabashed florescent cry into a public space, one that models the modern city and its sparkling nocturnal urbanity.

The setting is unmistakably a working city, but one in which goliath-sized billboards and sunburst neon have long been the purveyors of and towncriers for consumer desire. Yet, this expression of desire in Holzer's work is extreme to say the least, and in its extremity lies the conditions for its potential obliteration as something stable from which to make judgments of any type, including economic ones. The desire Holzer puts on blazing display is dangerous because excessive. It is a force that is thought to be so destructive as to require external, and not passive, restraints. A social straitjacket. *Protect Me From What I Want* can be read, once again, in participating in that continuing blare against the supposed "insatiability of human wants" thought to be what is unleashed by an always hungry and never-sated consumer capitalism. Yet, here, labor is not exactly calmly substituted as an alternative first principle for valuing commodities and regulating exchange. Indeed, perhaps it is simply the commodity-form that is indicted in Holzer's work since it elicits—creates— the very desires it is supposed to reflect (at least in the neoclassical economic tradition), but does so excessively. Holzer can be read as referring to the excesses of commodification and its effects in a landscape occupied by capitalist markets, but note that one irony consists again in her suggestion of one of the most familiar, and iconic, means of producing consumer desire, the neon sign, itself an icon of the cheapened since overinflated (think Las Vegas). So, what we

38   *Jack Amariglio*

can read here is individual desire so strong and potentially wild that it requires nothing short of social policing (who, we might ask, is being hailed by this wrenching plaint?). And this problematizing of desire is placed by Holzer—iconographically—exactly where desire is most often oversold, in the modern urban agora, where we now fix our eyes upwards, the level of sight centuries ago reserved for gods.

Flatness and the representation of not representing

I have spoken to this point about artworks that depict notions of economic value through scenes that denote the presence or absence of economic activities or institutions or sentiments. Of course, there are many examples of modern art in which there is a more recognizable economic content insofar as what is represented are the representations that are encountered daily in the world of market exchange: money and branded commodities. The cultural theorist Marc Shell devotes most of his book *Art and Money* (1995) to art that depicts money, including those artistic endeavors, like the work of J. S. G. Boggs (see Weschler, 1999), that verge on outright forgery and counterfeiting. While it may seem that what is being signified in these images is transparent, much of this work, rather than being commensurate with the association of economic value and its iconic and material representation, can be read as a means of escaping the idea that a sign of economic value is appropriate to the object it is thought to measure and represent.[14]

Producing readings of artworks in which one can find plausible the existence on the surface of the canvas representations of that which is valued economically is not particularly controversial when we believe that what we are looking at does have commonly identifiable images and signs. Yet, before leaving this terrain, I want to also acknowledge that even "representational art" was read, during much of the period of artistic modernism, as not "about" the image or content, but, rather, constituted a preoccupation with the surface of the canvas. This, at least, is the interpretation provided by T. J. Clark in his opus on Impressionism, *The Painting of Modern Life* (1999a). Clark asserts that modernism's concerns for "flatness" "were time and again recovered as a striking fact by painters after Courbet" (12). He asks the questions, "[W]hy [did] that literal presence of surface [go] on being interesting for art[?] How could a matter of effect or procedure seemingly stand in for value in this way?"

Clark's answers are illuminating and also bear reflecting upon for the analysis that follows. For Clark insists that "if the fact of flatness was compelling and tractable for art—the way it was for Manet and Cezanne, for example, that must have been because it was made to stand for something: some particular and substantial set of qualities which took their place in a picture of the world" (13). Clark advances three competing or adjacent (depending on your point of view) explanations on how, precisely, the flat surface of the artist's canvas could, in this way, take on representational value. In one case, "flatness was imagined to be some kind of analogue of the 'Popular' ... It was therefore made as plain, workmanlike, and emphatic as the painter could manage; loaded brushes and artisans' combs were

Tracing the economic 39

held to be appropriate tools; painting was henceforth honest manual labour" (13). In a second version, "flatness could signify modernity, with the surface meant to conjure up the mere two dimensions of posters, labels, fashion prints, and photographs" (13). In this view, "painting would replace or displace the Real, accordingly, for reasons having to do with subjectivity, or city life, or the truths revealed by higher mathematics" (13). And, in the third path, "unbrokenness of surface could be seen—by Cezanne par excellence—as standing for the evenness of seeing itself, the actual form of our knowledge of things. That very claim, in turn, was repeatedly felt to be some kind of aggression on the audience, on the ordinary bourgeois. Flatness was construed as a barrier put up against the viewer's normal wish to enter a picture and a dream" (13).

But, what comes through, in Clark's rendition, is that "flatness in its heyday *was* these various meanings and valuations; they were its substance, they were what it was seen *as*; their particularity was what made flatness a matter to be painted" (13). Thus, the putative representational imagery was either secondary or subsumed to this flatness, or the "content" itself was exclusively the representation of flatness, with all the possible permutations and interpretations of what it meant to live and experience such a flat world, at least visually. This lesson serves us well as we venture forward into the realm of the supposedly "non-representational" art that proceeds soon after Impressionism's golden years.

Despite Clark's edifications, it is often more difficult for contemporary viewers to render plausible readings of works that are allegedly "non-representational" or supposed to be either non-referential (understood as non-objective) or self-referential (that is, artwork that is self-contained in the sense of signifying only its own materials, forms, composition, and techniques).[15] How can we read such art as constructing, in a representational way, notions of economic value? And if we can dare to do this, then what kinds of notions of economic value can be gleaned in such modernist abstractions?[16]

The general proposition that non-representational art represents "nothing" or "no thing" (so, has no "objectivity" outside of itself) is strictly impossible. Three arguments come immediately to mind. One is that representing "nothing" is of course to represent precisely "something" (that is, the work in question is read as representing "not representing").[17] The artist and writer David Batchelor (1991) develops a somewhat orthogonal take (from mine) on the problem here in his commentary on the non-iconic and non-depictional, but still "meaningful" or representational, quality of abstract art: "It may be argued that a Mondrian or a Rothko or a LeWitt is an image of *something*, but not an image of some *thing*. It seems safer to think of the work as representing, or attempting to express, a kind of conception or understanding of the world, to be *like* that world in an abstract way" (55).

The second is that viewers recognize the representation of non-representation when we are faced with it. So, when we gaze at Malevich's *White on White*, for example, and see two white squares, one superimposed on the other, we "recognize" that we are viewing something that is supposed to be "non-representational" or at least not referring explicitly to an object, an emotion, an event, or a scene

40 *Jack Amariglio*

that would otherwise be obvious to us (the modernist art critic supreme Clement Greenberg (1940) called such referring to these "outside" things in art, "art as literature"). To "see" any painting or work as "non-representational" or "non-referential" is to acknowledge the fact that the painting signifies—represents—that which it is paradoxically refusing.

The third argument is that anything visual is always/already immersed as a sign in a world of references (that is, other signs). So when a reader/viewer comes into contact with a work of abstract or minimalist or conceptual art from the twentieth century, he or she locates (without necessarily being conscious of it) what is being viewed within an already existing social field of signs and meanings, many of which correspond to distinct affects. Most modern paintings are saturated sites; they have been picked over by many viewers for manifold meanings. In fact, the more supposedly opaque the text or canvas, the more its meaning is sought and debated and thereby saturates the text or canvas. In the face of such saturation, we need a "license to read" economic content—and to read it "differently"—in even the most referentially saturated, though non-representational, artwork.[18]

We need to take care, though, to avoid a reading that, at its core, displays a deep hostility to abstraction as an aesthetic production choice. In a short, trenchant essay, Gerardo Mosquera (1994) recounts the similar disdain that abstraction and the non-figurative evoked in many Marxist aestheticians during a large part of the twentieth century. Singling out Meyer Shapiro as an influential and relieving exception, Mosquera explains that "non-figurative art became a pole in contradistinction to the 'socialist realism' instituted as official doctrine in Eastern Europe, China, and North Korea" (76). Socialist realism was preferred in step with "*epistemologism*, an aesthetic discourse ... that valorized art as a form of knowledge through images, which differed from the knowledge that was acquired through concepts proper to science. Art was better according to the extent that it had the capacity to transmit knowledge that was external to art itself, especially when it was about society" (76). With "mimesis" as its chosen method, socialist realism in the Stalin era faced off against abstraction, which was viewed as "anathema not only as a form of individualism characteristic of a 'decadent society,' but also for being 'a chaos of marks, lines, dots, and sounds that neither signified nor expressed anything,' or rather, for its incapacity to convey knowledge by virtue of its presumed rhetorical vacuity" (76).[19] Of course, in a sense, such Marxist critics didn't precisely find the non-figurative vacuous since one of the more recycled complaints was that abstraction reflected or signified in some way the decadence of an internalized capitalism, a profit-driven, exploitative economy seemingly looking inward, or at least for outward display purposes.

In Mosquera's account, Shapiro stood out in the 1930s as a lone oppositional Marxist voice, willing not only to acknowledge the necessary significatory aspect of abstract art, thus rescuing it from accusations of either emptiness or pure ornamentation, but grounding this signification in the materialism of individual affect. Mosquera sees in Shapiro's appreciation and method toward abstraction "the basis for a semiology of the non-figurative," a system of communication

Tracing the economic 41

and expression that side-stepped solipsistic mystifications of the utterly unique aesthetic experience. If abstract art doesn't quite reflect directly something external to it, it can nonetheless "communicate" through the effects of colors and shapes and forms on states of mind and emotion. Or as Mosquera puts it, abstraction as a form of communication "did not result from representing something or from 'making seen,' but rather from 'making felt'" (80).

But, pace Shapiro, we insist that the significations of abstract forms—which work sometimes as the positivity left in the presence of what is "absent"—do not reside solely in the realm of the personal or even by reference to materially provoked affect, however broadly understood. So, with epistemologism as a possible warning signal, I return to the question, what of reading the supposedly non-representational work of art for the way it signifies "economic value"? And why, indeed, would anyone seek to do so?

Reading modern art for economic value

I want to answer these questions briefly and defensively, perhaps, by way of asking that, if psychoanalytic readings of the "symptoms" of a work of art can be justified,[20] and if references to the intentions of the artist as "showing up" in the painting can be justified, and if disquisitions on the formal principles of the work can be justified—if all these readings that introject some kind of representational strategy and implicit, even if indeterminate and deferred, content can be justified, then why not reading for economic content? More forcefully, though, as I argue above, there is much at stake in performing such readings if you believe, as I do, that viewers come to learn about economics at least partly through visual art and culture. And especially if you believe that the kinds of knowledge that are constructed by such works constitute important moments of criticism of and alternatives to dominant traditions within the field of official economic discourse.

Marc Shell (1995) has been equally adamant about the possibility of reading works of art for their economic content, whether or not they permit such immediate interpretation through more supposedly obvious signs of economic value, such as representations of money. Shell remarks that, "whether or not a painter depicts money or is aware of its role, monetary forms of meaning and value come to affect the meaning of meaning in painting. This participation of economic form in painting and in the discourses about painting is defined neither by what painting depicts (sometimes money, sometimes not) nor by why painting depicts it (sometimes for money, sometimes not), but rather by the interaction between economic and aesthetic symbolization and production" (4).

Shell's claim is consistent with Malevich's outlook. Malevich had no problem in arguing for an approach to his own and other Suprematist art that read the objectively economic into every nook and cranny of the work, as is implied in this quote: "now we have an army, faithful towards a new principle in economic life, and the vanguard of art. The economic life of the new world has produced the commune. The creative construction of the new art has produced the Suprematism of the square" (1992, 296–7).

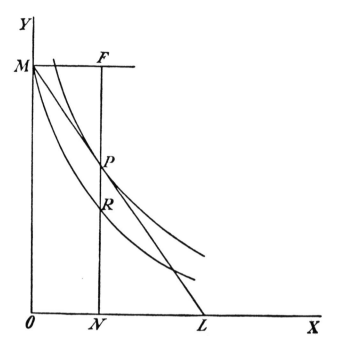

Image 5 John R. Hicks, Graph.

In conducting my research for this essay, I puzzled over how to read modernist abstract and other non-representational art for its economic content.[21] Or rather, how to make plausible an approach to such a reading. I considered many things, such as the economic significations that come with color (or lack thereof), or the hierarchy of materials used, the application of paint and other materials to the canvas, and much else.

Yet, there are some elements that seem more compelling than others, such as the experiments in form introduced by Malevich and Piet Mondrian, and others.

The formalism of a good deal of modernist art has, in fact, a close parallel in the history of economic thought. While I have been speaking of theories of economic value within the field of economics that focused attention on either labor or desire/utility as the source and substance of the determination of value, it is also true that, by the 1930s in economics, embarrassment with value theory and, in fact, all notions that market price reflects anything "deeper" than itself led to formal innovations in economic theory that began to purge altogether the value referent from the discipline. Here, I am thinking of the move within neoclassical economics away from utility as a cardinal measure and, therefore, as a necessary corporeal referent to "real" bodies. In the work of Sir John Hicks in *Value and Capital* in the 1930s (1939) and then with Paul Samuelson's *Foundations of Economic Analysis* (1983), reference to utility as that which was signified in price was dropped or at least considerably watered down in favor of a flatter and more formal technical apparatus.

The flatness of the economic analysis produced by Hicks, Samuelson, and then consequent generations and the obsession with the mathematical form of the argument treated economic value as a purely surface phenomenon, a signifier without a signified.

Samuelson's penchant for formalism and the intensifying efforts to mathematize mainstream economics from the 1940s onward has been compared by the cultural economist Arjo Klamer (2007) with the movements in art associated with experiments in geometry, calculation, placement, and formal structure only a few decades earlier, as exemplified by Mondrian, among others.[22] Klamer's take on Mondrian and Samuelson is to see them as two pioneers in high modernism in which references to an objective or even a subjective world disappear.

Mondrian's *Broadway Boogie Woogie* is frequently used in public presentations by Klamer to underscore a prior cultural history in which a desire for formal clarity and an erasure of mostly human referents become the passion and interest of economists from Hicks and Samuelson onward. Reading modern art, in this way, "into" economics (or at least reading the modernist spirit that motivated both fields of creative endeavor), Klamer leaves the door open for a feedback effect, one that implies that the work of abstract artists following Mondrian can also be seen as mimicking, even if unconsciously, the economist's obsessive concentration on finding the barest and most basic principles of formal analysis.

"Beware of the artists baring their gifts" (Lucy Lippard, 1984)[23]

Yet, even this approach still doesn't allow us to see, directly, how non-representational art may construct and inscribe notions of economic value. I stated above that I regard the idea of the gift—as it has been formulated and debated by a wide range of cultural theorists influenced by the anthropologist Marcel Mauss (1950)—as an appropriate catch-all term to discuss the kinds of notions of economic value that I believe can be read in modernist art, and particularly work that enshrines the idea of the autonomy of art, its self-referentiality, and its essential reduction to basic and abstract forms and principles. This may seem surprising, but the excess that I think can be read in the move to purify, simplify, and display the essence of art's medium is best understood in the context of ideas of the gift that emphasize forms of expenditure that are overflowing, destructive, bacchanalian, and most importantly, based on a superfluity of signification.[24] The gift, as it has been conceived by Georges Bataille (1991) among others, involves those aspects of a movement of goods, from a giver to a recipient, in which an object's economic value is overdetermined, and nearly annihilated (in the sense that no clear and unique quantitative value may emerge), due to a multiplicity of signs and symbols—many of them bound up with plays of cultural and political power. Gift theory has in fact been promulgated in the past 30 years by many cultural theorists and practitioners intent on seeing artworlds as being either outside

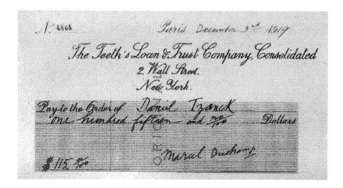

Image 6 Marcel Duchamp, *Tzanck Check*.

economics, or built upon principles of production and consumption that at the very least are opposed to a simplistic understanding of capitalist commodification.[25] It may also provide an appropriate lens to discuss the backfiring of some abstract art's essentialism, that is, the excessive focus on finding the core of artistic practice.

Recent commentators on the economics within artworlds have turned to gift theory as an escape from both classical Marxist labor theories and neoclassical utility theories of value to explain the workings of art markets or, alternatively, the non-workings of these markets, as these theories fail to capture what happens in the actual transactions that take place between artists and those that commission, sell, or consume their work. Gift theory also has been used to discuss the formation and distribution of aesthetic taste.

A good example of one variant of gift theory can be found in an article by the economic sociologist of art, Olav Velthuis (2005), talking about Marcel Duchamp's excursions into the production of semblances of monetary value, such as the *Tzanck Check*.

The *Tzanck Check* is a piece of handwork that Duchamp made as a form of "payment" to a Parisian dentist and avid art collector in 1919. Velthuis considers this turnabout: the check, intricately drawn to replicate a "real" check (drawn on the "teeth's loan and trust company, consolidated"), is neither legal tender, nor is it strictly intended as a disinterested work of art, since it was offered as a form of payment for dental work. The *Tzanck Check* blurs the distinction between art and money, and it also participates in the circuits within which both economic and aesthetic value are constructed and, in this instance, even exchanged (or change places). The playfulness that soaks the check with such ambiguity and uncertainty about the autonomy of art and economics calls out for a connection to some versions of gift theory, and so Velthuis fixes upon the simultaneous aspect of the check as a form of monetary exchange, barter, and finally an act of reciprocal gift-giving. What Velthuis notes is that, with the *Tzanck Check*, the nearly infinite social and cultural subtexts of any form

Tracing the economic 45

of transaction are made apparent. Whether Velthuis intends this or not, his discussion of Duchamp's *Tzanck Check* leads us, in an instance, to consider the proposition that the exchange value of any item—commodity or gift—may always be uncertain, saturated by a panoply of cultural signs, symbols, and ceremonies, and may only be determined in a case-by-case fashion (hence, they are not subject to a general theory of economic value à la modernist economics). The *Tzanck Check* is a prime example of the welter of social and cultural determinants and ironic twists and turns that constitute what is often considered the fundamental character of the gift.

While gift theory may be valuable for describing dealings in artworlds that don't easily fit into purified categories of market exchange or the omnipresence of consumer capitalism, still little has been written about gift *theory* (and not the gift itself) as an inscription on the face of contemporary art.

Abstract art and the representation of its production, or, "how much?"

One way we may approach the inscription of the notion of the gift as a sign of excess and intermixture is if we return to William Morris's idea of the work of art signifying its own conditions of production and thereby making enlightened labor the key aesthetic component of a piece. But let us now focus not on the figurative, representational art that still dominated in Morris's day, but instead on the abstract art (for example, Barnett Newman's *Vir Heroicus Sublimis*,[26] an iconic reference in Abstract Expressionism[27]). Here, my main thesis is that abstract art both announces almost exclusively and/or hides intensively the conditions of its production.[28]

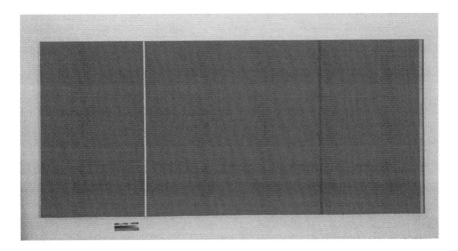

Image 7 Barnett Newman, *Vir Heroicus Sublimis*, 1950–51.

46 *Jack Amariglio*

What I mean in the first instance is that the turn to the purification of art that is associated with the turn to abstraction brings forth a displaying, on the flat surface, of the material elements of its composition, as well as some important clues as to the strategic choices the artist may have made in its execution.[29] In this important sense, some abstract art is overwritten by its desire to show what it's made of (from material to form).[30]

Yet, in the second instance, there is a sense that much modernist art "hides" its own labor—perhaps with some notable counter-tendencies, such as the art that Harold Rosenberg labeled "action painting" (Jackson Pollack, *et al.*)—in what viewers (even some critics) may see as subterfuge or even fraud.[31] That is, it remains commonplace to encounter reactions to modern art, even 60 or so years after its efflorescence, that are simply bafflements as to the level of skill, the number of labor hours that went into the doing of it, the prerequisites in training and schooling, and even the degree to which the work reflects any mental efforts other than randomness or highbrow pretentiousness.[32, 33]

Many pieces of modern art refuse to care about "looking" like what is expected of a good day's work. And they raise in this paradoxical way many more questions about the conditions of production and labor (both mental and physical) than other representational pieces. This paradox, then, determines to a large degree the signification of many works of abstract art, at least as they are read for their connection to and reflection of economic processes in the making of the work. These works display in a heightened way issues of the value of labor, the interiority of desire in a painting, and much else.[34] To put this otherwise, non-objective art, boiled down to basic principles and materials, makes eminently visible, by hiding, notions of economic value that pertain to its making as well as to its representation. The work itself comes to connote the problem of economic value, and this problem or puzzle greets viewers in every corner of the canvas.

So, the work of non-representational art comes to connote the problem of economic value (as in, "that mess of dripped paint, scribbles, and smudges is worth HOW MUCH?" and, of course, "hey, my kid could do a better job than that!").[35] But the piece does so in a rather hysterical, indeterminate, and excessive way.[36] I offer the view that the more abstract art dug deeper and obsessively for its underlying principles of composition, the more it became enmeshed in the practice of excessively signifying images and concepts that are thought to be both inside and outside of the work itself. The supposed coolness and lightness of modernist art was belied by a nearly hysterical performance, a veritable witch-hunt at times, to get rid of extraneous, non-pictorial elements in order to find the core of art practice itself. In a sense, non-representational art occupies and inscribes what Anthony Vidler (1998) has called "spatial anxiety," or, at the very least, a "psychological space"—one prone to phobias, in relation to the stretched canvas, for example, about perceived essential absences and presences. This kind of essentialism verges on fetishism. And, in perfect irony, sets off waves of speculative fever about meaning and value that most figurative works very rarely elicit.

This overloading of even the most austere and abstract modernist art by a jumble of signs, projected surely by viewers in their near panic to "make sense"

Tracing the economic 47

out of the canvas, is an apt configuration of the notion of the gift. The abstract work of art initiates "conversation" about meaning and value through the opacity of the canvas and invites, often despite itself, something almost approaching a crescendo of aggressive gift exchange, one in which what is being traded back and forth are the possible meanings of the work. The often indeterminate exchange of elements within and outside an artwork contributes to a shared perception that modern, abstract art is "difficult," both in the obscurity of its meanings, and in its relation to its surroundings and audience.[37] There is work involved to bridge internal semiotic and external intersubjective gaps, and this requires a praxis and ethos of (often resentful) gifting reciprocity.

Abstract art may signify a multiplicity of meanings over and against itself. There are also works that can be read a bit more easily as employing the tactics of abstraction but intermix them with explicitly representational materials. In those works we see a different kind of play of signs, also in tune with the concept of the gift.

Image 8 Kurt Schwitters, *Mz 1926, 7. Slagen.*

Schwitters: bridging the representational gap of economic value

A visit to the Stedelijk Museum in Amsterdam to see an exhibition by Kurt Schwitters provided an unexpected opportunity to consider how to bridge the gap between the representational works I discussed earlier and those that melt into abstract art. Schwitters is known, among other reasons, for his creation of artforms that he called "Merz." Schwitters coined the term "Merz" as a more or less random word fragment that, supposedly, he lit upon one day in an advertisement for a commercial bank. This explicit economic reference, which he used as an overarching title for many of his collages, coincided with what one critic has regarded as Schwitters's contempt for and rejection of bourgeois culture.

Schwitters's Merz works, like *Mz 1926, 7. Slagen* and *The Big I-Painting* composed in 1919, participated in the broader tendency of cubist collage, which in the words of the art critic Rosalind Krauss (1985) represented "the first instance within the pictorial arts of anything like a systematic exploration of

Image 9 Kurt Schwitters, *The Big-I Painting*.

representability entailed by the sign" (34). Schwitters's collages were built upon a certain abstractness, yet, as Rudi Fuchs (director of the Stedelijk) points out, they were different from that of Mondrian and others intent on purifying and reducing art to its supposed basic elements and principles. Fuchs (2000) lists these principles, among others, to include "extreme clarity, physical elegance, balance, intelligence, and perfection" (13)—no wonder that Arjo Klamer has compared formal experiments in art with those in high modernist economic theory; these principles are so often repeated in the defense of formal mathematical models in the discipline.

But Schwitters was, in Fuchs's words, a decidedly "impure" artist, and his Merz collages are examples of a near riot at times of shapes and textures and materials.[38] Rather than accede to the norm of orderliness—of American abstract art's stripping away of impurities that were thought to be the unnecessary "noise" of a figurative or superfluously decorative quality—Schwitters was a maker of disorder, of play, of mobility, of the saturated and fragmented surface.[39] In this way, Schwitters's compositions may too be entailed in the figure of the gift.

What is equally important, though, are the explicit references to and uses of economic iconography in some of the Merz collages. In the mode of composing his elements and in the materials he used, Schwitters provides us with a way to link the excessiveness and overworking of much modernist art (but here, of course, in playful rather than stern abstractions) with clearly visible representations of economic signs and symbols, suggesting a world of value that is, itself, a world of play (the play of valuing signs). *The Big I-Painting* is a paper collage with shreds of references to quantities, official commercial stamps (used in international transactions), bits of financial sheets (or account books), train fares, bills of lading, and much else. The much else includes moneylike shapes, in some cases cut out to reveal a commercial document or word underneath, or in other cases obscured by the same kind of material. Schwitters's work can be read as providing a guidepost linking the dense play of symbolic value in the work itself to the dense overdetermination of economic value, as fragments of economic documents and other elements are placed one on top of another or juxtaposed with no apparently logical order to render them meaningful in a single figure of value. As Fuchs says, Schwitters made the surface of his collages "opaque, dense, and heavy" (15), and this can be extended not just to a description of the materials, but also to the representational elements, including those that refer to economic data and, ultimately, back to economic value. But in a lighthearted, mobile way. In *The Big I-Painting*, economic value literally dances off the surface and takes us home Back to Malevich. To an altered Square One.

Conclusion: fade to black

Malevich's *Black Square*, which was painted, as was *Red Square*, in 1915, set off a revolution in art and in meaning. It stood in a line of work, though, that employed increasing "abstract" pictorial devices which, in their way, attempted

50   *Jack Amariglio*

to fuse a transformation in the conventions of art with a form of representation of new economic and political ideas and realities. As Paul Wood (1999) says, Malevich's *Black Square* "represented the only proper form of response to modernity; as it were, the first word of a new artistic language, purged of all worn-out convention" (200). Yet, in Malevich's view, this language did not consist of a retreat from economic life; to the contrary, it was mostly about a new form of (socialist) economy, and a new politics of art dedicated to building that economy. Malevich propounded, at least in his writings on Suprematism, an economic value theory that attempted to correspond, and vice versa, to the stripped-down reality he believed the pictorial space of *Black Square* to represent.

Yet, the excessiveness of this move, the "believing and not believing" that T. J. Clark (1999b) sees in Malevich's art, beckons toward the gift, and the indeterminateness of its value theory. As Clark recounts: "The *Black Square* is at once the strongest instance of the new belief-system and its *reductio ad absurdum*. Among its many other undecidables—is it figure?, is it ground?, is it matter?, is it spirit?, is it fullness?, is it emptiness?, is it end?, is it beginning?, is it nothing?, is it everything?, is it manic assertion?, or absolute letting go?—is it the question of whether it laughs itself to scorn" (254).[40]

I have argued that this anxious revolution, keynoted by Malevich's black, red, and white squares, gave rise to both a narrowing and a widening of the scope of the way "economics" came to be represented or alluded to within abstract modern art. In my view, the increased nervousness—first marked by a euphoria—about the liberation of the canvas from its "literary" meanings called increasing attention to the conditions of production of the artwork and its objecthood in an expanding world of aesthetic commodities. What, after all, is the value of something that, purportedly, doesn't "mean"? Artists, and, perhaps more importantly, their audiences, came to question, in loquacious excess, the very excess of nothingness, or related lack of skill, etc., that were perceived as adhering to the abstract canvas. The abstract work solicited, often against itself (and in line with a regime of studied silence), questions about and solutions to the value or worth of the work, its materials, the artist's labor, and much more. The overflow of discourse—corresponding to the overflow of meaning, or at least the surplus of reactions—allowed for an oblique economic referent to emerge. I have called that referent and the figuration or traces of that referent the gift. But, as an adjacent point, the journey from Malevich to Schwitters and beyond has carried along a dialectic of purity/impurity, a dialectic that has resisted a synthetic resolution into one or another of the well-known value theories and well-worn referents for "the economy." The gift is the impure, overwrought, hybrid, but also uncertain figure that haunts the abstract artifact. In an often indirect way, modern, abstract art has taught us something about the inside and outside of exchange and production (including its own) that earlier representations of economic theory and reality were constrained from showing; it has taught us how to trace the economic even when those traces do not add up to representation itself.

Acknowledgments

The research for this paper was begun in 1999–2000 with the support of a Ciejek Fellowship in the Humanities at Merrimack College. I wish to thank Linda and Dan Ciejek for their kind and generous backing of my project; I also thank former Merrimack administrators, Theodore Long and Arthur Ledoux, and my former Dean and co-instructor, Albert DiCiccio, for their strong institutional and personal encouragement of my efforts during the early years of research. This paper has been presented in a variety of versions and at different sites, including the "Aesthetics of Value" conference at the University of California-Riverside in 2001. Along the way, numerous colleagues have made helpful comments, incisive criticisms, and suggestions for improvement. I am indebted to Kerry Johnson, Rose-Mary Sargent, Ellen Longsworth, David Raymond, David Ruccio, Evan Watkins, Regenia Gagnier, Arjo Klamer, Olav Velthuis, Peter-Wim Zuidhof, Judith Mehta, Deirdre McCloskey, Christina Hatgis, Stephen Cullenberg, Joseph Childers, Kevin Salemme, Bregje van Eekelen, and Monica Kjellman for their unstinting support and inspiration.

Notes

1 Malevich used peasant life as a signifier, but also an index of transformation, as his work became more "non-objective." According to John E. Bowlt (1996), "Russia's modernism was a rural one, and Malevich with his peasants and fields is fully representative of this denominator. There is no question that the basic philosophical identification of the peasantry with the moral and spiritual wholeness that the Symbolists also sought was a constant element in Malevich's pictures, early and late, although it was supplemented by other considerations in the late 1920s. Certainly, these ulterior interests help to explain the apparent anonymity and uniformity of Malevich's peasants; that is, in reducing their faces and figures to geometric units, Malevich was concerned with their universal force and not with their personal peculiarities" (48). Bowlt goes on to say that "By 1919 Malevich was already speaking of practical applications of suprematist forms, from spaceships to clothes, and his return to figurative painting around 1928 is clearly connected with this philosophical expansion of Suprematism. Naturally, for Malevich these suprematist beings—larger than life, streamlined, and immortal—were descendants of the robust, vigorous peasants who also served as prototypes for his strong men in Victory over the Sun. Malevich's supermen of the late 1920s, therefore, are the new humanoids that are to inhabit the new architecture, pour tea from Suprematist teapots, and wear suprematist clothes" (49).
2 Barrett Watten (2003) reenvisions the spirit of that early optimistic Soviet moment in which palpably performing that one is showing and signifying via abstraction was linked by hope and pedagogy to an all-encompassing socialist socioeconomic formation: "The Soviet avant-garde's emphasis on the materiality of signification— the emphasis on the fabrication of painting for Malevich, the invention of an elementary vocabulary of visual representation for Lissitzky, the foregrounding of the literary device for Shklovsky, the construction of montage effects for Eisenstein, the materiality of social discourse for V. N. Voloshinov ... directly addressed the construction of social reality in the Soviet Union, in a collectively held fantasy that aesthetic form could be the model for a new social order" (xxi). Yet, Susan Buck-Morss (2000) notes that Malevich's fantasy of chasing the eternal through his Suprematist art eventually placed him, and like-minded Russian avant-gardists, in a

52 *Jack Amariglio*

chronological/political disjuncture with the notions of time and history of the vanguard Bolshevik party.

3 David Batchelor (2000) captures concisely the spirit of the age in his discussion of Alexander Rodchenko's monochromes (he credits Rodchenko as "arguably" executing "the first 'true'—but hardly pure—monochromes in 1921"). According to Batchelor, "for the artists of the Russian Revolution this was a revolutionary possibility. The end of representation. The end of easel painting. The end of art. The end of old inherited bourgeois norms and practices. The beginning of a new life, a new mode of production, a new culture" (153). Monochromes are often thought to be the epitome of abstraction's obsession with nihilistic "emptiness." This view of the monochrome as compositionally and/or representationally (or expressively) "empty" is challenged in an important essay from 1967 (reproduced in 2002) by Lucy Lippard. Focusing on both the canvas and the viewer, Lippard argues against the interpretation that such monochromes are nihilist in intention and effect. Lippard conjectures that "the experience of looking at and perceiving an 'empty' or 'colorless' surface usually progresses through boredom. The spectator may find the work dull, then impossibly dull; then, surprisingly, he breaks out on the other side of boredom into an area that can be called contemplation or simply esthetic enjoyment, and the work becomes increasingly interesting" (2002, 59).

4 While there are likely to be a zillion different definitions or explanations of "modern art" and "modernism" as they pertain to art and culture, here is a rudimentary one from Arthur Marwick's (2002) art history primer that serves the purposes of this paper adequately: "Among the characteristics of modernism … are: a conviction that a new era of cataclysmic change demands a new art; a rejection of mimesis (imitation of the 'real' world), representationalism (direct representation of that world), and figurism (direct representation of human figures and of objects); the explicit and self-conscious recognition that the arts are an artificial convention or game consisting of words on a page, paint on a canvas, etc., and the conviction that, instead of merely echoing 'reality,' art should create a separate 'reality' of its own" (14). But see also the engaging, whimsical periodization of modernism, its antecedents, and descendants, through self-drawn maps in James Elkins's *Stories of Art* (2002) and Susan Stanford Friedman's (2001) interrogative "definitional excursions."

5 When I wrote the first draft of this essay in 2000, I believed that connecting economic representation in art and "the gift" was a distinct and novel challenge. In revising my essay for this collection, I was alerted by my co-editor, Steve Cullenberg, to a fine paper published in 2004 in the *Review of Radical Political Economics* by Allan Moore in which he, too, connects "political economy" in and of art to the notion of the gift. One main difference in our approaches, though, is that Moore is more interested in discussing the gift as the basis for the "economy of artistic production" (471) and less (if at all) with the gift as the signified within the realm of artistic representations of the economy. See also my own earlier thoughts (Amariglio, 2002), and that of Antonio Callari (2002), on the excess and uncertainty—and the challenge for economic thought—that is embodied in the theory of the gift.

6 I do not wish to "solve" the issue of differentiating between "representing" and "reading," with some weight in the former placed on the properties of the object or author's intentions, and the latter implying an act of a viewer who is chronologically placed "after" the original "production" takes place. So, my language in this paper will move back and forth between "representation" and "reading" without any attempt to definitively locate the finding of expression, affect, meaning, etc., in any delinking of subjects and objects (or subjects at different moments in the life of an artwork). Having said this, I do appreciate Jean-François Lyotard's (1993) recounting of the historical shift that gave rise to aesthetics, and certainly to modern aesthetics, as it pertains to the notion of "the sublime." Lyotard states that the "transformation" that occurs with the modern

Tracing the economic 53

development of the sublime "explains why reflection on art should no longer bear essentially on the 'sender' instance/agency of works, but on the 'addressee' instance. And under the name 'genius' the latter instance is situated, not only on the side of the public, but also on the side of the artist, a feeling which he does not master. Henceforth it seems right to analyze the ways in which the subject is affected, its ways of receiving and experiencing feelings, its ways of judging works" (249). I should add, though, that my continued shuttling between "representing" and "reading" is meant to muddy the issue of aesthetic experience as connoting purely a matter of faculties of "feeling," and also as a matter of "reception" that is detached from "production." Mieke Bal (1996) has a fine discussion of the "difficulties of looking" at artifacts and artworks which often lead to the "need to read." And for a technical discussion of the distinction between the "drawing systems" and the "denotation systems" in the process of artistic representation, see Willats (1997).

7 I acknowledge that reading art for its economic meanings—including its value theories—is a longstanding tradition in art criticism. I should also add that my own tendency to read "gift" theory or its figuration in modern art, and especially abstract, non-objective painting, in a positive light is countered by others who see in the representation of excess or purity as the case may be the introjection, even in critique, of a consumerist culture that is ruled by a "culture industry" dedicated to the cooptation and commodification of all "styles" proposed by avant-gardes. Thus, hybridization and excess are the leisure values par excellence that express the unleashing of consumer desire both promoted and expressed by capitalist firms. This point is argued persuasively by Thomas Crow (1996) in his conspectus on the relationship between modernist avant-gardes and mass culture. As for the "negation" that comprises the content of modernist art, Crow states that "modernist practice sustains its claim to autonomy by standing, in its evident formal coherence, against the empty diversity of the culture industry, against market expediency, speculative targeting of consumers, and hedging bets. But it has achieved this contrast most successfully by figuring in detail the character of the manufactured culture it opposes" (32).

8 This paper is closely related to the larger project that can be found in David Ruccio's edited volume *Economic Representations: Academic and Everyday* (2008).

9 Lucinda Hawksley (1999) notes that "many early viewers saw it [*The Stonebreaker*] as an image of a weary worker sleeping at the end of a day's toil; it was not until the critics began writing about it that it became generally understood as a picture about death" (184).

10 Perhaps the labor of the future would be "attractive labor," a concept that, according to Ruth Kinna (2000), William Morris borrowed from Charles Fourier to portray "labor as art" and to equate, at a fundamental level, leisure and work. But stonebreaking, for Morris, was likely akin to "occupations, for example, ploughing, fishing, and shepherding [that] were inherently 'rough' and workers employed in these roles might need periods of complete 'dog-like' rest in order to recuperate from their activities" (496).

11 But consider, in contrast, the later development of abstract art, in which most artworks referencing the craft conditions of their production are, as Thierry de Duve (1991) puts it, to be avoided "like the plague" (155). In particular, de Duve credits Malevich and Mondrian as knowing that "the grand painting of the twentieth century could only be that which rejected 'grand painting,' and that the 'new craft' consisted in avoiding like the plague anything that connoted 'craft.' From this came the mechanical, 'clumsy' technique, voluntarily deprived of all virtuosity, of the works of Malevich and Mondrian. And from this, despite all the formal dissimilarities, came the profound affinity of these painters with Marcel Duchamp" (155). De Duve goes on to say about Malevich that "the know-how that *Black Square* demanded of its author is nil. This kind of craftsmanship is within the reach of anyone … Being no longer painting,

54   *Jack Amariglio*

it declared negatively that painting could survive its own death only by recognizing the cause of it. And it declared this cause positively by being an industrial object: industrialization, which had assassinated all the crafts, had assassinated the craft of painting as well. *Black Square* addressed itself to the ideological consequences of the same assassination" (155). Here, we see a dialectical turn in Morris's adage regarding the inscription of the conditions of production and labor (via craft) in the art object. For Malevich, if de Duve is correct, the space of the canvas now became the place to display "positively" the death of this specialized labor itself. It went beyond "creative destruction" to depict, of course in its materials, color, and discernible method of composition, a representation of a devalued but also revalued though ambivalent labor process. The contradiction in attitude to painterly labor or craft is therefore left in limbo, and its unresolved effects are productive in themselves and in relation to the viewer's reception.

12 In her important essay, Jennifer Ellen Way (2004) considers the possibility that "painterly abstract art" of the mid-twentieth century did, indeed, reflect and inscribe changes that were taking place in the "consumerist" economy after WWII. She states: "much of the vanguard painting being exhibited to acclaim did not visually represent consumer goods or images manufactured for, distributed to, and ultimately consumed by middle-class Americans, which raises a question. Barring images connoting consumer culture or the economy, what was it about the paintings that prompted so many commentators to discuss them in light of discourses not merely descriptive but also critical of consumer culture? As proof that consumer culture was beginning to dominate much about the contemporary American art world, commentators stressed the emphatic materiality of the painterly surfaces of painterly abstract paintings. Restaging their discourse brings to the fore a belief in the power of consumer culture to configure art to its forms, values, and uses, while it frustrates redress thereof. Yet, was it not possible that artists proposed an alternative to the sinister developments that their colleagues considered inevitable?" (489–90). Way goes on to posit that there was an explosion of artists coming from the ranks of the newly trained and interested middle class, and that this resulted in a supply of abstract paintings that reduced the claims to authenticity and unique creativity, but, rather, were increasingly read as commodities being churned out in near production line processes. The creating of an abstract expressionist genre, for example, made it easier for commentators to regard the overplus of such paintings as an expression of the economic needs but also the inscribed understandings of these newly minted artists. In this way, the art that was being produced in massive amounts took on the trappings of their production conditions. Their similarity and substitutability became *what* was being painted, and was not just the external conditions of their production. As Way states, "art writers accused artists of shunning longer and more deliberative and idiosyncratic processes for ways of working that promised quick profits" (490). Way, following Harold Rosenberg, characterizes this situation as "resemblances of surfaces." Thus art signified the very conditions of its resemblance and substitutability and its overall surplus, and increasingly surfaces were read as "packages," indistinct from forms of advertising and commercial graphic design. One wonders, then, what notion of economic value was being portrayed in this development. It seems more like a combination of standard mainstream "product-cycle" theory along with strains of a Marxian-inspired view of the leveling of aesthetic value and its replacement or its constitution by profit-driven heightened exchange-value (due to the cheapening of the living labor involved and the dead labor embodied in the materials, and the maintenance of a sale price, despite the fact of increased competition). Then, of course, as I argue below, there are also elements of gift theory in all of this, particularly in the excess that was being both performed and represented in these "production-line" paintings. Without reproducing her argument here, it should be said that, in the works of Claes Oldenburg, Way finds a

critical sensibility able, by a strategy of deliberate reification, to challenge the introjected commodification of the art object and its appearance as the content of that same object.

13 For a more recent survey of the influence of a now-battered Marxism on the prevailing "social history of art" and its two somewhat conflicted, dominant strands (one more orthodoxly intent on revealing the social context of the individual work of art, the other more Foucauldean and focused on the socioanthropology of institutional power for art in general), see Hemingway (1996). It is relieving to still find art historians and critics who are neither vulgar non- or anti-Marxists, nor orthodox Marxists in reaction. Gen Doy (1998), citing Marx on the symbolism of coins and painting, concludes that, "for Marx, painted forms are not symbols of things in nature. They have an ontological status of their own, and their being made in a 'realistic' way should not alter this fact. Any painted representation will have its own status whether it is naturalistic or non-figurative, although there was obviously no non-figurative art in Marx's day. Thus, we should not assume that Marxists would advocate realistic art as a form of privileged knowledge above other types of art" (30–1).

14 Richard Leppert (1996) explains that, in the late nineteenth century, "paintings of money, paper money especially, were produced in large numbers" (35–6). Leppert's explanation for this outpouring of what was considered, at best, "middlebrow art" is that there was considerable social anxiety about counterfeiting "which exacerbated the uncertainties surrounding paper money's worth and brought into sharp focus the suspicious nature of an economy so apparently dependent on representation" (37). "Paintings of money," Leppert continues, "joined the debate both by their subject and by their very nature. Paintings of paper money, after all, were representations *of representations*; they themselves, in other words, referenced the troubled relation between representation and fakery, or counterfeiting" (38).

15 A good, basic introduction to twentieth-century abstract art is Whitford (1987).

16 The possibility of reading economic, or any, represented "content" in non-representational art is foreclosed by Anne Sheppard in her primer, *Aesthetics* (1987). In a brief and too simplistic survey of Marxist views on the connection between art and "morals," Sheppard states that "the simple view that art reflects social and economic reality, although it can offer reasonably satisfying accounts of realist art forms such as the nineteenth-century novel, cannot cope satisfactorily with modernist art" (143). By "modernist art," I take Sheppard to mean the art of the twentieth century, starting with Cubism and moving forward. This is made clearer when one reads the first chapter of Sheppard's book, in which she rules out applying the notion of "representation" to abstract or any similar art forms. As she claims, to "argue that emotions or states of mind can be represented is to extend the notion of representation too far" (17). For Sheppard, the "reading into" non-representational art that which bears no ostensible (in her view) "resemblance" to an objective world, nor which corresponds in some way to what an artist intended to place on view, is illegitimate insofar as this "reading into" involves a statement about representation. In place of representation, though, Sheppard does allow for viewers to be able to apprehend expression, form, and beauty, none of which imply "representation."

17 Perhaps, instead, it's useful to think that the presumable alternative to "not representing" is "presenting" or "immanence." This is Johanna Drucker's (1994) reading of the self-claims of Malevich, Mondrian, and other abstract artists, for whom she argues "material presence was fully equated with ontological completeness. No matter what else was to be signified by the visual elements—the manifestation of cosmic principles, geometric truths, or visual dynamism, etc.—it was on the basis of their visual existence that these images exemplified a belief in the self-sufficiency of visual presence. The very concept of presence, as the manifestation of being, as replete immanence, becomes a primary foundation for the construction of these works. By giving up the overt need

56   Jack Amariglio

for a referent, they assert the capacity of visual forms to function in themselves, on the basis of their visuality, and, again, with the premise that their appearance *is* a form of presence" (77–8).

18 I owe this idea of a "license to read" to the anthropologist Bregje van Eekelen.

19 But the worm often turns; upon the death of Stalin, at least in the Soviet Union, the artistic avant-garde resumed its assault on forms of realism and representation that now were associated with inexcusable "bad taste." A "contemporary style" emerged in the "reassessment of indigenous Constructivism and international modernism" (Reid, 1997, 178). This "contemporary style" not only visually differentiated the Khrushchev period from Stalinism, but, "by the end of the 1950s, the Khrushchev regime fully endorsed the reformist campaign for aesthetic quality as part of its effort to rejuvenate the legitimating ideology of Marxism-Leninism" as well as "the purpose of Communism" (178). For discussions of "unofficial art" in the Soviet Union after the death of Stalin, see the essays by Aleš Erjavec and Boris Groys in Erjavec (2003).

20 Summing up the state of contemporary art criticism under the influence of "the French," Jeremy Gilbert-Rolfe (1999) asserts that for a sizable number of critics "while Freud may not be quite adequate to human psychology, all artworks are Freudian" (78). In his essay on Andy Warhol and his break from the high pretensions of mid-century abstract expressionist art, Arthur Danto (1999) explains as well that, among earlier surrealist and especially New York School Abstract Expressionist artists and their followers, Freudian and Jungian deep readings of their own work and their "unconscious" meanings (or better said, the meanings of the Unconscious that they unconsciously but, ironically, self-consciously tapped, if only abstractly) were *de rigueur* and were a necessary rite of passage into their midst. On the abiding attachment of artists, art historians, and critics to psychoanalytic readings of art, see also Elkins (1999).

21 I also puzzled, as the discussion that follows suggests, over the "forms" of non-representational art, and the impossibility of retaining the form/content distinction in tracing "the economic." For, form is itself, if nothing else, materially specific and historically constituted, and there is a story to be told about each particular formal innovation and its appearance—in economics as well as in art—a story that is always/already linked to the concrete overdetermination of form(s). For this point, see the "Introduction" to Yve-Alain Bois's *Painting as Model* (1993).

22 See also, by comparison, Vargish and Mook (1999), an English professor and physicist respectively, who relate modernist art (with an emphasis on Cubism, Futurism, and Abstract Art) to developments in math and physics during the early and mid-twentieth century.

23 No, to the contrary. Of course, Lippard's adage (1984, 345) appears in an energetic defense of the "activist art" of the 1980s, and her commentary focuses on the possibility that artists could avoid, in some way, "co-optation" by the powers that be.

24 It should be noted that the excess and expenditure of Maussian-inspired gift theory need not displace Marxist conceptions of "surplus value" insofar as these notions are relocated to a new metaphorical and ontological sphere: the realm of signification. Something like this translocation is recorded by Gilbert-Rolfe when he claims that, "while Marx may have been subsumed or displaced, art may still be said to employ a Marxist attitude to surplus value, where it plays with a marginal surplus squeezed out of the signs it appropriates" (1999, 78).

25 Some of the essays (rendered first in German, and then translated as an appendix—I will refer only to these translations) that are included in the marvelous catalogue of the German exhibition *Art & Economy* (2002) discuss, either directly or indirectly, the excess over and within the strict economic rationality presumed to have existed, once upon a time, in commodity exchange. The essays are part of a project that take as its point of departure a new, more directly engaged, if still critical, relationship between contemporary artists who were involved in the exhibition and successful corporations, including these same artists' sponsors and patrons. Yet, the writers asked to both

comment upon and accompany the visual art of the exhibition tend toward the view that, to the extent artists engender distinct economic ideas and visions, these ideas and visions may encompass notions of waste, of restricted and general reciprocity, of the high importance of the "non-" or "im-material" in economic activity, of creativity and incessant innovation as economic intangibles that must now be incorporated into the businesses' bottom line, and so forth. Christopher Kihm, for example, mentions the "economy of gifts" that have always been a dimension of economic exchange, that is, within the transactions performed by businesses, consumers, and other economic agents (a point I make in Amariglio, 2002). In this sense, then, perhaps gift theory *in* art corresponds to the realization that the form of exchange in capitalist economies has never worked outside the elements of the gift, but always/already inscribed them, though often kept them hidden. See also the essays by Wolfgang Ullrich, Helen Karmasin, and Michael Hutter for elaborations of and sidebars to this argument that art may, respectively, increasingly reflect the aspects of excessively libidinal and destructive potlatch as characterized by "irrational" corporate spending on art; a semiotic achieved by today's artists of "openness," non-materiality, and non-utilitarian values that are instantiated by businesses seeking to sell themselves and their products globally in a diversely constituted consumer culture, certainly through advertising, via this artistically constituted semiotic; and the primary role of power (and not just preferences) in determining how art and economic agents are positioned, economically and culturally, vis-à-vis each other. These fragments, I would argue, are all components of a more developed theory of the gift, one that is meant to escape the constraining bounds of traditional economic value theory.

26 For one reading of Newman's painting, see de Bolla (2003). De Bolla states, "Perhaps the most common reaction to this canvas is bemusement. What does it mean, what does it represent? What is it trying to say? Even viewers familiar with abstract expressionist art, or with what has come known to be 'color field' painting, may find this canvas too instant, too cool, too intellectual. And if this is so, bemusement may quickly transform into stronger negative reactions such as disappointment, boredom, or resentment" (29–30). Never fear, though. Predictably, de Bolla asserts that these "are the wrong questions to ask" (31). Instead, reception in the form of affect or feeling is what is decisive. Newman's painting is obviously "empty of representational content; the image is 'abstract,' which is to say that it does not depict anything except, perhaps, color" (32). As I have argued above, being empty of representational content or depicting "nothing" is to represent or depict exactly that supposed absence. In any event, de Bolla does have a more interesting discussion of the affect, which seems more and more as his discussion proceeds to being "in" the painting itself; he conceives of the painting as introducing a feeling for or sensation of "time" or timeliness (42–3). Time is of the essence of some versions of gift theory—for example, the time of return, as in Derrida's conception (1992), but I cannot draw out these connections in this essay. On Newman's work more generally, and the claim that, for Newman, at least in some of his paintings, ideas were indeed intended to be directly represented through what we are calling abstraction, see Bois (1993).

27 Jonathan Harris (1999) has an excellent discussion of the cold-war influenced "Americanism" of Abstract Expressionism that emerged after WWII. Within the "triumphalist" context of the autonomy and purity of the turn modernist, abstract art took in that period, Harris also has this striking quote about political representation from Barnett Newman in an interview on one of his most influential paintings, *Covenant*. "Harold Rosenberg challenged me to explain what one of my paintings could possibly mean to the world. My answer was that if he and others could read it properly, it would mean the end of all state capitalism and totalitarianism" (65). For a full documentary and critical accounting of Abstract Expressionism, see the collection by Landau (2005). In that collection, Ann Gibson (2005) contributes a provocative analysis of the "rhetoric" of Abstract Expressionist artists (such as Pollack, Newman, and others). She concludes

58 *Jack Amariglio*

that, in point of fact, the rhetoric and practice of Abstract Expressionist art can be seen largely as a form of postmodern allegory, which she attributes to "the switch [by the 1950s] to multiple and simultaneous kinds of signification" rather than a search for essential elements and pictorial totality (473).

28 My argument is different from those critics who see in "abstraction" the general semiotic of capitalist society and the dominance of capitalist economic relations as reflected in art and culture (the most influential and brilliant exposition of this can be found in Lukács, 1971). While not explicitly discussing "abstract art," Wolfgang Haug nicely renders one version of such an argument in his pathbreaking text (1986) on "commodity aesthetics." Haug claims that, "in bourgeois society," it is necessary for "the ruling class ... to create a kind of expression and justifying scenario, to produce the illusion that social relations really do serve the vital needs of all. This illusion must convey complete classlessness, justice, humanity, welfare, etc., and/or make subjugation, service, discipline and sacrifice, appear to be natural and the highest fulfillment. Every expression which gains the trust of the masses ... will be brought into play and stripped of the concrete endeavors it once expressed. Hence, it is necessarily the mere abstraction of an expression which is nothing other than aestheticization" (134). Translating (and subverting) Haug's statement into the terms of this paper, "abstract art" could therefore be read as a crowning moment of modernist (and capitalist) "aestheticization," the emptying of all putative content in art and culture in order to sublate the possibility of radical critique.

29 Kobena Mercer's (2006) collection of essays on "discrepant abstraction" counters a particular ideological history of abstract art, one that emphasizes the search for and actualization of "purity" involved in this putatively Western movement. Mercer and his collaborators point out, instead, the incessant borrowing internationally (and certainly from colonial and post-colonial traditions) that inspired all movements toward twentieth-century abstraction. In the "Introduction" to the collection, Mercer also illuminates art critical studies that concern the critical edge of abstract art, its disruptive moment. He cites Rosalind Krauss, Michael Leja, and Briony Fer "who each employ post-structuralist, psychoanalytical and deconstructive concepts to reveal how abstraction resists the fixity of 'meaning' that essentialism requires and gives rise instead to a plurality of readings which are generated by a process of semiosis that cannot be fully closed by any one singular interpretation" (17).

30 In a collection of essays written mostly in the late 1970s, Peter Fuller (1980) sought a position beyond what he called the "physicalism" of critics like Clement Greenberg, with Greenberg's emphasis on the flatness or materiality of the painted canvas, and an idealism that he associated with 1960s and 70s conceptual art, in which, as he claimed, the essential medium of art altogether is abandoned. Though I don't share what was then Fuller's anti-Althusserian, Marxist humanism (he later espoused an anti-left conservatism), I do share his attention to the corporeality and materiality of art practices (and art practitioners) *and* their objects. It is too bad, in my view, that Fuller sought to reduce this bodily focus more often than not to universal biological expressions and emotions.

31 Though it must be said that "action" is not exactly "labor" and, indeed, was not meant by Rosenberg or others to be its simple equivalent, since it avoids labor's somewhat Marxian connotations. In her chapter on Rosenberg, Marjorie Welish (1999) discusses the attraction for artists and critics alike of "action" and "activism" as opposed to the contemplative stance that some identified with approaching a work of abstract art.

32 Speaking for "teachers of aesthetics," David Fenner (2005) wearily acknowledges that, when it comes to abstract expressionism and other modern art, "students in aesthetics courses ... deny the value of it, together with claims about their artistic abilities during their kindergarten years" (13). Indeed, Fenner links together what he calls "two of the most common challenges" that these teachers face from their students: 1) "every

Tracing the economic   59

aesthetic judgment is as good as every other one," and 2) modern art "is made up 'of stuff I could have done when I was four years old'" (13).

33 On a practical level, many artists are defensive and also clear about the labor time and skill level they believe go into their work. Some, relying on the old saw of the "impulsion" to have to do their art as creative people, indicate that they spend very long hours in their studios or other work places. I'm not aware of studies that document in detail the labor hours of artists, but I do accept that the numbers could be extraordinary for some if not most (that is, when they're not "working" on a different wage-paying job). Stuart Plattner (1996) has a nice quote from a painter in St. Louis who he says, as a full professor, gave the following information about his "standard orientation lecture to beginning graduate students" in his classes: "I usually tell students that the artist is ... the only profession in our society where you have to be, first of all, a common laborer; second, a highly skilled technician; third, a highly skilled and/or a marginally skilled technician in other crafts than your own. That is, if you're a painter, you have to know about making slides ... carpentry, matting, crating. Technical skills in other professions than your own, unless you can hire them done. Most artists can't. Fourth, a small-business person, an entrepreneur, a manager of your own career, which is part of that. But, to deal with dealers, you have to at least prepare your accounting practices for your accountant when you file your income tax and so forth. Then, finally, an intellectual. In addition to that—not finally, in addition to that—you have to find a second profession to make a living" (85–6).

34 Let's compare this to Marx Wartofsky's claim (1993) that, today, "Art is about art; art has taken itself as its own object, and has subordinated both form and content to this object. Artists have become preoccupied with the representation of their own activities as the very object of their activities. The painting is *about* painting; it is about the very process of its own production ... In this context, art takes itself as its own concrete object. It represents itself. It presents its own immediacy and its own mode of production in an iconic way" (218). In relation to my argument, Wartofsky hits on something similar insofar as he avers that the conditions of production of the art piece are, directly or by "negation" and supposed erasure, pushed to the center of a representational matrix. Yet, there is nothing iconographically straightforward about the primacy of questions of labor and production, and there is likewise a surplus of meanings left dangling quite often due precisely to the labored effects of production's materiality and/or its disappearance. Once again, I think we are in the register of the gift, or, at minimum, an internal economy of alternating austerity (art is *only* about art's production) and excess (art is *all, and then some* about art production).

35 Pam Meecham and Paul Wood (1996) point out that "a practice which on the one hand continues to be surrounded by a high-flown rhetoric of creativity, insight, and value, yet which on the other hand has abandoned most of the criteria by which such value has traditionally been judged (skill, beauty, effective story telling, etc.), stands in an exposed position when the resulting products continue to be exchanged for what to most people seem exorbitant sums of money. 'The emperor's new clothes' is one of the most persistent refrains in lay criticism of modern art: and not always without justification" (31). See also Varnedoe (2006) for his rejection of the thesis (he calls it tiresome "whistling in the dark") of the "emperor's new clothes" syndrome in audience reception of abstract art (28–9).

36 The hysteria set off by non-representational artwork shows up, not surprisingly, in contemporaneous art criticism and art history. James Elkins (1999), though not confining himself to abstract art, comments that "much of modern and postmodern art history and criticism would then be a kind of collective hysteria about pictures, brought on by the fact that pictures do not speak and do not mean anything aside from their trappings as legible signs. The simplicity and irreducible nature of visual meaninglessness would make pictures even more exasperating for minds bent on understanding" (16).

60   Jack Amariglio

37 The artist/writer Derek Whitehead (2007) reflects on this perception of difficulty: "Much contemporary art is seen as a drive toward obscurity, having a will to enigma, to unintelligibility or to uninterpretability, as Donald Kuspit has claimed. But is this so? Defenders of contemporary art speak of the ways in which assemblage art, installation and multi-media art (video, audio, and film art) and certain modes of performance art manage to instate some guiding motif at the organizational centre of its perceptual field, such that new resonances, balances and tensions emerge, thus saving its composition, or design, as Charles Altieri would have it, from 'willfulness' or mere 'ornamental status.'"

38 Harold Rosenberg (1973) accords Schwitters a high honor in placing him in the (gift-imbued—in my terms) context of what Rosenberg called "the de-definition of art." To wit, "Painting, sculpture, drama, music, have been undergoing a process of de-definition. The nature of art has become uncertain. At least, it is ambiguous. No one can say with assurance what a work of art is—or, more important, what is not a work of art. When an art object is still present, as in painting, it is what I have called an anxious object: it does not know whether it is a masterpiece or junk. It may, as in the case of a collage by Schwitters, be literally both" (12). As for Schwitters's "impurity," this may be contrasted with the "purity" attributed to others, such as Mondrian and Kandinsky, for whom, in the opinion of Mark Cheetham (1991), painterly abstraction constituted pious essentialist transcendence.

39 Elizabeth Gamard (2000) argues that Schwitters had a decidedly "developmental and incorporative" approach to his art: "He did not operate according to a fixed stratagem, but rather forged his material from events and circumstances as they presented themselves. Accordingly, there is no obvious fixed point or referent from which his overall approach might be apprehended" (4). In Gamard's description of Schwitters's evolving work, "results could not be predicted but could be found as the evidence is gathered, assembled and de-assembled. There were no rules or fixed principles for either life or art, but an ongoing research that was itself developmental and generative, in effect mirroring the constantly fluctuating circumstances and contingencies by which and through which it was formulated" (36). Gamard thus sees Schwitters as a forerunner of "the postmodern" in art, at least as it is described by Lyotard.

40 Margarita Tupitsyn (2002) takes *Black Square* as the premise of a wide-ranging dissertation on Malevich's work, most pointedly the ultimately "filmic" quality of his most non-objective paintings and of the sequencing with which he often showcased/exhibited them. Starting with a brief discussion of how Clement Greenberg dismissed Malevich's influence—which Tupitsyn sees as evidence supporting Clark's thesis that *Black Square*, and other paintings in its wake, was just too uncertain and possessed too many undecidables to make it the basis of a reductionist thesis (Greenberg's) that saw flatness and purity as the essential elements of abstraction— Tupitsyn proceeds to elaborate upon the "code" of painting that Malevich inscribed in contrast to what his opponents among the Constructivists derided as "colorless writing" or a "painting-over" in *Black Square*. Much has also been made of the so-called "mysticism" of Malevich (and Mondrian later) that inspired and actualized *Black Square, White on White*, and his other Suprematist compositions, yet I suspect that this resort to reading Malevich as a deep-down mystic during this period of his work is partly the result of the dialectic of excess and absence of meaning—all those undecidables—that Clark, Tupitsyn, and others have highlighted. In this way, again, Malevich's semiotic overloading and literal over-painting of the canvas (or, alternatively, his painting "degree zero"), and, simultaneously, his playing within the picture's frame, initiate an internal "economy" of painting that, not unlike the "economic principle" that Malevich proposed as the expressive goal of Suprematist art, invokes and combines seemingly opposed but also excessively rendered values (understood both in the aesthetic and economic sense).

References

Amariglio, Jack. 2002. "Give the Ghost a Chance! A Comrade's Shadowy Addendum." In *The Question of the Gift: Essays Across Disciplines*, edited by Mark Osteen, 266–79. New York: Routledge.

Bal, Mieke. 1996. *Double Exposures: The Subject of Cultural Analysis*. New York: Routledge.

Bataille, Georges. 1991. *The Accursed Share: An Essay on General Economy, Vol. 1*, translated by R. Hurley. New York: Zone Books.

Batchelor, David. 1991. "Abstraction, Modernism, Representation." In *Thinking Art: Beyond Traditional Aesthetics*, edited by Andrew Benjamin and Peter Osborne, 44–57. London: Institute of Contemporary Arts.

Batchelor, David. 2000. "In Bed with the Monochrome." In *From an Aesthetic Point of View: Philosophy, Art and the Senses*, edited by Peter Osborne, 150–76. London: Serpent's Tail.

Bois, Yve-Alain. 1993. *Painting as Model*. Cambridge: MIT Press.

Bourdieu, Pierre. 1984. *Distinction: A Social Critique of the Judgement of Taste*, translated by Richard Nice. Cambridge: Harvard University Press.

Bourdieu, Pierre. 1993. *The Field of Cultural Production*. New York: Columbia University Press.

Bourdieu, Pierre. 1995. *The Rules of Art: Genesis and Structure of the Literary Field*, translated by Susan Emanuel. Stanford: Stanford University Press.

Bowlt, John E. 1996. "Body Beautiful: The Artistic Search for the Perfect Physique." In *Laboratory of Dreams: The Russian Avant-Garde and Cultural Experiment*, edited by John E. Bowlt and Olga Matich, 37–58. Stanford: Stanford University Press.

Brettell, Richard R. 1999. *Modern Art 1851–1929: Capitalism and Representation*. Oxford: Oxford University Press.

Buck-Morss, Susan. 2000. *Dreamworld and Catastrophe: The Passing of Mass Utopia in East and West*. Cambridge: MIT Press.

Callari, Antonio. 2002. "The Ghost of the Gift: The Unlikelihood of Economics." In *The Question of the Gift: Essays Across Disciplines*, edited by Mark Osteen, 248–65. New York: Routledge.

Cheetham, Mark A. 1991. *The Rhetoric of Purity: Essentialist Theory and the Advent of Abstract Painting*. Cambridge: Cambridge University Press.

Clark, T. J. 1999a. *The Painting of Modern Life: Paris in the Art of Manet and His Followers*. Revised Edition. Princeton: Princeton University Press.

Clark, T. J. 1999b. *Farewell to an Idea: Episodes from a History of Modernism*. New Haven, CT: Yale University Press.

Crow, Thomas. 1996. *Modern Art in the Common Culture*. New Haven, CT: Yale University Press.

Csikszentmihalyi, Mihaly, and Eugene Rochberg-Halton. 1981. *The Meaning of Things: Domestic Symbols and the Self*. Chicago: University of Chicago Press.

Danto, Arthur C. 1999. *Philosophizing Art: Selected Essays*. Berkeley: University of California Press.

de Bolla, Peter. 2003. *Art Matters*. Cambridge: Harvard University Press.

de Duve, Thierry. 1991. *Pictorial Nominalism: On Marcel Duchamp's Passage from Painting to the Readymade*. Minneapolis: University of Minnesota Press.

Derrida, Jacques. 1992. *Given Time: 1. Counterfeit Money*, translated by Peggy Kamuf. Chicago: University of Chicago Press.

62   Jack Amariglio

Doy, Gen. 1998. *Materializing Art History*. Oxford: Berg.

Drucker, Johanna. 1994. *Theorizing Modernism: Visual Art and the Critical Tradition*. New York: Columbia University Press.

Elkins, James. 1999. *Why are Our Pictures Puzzles? On the Origins of Pictorial Complexity*. New York: Routledge.

Elkins, James. 2002. *Stories of Art*. New York: Routledge.

Erjavec, Aleš. 2003. "Introduction." In *Postmodernism and the Postsocialist Condition: Politicized Art in Late Socialism*, edited by Aleš Erjavec, 1–54. Berkeley: University of California Press.

Fenner, David E. W. 2005. "Why Was There So Much Ugly Art in the Twentieth Century?" *Journal of Aesthetic Education*, 39(2), 13–26.

Friedman, Susan Stanford. 2001. "Definitional Excursions: The Meanings of Modern/ Modernity/Modernism." *Modernism/Modernity*, 8(3), 493–513.

Fuchs, Rudy. 2000. "Conflicts with Modernism or the Absence of Kurt Schwitters." In *I is Style*, Kurt Schwitters, 7–16. Rotterdam: NAI Publishers.

Fuller, Peter. 1980. *Beyond the Crisis in Art*. London: Writers and Readers Publishing Cooperative Society, Ltd.

Gagnier, Regenia. 2000. *The Insatiability of Human Wants: Economics and Aesthetics in Market Society*. Chicago: University of Chicago Press.

Gamard, Elizabeth Burns. 2000. *Kurt Schwitters' Merzbau: The Cathedral of Erotic Misery*. New York: Princeton Architectural Press.

Gibson, Ann. 2005. "The Rhetoric of Abstract Expressionism." In *Reading Abstract Expressionism: Context and Critique*, edited by Ellen G. Landau, 442–86. New Haven, CT: Yale University Press.

Gilbert-Rolfe, Jeremy. 1999. "Nietzschean Critique and the Hegelian Commodity, or the French Have Landed." *Critical Inquiry*, 26(1), 70–84.

Grampp, William. 1989. *Pricing the Priceless: Art, Artists, and Economics*. New York: Basic Books, Inc.

Greenberg, Clement. 1940 (reprinted 1992). "Towards a Newer Laocoon." In *Art and Theory: 1900–1990,* edited by Charles Harrison and Paul Wood, 554–60. Oxford: Basil Blackwell.

Groys, Boris. 2003. "The Other Gaze: Russian Unofficial Art's View of the Soviet World." In *Postmodernism and the Postsocialist Condition: Politicized Art under Late Socialism*, edited by Aleš Erjavec, 55–89. Berkeley: University of California Press.

Halle, David. 1996. *Inside Culture: Art and Class in the American Home*. Chicago: University of Chicago Press.

Harris, Jonathan. 1999. "Modernism and Culture in the USA 1930–1960." In *Modernism in Dispute: Art since the Forties*, edited by Paul Wood, Francis Frascina, Jonathan Harris, and Charles Harrison, 3–76. New Haven and London: Yale University Press.

Haug, Wolfgang Fritz. 1986. *Critique of Commodity Aesthetics: Appearance, Sexuality and Advertising in Capitalist Society*, translated by Robert Bock. Minneapolis: University of Minnesota Press.

Hawksley, Lucinda. 1999. *Essential Pre-Raphaelites*. Bath: Parragon Publishing.

Hemingway, Andrew. 1996. "Marxism and Art History after the Fall of Communism." *Art Journal*, 55(2), 20–7.

Hicks, John R. 1939. *Value and Capital*. Oxford: Oxford University Press.

Hutter, Michael. 2002. "Art Shows Power." In *Art & Economy*, edited by Felix Zdanek, Beate Hentschel, and Dirk Luckow, 248–53. Ostfildern-Ruit: Hatje Cantz.

Tracing the economic 63

Karmasin, Helene. 2002. "Art and Advertising." In *Art & Economy*, edited by Felix Zdanek, Beate Hentschel, and Dirk Luckow, 272–5. Ostfildern-Ruit: Hatje Cantz.

Kihm, Christopher. 2002. "Art and Business: A Capital Relationship." In *Art & Economy*, edited by Felix Zdanek, Beate Hentschel, and Dirk Luckow, 264–5. Ostfildern-Ruit: Hatje Cantz.

Kinna, Ruth. 2000. "William Morris: Art, Work, and Leisure." *Journal of the History of Ideas*, 61(3), 493–512.

Klamer, Arjo. 2007. *Speaking of Economics: How to Get in the Conversation*. New York: Routledge.

Krauss, Rosalind. 1985. *The Originality of the Avant-Garde and Other Modernist Myths*. Cambridge: MIT Press.

Landau, Ellen G., ed. 2005. *Reading Abstract Expressionism: Context and Critique*. New Haven, CT: Yale University Press.

Leppert, Richard. 1996. *Art and the Committed Eye: The Cultural Functions of Imagery*. Boulder, CO: Westview Press.

Lippard, Lucy. 1984. "Trojan Horses: Activist Art and Power." In *Art After Modernism: Rethinking Representation*, edited by Brian Wallis, 341–58. Boston: David R. Godine.

Lippard, Lucy. 2002. "The Silent Art." In *Abstract Art in the Late Twentieth Century*, edited by Frances Colpitt, 49–60. Cambridge: Cambridge University Press.

Lukács, Georg. 1971. *History and Class Consciousness: Studies in Marxist Dialectics*, translated by Rodney Livingston. Cambridge: MIT Press.

Lyotard, Jean-François. 1993. "The Sublime and the Avant-Garde." In *Postmodernism: A Reader*, edited and introduced by Thomas Docherty, 244–56. New York: Columbia University Press.

Malevich, Kasimir. 1992. "The Question of Imitative Art." In *Art in Theory 1900–1990: An Anthology of Changing Ideas*, edited by Charles Harrison and Paul Wood, 292–7. Oxford: Blackwell.

Marwick, Arthur. 2002. *The Arts in the West since 1945*. Oxford: Oxford University Press.

Mauss, Marcel. 1950. *The Gift: Forms and Functions of Exchange in Ancient Societies*, translated by I. Cunnison. London: Routledge and Kegan Paul.

Meecham, Pam, and Paul Wood. 1996. "Modernism and Modernity: An Introductory Survey." In *Investigating Modern Art*, edited by Liz Dawtrey, Toby Jackson, Mary Masterson, Pam Meecham, and Paul Wood, 1–33. New Haven, CT: Yale University Press.

Mercer, Kobena, ed. 2006. *Discrepant Abstraction*. Cambridge: MIT Press.

Moore, Allan W. 2004. "Political Economy as Subject and Form in Contemporary Art." *Review of Radical Political Economics*, 36(4), 471–86.

Morris, William. 1993. *Art and Society: Lectures and Essays by William Morris*, edited by Gary Zabel. Medford, MA: George's Hill Publications.

Mosquera, Gerardo. 1994. "Meyer Shapiro, Marxist Aesthetics, and Abstract Art." *Oxford Art Journal*, 17(1), 76–80.

Plattner, Stuart. 1996. *High Art Down Home: An Economic Ethnography of a Local Art Market*. Chicago: University of Chicago Press.

Reid, Susan E. 1997. "Destalinization and Taste, 1953–1963." *Journal of Design History*, 10(2), 177–201.

Rosenberg, Harold. 1973. *The De-definition of Art*. New York: Collier Books.

Ruccio, David F., and Jack Amariglio. 2003. *Postmodern Moments in Modern Economics*. Princeton: Princeton University Press.

64 *Jack Amariglio*

Ruccio, David F., ed. 2008. *Economic Representations: Academic and Everyday*. New York: Routledge.

Samuelson, Paul. 1983. *Foundations of Economic Analysis*. Cambridge: Harvard University Press.

Schwitters, Kurt. 2000. *I is Style*. Rotterdam: NAI Publishers.

Shell, Marc. 1995. *Art and Money*. Chicago: University of Chicago Press.

Sheppard, Anne. 1987. *Aesthetics: An Introduction to the Philosophy of Art*. Oxford: Oxford University Press.

Tupitsyn, Margarita. 2002. *Malevich and Film*. New Haven, CT: Yale University Press.

Ullrich, Wolfgang. 2002. "The Cycle of Money and Art: The Economics of Anti-Economics." In *Art & Economy*, edited by Felix Zdanek, Beate Hentschel, and Dirk Luckow, 244–5. Ostfildern-Ruit: Hatje Cantz.

Vargish, Thomas, and Delo E. Mook. 1999. *Inside Modernism: Relativity Theory, Cubism, Narrative*. New Haven, CT: Yale University Press.

Varnedoe, Kirk. 2006. *Pictures of Nothing: Abstract Art since Pollock*. Princeton: Princeton University Press.

Velthuis, Olav. 2005. *Imaginary Economies: Contemporary Artists and the World of Big Money*. Rotterdam: NAI Publishers.

Vidler, Anthony. 1998. "Interpreting the Void: Architecture and Spatial Anxiety." In *The Subjects of Art History: Historical Objects in Contemporary Perspective*, edited by Mark A. Cheetham, Michael Ann Holly, and Keith Moxey, 288–307. Cambridge: Cambridge University Press.

Wartofsky, Marx. 1993. "The Politics of Art: The Domination of Style and the Crisis in Contemporary Art." *Journal of Aesthetics and Art Criticism*, 51(2), 217–25.

Watten, Barrett. 2003. *The Constructivist Moment: From Material Text to Cultural Poetics*. Middletown, CT: Wesleyan University Press.

Way, Jennifer Ellen. 2004. "Negotiating the 'Resemblances of Surfaces': Painterly Abstract Painting and Consumer Culture, circa 1945–1965." *Review of Radical Political Economics*, 36(4), 487–505.

Welish, Marjorie. 1999. *Signifying Art: Essays on Art after 1960*. Cambridge: Cambridge University Press.

Weschler, Lawrence. 1999. *Boggs: A Comedy of Values*. Chicago: University of Chicago Press.

Whitehead, Derek. 2007. "Artist's Labor." *Contemporary Aesthetics*, 5(5).

Whitford, Frank. 1987. *Understanding Abstract Art*. New York: E. P. Dutton.

Willats, John. 1997. *Art and Representation: New Principles in the Analysis of Pictures*. Princeton: Princeton University Press.

Wood, Paul. 1999. "The avant-garde in the early twentieth century." In *The Challenge of the Avant-Garde*, edited by Paul Wood, 182–203. New Haven and London: Yale University Press.

2

Meaning to say ...

Judith Mehta

■ Frame/Lemmata

This essay is part of a continuing programme of investigation into what it means to do economics, or what is inscripted in economic practice. At issue in the essay is *the relationship between form and content* in journal articles and texts. My perception of this relationship as complex and deeply problematic, and, hence, as open to critique, is often challenged. In one case, a publishing house asserted that it simply wasn't possible to publish an essay I had written in the two parallel columns in which it was submitted, it being imperative that academic convention, house style, and printing and typographical constraints determine the form of the printed text. In another case, a copy editor unilaterally decided to change the headings I had assigned to the various sections of text, together with the typeface, punctuation, and much else besides in order to bring the work in line with 'good practice'.

Now let us be clear that there is meaning in the form of the text, that so-called 'presentational features' are not somehow detached and apart from the theoretical endeavour taking place in the interior of the text but are integral to that endeavour. Accordingly, these attempts to change so-called 'presentational features' of the text would have seriously interfered with its meaning. Of course, copy editors cannot be blamed for observing the diktats of their publishing houses. But, however benign the motives of academic publishers, such interventions constitute part of the enforcement process in which the rules of engagement in economic discourse are elliptically inscribed. It is only when there is a movement against the rules that they emerge from concealment and the limits of disciplinary practice make themselves known.

Economists have a multiplicity of conceptual tools and aesthetic protocols at their disposal with which to negotiate and construct economic realities, only some of which are deemed to be legitimate. Each selected device leaves its imprint upon the work. Mathematics is a case in point. Mathematics provides a logic that can be helpful in the organization of phenomena. There is also pleasure to be had from the act of quantification, such as joy in the aesthetics of mathematical forms and satisfaction in the orderliness that results when a messy world comes under the thumb of brackets. Given these seductions, it's unsurprising that mathematical logic has come to be reified in the neoclassical tradition – it has become an intrinsic constituent of economic knowledge. Yet this thing that began as an adjunct or embellishment is at the same time imposing its own limits and importing its inadequacies.

The deleterious effect of mathematics on the form and content of economic knowledge has been taken up by economists critical of the neoclassical tradition. Yet this particular area of contention merely points to a wider issue. More generally, I would say a tension arises whenever something regarded as a *surplus* in economic theorizing appears to be collapsing into what is apparently the *interior* of the work. Under these conditions, the limits of the discipline are placed in question, whether through a desire to break through those limits or a desire to defend them from incursions. Whichever the case, I suggest no theoretical practice can intervene effectively in its field of operation if *"it does not weigh up and bear on the frame, which is the decisive structure of what is at stake"* (Derrida, 1987, p.61). And this is the point of my essay.

The *parergon* is a concept I find helpful in taking up Derrida's injunction. The parergon is a supplement (*para*) to the work in question (*ergon*) which appears to lie beyond or outside the work, rather like the frame around a painting or the columns around a building. But the parergon is not merely ornamental. According to Kant, the parergon separates that which is integral to, or a part of, the work, and that which is extraneous to it, while having no part in determining the meaning and value of the work. It is this implicit assumption that might justify the enforcement of protocols relating to house style and 'good practice' on the part of copy editors and journal referees. But in a seminal text, *The Truth in Painting* (*ibid*), Derrida brings into question this distinction between the interior and the exterior. He finds it problematic to determine the limits to a work, and asks: what is this thing that is neither essential nor mere accessory? where does it begin? where does it end? what is it that is being framed? and what is it that is being excluded as frame?

Derrida proposes that the parergon announces some lack or inadequacy on the part of the work; after all, without this lack, the *ergon* would have no need of a *par-ergon*. Thus, it is an internal structural link which rivets the parergon to a lack in the interior of the work. The parergon is, therefore, at one and the same time both a separable and particular part of the work, and also a nonparticular, nondetachable part. As Taylor (2001, p.273) points out in his commentary on the parergon:

> "Parerga are elements which are more difficult to see entirely apart from the work because they may seem to be required for the work's articulation. One senses perhaps that the work cannot quite do without them, or that the work's definition would not be entirely clear without them. Thus, it is as though the work which requires parerga is lacking somehow.... Parerga make up for this lacking in the interior of the work, but still they remain, somehow, exterior to the work."

Meaning to say ... 67

This critique of the parergon can be put to work to examine the relationship between two domains that are held to be distinct in neoclassical thinking: the cultural and the economic. In summary form, the argument is as follows.

Neoclassical economics sees itself as a closed field, as supplying all the conceptual tools required to fix the identities, and the relations between identities, at issue in the activities of production, exchange and consumption. But some lack in the neoclassical apparatus emerges when culture must be admitted as a supplement.

Culture is assigned the minor and subservient role of performing as a kind of error term, soaking up the 'white noise' of inconsistent or otherwise inexplicable elements of economic behaviour. But culture exceeds the task ordained for it. As it becomes clear that *all* the objects of disciplinary practice are cultural constructs, it also becomes apparent that the interior of the work has been contaminated.

Yet if every thing can be conceived as a cultural construct, the economic domain must surely collapse into the cultural domain and *il n'y a pas de hors-culture*. By the same token, as the cultural field itself admits concepts and ideas appropriated from economics, so, too, *il n'y a pas de hors-economie*. Each term has reproduced itself to the point at which all meaning has been evacuated. Thus, culture and economics each appear as a simulacrum, that is, as some reflection of a 'reality' which bears no relation to any reality whatever (Baudrillard, 1995). Devoid of a referent, the idea of culture, and the idea of economics, must exist solely in nostalgia or, in deference to our compulsion to speak of them, under erasure.

The collapse of form into content, of the interior and the exterior of the work, is necessarily invoked in the representation of ideas of which this Introduction is a part. Consider the task performed by an Introduction: it presents itself as a frame to the work; but is it merely an accessory to the work? something more? something less? can we dispense with it? what are its effects upon the work? what *is* the work: where does it begin and where does it end?

Parergon

The Truth in Painting Passe-Partout

This connection [*trait*] between the letter, discourse, painting is perhaps all that happens in or all that threads its way through *The Truth in Painting*.

...

I write four painting.
The first with folding the question of the art?" "The "Representation?" work of art?" etc.) atopics of the work (*ergon*) nor (*hors d'oeuvre*), outside, neither disconcerts any does not remain it *gives rise* to the longer merely That which it puts instances of the signature, the not stop disturbing of discourse on its commerce, its surplus-values, its law, and its what conditions, if can one exceed, displace the great philosophies dominate this above all those of in another respect, These prolegomena *Painting*, *parergon of this together by a circle.*

...

Discourses perhaps destined to which constitutes they do and there is for them an

■ **Wait for the title – it's already causing trouble ...**

■ Within the modern theoretical tradition, *the economy* is commonly understood as the site at which *value* is determined and *economics* as value's master discourse. Yet modern economic ideas reveal themselves to be inadequate to the task of making sense of value. This *lack* in economics surfaces when notions of *culture* seep into the conversation. While modern economists would preserve the integrity of the discursive regime from culture's excesses, it becomes increasingly difficult to do so in the face of recent developments in philosophy. This essay examines the boundaries between the economic domain and the cultural domain; it takes place in the event of a collapse of the interior of the work (*ergon*) into its exterior (*parergon*).

The essay is framed by excerpts from Derrida's (1987) text The Truth in Painting in which he writes around painting. The frame regulates and insinuates itself into what is being said. Derrida says that to keep to the frame, to the limit, he writes four times around painting. Here from the inside, I write three times around his writing around painting:

- in order to make a disturbance in the aesthetic regime which dominates economic discourse; to disrupt in the practice of writing that which is entailed in the practice of writing, that is, the presumed opposition between meaning as inner content, and form as its neutral frame.

- in thinking through the relationship between the economic domain and the cultural domain to recuperate

times here, *around* time I am occupied great philosophical tradition (Awhat is beautiful?" "The origin of the on to the insistent *parergon*: neither outside the work neither inside nor above nor below, it opposition but indeterminate and work. It is no around the work. in place - the frame, the title, the legend, etc. - does the *internal* order painting, its works, evaluations, its speculation, its hierarchies. On it's even possible, dismantle, or heritage of the of art which still whole problematic, Kant, Hegel, and, that of Heidegger? of *The Truth in* themselves the book are ringed (P.9.)

on painting are reproduce the limit them, whatever whatever they say: inside and an

outside of the work as soon as there is work. A series of oppositions comes in the train of this one, which, incidentally, is not necessarily primary (for it belongs to a system whose edging itself reintroduces the problem). And there the trait is always determined as an opposition-slash. (P.11.)

...

One space remains to be broached in order to give place to the truth in painting. Neither inside nor outside, it spaces itself without letting itself be framed but it does not stand outside the frame. It works the frame, makes it work, lets it work, gives it work to do (let, make, and give will be my most misunderstood words in this book). The trait is attracted and retrac(t)ed there by itself, attracts and dispenses with itself

there [*il s'y attire et même*]. It is situates between and the phantom in which we *fascinate*. this word one would say "we salivate", "you a hard-on", or "the anchor" [*le bateau Between* the inside, between the internal edge-line, the framed, the ground, form and and signified, and two-faced trait thus divides in it takes place. The *topos* seems shall borrow it from nomenclature of *passe-partout*.

... To that partout remains a movable base; but something appear, frame in the strict **frame within the**

...

PARERGON

Lemmata [a indicating the argument of an motto appended to If, therefore, one lessons on art or question of this art?" "What is the works of art?" meaning of art?"

some of *the pleasure of the text*, that is, some thing of value which somehow seem to lies beyond price or utility and, hence, which eludes the utility function and defies neoclassical modes of representation. I think it's to be found in here and there letting the parerga get the upper hand (not something which is wholly under my control).

- and then to question the point of departure. Can a work be untitled? If I was to say by way of an *introduction* that 'economics and culture' is to be the title of the play that I am performing today, what would be happening? what kind of economics-and-culture would already be the object of my discourse? what rules and categories would already be defined? I can't make up these things as I go along, however I might try. Lyotard (1986) says that rules and categories are what the work itself is looking for, that the writer is writing without rules in order to formulate the rules of what will have been done; he sets a hard task.

———

■ *Sentence* I've been trying for years to speak of culture and economics within the same sentence and it always seems to get me into trouble. It marks me down as not-a-proper-economist, and impinges on the status of my work in game theory and industrial organization theory. So much for pluralism and inclusivity. So much for the pleasure of the text. From where I stand, culture announces a death sentence on my career as an economist. [The Concise Oxford Dictionary (COD) (1990) reminds me that a *sentence* is the decision of a lawcourt, especially the punishment allotted to a person convicted in a criminal trial.]

Let's say, however provisionally, and in keeping with the rules of the regime itself, that *the economic field* is given by the focii of the neoclassical paradigm, that is, with the

*s'y passe, de lui-*situated. It the visible edging the center, from I propose to use intransitively, as hallucinate", "I expire", "she has boat lies at *mouille*]. outside and the external and the the framer and figure and the content, signifier *so on* for any opposition. The this place where emblem for this undiscoverable; I the framing: the extent, the passe-structure with a although it lets it does not form a sense, **rather a frame.** (P.12.)

I.

heading subject or annotation; a a picture. JM] ... were to broach aesthetics by a type ["What is origin of art or of "What is the "What does art

mean?" etc.), **the form of the question would already provide an answer.** Ar**t** would be predetermined or precomprehended in it. **A conceptual opposition which has traditionally served to comprehend art would already, always, be at work there: for example the opposition between meaning, as inner content, and form.** Under the apparent diversity of the historical forms of art, the concepts of art or the words which seem to translate "art" in Greek, Latin, the Germanic languages, etc. (but the closure of this list is already problematic), **one would be seeking a one-and-naked meaning [*un sens un et nu*] which would inform from the inside, like a content, while distinguishing itself from the forms which it informs.** In order to think art in

70 *Judith Mehta*

general, one thus accredits a series of oppositions (meaning/form, inside/outside, content/container, signified/signifier, represented/representer, etc.) which, precisely, structure the traditional interpretation of works of art. One makes of art in general an object in which one claims to distinguish an inner meaning, the invariant, and a multiplicity of external variations *through* which, as through so many veils, one would try to see or restore the true, full, originary meaning: one, naked. Or again, in an analogous gesture, by asking what art *means* [to say], one submits the mark "art" to a very determined regime of interpretation which has

supervened in history: it *tautology* without reserve, *vouloir-dire* of every work if its form is not that of one wonders what a plastic means (to say), submitting the aut hority of speech and the (Pp21-2.)

...

Like the figure of figure of the circle asserts beginning of the *Lectures* the *Origin of the Work of* and Heidegger, very different in their aim, their style, these two common, as a common exclude - (that) which then and bound them from alike.

And if it were a

objects and arrangements of production, exchange and consumption within a market society in which resources are perceived to be scarce. It's this regime which would like to dispense with culture altogether, to keep its *ergon* all to itself, intact and unified. So where does exclusion take place?

I would say, in rational choice theory, which lies at the heart of neoclassical economics. Rational choice theory is in the frame because it supplies the axiomatic account of individual decision-making behaviour which informs the edifice of micro- and macroeconomics. Experimental tests reveal that people systemmatically deviate from the theory's predictions and so the theory has its problematic moments, even from the point of view of those committed to the neoclassical agenda (see, for example, Davis & Holt, 1993). But since it has not yet been possible to develop a more powerful account of individual decision-making, rational choice theory continues to hold sway (and even to colonise the cognate disciplines). Briefly stated, the theory runs as follows.

Every individual is endowed with a set of preferences over the objects of choice (say, whether to buy a ticket to the cinema or dinner at

consists, in its in interrogating the of so-called art, even saying. In this way, or musical work all productions to

"discursive" arts.

the third term, the itself at the *on Aesthetics* and *Art*. [Texts by Hegel respectively. JM] So their procedure, discourses have in interest, that they comes to form, close inside and outside

frame. (P.23.)

■The *parergon* inscribes something which comes as an extra, *exterior* to the proper field but whose transcendental exteriority comes to play, abut onto, brush against, rub, press the limit itself and intervene in the inside only to the extent that the inside is lacking. P.56.

Frame v. concoct a false charge or evidence against, devise a plot with regard to. C.O.D., ibid.

... **What happens when one entitles** a "work of art"? What is the *topos* of the title? [*topos*: a stock theme in literature, etc. JM] Does it take place (and where?) In relation to the work? On the edge? Over the edge? On the internal border? In an overboard that is re-marked and reapplied, by invagination, within, between the presumed

center and between that that which is **Does the** that of a scroll-like imitating, or with rolled-ornamentally inscription; **command discursive of an *hors*-outside the exergue of directly statement,** definition of a does the title the "work", with its in an longer constitutes it effect? If I circle and title of the performing doing and the circle object of my by it? Or the form discourse, object, and away by the discourse on *describe* a very one describe a the very

a restaurant); this is the only aspect of subjectivity required to individuate one person from another. A 'rational' individual is one who, when choosing between feasible options, seeks to achieve the highest possible level of satisfaction - or *utility* - by drawing on their preferences in a consistent fashion. This amounts to saying that the individual is an autonomous agent; s/he's a utility maximiser for whom self-interest provides the motive force on behaviour. The theory doesn't preclude the possibility that an individual has preferences relating to the welfare of another person; but it does require that these preferences are refracted through self-interest. That is, as long as A's concern for B's welfare is constituted by a consistent set of preferences, the rational choice theorist will admit any such concerns to the objective function which A seeks to maximise.

The form and content of the discourse is exemplified in this excerpt; it's short, but will suffice to provide a sense of the protocols at work in modelling choice behaviour.

• "... When [axioms 1-3] hold, the individual has a preference ordering, and when [axioms 1-4] hold the preference ordering can be represented by a utility function which is unique up to a positive monotonic transformation. This means that if a function $U(x)$ represents this preference ordering, the function $V(x)$ will also represent the ordering when $V(x) = T(U(x))$, where T is any transformation which satisfies the condition of V increasing when U increases. Thus, an individual, when acting in accordance with this preference ordering, can be represented as maximising his or her utility." Hargreaves Heap *et al*, 1992, p.6.

Clearly, culture, however one defines the term, is not a part of the picture. It is recognized that cultural factors may influence a person's preferences; but since preferences are taken as given and stable (and so supply the raw datum), an account of where they come from, or how they might change over time, is unnecessary for a theory of decision-making. What matters in to the neoclassical tradition above

work? On the edge? Over the edge? On the internal border? In an overboard that is re-marked and reapplied, by invagination, between the presumed the circumference? Or which is framed and framing in the frame? *topos* **of the title,** like *cartouche* [*cartouche:* a ornament; a tablet a drawing of, a scroll up ends, used or bearing an an ornate frame. JM], **the "work" from the and juidical instance *d'oeuvre*, a place work, from the a more or less definitional** and even if the operates in the manner performative? Or else play *inside* the space of inscribing the legend, definitional pretension, ensemble that it no commands and which - the title - as a localized say for example that the the abyss will be the play that I am today, as an introduction, what am I what is happening? Will and the abyss be the discourse and defined else do they describe which constrains my its scene rather than its moreover a scene stolen abyss from present representation? As if a the circle also had to circle, and perhaps the that it describes, circular movement at moment that it

describes a circular movement, describe it displacing itself in its meaning [*sens*]; or else as if a discourse on the abyss had to know the abyss, in the sense that one knows something that happens to or affects one, as in "to know failure" or "to know success" rather than to know an object. ... (p.24.)

Now the problem of the introduction causes no difficulty in the case of the natural or mathematical sciences:

their object is determined in it the method that on the contrary, on the products of Aneed for an preface makes the object of such produced by the which knows, the have engaged in a the knowledge of of the product of This poses singular priority. The mind its own product, discourse on what introduce itself of This circular reduction to what Hegel names In the science of mind presupposes itself, precipitates **Everything with commences is a *work*, an projection of *resultare.* Every** justification will this is, as you mainspring of the dialectic. must proceed from demonstrated Hegel. "In nothing must be does not possess necessity, which everything in have the value of a

We are, the

all is the *outcome* of behaviour; *process* is only of interest insofar as it helps to explain or predict the end result.

Yet neoclassical economics finds itself compelled to call upon the services of culture in treating the residue of economic behaviour. A review of nine leading mainstream economics journals for the sample years 1970, 1985 and 2000 reveals that the term occurs most commonly in the literature on wage differentials and economic achievement where culture enters as an explanatory variable. Within this literature, there is little attempt to explicate culture; most economists deem it sufficient simply to refer to "cultural factors", "cultural differences", "cultural environment", or even just "culture" ,without further clarification.

The forms in which culture is admitted to the discourse are, of course, determined by economics such that its performance obeys the logic of the master discipline. For example, notions of *social* or *cultural capital* are invoked to explain the investments of economic agents in relationships which exceed the parameters of market exchange; consumption of the objects of *cultural production* (say, music or painting) is expressed according to the laws governing normal, merit or public goods; while *cultural institutions* such as the art museum are treated as: "... a large stock of capital held in the form of works of art and of buildings in which the art is either displayed or stored" requiring that we: "... compare at the margin the benefits to be obtained by investing an additional dollar in building gallery space as compared with the benefit of investing that dollar in additional works of art and then spending the money where the benefit per dollar is greatest." (Heilbrun & Gray, 1993.)

Culture can be spoken, then, if it soaks up the residue in economic behaviour, but only in ways in which the sanctity of the utility function (and, by implication, the centrality of the individual) is preserved, and only provided the rules of the *equi-marginal principle* are

given or advance, and with it requires. When, the sciences bear the mind, the introduction or itself felt≥. Since sciences is mind, by that mind will have to self-knowledge, in what it produces, its own production. autodetermination problems of must put itself into produce a it produces, itself into itself. duction, this intro- oneself calls for a "presupposition". the beautiful, the itself, anticipates itself. *Head first.* **which it already a result, effect of a the mind, a** foundation, every have been a result - know, the speculative Presuppositions a "proven and necessity", explains philosophy, accepted which the character of means that philosophy must result."

right from

introduction, encircled. (P.26.)

Meaning to say ... 73

... **The chosen point of departure**, in everyday *representation*: *there are* works of art, we have them *in front of us* in representation. But how are they to be recognized? This is not an abstract and juridical question. At each step, at each example, in the absence of enormous theoretical, juridical, political, etc. protocols, there is a trembling of the limit between the "there is" and the "there is

not" "work of art", between a "thing" and a "work", a "work" general and a "work of art". Let's leave it. What does "leave" [*laisser*] mean ((*laisser*) *voir* [allow to see (or be seen)], (*laisser*) *faire* [allow to (or be done)], *voir faire, faire voir, faire faire* [cause (something) to done], leave as a remainder, leave in one's will), what does "leave" do? etc. (Pp.28-9.)

Why a circle? Here is the schema of the argument: to look for the origin of the thing is to look that from which starts out and whereby it is what it is, it is to look for its essential provenance, which is not its empirical origin. The work art stems from the artist, so

upheld. For example, one consumes or produces a cultural artifact like a painting until the marginal benefit derived from the activity exactly equals the marginal cost of so doing. In this way, culture is restricted to a relationship of subservience to the neoclassical economic regime. The cultural domain, whatever that might be, can only have presence in the interior of the body of economics in the form of commodity, capital or investment. Thus, it can be accessory to the fact of economic behaviour when it cooperates in the mobilization of economic ideas, but it cannot be constitutive of that fact; it is, as Derrida would say: *"neither simply outside nor simply inside. Like an accessory that one is obliged to welcome on the border."*

■ *Culture* ...

This mischievous term. *Culture*. I don't claim to understand it. Indeed, the more I think about it, the more ephemeral the meaning and effects of culture become. There is a convention – a cultural convention – in academic discourse which says that text ought to constitute a finished product, that a conclusion should be reached so that matters can be brought to a close. But some words refuse to lie low in a well-behaved text; they won't take closure. Culture is one of those words.

Culture is especially troubling to neoclassical economists. They are happy to invoke it to perform, even to pay a small fee for its services. But they refuse to be responsible for it beyond the transaction and then wonder why this loose-living concept, this street-walker, returns to haunt them.

I guess Raymond Williams (1983) was right when he said ... "Culture is one of the two or three most complicated words in the English language ... This is so partly because of its intricate historical development, in several European languages, but mainly because it has now come to be used for important concepts in several distinct intellectual disciplines and in several distinct and incompatible systems of thought."

in

do

be

for it

of

Parergon Do you, like me, sometimes write in the margins of the text? do you frame what is taking place with your own interventions? I think of this practice as *Writing back.*

they say. But what is an artist? The one who produces works of art. The origin of the artist is the work of art, the origin of the work of art is the artist, "neither is without the other". Given this, "artist and work *are* in themselves and in their reciprocity by virtue of a third term which is indeed the first, namely that from which artists and work of art also get their name, art". What is art? As long as one refuses to give an answer in advance to this question, "art" is only a word. And if one wants to interrogate art, one is indeed obliged to give oneself the guiding thread of a representation. And this thread is the work, the fact that *there are* works of art. Repetition of the Hegelian gesture in the

74   *Judith Mehta*

necessity of its lemma: there are works which common opinion [*l'opinion courante*] designates as works of art and they are what one must interrogate in order to decipher in them the essence of art. But by what does one recognize, commonly [*couramment*], that these are works of art if one does not have in advance a sort of precomprehension of the essence of art?

This hermeneutic circle has only the (logical, formal, derived) appearance of a vicious circle. It is not a question of escaping from it but on the contrary of engaging in it and going all round it: "We must therefore complete the circle. It is neither a stop-gap meaure nor a lack. To engage upon such a road is the force of thought and to remain on it is the feast of thought, it being admitted that thinking is a craft. ... Not only the chief step of the work toward art, *qua* step of the work toward art, is a circle, but each of the steps we attempt to take here circles in that circle." (Pp.32-3.)

Index of a discrepancy: in relation to all the machinery of the *pose* (position/opposition). By giving it the philosophical name of *art*, one has, it would seem, domesticated it in onto-encyclopedic economy and the history of truth (P.34.)

However many different notions of culture there are, neoclassical economists are oblivious to the complexity of the term, while theorists in the cognate disciplines are acutely aware of culture's subtleties and its excesses (see, for example, Eagleton, 2000). Stuart Hall (1997) is one of those attempting to organise the field, identifying five notions of culture which will suffice to demonstrate its tendency to replicate and mutate; these are: the traditional, the modern, the social-scientific, the sociological, and the 'cultural turn'.

In *traditional* usage, culture is a way of describing 'the best' that has been said and thought in a society. It is the sum total of 'great ideas' to be seen expressed in literature, painting, music and philosophy, which are sometimes referred to as 'the culture of the age'. This usage clearly invokes taste and judgement into culture's sphere, concepts which are themselves aporetic.

In *modern* usage, culture embraces the widely distributed forms of popular music, publishing, art, design and literature, or the activities of leisure-time and entertainment which comprise the everyday lives of so-called ordinary people. Some cultural theorists assemble these forms under the heading of 'mass culture' or 'the popular culture of the age'; others distinguish between 'popular culture' as all cultural forms not valorized as High Culture, and 'mass culture' as the products of large-scale cultural industries (Driscoll, 2001). Note that in making this distinction, cultural studies effectively legitimates colonisation of their domain by neoclassical economists; the so-called 'cultural economists' now regard the activities of the popular music, heritage and leisure industries, etc., as justifiably part of their domain.

The *social-scientific* use of the term is nuanced by nineteenth century anthropological interests in that culture emerges as whatever is perceived to be distinct about the way of life of a people, community, nation, or other identifiable social group. Culture thereby invokes a position of Otherness, of the theorist as Transcendental Observer. Only someone well-versed in the Western traditions of modern social theory can identify and distinguish between one culture and its Others.

II. The Parergon   economize on the abyss: not only save oneself from falling into the bottomless depths by weaving and folding tback the cloth to infinity, textual art of the reprise, multiplication of patches within patches, but also establish the laws of reappropriation, formalize the rules which constrain the logic of the abyss and which shuttle between the economic *and* the aneconomic, the raising [*la relève*] and the fall, the abyssmal operation which can only work toward the *relève and* that in it which regularly reproduces collapse. (P.37.)

what then is the object of the third *Critique*? [Kant's text. JM] The critique of pure theoretical reason assumes the exclusion of all that is not theoretical knowledge: the effect in its two principal values (pleasure/unpleasure) and the power to desire. It cuts out its field only by cutting itself off from the interests of desire, by losing interest in desire. (P.37.)

In *sociological* discourse, culture has traditionally been treated as synonymous with the shared values of a group or society; this is the kind of 'culture' which economists have imported into the literature on wage differentials and economic achievement. The term *sub-culture* is invoked to describe some smaller group subscribing to a set of values which are distinguishable from, but in oppositional relation to (and usually parasitic upon), those of the larger group within which the smaller group is located.

The kind of culture which features in the so-called *cultural turn* in a variety of late twentieth century academic endeavours (particularly, cultural studies) emphasizes shared meaning. Here, culture is not so much a set of objects (books, paintings, television programmes, etc) as a process, or a set of practices. Culture then becomes concerned with the production and exchange of meaning between members of a society or group. So to say that two people belong to the same culture is to say that they interpret the world in broadly similar ways, and that they can express themselves and their ideas in ways which will be mutually understood. Language is necessarily heavily implicated. But language is taken to refer to a multitude of discursive forms – text, pictures, photographs. On this reading, culture is:

"involved in all those practices which are not simply genetically programmed into us - like the jerk of a knee when tapped - but which carry meaning and value for us, which need to be meaningfully interpreted by others and which depend on meaning for their effective operation." Hall. 1997.

... Since the *Mittelglied* [an intermediary member, a third faculty between understanding and reason: judgement. JM] also forms the articulation of the theoretical and the practical (in the Kantian sense), we are plunging into a place that is *neither* theoretical *nor* practical or else *both* theoretical *and* practical. Art (in general), or rather the beautiful, if it takes place, is inscribed here. But this *here*, this place is announced as a place deprived of

place. It taking place, proper	runs the risk, in of not having its own domain. (P.38.)

Lemmata

"... pictures to be sure, are more imperative than writing, they impose meaning at one stroke, without analysing or diluting it. But this is no longer a constitutive difference. Pictures become a kind of writing as soon as they are meaningful: like writing, they call for a lexis. ... We shall therefore take language, discourse, speech, etc., to mean any significant unit or synthesis, whether verbal or visual: a photograph will be a kind of speech for us in the same way as a newspaper article; even objects will become speech, if they mean something."
Barthes, 1993.

Philosophy, Kant's third think art general and its field or of	which in this book [ie *Critique*. JM] has to through - art in fine art - as a part of its edifice, is here *representing itself* as
a part of its an art of represents *itself*, proxy, a part in order to philosophy	part: philosophy as architecture. It itself, it *detaches* detaches from itself a of itself beside itself
fundamental unpleasure, be a	

think the whole, to saturate or heal over the whole that suffers from detachment. The of art presupposes an art of philosophizing, a major art, but also a miner's art in its critical preliminaries, an architect's art in its edifying erection. ... Finally, if this pure philosophy or metaphysics here proposes to account for, among other things, desire, pleasure and it exposes itself and represents itself first of all in its own desire. The desire of reason would fundamental desire, a desire for the fundamental, a desire to go to the *bythos*.

76   *Judith Mehta*

"Great difficulties" arise. ... The only concept which it [judgement] can produce is an empty concept, in a sense, and one which does not give anything to be known. By it, 'nothing is properly known'. It supplies a rule of usage which comprises no objectivity, no relation to the object, no knowledge. The rule is subjective, the faculty of judgement gives itself its norms, and it must do so, failing which it would be necessary to upon another faculty **or** arbitration, *ad infinitum*. And this *subjective* is applied to judgements, to statements which by their structure lay claim to universal objectivity. (P.41.)

own

■ *Il n'y a pas de hors-culture*

call

yet
rule

Even with just five notions of culture, it would seem that culture is here, there and everywhere. But in virtue of its excesses, culture may be playing out its own disappearance. If everything can be understood as a cultural construct, then there is nothing outside of the cultural domain and the idea of culture is vacant. Consider the objects of economic discourse: every industry can be understood as a cultural industry, every action or event as a cultural practice, and every object as a cultural artifact; every mode of thinking – including methodological individualism and its inheritance in rational choice theory – becomes culturally determined. At the limit of these hyperinflationary forces, even 'the jerk of a knee when tapped' must be understood as cultural phenomenon since our concept of the body is inevitably a cultural construction. On these grounds it can be argued that the 'cultural turn' announces the demise of the idea of culture, that the term no longer has currency, or value. Where then is the subversive edge, the cut, the critique of everyday material existence, once the seam between culture and its Other-in-Economics has been lost?

... this discourse on the beautiful and on art, judgement, gets tangled up in the - derived - opposition ... This critique of taste does not concern production; it which can very well do without it. And as the *Critique* rules to the beautiful, it will not be a question of

Lemmata

"As Andrew Milner points out, *'it is only in modern industrial democracies that 'culture' and 'society' become excluded from both politics and economics ... modern society is understood as distinctively and unusually asocial, its economic and political life characteristically 'normless' and 'value-free', in short, uncultured.'* Our very notion of culture thus rests on a peculiarly modern alienation of the social from the economic, meaning from material life. Only in a society whose everyday existence seems drained of value could 'culture' come to exclude material production; yet only in this way could the concept become a critique of that life." Eagleton, 2000.

depend on? What lack is it?

because it remains at the stage of a theory of of subject and object**.**
has in view neither 'education' nor 'culture', **will show that** one cannot assign conceptual constituting an *aesthetic*, even a general one, but of analyzing the formal conditions of possibility of an aesthetic judgement in general, hence of an aesthetic objectivity in general. With this transcendental aim, Kant demands to be read without indulgence. But for the rest, he admits the lack, the lacunary character of his work. This is the word Hegel uses too.

What does this lack

Meaning to say …   77

And what if were the frame. What if the lack formed the frame of the theory. Not its accident but its frame. More or less still: what if the lack were not only the lack of a theory of the frame but the place of the lack in a theory of the frame. (Pp.42-3.)

… Now you know what talking about, *intrinsically* the value and what external to your sense of beauty. permanent requirement - distinguish the internal or sense and the circumstance of being talked organizes all philosophical on art, the art and such, from Hegel, Husserl Heidegger. This requirement presupposes a on the limit the inside and the art object, *discourse on the frame.* Where is it

Even what is called intrinsic constituent in the delight of taste does so only drapery on statues, or the into the composition of the approval for the picture my means beauty (Meredith, 65, 67-68).

■ *Il n'y a pas de hors-économie.*

In parallel, it can be argued that economics has been seduced by its own desire for excess – which is ironic for a discipline grounded in scarcity and preaching the virtues of parsimony. The discourse can be observed replicating itself – and, necessarily, its inadequacies – both as neoclassical analyses colonise areas hitherto regarded as the province of the cognate disciplines (art-worlds, familial relations, popular culture, etc.) and, in a reciprocal arrangement, as economic concepts and ideas are appropriated into cultural theory, literary theory, semiotics and aesthetics as value-adding adjuncts (now it is said that meaning is something which is produced, exchanged and consumed, invoking analogies with the circular flow of income or the income-expenditure model). This inflation of hitherto separable fields of operation suggests there are no margins, that economics and culture are each losing their Other. Both terms exist solely in our nostalgia for them.

All this replication, all these supplements; what does it mean for *writing*? what kind of ~~economics~~ and what kind of ~~culture~~ is produced by the necessity to strike out terms? I think what we need is a theory of the frame, of the supplement.

have to you're what concerns "beauty" remains immanent This

to between proper

the object about -

discourses meaning of meaning as Plato to and

discourse between outside of here a

to be found? (P.45.)
ornamentation i.e., what is only an adjunct, and not an complete representation of the object, in augmenting the by means of its form. Thus it is with the frames of pictures or the colonnades of palaces. But if the ornamentation does not itself enter beautiful form - if it is introduced like a gold frame merely to win of its charm - it is then called *finery* and takes away from the genuine

What does the lack were the frame. theory. Not its what if the lack were but the place of the   depend on? What lack is it? And what if it What if the lack formed the frame of the accident but its frame. More or less still: not only the lack of a theory of the frame lack in a theory of the frame?

clothes on statues - for example -   would thus be ornaments: *parerga.*

… In the search for the *parerga* get the upper hand over the *parergon.* But what about this   cause or the knowledge of principles, *one must avoid* letting the the essentials. Philosophical discourse will always have been *against against.* (P.54.)

78   *Judith Mehta*

A parergon comes against, beside, and in addition to the *ergon*, the work done [*fait*], the fact [*le fait*], the work, but it does not fall to one side, it touches and cooperates within the operation, from a certain outside. Neither simply outside nor simply inside. Like an accessory that one is obliged to welcome on the border, on board [*au bord, à bord*]. It is first of all the on (the) bo(a)rd(er) [*Il est d'abord l'à-bord*].

... These questions of wood, of matter, of the frame, of the limit between inside and outside, must, somewhere in the margins, be constituted together.

The *parergon*, this supplement outside the work, must, if it is to have the status of a philosophical quasi-concept, designate a formal and general predicative structure, which one can transport *intact* or deformed and reformed *according to certain rules*, into other fields, to submit new contents to it.

... The *parergon* inscribes something which comes as an extra, *exterior* to the proper field but whose transcendental exteriority comes to play, abut onto, brush against, rub, press against the limit itself and intervene in the inside only to the extent that the inside is lacking. It is lacking *in* something

In Derrida's (1993) treatment of the term, the *supplement* is a thing that must be added to the work in order to treat its lacunary character. The supplement appears to stand outside the work as something other than the work itself and independent of it; hence, it would seem that the supplement is unable to intervene in the work in any way, other than to bring about the closure and completeness which is intended by its introduction.

But the supplement only draws attention to the lack or inadequacy in the work since, if it were not for that lack, there would be no need for the supplement. In this sense, the supplement endlessly reinforces, replicates and extends the work's lacunary character. This *economy of supplementarity* makes it apparent that the work never existed other than in its encounter with the supplement and, moreover, that supplementarity is endless; that is, the encounter of the work with the supplement is always immanent. Thus, work and supplement exist in each other, each being co-produced, or a party to, the other.

and it is lacking *from itself*. Because reason is Aconscious of its impotence to satisfy its moral need≅, it has recourse to the *parergon* ... It needs the supplementary work. This additive, to be sure, is threatening. Its use is critical. It involves a risk and exacts a price ... (P.56.)

So, as an example among examples, the clothing on statues would have the function of *parergon* and an ornament. This means, as Kant makes clear, that which is not internal or intrinsic, as an integral part, to the total representation of the object but which belongs to it only in an extrinsic way as a surplus, an addition, an adjunct, a supplement. ... Hors-d'oeuvres

This collapse into one another of the interior of the work and its exterior, of form into content, transforms the field of ~~economics~~; it exposes a kind of post-cultural post-economic *writing* in which new conversations can take place, conversations which decentre neoclassical authorities and reconfigure the objects of disciplinary practice. These conversations appear under the auspices of the heterodox and post-autistic movements, and in the ~~economic~~ theorizing conducted outside of the official discipline of neoclassical economics (see, for example,

stuck onto the edging of the work nonetheless, and to the edging of the represented body to the extent that - such is the argument - they supposedly do not belong to the whole of the representation. What is represented in the representation would be the naked and natural body; the representative essence of the statue would be related to this, and the only beautiful thing in the statue would be that representation; it alone would be essentially, purely, and intrinsically beautiful, "the proper object of a pure judgement of taste".

This delimitation of the center and the integrity of the representation, of its inside and its

Community Economies Collective, 2001; Ruccio & Amariglio, 2003; Mehta, 1999; and Mehta, 2001). But remember the parergon: the surplus, addition, adjunct, supplement, never leaves the text except under the illusion that it has done so.

Par/ergon

Meaning to say …   79

outside, might already seem strange. One wonders, too, where to have clothing commence. **Where does a *parergon* begin and end**. Would any garment be a *parergon*. G-strings and the like. What to do with absolutely transparent veils. And how to transpose the statement to painting. For example, Cranach's Lucretia holds only a light band of transparent veil in front of her sex: where is the *parergon*? Should one regard as a *parergon* the dagger which is not part of her naked and natural body and whose point she holds turned toward herself, touching her skin (in that case only the point of the *parergon* would touch her body, in the middle of a triangle formed by her two breasts and her navel)? A *parergon*, the necklace that she wears around her neck? The question of the representative and objectivizing essence, of its outside and its inside, of the criteria engaged in this delimitation, of the value of naturalness which is presupposed in it, and, secondarily or primarily, of the place of the human body or of its privilege in this whole problematic. If any *parergon* is only added on by virtue of an internal lack in the system to which it is added, what is it that is lacking in the representation of the body so that the garment should come and supplement it? And what would art have to do with this? What would it give to be seen? Cause to be seen? Let us see? Let us cause to

be seen Or let itself be shown?

Par/ergon

… The example immediately following is that of the columns around sumptuous buildings. These columns are also, then, supplementary *parerga*. And the garment, the column? Why would the column be external to the building? Where does the criterion, the critical organ, the organum of discernment come from here? It is no less obscure than in the previous case. It even presents an extra difficulty: the *parergon* is added this time to a work which *does not represent anything* and which is itself already *added* to nature. We think we know what properly belongs or does not belong to the human body, what is detached or not detached from it – even though the parergon is precisely an ill-detachable detachment. …

■ These texts are amongst those in circulation here:

Barthes R, 1993, Mythologies, London: Vintage.

Baudrillard J, 1995, The Gulf War did not take place, trans. by Patton P), Sydney: Power Publications.

Community Economies Collective, 2001, 'Imagining and Enacting Noncapitalist Futures', Socialist Review, vol.28.

With this example of the columns is announced the whole problematic of inscription in a milieu, of the marking out of the work of the field of which it is always difficult to decide if

it is natural or artificial and, in this latter case, if it is *parergon* or *ergon*.For not every milieu, even if it is contiguous with the work, constitutes a *parergon* in the Kantian sense. The natural site chosen for the erection of a temple is obviously not a *parergon*. Nor is an artificial site: neither the crossroads, nor the church, nor the museum, nor the other works around one or other. But the garment or the column is. Why? It is not

Concise Oxford Dictionary, 1990, Eighth Edition, Oxford: Oxford University Press.

Davis D & Holt C, 1993, Experimental Economics, Princeton NJ: Princeton University Press.

Derrida J, 1976, Of Grammatology, Baltimore, Maryland & London: John Hopkins University Press.

Derrida J, 1987, The Truth in Painting', Chicago & London: University of Chicago Press.

Derrida J, 1993, Memoirs of the Blind, Chicago & London: University of Chicago Press.

Driscoll C, 2001, 'Cultural Studies', in Taylor VE

80   *Judith Mehta*

because they are detached but on the contrary because they are more difficult to detach and above all because without them, without their quasi-detachment, the lack on the inside of the work would appear; or (what amounts to the same thing for a lack) would not appear. What constitutes them as *parerga* is not simply their exteriority as a surplus, **it is the internal structural link which rivets them to the lack in the interior of the *ergon*. And this lack would be constitutive of the very unity of the *ergon*.** Without this lack, the *ergon* would have no need of a *parergon*. The *ergon*'s lack is the lack of a *parergon*, of the garment or the column which nevertheless remains exterior to it. ...

& Winquist CE, (eds.), Encyclopedia of Postmodernism, London & New York: Routledge.

Eagleton T, 2000, The Idea of Culture, Oxford: Blackwell.

Hall S, 1997, Representation: Cultural Representations and Signifying Practices, London: Sage/Open University.

Hargreaves Heap S, Hollis M, Lyons B, Sugden R, & Weale A, 1992, The Theory of Choice, Oxford: Blackwell.

... *Parerga* have a thickness, a surface which separates them not only (as Kant would have it) from the integral inside, from the body proper of the *ergon*, but also from the outside, from the wall on which the painting is hung, from the space in which statue or column is erected, then, step by step, from the whole field of historical, economic, political inscription in which the drive to signature is produced. **No "theory", no "practice", no "theoretical practice" can intervene effectively in this field if it does not weigh up and bear on the frame, which is the decisive structure of what is at stake, at the invisible limit to (between) the interiority of meaning (put under shelter by the whole hermeneuticist, semioticist, phenomeno -logicalist, and formalist tradition) *and* (to) all the empiricisms of the extrinsic which, incapable of either seeing or reading, miss the question completely...**

Heilbrun J & Gray CM, 1993, The Economics of Art and Culture, Cambridge UK: Cambridge University Press.

Lyotard J-F, 1986, The Postmodern Condition: A Report on Knowledge, Manchester: Manchester University Press.

McCloskey D, 1986, The Rhetoric of Economics, Brighton, Sussex: Harvester Press.

... The *Critique* presents itself as a work (*ergon*) with several sides, and as such it ought to allow itself to be centred and framed, to have its ground delimited by being marked out, with a frame, against a general background. But this frame is problematical. I do not know what is essential and what is accessory in a work.

And above all I do not know what this thing is, that is neither essential nor accessory, neither proper nor improper, and that Kant calls *parergon*, for example the frame. Where does the frame take place. Does it take place. Where does it begin. Where does it end. What is its internal limit. Its external limit. And its surface between the two limits. .. (P.63.)

Meaning to say ... 81

McCloskey D, 1994, Knowledge and Persuasion in Economics, Cambridge UK: Cambridge University Press.

Mehta J, 1999, 'Look at me look at you', in Garnett RF, (ed.), What Do Economists Know? New Economics of Knowledge, London: Routledge.

Mehta J, 2001, 'A Disorderly House – Voicing the Noise', in Amariglio J, Cullenberg S, & Ruccio D, (eds.), Postmodernism, Economics and Knowledge, London: Routledge.

Ruccio D & Amariglio J, forthcoming 2003, Postmodern Moments in Modern Economics, Princeton: Princeton University Press.

Taylor C, 2001, 'Parergon', in Taylor VE & Winquist CE, (eds.), Encyclopedia of Postmodernism, London & New York: Routledge.

"... the economy of a written text, circulating through other texts, leading back to it constantly ...". Derrida, 1976, p.149.

■ Thanks are due to Jon Cook and Peter Womack for conversations contributing to the development of ideas, and to Jon and Peter, and Jack Amariglio for assistance with a performative version of this essay at the University of California Riverside.

3 Use, value, aesthetics
Gambling with difference/speculating with value

Joseph W. Childers and Stephen E. Cullenberg

This essay begins by addressing the value side of the rubric of value/aesthetics, to the extent that such a rubric exists, as an ongoing conversation between mutually informing discourses. Our intent on focusing in this way is not to marginalize a discussion of the aesthetic; neither is it a gesture toward privileging value. Rather, we view it as the theoretical starting point for our project, since the concept of value is tied so firmly, especially by Marxist and many post-Marxian theorists, to particular understandings of labor and exchange. A good deal of what we want to accomplish involves rethinking, though by no means entirely abandoning, the connection between value and labor. We want to attempt a beginning of new ways to think through value and labor, and thus also consider the political and aesthetic implications of a more flexible realignment of these two fundamental concepts.

We frame the problem we are approaching with two brief quotations. The first, from Gayatri Spivak, serves as an epigram: "Marx left the slippery concept of use value untheorized" (Spivak, 1993a: 97). The second is from a more accessible, and for some perhaps more compelling, source—talk radio. A famous athlete's voice comes over the airwaves in an advertisement for tires. He assures us that by purchasing these tires we also receive value, which, of course, is "quality plus price." While it is certainly not uncommon to get economics lessons, of a sort, on the radio or television or even to have those lessons come from a celebrity, it is unusual to have an equation offered to us so directly and unequivocally. Would that value, which seems such an easy concept to grasp, were so easily defined, so readily fixed, so effortlessly applied.

But of course it is not. Once we begin to push upon the concept of value we find in *Capital* and elsewhere in Marx, and once we begin to use some of the tools bequeathed us by post-structuralist incursions into Marxist theory, we discover that not only is the concept—indeed one might say *concepts*—of value vexed, but sometimes mulishly so. Linked as it is to understandings of commodity fetishism and labor that are often too quickly essentialized by those unwilling to challenge the boundaries of traditional Marxist inquiry, value becomes the marker, the sign, that which is to be seen in the speculations on Marxism that arise from within the academy.

Use, value, aesthetics 83

Gayatri Spivak has been one of those who has taken up the concept of value in its function of difference, as a means of signifying yet also of always falling short of representing. Unwilling to sever completely value's connection to labor, Spivak instead asks us to think value as both more inclusive and as limited in its representational abilities. In its textual function, then, "value" is as catachresis— a rather grand "failure" to fully represent labor. From the Greek $\kappa\alpha\tau\acute{\alpha}\chi\rho\eta\sigma\iota\varsigma$, "catachresis" literally refers to the improper or incorrect use of a term; it can also mean the use of a term for something it does not properly denote, but without which there would be no name, such as the "foot" of a bed. Rhetorically, catachresis is typically used intentionally, for effect. The consequence of such usage is to draw attention to the approximation of language, to its inability to convey meaning unambiguously or completely. Indeed, catachresis underscores rather vigorously the *difference* between a thing, concept, activity, *et cetera* and the language used to attempt to convey its meaning.

With the term "value," the difference between its naming and its meaning is further complicated. Because "value" is usually seen as the expression of social abstract labor, it consistently occupies an essentialized position, for abstract labor is itself an essence, never extant in the particular, only in the virtual. In this respect, "value" is representationally yet another step removed from concrete, individuated labor, since it is equated with labor in both its abstraction and its social or exchange function. At the realization of this dual signification of value and its nearly simulacrum-like distance from labor, where value becomes simultaneously its own spectacle and delimiter, Spivak asks us to examine that which is not articulated and cannot be contained in conventional Marxist constructions of value. As first Saussure and later Derrida have taught us, to stand for something, to represent, especially in language but in other kinds of signification as well, is based upon difference. That which signifies something else can only represent the other because of difference, because it is NOT the other. Indeed our entire rhetoric of representation from mimesis to identification depends upon that difference, remarking not so much on what something is but what it is not and how closely its substitute—its signifier—approximates it. And there is much that the term value excludes, that it cannot stand for. First, it does not consider the use value function of items, except as a prerequisite to exchange value, and thus commodification, or as part of the value form in which the value of one commodity is expressed as the use value of another commodity. Yet even in the value form, emphasis is on exchange, equivalency based upon difference. The similarities to language's strategies of representation are palpable. "Value" in its representational capacity once more falls far short of inclusiveness, and relies upon approximation and catachresis to express meaning. Thus, despite an admitted reliance on its connection to labor, the concept of value cannot stand for the labor that goes into the production of items for use value. Labor that does not immediately enter into exchange, or does not produce exchange value, is outside the conventional representational purview of value. Yet, as we know, a considerable amount of labor—what we might call "unremarked labor"—goes into the production of items. Women's labor, much

84 *Joseph W. Childers and Stephen E. Cullenberg*

"third world labor," children's domestic labor, are supplements to value as we usually conceive it.

But what can this portend for Marxist analysis? If value is a site of excess beyond its representational capabilities, where can we go in our own thinking about it? Here it is salutary to turn to Spivak's own suggestions, such as they are, and consider whether she is really calling for a rethinking of the value–labor connection in a way that can have positive effect. In her essay, "Scattered Speculations on the Question of Value," she foregrounds the "textual chain" of value as construct, noting that, in her "reading, it is use-value that puts the entire textual chain of value into question" (Spivak, 1988b: 162). Rather than consider Marx's theory of value in the "continuist" tradition, which has come to describe it in terms of the transformation from labor to value to money to capital, she suggests that we should read Marx's account of value as an "analysis of the ability of capital to consume the use value of labor power" (McCabe, 1988: xv). In so doing, use value becomes the indeterminate moment in the formation of value determinations, the moment in the movement from labor to capital that the representational connection between the two becomes murky, even untenable. As Colin McCabe tells us, such a move breaks open that "continuist," signifying chain so vital to most labor theories of value (McCabe, 1988: xv), allowing us a glimpse of the possibility that even textualization, "which is already an advance upon the control implicit in linguistic or semiotic reductionism, may be," as Spivak puts it, "no more than a way of holding randomness at bay" (Spivak, 1988b: 162).

Spivak's statement offers up a number of interesting possible readings. First, the recognition of a randomness (of value) that is always seeking to break the bounds of textualization and representation speaks to issues of control, even discipline, that continue to bedevil discussions of the aesthetic as well as of value. As Jack Amariglio asks in his essay in this volume when discussing certain forms of "modern" art: "What, after all, is the value of something that, purportedly, doesn't 'mean'?". Or, which can "mean" excessively, that is whose meanings are not moored inextricably to the demands of representation? Indeed, we should go farther. What *is* value if it is always haunted by the undecidability that is imbued in value as a sign? Further, despite Spivak's self-identification with strategies of resistance and opposition, her characterization of textualization's role as mediator (and therefore regulator) of value in all its vagaries hardly seems to open the door to ways in which that randomness can be explored. In some instances, the *jouissance* of the text may be the very goal of reading—or more problematically, the *value* of reading. In the matrix of economic and cultural forces that combine to create the exigencies with which she is concerned, however, Spivak hints at the need and even the desire—though never the promise—of a teleology that is not the product of randomness. At the same time, she implies that the control that abides in textualization, though not as draconian as the reductionism she dismisses, is nonetheless an impediment to our understanding of the full complexities of the connections of labor to value.

It is the point where "randomness is held at bay," where textuality appears simultaneously to challenge the boundaries of the semiotic and linguistic reductionism

Use, value, aesthetics   85

of value and to provide a moment of rest from continual deferral, to offer, however fleetingly, a trace of meaning, that we can most clearly see the links between value and the aesthetic. As Terry Eagleton has pointed out, for Kant, the aesthetic experience functions as a bridge between the mechanical, causal processes of the world revealed to us by "pure" reason on the one hand and the knowledge of ourselves as free, purposive agents provided us by "practical" reason on the other. Eagleton goes on to say, it is "in the act of aesthetic judgment" that "a piece of the external world momentarily appears to have some kind of purposive point to it, thus assuaging our rate for meaning" (Eagleton, 1991: 162).

Although Spivak would likely refuse the essentialist aspects of Kant's conception of the aesthetic, the residue of its function as a moment of "meaning" or rest from the never-ending dance of differentiation is notable. In a nearly Foucauldian move reminiscent of his later pronouncements on the "aesthetic of existence," Spivak records her personal difficulties with the contingencies of existence that make it both necessary and impossible to claim a momentary place of universality. In her own struggles with political—and to this end aesthetic— self-fashioning, textuality itself becomes a catachresis in Spivak's positioning. It suggests new understanding, yet also functions as a delimiter to the free play of randomness. In its double-edged role it engenders aporetic moments of its own, as she points out:

> This expansion of the textuality of value has often gone unrecognized by feminists as well as mainstream Marxists, when they are caught within hegemonic positivism or orthodox dialectics. They have sometimes tried to close off the expansion, by considering it as an opposition (between Marxism and feminism) or by way of inscribing, in a continuist spirit, the socializing or ideology forming function of the family as direct means of producing the worker and thus involved in the circuit of the production of surplus value for the capitalist. They have attempted to legitimize domestic labor within capital logic. Most of these positions arise from situational exigencies. ... That these closing off gestures are situationally admirable is evident from the practical difficulty of offering alternatives to them.
>
> (Spivak, 1988b: 163)

This "expansion of the textuality of value" that Spivak recognizes does not offer readily apparent solutions to the problems that arise in everyday life and seemingly mundane personal political decisions. Citing her own inability to attain "a critical distance" because of her involvement with those positions arising from situational moments that she points to, Spivak leaves textuality more as a problematic than as an opening to innovative solutions. Indeed, in as much as textuality expands not to articulate difference, but "to hold randomness at bay," it functions in very nearly the same way as the relationship of value to labor always has—as a virtual, homogenizing, totalizing condition that points to difference even as it writes in similitude.

86   *Joseph W. Childers and Stephen E. Cullenberg*

Thus Spivak is able to assess the "closing off" gestures of various feminist and post-structuralist informed Marxists with a certain amount of admiration. Yet her assertion that such gestures apparently arise less the inability or refusal to recognize the chain of textuality of value seems to us much less persuasive than recognizing them as resistance to textualization's homogenizing and limiting force. Within the "Scattered Speculations on Value" essay, and in others in which she discusses value, such as "Marginality in the Teaching Machine" and "Can the Subaltern Speak?," Spivak's own interventions resemble a Foucauldian strategy of local situations, local solutions, and do not offer either a dramatic, all-encompassing theory of value as text or deconstructive readings which emphasize the ambivalence of the subject, placing her/him in the *mise en abyme* of play without the possibility of action or—conversely and perhaps more paralyzingly— with the possibility of all actions. Despite her protestations to the contrary, Spivak does indeed retain some aspect of the metaphysical notion of value that echoes back to that athlete's pitch about "quality." And for her, this quality resides in certain ethical and moral imperatives to act. This is not to say that Spivak condones or ascribes to some universal ethos; yet neither does she present herself as a radical relativist or a pragmatist in the Rortian sense of the term. For Spivak, there is a political agenda that is clear and defined, one that demands action AND theorizing and that informs her choices in these arenas.

This agenda becomes particularly interesting when she takes up the issue of identity politics in her "Marginality" essay collected in *Outside in the Teaching Machine*. Beginning with the notion of cultural value coding she writes:

> "Marginality," as it is becoming part of the disciplinary-cultural parlance, is in fact the name of a certain constantly changing set of representations that is the condition and effect of it. It is coded in the currency of the equivalencies of knowledge. That currency measures the magnitude of value in the sphere of knowledge.
>
> (Spivak, 1993b: 62)

She acknowledges that in many ways this is unavoidable. The practicalities of the academy transform questions such as "what is worth studying teaching and talking about" into "what can best be parceled out into a fourteen-or-ten week format"; or "How best can it be proved that this can be integrated into the English curriculum without disturbing the distribution requirements?" (Spivak, 1993b: 62). She goes on to say that we cannot grasp value as "that currency of the equivalencies of knowledge," that is, in its form alone, without content. Rather we tend to position ourselves "as *identities* in terms of links in the chain of value-coding as if they [the links] were persons and things, and [we] go on to ground our practice on that positioning" (Spivak, 1993b: 63). The result, she claims, is that "we become a part of the problem" in those practical ways she describes (Spivak, 1993b: 63). Just as with value, whose randomness is "kept at bay" by the strictures of textualization, and just as the aesthetic is also looking for that moment—however fleeting—of

Use, value, aesthetics 87

universalism, so too is identity, for Spivak, grounded—if only for a moment—by our practice of textualizing, of linking it to representation.

From this observation, Spivak moves back to her own now famous, often-confusing, stance on "strategic essentialism," once again taking up the demands of the contingencies of being in the world. Insisting on the arbitrary and unfixed relation between value and labor, it is a predictable move to loosen the claims that the value form itself has on our agency. In a nearly nominalist moment she asserts that "the operation of the value-form makes every commitment negotiable, however urgent it might seem or be" (Spivak, 1993b: 62). For Spivak, if indeed we have understood her argument, the very functioning of the value form as a means of expressing equivalencies in terms first of social relations and second of commodities in exchange (a definitional redundancy of which we are aware) is precisely the site where the cultural and the economic are ineluctably imbricated and must be seen through a lens that focuses on capitalist abilities to consume the use value of the cultural capital it has also helped to produce. Her own example, identity, then is rewritten and rethought in a sphere outside the usual *liberal* notions of tolerance or redress as such. As she points out, "For the long haul, emancipatory social intervention is not primarily a question of redressing victimage by the assertion of (class- or gender- or ethnocultural) identity. It is a question of developing a vigilance for systemic appropriations of the unacknowledged social production of a differential that is one base of exchange into networks of the cultural politics of class- or gender *identification*" (Spivak, 1993b: 63). In an apt description of her own position within the academy, she explains how such a strategy might work by arguing that "the postcolonial teacher can help to develop this vigilance rather than continue pathetically to dramatize victimage or assert a spurious identity. She says 'no' to the 'moral luck' of the culture of imperialism while recognizing that she must inhabit it, indeed invest it, to criticize it" (Spivak, 1993b: 62).

Spivak calls this the deconstructive dilemma of the postcolonial, but it might well serve, if taken as a general strategy, as the dilemma for any political activity. Her double move of rejecting the commodification of identity, especially in terms of victimage, while working to enable a new kind of sight, what she refers to as "vigilance," from within the culture of imperialism, redirects the vectors of agency within discourses of power, allowing them to produce activity that is disruptive, reformulative, and potentially, she tacitly claims, "liberating." The invocation here is less the ghost of Marx than the spectre of Foucault, especially when she claims that such a strategy allows us to understand that "no historically (or philosophically) adequate claims can be produced in any space for the guiding words of political, military, economic, ideological emancipation and oppression" (Spivak, 1993b: 63). Her dilemma then gets written in Foucauldian as much as Derridian terms, in which the particular discourse of power, in this instance imperialism, constrains as well as produces its subjects, yet also always reabsorbs them into new configurations of power relations.

This short digression into identity-politics theories of resistance and opposition, may seem a long distance from issues of value or aesthetics, but the ways

88   *Joseph W. Childers and Stephen E. Cullenberg*

Spivak in her "Marginality" essay includes value form and its chain of coding in her discussion of postcolonial identity (and its commodification) help us to emphasize our own observation about value, its function, and its analogous status with subjectivity, an observation taken from our reading of Spivak on value, but one which we believe needs a more direct articulation than she seems willing to offer. The most provocative theoretical undertakings today begin with a set of assumptions about the subject that separate subjectivity and agency and emphasize the multiply constituted formation of the subject. Chantal Mouffe, who is by no means alone in holding these assumptions, offers a succinct expression of that position:

> Within every society, each social agent is inscribed in a multiplicity of social relations—not only social relations of production but also the social relations, among others, of sex, race, nationalism, vicinity. All these social relations determine positionalities or subject positions, and every social agent is therefore the locus of many subject positions and cannot be reduced to only one. Thus, someone inscribed in the relations of production as a worker is also a man or a woman, white or black, Catholic or Protestant, French or German, and so on ... [T]he subjectivity of a given social agent is always precariously and provisionally fixed or, to use the Lacanian term, sutured at the intersection of various discourses.
>
> (Mouffe, 1988: 90)

This is not a new formulation to anyone reading this, and many social theorists operate with a similar conception of subjectivity and agency. As we can see from even a cursory reading of this quotation, the subject is the site where a number of different ideological and material forces intersect. But because the social, economic, and cultural activities that produce these possibilities are themselves dynamic and in multilateral engagement with one another, and because the subject itself is no longer tightly bound to an essence of self, or a metaphysical totality, that intersectional space is always shifting in its shape, its place, indeed in the very possibility of combinations it can contain (or proscribe), and the social agent's subjectivity is materially, as well as ideologically, linked to any number of material and ideological conditions.

In a very real sense, then, the subject is a kind of text in which the possibilities of agency are written, and also always already being re-written. It is in this sense, too, that we can reintroduce the idea of the aesthetic, for, at any moment, there is a possibility for stopping, for reconciling our relative agency to our relative subjection. In insisting on the textual chain of value, Spivak offers us a situation for it that is analogous to that of the subject. And, if we are correct in our own reading of value as the space of intersection between culture—in all its possible manifestations—and economics (as science or discipline), then we should also consider value as an overdetermined site, not reducible only to a representation of labor. We must also consider the cultural constitutions of value—desire, perceived need, the privileging of one commodity over another, etc. Put perhaps too simply,

Use, value, aesthetics 89

if we can return to the value is price plus quality equation we whimsically began with, value partakes not only of the economic ("price"—whether in terms of labor or a universal equivalence such as money) but also of the cultural ("quality," in whatever ways that might be expressed). Conceiving of value in such terms thus marks it as a site of multiple, overdetermined, possibilities that produce and disseminate meaning as well as create both limits and openings for political intervention. Multiply determined, and understood, in this way, value retains an aesthetic aspect—the quality if you like—of the moment of negotiation between practical and pure reason—between what we desire to do and what we cannot help but do—that moment we often call the political.

This move, at the outset, may seem potentially devastating for Marxism as we have come to know it. But before that judgment is pronounced, let us consider some of the implications that obtain from this argument. First, let us point out that Spivak needs to retain a connection between value and labor, yet is unwilling to preserve a labor essentialism as the basis of value. The result is the problematization of abstract labor as the "essence" of value—an argument we have already briefly rehearsed. In order to retain the connection to labor, however, she privileges the use-value moment of value. Consequently, as McCabe has pointed out, labor becomes "endlessly variable." Further, by continuing the refusal of abstract labor as originary to value, surplus value also becomes variable, indeterminate, loosed from its chain of signifiers—as does value form. The consequences of this way of thinking are twofold, at the very least. On the one hand it allows a consideration of certain kinds of labor that have conventionally been ignored, since they operate outside the sphere of circulation, and thus are not incorporated into the totality of "abstract labor," do not contribute to the constitution of exchange value, and cannot be represented in value. This, the catachrestic moment, is the opening Spivak is looking for in examining, especially, "the normative accounts of modes of production" that "have impeded third world struggles" (McCabe, 1988: xv). But because surplus value is no longer tied to the totalizing conception of abstract labor—a totality that loses its force within this schema—the fundamental Marxist ethico-political critique of exploitation—tied as it is to surplus value—is undermined. The question that remains at such a juncture is whether a critique of exploitation can still edure. We believe it can.

In order to make our point, we rely on G.A. Cohen's discussion of exploitation in his 1988 *History, Labour and Freedom*. With similar reservations about the connections of labor to value, Cohen begins his series of observations with a significant difference. For him, the laborer is the person who creates the product, that which *has* value. It is important to note that Cohen's formulation implies the accretion of value in the product, and does not rely on value as intrinsic to the product because of the labor invested in the commodity. It is at this moment in Cohen's argument that we can see that value is, again, overdetermined, resulting from factors external to labor as well as connected to labor. This, for lack of a better term, is the aesthetic moment of the creation of value. It is, again, the intersection of culture and economics. From there, the sequence follows that the capitalist appropriates some of the value of the product; the laborer receives less

90   Joseph W. Childers and Stephen E. Cullenberg

value than the value of what she creates; the capitalist thus also appropriates some of the value of what the laborer creates; and the laborer is consequently exploited by the capitalist (see Cohen, 1988: 229). It is important to note several theoretical inferences of this analysis. First, the attention is on the creation of the product's use value, not value per se. Second, the creation of value is not (completely) attributed to labor; it is overdetermined in "essence" and thus operating as a sign of both economic and cultural imperatives. Third, because the word "capitalist" could be replaced by feudal lord, slave owner, state, etc., this formulation is appropriate for explaining different forms of class exploitation in different sites, whether the household, the third world, or cyberspace. Finally, we see that the fundamental Marxian critique of exploitation retains its explanatory function, although it is now formulated differently and not in such a totalizing fashion as when linked to the abstract labor/value/surplus value nexus.

In many ways, we believe that this moves us a bit farther along in drafting a strategic outline of the possibilities of speculating with value and gambling with difference that Spivak sometimes tentatively suggests. It considers the consequence of the privileging of use value that McCabe identifies when he remarks that without a fixed relation between value and labor it is impossible to understand the appropriation of surplus outside a full understanding of the organization of value within a particular community. That is to say, the "social" is once again a complex, multiple set of possibilities that cannot be reduced simply to its function in exchange or in the value form. And while value itself may indeed be destabilized within the traditional Marxian metric, the openings such a destabilization offers allow us to consider exploitation and its concomitant results in relation to the formation of value in its many manifestations—from the surplus value that derives from capitalist appropriation of both the labor and the cultural accretion of value in a commodity to the use value of products that are produced by labor usually written out of theorizations of exploitation, because they are not part of the generally recognized sphere of exchange. At this point in our own deliberations on such speculations, we have no general theory, no grand narrative to offer for political intervention. Indeed, even to assume that we might produce one would be to subvert the anti-essentialist, anti-totalizing theoretical impulses that underwrite many of our assumptions and arguments. On the other hand, we do think that, by beginning to rethink value as non-derivative and as a function of both the economic and cultural spheres (a binary that functions only heuristically for us), it may be possible to keep in mind the ever negotiable characteristics of our own commitments while still striving to reverse, displace, and seize the very apparatus of value coding. Perhaps it will allow us to instigate change that we can commit to, however briefly.

References

Cohen, G.A. 1988. *History, Labour and Freedom: Themes from Marx*. Oxford: Clarendon.
Eagleton, Terry. 1991. *Ideology: An Introduction*. London: Verso.
Marx, Karl. 1992 [1867] *Capital, Volume I*. London: Penguin.

Use, value, aesthetics 91

McCabe, Colin. 1988. "Preface." In *In Other Worlds*, Gayatri C. Spivak. London: Routledge, ix–xx.

Mouffe, Chantal. 1988. "Hegemony and New Political Subjects: Toward a New Concept of Democracy." In *Marxism and the Interpretation of Culture*, ed. Cary Nelson and Lawrence Grossberg. Urbana: University of Illinois Press, 89–104.

Spivak, Gayatri Chakravorty. 1988a. "Can the Subaltern Speak?" In *Marxism and the Interpretation of Culture*, ed. Cary Nelson and Lawrence Grossberg. Urbana: University of Illinois Press, 271–316.

Spivak, Gayatri Chakravorty. 1988b. "Scattered Speculations on the Question of Value." In *In Other Worlds*. London: Routledge, 154–78.

Spivak, Gayatri Chakravorty. 1993a. "Limits and Opening of Marx in Derrida." In *Outside in the Teaching Machine*. London: Routledge, 97–119.

Spivak, Gayatri Chakravorty. 1993b. "Marginality in the Teaching Machine." In *Outside in the Teaching Machine*. London: Routledge, 53–76.

Part II

Sublime intercourse

Economics meets aesthetics (and vice versa)

4 Reluctant partners

Aesthetic and market value, 1708–1871

Neil De Marchi

Intrinsic and economic values

Intrinsic value has a nice ring to it. It picks up on "essential" properties supposedly existing in an object, and implies greater stability than external evaluations, which can be attached, modified, even withdrawn altogether, on whim. The precious metals have intrinsic value, based on undeniable properties—sheen and feel, durability, malleability, resistance to corrosion, and so on—plus accepted standards for measuring weight and purity in the metal itself. When coins were made of precious metals, weight and purity were all that mattered, but intrinsic value dominated even when gold, or silver, was fashioned into objects of use and beauty. Typically there was a second value attached for the fashioning. But it was understood that, in time of crisis, fashioning would be discounted to zero, beautiful objects being melted down for their metal content.[1] Yet when a fashioned object had been smashed or melted down to its metallic core, this still had to be valued. Measures of purity and weight are just that, they affect but do not in themselves establish an external exchange value for metal of specified standards. An exchange value is derived from the metals markets, or established by government edict.

So it has been, though with significant differences, with art. The makers and traders of paintings, for instance, have often pretended that their wares embody intrinsic value. Historically, appeals have been made to essentials, as in the tradition that paintings are imitations of Nature, or that they embody timeless ideals of Beauty. In addition to such core values, however, there have always been standards, often imposed by some designated or self-appointed authority, as to what constitutes "excellence" in any particular work. These standards are the aesthetic equivalent of special systems for weighing and measuring the fineness of precious metals. They refer to the aspects or properties deemed to constitute the art of painting—composition, design, coloring, etc.—and once these are scored along some arithmetic scale they serve like Troy weight and degrees of purity in a refined metal.

Often enough the temporary keepers of standards for painting, and those who define paintingness, have behaved like sovereigns or governments with respect to coins, dictating what the relative worth of works of different sort will be. But gold

96   *Neil De Marchi*

or silver coins have a certain universal acceptability, and a sovereign issuing them could control the supply, so that decreed and market values might stay close to one another for long periods. Neither condition has ever prevailed with respect to paintings. Precious materials costs (gold leaf, lapis lazuli) began to make up a decreasing share in the cost-value of a painting as medieval church notions of what is proper subject matter and technique gave way in the West to new media, modern ideas on drawing, rediscovered classical ideals of representation, and invention as an economic category.[2] Although guilds took on the job of controlling supply and overseeing quality, they could not count on buyers accepting their norms. As a result of all this, over time, the content in the claim that paintings have an intrinsic value came to seem more difficult to locate.

While the market kept imposing its own valuations on paintings, however, the guardians of intrinsic value walled themselves off, claiming that, though there are market considerations, these are of no concern to a person of taste, a true connoisseur. My story begins in the early eighteenth century, when walling-off was well established. Nevertheless, it was masons of taste who introduced the idea of a numerical scale for measuring achievement on each of several designated aspects of the art of painting. This, understandably, was portrayed by its inventors as either a plaything of no real consequence, or as a tool for making connoisseurship into a science. Either way, there was still lacking a bridge from such aesthetic exercises to market valuation. If we write the history backwards, however, it might seem that the scale idea held within it the possibility of connecting the two.

The logic of this is spelled out by Ginsburgh and Weyers in their contribution to this volume. Briefly, the idea is that, once the aspects of an art are scaled and scored (drawing, relative to coloring, and so on, for the art of painting), aspects can be compared. This requires the imposition of a weighting scheme. Thus coloring might be said to count twice as much as design, and expression for nothing. If, then, we multiply each weight by the numerical score of a painting (or an artist) aspect by aspect, we will have a measure of the contribution of each to value. We still do not know what "value" is; but various measures are possible, ranging from the number of lines given to artists in catalogues or dictionaries of artists to (for living artists) hanging position and space in an annual official exhibition. Both of those measures are likely still to reflect basically aesthetic criteria. But we could also decide to call value prices at auction. Then, using either aesthetic criteria or the market or, as Ginsburgh and Weyers illustrate, *both*, the method of regression allows us to identify the weights implicit in a given set of scores, linking a (known) value outcome to its contributing component parts. The modern name for this is hedonic regression.

The actual history is less neat than this, and I wish to say something here about the reasons for that messiness. The innovation of measuring performance on a numerical scale, aspect by aspect, was eighteenth century, the work of a Frenchman, Roger de Piles (1635–1709). De Piles treated it as a provocative joke. When the English took over the idea of quantifying degree of excellence, they too were inclined to turn it into a game. As such it might be adopted for private use, like the diary version devised by Hester Thrale in which the merits of her friends, the members of Samuel Johnson's circle, were compared (Balderston, 1942). Or, if deployed in the public sphere, the quantifying idea could be adapted to sharpening satirical attacks on Establishment foibles and pomposity. Bentham mentions one such exercise, where prominent judges were assessed according to several characteristics (Bentham, 1827). In the hands of its English co-developer, the portraitist and art theorist Jonathan Richardson, however, the scale technique was adapted to strengthening a claim that connoisseurship be regarded as a "science." Richardson saw in it a way to heighten the walls blocking off intrinsic value from the market.

Separating out the aspects of an art such as painting was a natural extension of the analytical method itself, and did not require numerical scaling. Analysis was used in eighteenth-century inquiry of many kinds, and it was this aspect that attracted Adam Smith, not the possibility of measuring degrees of excellence. Certainly Smith was fascinated by rankings of all sorts—of the propriety of actions, of the imitativeness of the various arts, and so on—but his efforts in these directions had a purely ordinal character. Perhaps not surprisingly, his exploration of pricing in the market did not result in his directly comparing the properties of, say, paintings with their relative values in exchange. I will argue that he was open to such a move—much more so than Richardson, for example—but simply did not see very clearly a way to compare artistic excellence with market forces, as done, for instance, by Ginsburgh and Weyers. A link could have been forged, perhaps, through an index of pleasure, to quantify our "admiration" for the products of the arts along with objects in general. Smith, as I will show, was taken with the possibility of analyzing objects in terms of their pleasure-yielding properties. And he insisted that relative wages, whether for artistic or other services rendered, are determined by a single set of forces. But he did not integrate his analysis of wages in general with his "pleasure" analysis of the arts and of objects, much less with an aesthetic ranking. As a result such integration as was achieved was entirely on one side, the economic.

The Smithian moment, during which pleasure in objects and our admiration for the arts might have become part of a general approach to valuation, passed quickly and without yielding much beyond unfinished explorations. Smith did not explain artists' wages in terms of the pleasure-giving properties of their services, though these lurked in the background. And ingenuity itself, for example, which he acknowledged will affect the degree of admiration we feel for the labor embodied in particular objects, suffered under the difficulty that "it is not easy to find any accurate measure" for it (Smith, 1976a). After Smith, in any event, pleasure in consumption all but disappeared from the (British) economic agenda. The mid-nineteenth century in Great Britain was dominated by the economics of John Stuart Mill, whose reformist inclinations led him to emphasize distribution over consumption. Consumption rejoined the agenda in 1871, with the work of William Stanley Jevons, but as the problem of how to optimize consumption expenditure, not as a problem of how to quantify consumption pleasures; least of all, how to quantify the pleasures of consuming the arts. Jevons had already judged it impossible to ascribe any rule to the pleasures excited by "interest[,] beauty,

98   *Neil De Marchi*

or grandeur" (Jevons, undated).[3] Indeed, the economic analysis of consumption confined itself, until the introduction of the characteristics approach to demand by Kelvin Lancaster, in the 1960s, principally to basics: generic food and other necessities (Lancaster, 1966, 1971).[4] Art was off the economist's list.

My period ends at the point (1870) where the organizers of the "Aesthetics of Value" conference at the University of California, Riverside thought it might be fruitful to begin exploring examples of value-thinking which originated in the arts/humanities and afterwards had an impact beyond those disciplines, perhaps through interactions with economics. I hope to persuade that the earlier history is also instructive, though more for clarifying some of the obstacles to finding a language both groups feel reasonably comfortable with than issuing in positive suggestions. My history, as might already be apparent, will comprise three selected episodes, and will slight their contexts as well as intervening developments.

Richardson, de Piles, and the assessment of excellence

The first homegrown British treatment of how to assess the excellence of works of art is that by Jonathan Richardson (1665–1745), portrait painter and mentor to the teacher of Joshua Reynolds. In two essays, both published in 1719, Richardson dealt with "the whole Art of Criticism as it relates to Painting" and then incorporated his practical conclusions into "An Argument in behalf of the Science of a Connoisseur." Richardson borrowed his framework from Roger de Piles. De Piles was an art critic, served as artistic adviser to the duc de Richelieu, and, late in life, gave lectures at the Royal Academy of Painting and Sculpture in Paris. He is remembered for advocating that "coloring" be given a place among the criteria defining painting alongside the more traditional academic aspects: design, composition and expression.[5]

De Piles appended to his *Principles of the Art of Painting*, which first appeared in London in 1708, though in French (English translation 1743), what he called a *Balance des Peintres*. In this "balance" he set out to assign a score to 56 of the best-known painters (none living), for their performance in the four dimensions, composition, design, coloring, and expression, each on a scale of zero to twenty. The page reproduced in Figure 1 shows his scores for individual artists in the alphabetical range P to U. De Piles did not aggregate the scores across his four columns, perhaps indicating that he was aware that such averaging would require him first to impose a set of relative weights on the four aspects. Given what we know of his own preferences, however, it would not surprise us had he explicitly weighted coloring as heavily or perhaps even more heavily than design, and both heavier than the other two aspects or properties of painting. Both de Piles and Richardson allowed that an artist might be deemed good, even outstanding in certain respects, even if performance was poor on others.

Richardson, however, complained that aside from this nuance de Piles had done nothing with the balance, and he undertook to correct that. He extended the number of aspects to seven: composition, coloring, handling, drawing, invention,

The Balance *of* PAINTERS. 299

NAMES.	Composition.	Design.	Colouring.	Expression.
	Deg.	*Deg.*	*Deg.*	*Deg.*
Parmefan	10	15	6	6
Penni, Francifco il Fattore	0	15	8	0.
Del Piombo, Baptifta	8	13	16	7.
Perugino, Pietro	4	·12	10	4.
Pordenòu	8	14	17	5
Pourbus	4	15	6	6.
Pouffin	15	17	6	15.
Primaticcio	15	14	7	10
R.				
Rembrant	15	6	17	12
Reni, Guido	0	13	9	12
Romano, Julio	15	16	4	14
Rubens	18	13	17	17
S.				
Salviati, Francifco	13	15	8	8
Santio, Raphaele	17	18	12	18
Del Sarto, Andrea	12	16	9	8
Le Seur	15	15	4	15
T.				
Teniers	15	12	13	6
Tefta, Pietro	11	15	0	6
Tintoret	15	14	16	4
Titian	12	15	18	6
U.				
Del Vago, Pierino	15	16	7	6
Vandyke	15	10	17	13
Vanius	13	15	12	13
De Udine, John	10	8	16	3

Vero-

Figure 1 Portion of De Piles's 'Catalogue of the Names of the most noted Painters, and their Degrees of Perfection, in the Four principal Parts of *Painting*; supposing absolute Perfection to be divided into twenty Degrees or Parts.'

Countefs DOWAGER *of*
Exeter.

V. DYCK.

OCTOBER *the 16th,* 1717.

FACE.

Compofition	10	18.
Colouring	17	18
Handling	17	18
Drawing	16	17
Invention	18	18
Expreffion	18	18
Grace and Greatnefs	18	18

Advantage		*Pleafure*
18	*Sublime.*	16

Figure 2 Richardson's modified de Piles table, with added column for portrait.

Source: From *Science of a Connoisseur* (1719).

expression, and grace and greatness, though some of these had been subsumed by French and Italian writers under the more economical four- (sometimes three-) aspect approach. Richardson was also much more explicit in imposing the academic hierarchy of genres, with history painting on top, portraiture (as a sort of history of the person represented) just below, and both far above landscapes, sea-pieces, animal pictures, fruit, flower and other sorts of still-life, and "pieces of drollery" (Richardson, 1719: 44).

100   *Neil De Marchi*

In addition Richardson attached quality rankings to the strictly numerical scores. Thus (here following de Piles) a 17 or 18 is the maximum any artist could be said to have attained to; in a practical sense, then, it was the "sublime." Once again, this degree of perfection was thinkable only "in those Parts of Painting that are capable of it" (55) (which drollery, for example, is not). Slightly below the sublime, the range 13–16 denoted high excellence, and 5 through 12 the mediocre, while the numbers 4 and below were reserved for pictures worthy of notice but truly bad in some one respect. For portraiture, his own specialty, Richardson added a separate column to allow for an assessment of an artist's performance on the face alone, creating a distinct set of boxes, row by row, for all seven aspects (see Figure 2). Finally, though without actually attaching relative weights to the aspects, Richardson nevertheless provided for a summary judgment in terms of the "advantage" and "pleasure" afforded by a painting. In terms of these two, what we might call meta-criteria, handling, and drawing (from nature) "can only please," as can coloring, though more so. But composition, which pleases at least as much as coloring, also instructs, and that is also the great advantage of expression and invention, grace and greatness, in ascending order (48–9).

Richardson recommended to would-be connoisseurs that, since they should see as many examples as possible, and keep a record of their judgments, his complete scale should be transferred to every page of a little pocket-book, which they would keep by them and bring out as occasion (a painting) presented itself. In this way, "when one considers a Picture an Estimate might be made of it by putting such Figures under each Head as shall be judg'd proper (56)."

Richardson thought of his methods for assessing worth as empirically based. The connoisseur must judge directly and for himself of "the Intrinsic Qualities of the thing itself," not just mouth another's opinion (23). It is true that he considered the superiority of history painting as beyond question, but all else, in principle, was examinable and was to be examined without prejudice or dependence on authority. There was, however, one other exception. Richardson also took as self-evident the superiority of instruction over mere sensual pleasure. This was a view widely advertised by British writers on "taste" in the eighteenth century. The first President of the Royal Academy, Joshua Reynolds, gave the position some official warrant through his *Discourses*, later in the century, but it is also to be found in many of the essays on taste that appeared in earlier decades. Among these the essay of Alexander Gerard is particularly interesting, since it is probable that Adam Smith helped judge it as a member of the Committee on belles lettres and criticism, of the Select Society of Edinburgh, whose Gold Medal it was awarded in 1758 (Hipple, 1963: vi; Ross, 1995: 141). Gerard's introductory words on the subject of the relative value of intellectual versus sensual pleasure leave no room for doubt about what would follow: "... the pleasures of taste [he began], though less improving than such as are intellectual ..." (Gerard, 1780 [1759]: 182). The convention was powerfully challenged, though not at once, by Smith.

Although he emphasized the importance of sense impressions to knowledge, Smith also accepted that in the existing state of science it was impossible to

Reluctant partners 101

indicate how the sense organs and a "principle of perception" might be linked.[6] He was inclined therefore to regard pleasures of both sorts, sensual and intellectual, as things that "the *mind* in reality enjoys" (Smith, 1980b: 205; my emphasis). This simplified the consideration of pleasure and may help explain Smith's willingness to investigate the pleasure-giving potential of objects as a pre-condition to understanding choice in consumption.

Smith on the pleasure-giving properties of goods and services

In a section of his early-1760s lectures on law at Glasgow University Smith explored, in prefatory remarks to a statement about how price is formed, the properties of objects which give us pleasure. The "ground of preference," he explained, that which directs our choice, whether in pursuits or purchases, is the *qualities* we ascribe to objects, "differences of things which no way affect their real substance" and which are irrelevant to our basic needs (Smith, 1978: 488; cf. 335).[7] These inessential, non-intrinsic differences are of four sorts. Smith summarized them under the heads of color, figure (form), rarity and singularity (he called it variety, the lack of which is commonness), and "imitation." Imitation refers to the ingenuity which enables artificers and artists to retain something natural in made objects, as when perspective is preserved in a two-dimensional plane (336). The four sources of pleasure in difference are of crucial economic importance: since "frivolous distinctions ... in things otherwise equall (sic)" are what give rise to pleasure or pain, they also drive "the whole industry of human life" (336; cf. 488).

Smith's identification of four pleasure-yielding properties of objects exactly parallels Roger de Piles's analysis of painting into the four aspects of composition, design, coloring, and expression. That the number of aspects identified was the same, however, is surely coincidental; Smith did not need to draw on de Piles as inspiration for this bit of analysis.[8] But having determined the aspects for objects in general, Smith was in a position to explore whether, supposing them to be of equal importance, scoring their respective contributions to pleasure might not open a way to comparing aesthetic value with exchange value. What steps would be involved?

First, a reminder of the approach outlined by Ginsburgh and Weyers. They take as given de Piles's scores, on the four dimensions or aspects defining painting, for his group of artists. They then set about acquiring two sorts of valuations of those same artists. The first sort is an aesthetic value ranking, for which they use the number of lines given to each artist in a prominent modern dictionary of art; the second is an economic value ranking, for which they take sales prices for works by the artists in auctions between 1977 and 1993. With a common set of scores, the regression method then generates two sets of weights for the aspects, one implicit in the aesthetic value ranking, the other in the market value ranking. These two sets can be compared, to see where there is agreement between the implications of the aesthetic and the economic rankings, and where the two fail to coincide. The hedonic regression method, used in this way, offers a framework

102   *Neil De Marchi*

for discussing the relative weights implicit in judgments from an aesthetic and a market perspective.

Now imagine that Smith engaged in a comparable exercise. How might he have gone about it? Let us suppose him to have been interested – as we know he was, casually – in watches. Further suppose that he was in possession of a set of scores for a group of watchmakers from the recent past on the several aspects of "watchness," properties such as accuracy; ingenuity of mechanism; workmanship on the case; proofness against shock, and so on. The scores might be the work of an expert, "one curious in watches."[9] To complete the exercise, Smith would have to have come up with two value rankings of the performance of his group of watchmakers. One of these might have been a pleasure index and the other perhaps prices at estate and other auctions over a specified period, of watches made by the group. With the common set of scores, Smith could then infer (informally, in the absence of the method of regression) the weights for each aspect implicit in the pleasure ranking versus the market ranking of the watchmakers.

Had Smith wished to modify the exercise to make the comparison between an *aesthetic* ranking and an economic, he need only have slightly altered the properties of watches. Thus, he might have emphasized the design of face, hands, and numerals; the exquisiteness of the movement; coloring (reflecting the materials chosen, and the way they combine together); and the uncommonness of the whole (perhaps reflecting the use of precious stones, chasing, or engraving on the dial or cover, the relative uniqueness of components, and so on). Those properties are close to his general four pleasure-giving aspects of objects in general, but with an aesthetic twist. He could have made do with the original set of scores on the aspects, since one who is curious in watches, Smith observed, is often as intrigued by their art as by their usefulness as timepieces.

The conceptual element in this exercise is surprisingly straightforward and is something Smith could easily be imagined toying with. But only up to a point. That he didn't actually conduct any such exercise (in print) is probably due to a well-known reluctance to apply measurement in any situation where an accurate measure is hard to produce. We saw this already in the case of ingenuity. Further evidence of Smith's reluctance is to be found scattered throughout his writings. I offer three additional illustrations. First, Smith was skeptical about "political arithmetick." On one occasion he questioned the "exactness" of computations of the volume of British grain exports, on another, estimates of the "precise" number of souls in Scotland (Smith, 1976a, 1977). In both instances Smith rejected the best available numerical estimates, unless they were to be employed solely for making broad, ordinal comparisons. A second illustration comes from his *Theory of Moral Sentiments* (1976b). After an extended discussion of virtue as "propriety," Smith concluded that none of the systems based on this principle was able to give "any precise or distinct measure by which ... fitness or propriety of affection can be ascertained or judged of" (294). He went on to say that the missing measure is given only by the sympathetic feelings of the "impartial spectator." But that measure functioned for him as an ideal to strive for, not as a present or attainable reality. For the supposedly impartial

Reluctant partners 103

spectator is subject to several sorts of bias, while the mechanism associated with the spectator device works at the level of the individual and is therefore much less objective than the notion of measurement might imply. My third illustration derives from the realm of taste. In matters of taste Smith was even more forthcoming about the elusiveness of a reliable measure. Appropriateness enters into taste in several ways. For example, in choosing combinations, or intensities, of colors; or in opting to apply or not apply paint to a statue. In such matters, Smith acknowledged, "decisions ... appear always, in some measure, uncertain" (123).

We know then that Smith did not take the steps necessary to conduct comparisons between the aesthetic and the economic, and we can be fairly confident that measurement difficulties figured prominently in his failure to do so. Nonetheless, it is worth looking at what he said on the pleasure-giving properties of objects. This lies at the heart of the modern characteristics approach to demand, the operational version of which is the hedonic regression. Moreover, the undeniable fact of the pleasure we take in the arts was, I believe, Smith's excuse for giving artistic performance equal treatment in the *Wealth of Nations* with so-called "productive" labor. In this Smith shows himself to have been an explorer in ways of enlarging the economic to embrace the arts, in contrast to, say, Richardson, who insisted on keeping the two apart. We can proceed through each of the four properties of objects Smith mentioned in his *Lectures on Jurisprudence* and which I listed briefly at the start of this section.

First, as to figure or form, Smith noted that we find plainness and repetition monotonous, therefore we want "A sort of uniformity mixd at the same time with a certain degree of variety" (Smith, 1978: 335). But if uniformity "tires the mind, too much variety, too far encreased, occasions an overgreat dissipation of it" (488). In other words, pleasure increases with variety, but there is a maximum, beyond which it once again decreases.

Concerning rarity and variety, we enjoy surprise, so singularity and differentiation among goods pleases us (488). Yet, from what Smith says in the *Moral Sentiments* about the troublesomeness of possessions—the loss of tranquility suffered in acquiring them, and the "most anxious attention" they demand once in our possession (Smith, 1976b: 181–3)—it also follows that too many goods, of too great a nicety or refinement, must decrease pleasure.

Color, thirdly, or rather "certain shades and combinations of Colour," is the means by which we discern depth, by which we govern our movements safely, and so on (Smith, 1980a: 151, 156). Moreover, certain visualizations are better fitted than others to stand for the corresponding tangible objects, and color plays a crucial role in these representations (156–7). While some of our responses to color, therefore, may reflect mere prejudice—we esteem Pinchbeck (an alloy of copper and zinc) much less than gold, yet the color is comparable (Smith, 1978: 336)—in some degree they are also reflections of our sense of what is right, fitting. For this very reason, however, while color can please it may also offend. Thus, "Certain colours are more agreeable than others," yet sometimes "the very colour of an object hurts" (Smith, 1976b: 199; Smith, 1978: 488).

104 *Neil De Marchi*

Finally, as to ingenuity (imitation), it can render objects agreeable, so that, "In painting, the very imitation of so very inferior an object as a suit of clothes is capable of pleasing" (Smith, 1978: 488; Smith, 1980b: 180). On the other hand, "In Statuary, scarcely any drapery is pleasing"; indeed, the best drapery is that "nearest to no clothing at all" (Smith, 1980b: 180). In short, imitation carried out mechanically, and applied without discrimination, can turn pleasure into its opposite.

The rule, then, in each of the pleasing aspects or properties of objects, is to make sure that the stimulus increases in appropriate degree *and* manner, lest pleasure be thwarted, or reach a maximum and be reversed. Smith, we are beginning to learn, was interested in efforts made by some of his contemporaries to produce a sort of physiology of sensibility, even if these did not come to fruition until late in the nineteenth century, with the work of Wilhelm Wundt and others who called themselves psycho-physicists.[10] I mention this only to indicate that degree was a problem that admitted of solutions, eventually. The more difficult measurement problem here was that of the manner, or the appropriateness, with which a stimulus was applied. We have encountered this already (to clothe and paint, or not to clothe and paint, statues). But take the case of variety in form or design. Variety of form achieved by introducing discontinuities in the form of sharp angles interrupting a line, or complicated constructions that prevent a figure, prospect, building, or interior "being easily and distinctly comprehended on the first sight," Smith asserted, must be eschewed (Smith, 1978: 335). But how could such a guiding principle be translated into quantitative terms? The best Smith himself could do was suggest that the circle is to be preferred above an ellipse, parabola, hyperbola, or "Archimedean spirall," all of which are more varied but also more difficult to grasp at a glance (336). This makes the point that it matters *how* variety is sought, but doesn't get us any closer to having an exact measure of appropriateness in a figure.

Smith retained his interest in analyzing pleasure, especially the pleasures we experience in artistic performances, on which he was still writing shortly before he died (Smith, 1980b). But he never got beyond discrete, qualitative statements. Thus, repetition in a piece of instrumental music can, by subtly altering a sense, a combination of sounds, eventually "move … agitate … and transport us." Comic opera, on the other hand, inspiring as it does "agreeable gaiety" and "temperate joy," produces in us "not only an elegant, but a most delicious pleasure" (Smith, 1980b: 192, 195). The two pleasures are thus differentiated in words, but how should they be measured and ranked? Despite offering no answer to this question Smith managed to integrate pleasure with economic considerations. He acknowledged, as noted earlier, that in those arts, and in the liberal professions, labor issues in no concrete product, so that "the work … perishes in the very instant of its production," yet "the labour … has a certain value." He even showed how this value is appraised in the market. The wage in those occupations, he insisted, is regulated "by the very same principles which regulate that of every other sort of labour" (Smith, 1976a: 331).

Reluctant partners   105

The factors Smith lists as determining relative wages, however, emphasize cost and supply factors—length and cost of training, probability of success, and so on—leaving the demand side relatively unexplored. He all but brought the two sides together, for if the rewards paid for artistic services reflect the esteem in which we hold the talents involved, they must also be a proxy for our pleasure, since the pleasure we experience is founded on our wonder and admiration "of the art" displayed (Smith, 1980b: 185). Here pleasure, aesthetic judgment, and wages come about as close together as one is likely to see in economics. Closing the circle is blocked in two ways. First, whereas costs can be measured—even the probability of success is quantifiable—pleasure is more problematic in this respect. Second, esteem for "the art" is only one of many factors entering into relative wages. Smith talked about pleasure, and he pointed to all the causal factors entering into relative wages, but he did not develop a pleasure index, nor did he try to quantify the role of any one of the causal factors.[11]

William Stanley Jevons and the turn away from pleasures of the mind

After the Millian hiatus, late in the nineteenth century British economics turned again to pleasure in consumption. This time there was a more explicitly quantifying goal in view. Pleasure, though submerged under the generic "utility," was central to the work of William Stanley Jevons. At the same time, he sought to apply the standards and methods of the sciences to political economy and, perhaps even more sensitive than Smith to measurement difficulties, restricted his analysis of pleasure to what could unequivocally be reduced to mathematical relations between measurable entities. This resulted in the relegation of aesthetic pleasures to metaphysical inquiry. It also restricted economic analysis to basic goods—strict necessaries.

The process at work here is both interesting and set a pattern for generations of economists, so it is worthwhile trying to identify the whole sequence of moves that Jevons made. As early as 1860 he posited a certain regularity in what he represented as universal experience in consumption, calling it an axiom. The axiom reads: "as the quantity of any commodity, for instance, plain food, which a man has to consume, increases, so the utility or benefit derived from the last portion used decreases in degree" (Jevons, 1860). A decade later, in his *Theory of Political Economy* (1871), Jevons wrote: "My principal work now lies in tracing out *the exact nature* and *conditions* of utility" (105; my emphasis). We may read this as the dual task of finding the measure proper to the entities "commodity" and "utility" and the precise relation between them.

An important step, though it turned out to be something of a misstep, was an attempt to generate experimental data in a sphere where quantification definitely was possible. As he was composing his *Theory*, Jevons conducted some experiments using men to throw weights, lift and lower weights by a pulley and cord, or hold a weight with an extended arm. The measured output of these

106   *Neil De Marchi*

activities was "force" or what Jevons dubbed "useful effect." Lying behind the experiments was the assumption that there is a limited amount of muscular force that can be developed in a given time, plus the presumption that, because fatigue increases rapidly with the intensity of exertion, there will be observed a point of maximum efficiency. Without crossing into the area of physiology Jevons hoped his observations would give "definiteness … to some of the principles and which form the basis of the science of political economy" (Jevons, 1870: 159).[12] Though there is a certain analogy to consumption here via "useful effect," the chief principle to be made more definite, unsurprisingly, had to do with labor. The proposition, as it appears in the *Theory*, is that, whereas exertion in its early stages produces net pleasure, a maximum of net pleasure over pain is soon reached; thereafter pain begins to dominate and presently it overwhelms any pleasure that might be felt (Jevons, 1871: 191–2).

That proposition was not in fact rendered more exact with help from the experiments. A correspondent pointed out to Jevons that his observations, expressed mathematically, did not generate any "real" value for the weight thrown (experiment no. 1) which would make useful effect a maximum, while in the other two experiments there was simply no maximum of useful effect at all. The second and third experiments generated observations best described by rectangular hyperbolae, with weight on the horizontal and useful effect on the vertical axis (Haughton, 1871). Jevons was not deterred, though he ended up having to rest his case on the commonsensical account of exertion given above.

It was the same when it came to finding the law of utility. Divide the food a man consumes during a twenty-four-hour period, Jevons suggested, into ten equal portions. If one portion is removed it will scarcely be noticed; the loss of the second will be felt; that of the third may cause harm; and so on, "until at length he will be on the verge of starvation" (Jevons, 1871: 106). Next, turn this around and consider each portion not as a decrement but as an addition. Each increment, it is obvious, "is less necessary, or *possesses less utility*" (106; my emphasis). Without knowing the exact nature of the law involved here, Jevons could conclude that any graphical expression of the underlying though unknown mathematical relation between quantity of food consumed (on the horizontal axis) and incremental utility (on the vertical axis) must be downward sloping. An implicit mathematical relation here was as much precision as Jevons ever got.

At this point, and even though "pleasurable effect" was the obvious corresponding term in consumption for "useful effect" in the analysis of work, Jevons pushed it aside, replacing it by "utility." The two, he insisted, are equivalent (106, 119–120). In fact there are three entities involved: some "mass" of commodity (M), producing a certain amount of pleasurable effect (E), in a given amount of time (T). Both quantity of commodity used and pleasurable effect have a time dimension, but the supply of commodity is properly a rate, M divided by T, whereas pleasurable effect is properly E multiplied by T. Time is thus self-canceling, and we are left with $(E \times M)$ for the exact "quantity of utility" (120). Jevons at this point did incorporate the results of his second and third experiments with weights. They displayed no maximum, recall; the same, he asserted, is strictly true of the total quantity of

Reluctant partners   107

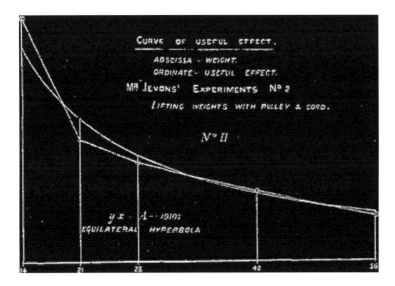

Figure 3 Jevons's experiment no. 2: useful effect from lifting weights (observations and fitted curve).
Source: From Samuel Haughton, "On the Natural Laws of Muscular Exertion. II," *Nature*, Feb. 9, 1871.

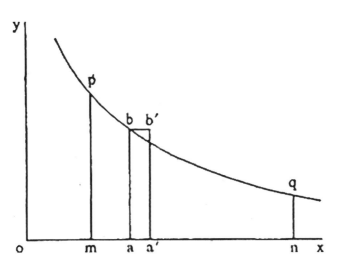

Figure 4 Jevons's graph of diminishing "intensity of effect" as quantity consumed increases.
Source: From *The Theory of Political Economy* (1871).

108   *Neil De Marchi*

utility. However, what matters is the *degree* of utility, or the "comparative utility of the several portions" of food in his thought experiment above (107). Thus, if we measure vertically the effect on the consumer of increments of the commodity (food in the mental experiment), by imagining the increments to be infinitely small, we generate a continuous curve of pleasurable effect or utility which is downward sloping and asymptotic to the horizontal axis (108).

The substitution of utility for pleasurable effect here appears to have been just a matter of convenience; in fact it was something more. Utility is generic; it abstracts from the peculiarities of whatever commodity happens to be involved in consumption. The result Jevons reached with the help of the terminological change, in short, is general, not commodity-specific.

Having replaced pleasurable effect, which is necessarily commodity-specific, with the generic utility, and having established an appearance of mathematical exactness with a posited continuous curve generated in the example involving "food"—itself a generic—Jevons reverted to his initial axiom. This he re-stated as the proposition "that *utility is not proportional to* [quantity of] *commodity*" (106; emphasis in the original). What holds for food is then said to hold for water, numbers of suits of clothing, indeed any commodity for which we can imagine consuming "further supplies of the same substance." This is then fully generalized to: "Exactly the same considerations apply more or less clearly to every other article," and: "No commodity can be named" to which satiety does not apply (105, 111). The "general law" is: "that *the degree of utility varies with the quantity of commodity, and ultimately decreases as that quantity increases.*"

However, not only were there no further actual examples given in Jevons's exposition, but he immediately restricted his own law to something considerably less than a general proposition. The law applies, he admitted, to "simple animal requirements ... food, water, air, etc.," but our more refined and intellectual needs are not subject to satiety. "To the desire for articles of taste, science or curiosity, when once excited, there is hardly a limit" (111–21). This accords with other, unpublished, statements Jevons made, in particular statements about the arts. Thus music, for example, has utility, but also something more. This something more Jevons called "perceptive pleasure," which makes it sound like Smith's pleasures of the mind, except that Jevons maintained something of the old distinction between sensual and intellectual pleasures, whereas for Smith both are "in reality" pleasures of mind. Enlarging his sweep to aesthetic pleasures in general Jevons added that the pleasure excited by "interest beauty or grandeur" is beyond investigation, or at least it is outside the realm of the physical and its laws. "To investigate it would be to enter one of the most difficult and least certain of metaphysical subjects" (see Mosselmans and Mathijs, 1999: 152). Putting these various statements together, precision cannot be expected in this area, but, in any case, pleasures of the mind, rather than of the body, display increasing, not diminishing, marginal satisfaction.

This is where the economic analysis of pleasure in consumption was left after Jevons, in the realm of physical "necessities," until Lancaster re-introduced the notion that we choose on the basis of pleasure-giving bundled characteristics.

Conclusion

I set out to trace the course and possible influence among economic thinkers of de Piles's initial introduction of the idea of measuring performance in the art of painting on a numerical scale, in the four dimensions of design, composition, expression, and coloring. I showed that Adam Smith employed a somewhat comparable analysis of objects in terms of their pleasure-yielding properties—though without scoring "performance"—along the four dimensions of form, color, ingenuity, and rarity or variety. Smith's approach seems to lend itself to adaptation in ways that amount to an informal variant of the exercise undertaken by Ginsburgh and Weyers in this volume. They have demonstrated that a set of scores such as those assigned by de Piles to a group of artists can be linked to value rankings, both artistic and economic, so as to yield two sets of implied weights of the four aspects of the art of painting. Comparing these relative weights clarifies the similarities and differences between artistic and market value thinking, via their rankings. Smith even went some way down this path, suggesting that our pleasure in the various arts, since it gives rise to admiration for the talents involved, will be reflected in the relative rewards that are paid to those talents (or artistic services). Thus relative wages function as value rankings for our admiration. If admiration, or the pleasure which underlies it, could be scored, in several appropriate dimensions, we would be well on the way to having a framework for arriving at the implied relative importance or weight attached to those dimensions.

Smith did not take matters that far, partly, I have suggested, because he was wary of seeking exact measurement where it was not obviously attainable. The prospect, however, was there, and it contrasts sharply with that presented by the leading artist-developer of de Piles's framework, Jonathan Richardson, who exploited the scoring idea, but only to give an appearance of greater scientificness to connoisseurship. Richardson in fact strengthened the barriers between art and the market.

Pleasure in consumption, including consumption of the arts, re-emerged in the late nineteenth century, in British economics. But the Smithian prospect of rendering the *implications* of artistic and market valuation somewhat comparable was destroyed by Jevons's insistence that the pleasure or utility we take in basic necessities, and the investigation of aesthetic pleasures, belong to completely different spheres. The one was supposedly quantifiable, by analogy with physical phenomena, whereas pleasures of an intellectual or artistic sort were a matter for metaphysical investigation. By confining the economic analysis of pleasure to necessaries, Jevons created a barrier as effective as Richardson's separation of intrinsic from market value, to the integration into a single framework of artistic and market value rankings.

An operational version of such a framework, the hedonic regression as interpreted by Ginsburgh and Weyers, is available, backed by the Lancastrian theory of objects as bundled characteristics, and warrants further investigation. I have not attempted to tell the story of how this theory or its operational counterpart

110 *Neil De Marchi*

came into being, but I hope to have highlighted some of the elements in aesthetic and economic thinking that have made conjunction difficult and probably will continue to do so unless tackled openly.

Notes

1 For an illuminating discussion of these matters see Clifford (1999).
2 The latter aspect in particular is emphasized in De Marchi and Van Miegroet (1996).
3 The original Jevons manuscript is in the John Rylands Library of Manchester University, JA 6/47/8.
4 Lancaster did not invent the method of hedonic regression. For early applications of that method see Waugh and Court (1939).
5 These aspects of the art of painting are discussed by Montagu (1994). On "coloring" (*coloris*) in particular, see de Piles.
6 See, for example, Smith's remarks on sound and hearing in his essay "Of the External Senses" (Smith, 1980a).
7 Smith's edited work comprises two sets of student notes, for the sessions 1762–3, and, in all likelihood, 1763–4.
8 Smith owned copies of de Piles's *Cours de Peintre par Principes* and his *Abregé de la Vie des Peintres*, but there is little to suggest that he was greatly influenced by de Piles's ideas.
9 The phrase occurs in a passage devoted to watches, in Smith (1976b: 180).
10 For a recent statement on Smith's interest in physiology see Forget (2002). On Wundt and German psychophysics see Murray (1993).
11 *Wealth of Nations*, Book I, ch. x, a and b, identified five principal circumstances affecting relative wages, of which public admiration is just a sub-element of one, the probability or improbability of succeeding in a profession.
12 I am indebted to Harro Maas for having drawn my attention to these experiments.

References

Balderston, Katherine C. (ed.) 1942. *Thraliana. The Diary of Mrs Hester Lynch Thrale*, 2 vols. (Oxford: Clarendon Press).
Bentham, Jeremy. 1877. *Rationale of Judicial Evidence*, edited by John Stuart Mill, 5 vols. (London: Hunt and Clarke).
Clifford, Helen. 1999. "A Commerce with Things: The Value of Precious Metalwork in Early Modern England," in Maxine Berg and Helen Clifford (eds), *Consumers and Luxury. Consumer Culture in Europe 1650–1850* (Manchester: Manchester University Press), 147–68.
Court, A.T. 1939. "Hedonic Price Indexes with Automotive Examples," in *The Dynamics of Automobile Demand* (New York: General Motors Corp.), 99–119.
De Marchi, Neil and Hans J. Van Miegroet. 1996. "Pricing Invention: 'Originals,' 'Copies' and their Relative Value in Seventeenth-Century Netherlandish Art Markets," in V.A. Ginsburgh and P.-M. Menger (eds), *Economics of the Arts. Selected Essays* (Amsterdam: North-Holland), 27–70.
de Piles, Roger. 1673. *Dialogue sur le Coloris* (Paris).
Forget, Evelyn. 2002. "Evocations of Sympathy: Sympathetic Imagery in Eighteenth-Century Social Theory and Physiology," mimeo, University of Manitoba.
Gerard, Alexander. 1780 [1759]. *An Essay on Taste* (Gainesville, Florida: Scholars' Facsimiles & Reprints, 1963).

Reluctant partners 111

Haughton, Samuel. 1871. "On the Natural Laws of Muscular Exertion. II," *Nature* (Feb. 9), 289–93.

Hipple, Walter J. 1963. "Introduction." In *An Essay on Taste*, Alexander Gerard (Gainesville, Florida: Scholars' Focsihiles & Reprints).

Jevons, William Stanley. 1860. "Letter to his brother," June 1. In R.D. Collison Black (ed.),

Jevons, William Stanley. 1870. "On the Natural Laws of Muscular Exertion," *Nature* June 30, pp. 158–60.

Jevons, William Stanley, The Theory of Political Economy, edited with an introduction by R.D. Collison Black (Harmondsworth: Penguin Books, 1971; originally published in 1871).

Jevons, William Stanley. 1871. *The Theory of Political Economy*, edited with an introduction by R.D. Collison Black (Harmondsworth, Middlesex: Penguin Books, 1970).

Jevons, William Stanley. Undated. "On the Functions of Music," published as Appendix 1 in Bert Mosselmans and Emest Mathijs, "Jevons's Music Manuscript and the Political Economy of Music," in Neil De Marchi and Craufurd, D.W. Goodwin (eds), *Economic Engagements with Art*, Annual Supplement to Volume 31 of *History of Political Economy* (Durham, NC: Duke University Press), 121–56, p. 152.

Lancaster, Kelvin. 1966. "A New Approach to Consumer Theory," *Journal of Political Economy* 74, 132–57.

Lancaster, Kelvin. 1971. *Consumer Demand: A New Approach* (New York: Columbia University Press).

Montagu, Jennifer. 1994. *The Expression of the Passions. The Origin and Influence of Charles Le Brun's Conférence sur l'expression générale et particulière* (New Haven and London: Yale University Press).

Mosselmans, Bert, and Emest Mathijs. 1999. "Jevons's Music Manuscript and the Political Economy of Music," in Neil De Marchi and Craufurd, D.W. Goodwin (eds), *Economic Engagements with Art*, Annual Supplement to Volume 31 of *History of Political Economy* (Durham, NC: Duke University Press, 1999), 121–56.

Murray, David J. 1993. "A Perspective for Viewing the History of Psychophysics," *Behavioural and Brain Sciences* 16, 115–86.

Richardson, Jonathan. 1719. *An Argument in Behalf of the Science of a Connoisseur* (London: W. Churchill).

Ross, Ian Simpson. 1995. *The Life of Adam Smith* (Oxford: Clarendon Press).

Smith, Adam. 1976a. *An Inquiry into the Nature and Causes of the Wealth of Nations*, edited by R.H. Campbell and A.S. Skinner, 2 vols., volume II of Glasgow edition (Oxford: Clarendon Press).

Smith, Adam. 1976b. *The Theory of Moral Sentiments*, volume I of the Glasgow edition, edited by D.D. Raphael and A.L. Macfie (Oxford: Clarendon Press).

Smith, Adam. 1977. "Letter to George Chalmers", 10 Nov. 1785, no. 249, in *The Correspondence of Adam Smith*, edited by E.C. Mossner and Ian Simpson Ross, volume VI of Glasgow edition (Oxford: Clarendon Press).

Smith, Adam. 1978. *Lectures on Jurisprudence*, edited by R.L. Meek, D.D. Raphael and P.G. Stein, volume V of Glasgow edition (Oxford: Clarendon Press).

Smith, Adam. 1980a. "Of the External Senses," in *Essays on Philosophical Subjects*, edited by W.P.D. Wightman and J.C. Bryce, volume III of Glasgow edition (Oxford: Clarendon Press).

Smith, Adam. 1980b. "Of the Nature of that Imitation which takes place in what are called the Imitative Arts," in *Essays on Philosophical Subjects*, 176–213.

Waugh, F.V. 1928. "Quality Factors Influencing Vegetable Prices," *Journal of Farm Economics* 10, 1–10.

5 On the contemporaneousness of Roger de Piles' *Balance des Peintres**

Victor Ginsburgh and Sheila Weyers

Roger de Piles (1635–1709), the French art theorist and critic, without being "revolutionary," (Rosenberg, 1967) does not share the views of the French artistic establishment of his time. He advocates the importance of color, going as far as writing that "there is no painting if color does not go with drawing," or that "color is the soul of painting," while the Académie Royale de la Peinture et de la Sculpture created in 1648 by the French Court, considers drawing to be the most important element. This is not new, but merely pursues a debate that had already started during the sixteenth century in Italy.[1] While Vasari complained that Titian should have been more careful in drawing, Dolce considered color as being as important as drawing. The official French doctrine pursued by the Academy is Poussinisme, after Poussin, who had written that "colors in painting are blandishments to lure the eyes." Le Brun, Louis XIV's official painter "associate[s] true value in art with drawing, which exemplifies 'reason', with color being of lower account because it is concerned with the senses."[2] These views are supported by André Félibien (1619–1695), the official art historian of the Académie Royale. His *Entretiens* (1686) published between 1666 et 1686, celebrates classicism, glorifying Poussin and Raphael.

In his *Dialogue sur le coloris* published in 1673, de Piles, on the contrary, blames Poussin for neglecting color. His admiration goes to Rubens, Van Dijck, Corregio and Titian,[3] and he is probably the initiator of what came to be called Rubénisme, in opposition to Poussinisme. In an appendix to his *Cours de peinture par principes* (1708), he publishes a table, the so-called *balance des peintres* in which he decomposes painting into four fundamental characteristics: composition, drawing, color, expression, and grades each of these on a scale between zero and twenty for 56 painters from his own and earlier eras. Rembrandt, for example, is very low on drawing and obtains 15, 6, 17 and 12 on the characteristics just mentioned, while Michelangelo is very high on drawing, with scores of 8, 17, 4 and 8 respectively.[4]

Though de Piles himself looked on this as a game, his contemporaries considered it a "clever way to characterize genius."[5] Later, this view changed. Schlosser (1924) hates it. Gombrich (1966, p. 76) describes the exercise as a "notorious aberration." In his book on de Piles' theory of art, Puttfarken (1985) thinks of de Piles as having been "at his worst when he tried to be most systematic."

On the contemporaneousness of Roger de Piles' Balance des Peintres   113

The originality of the *balance* is that it introduces a view of aesthetics that may be thought of "as either breaking up beauty into its parts or supplementing beauty with additional concepts" (Dickie, 1997: 3).[6] This is of course the very same idea as the one expressed by the economist Lancaster (1966) according to whom a commodity can be thought of as a bundle of characteristics, purchased by consumers not for itself, but for the value it provides by combining such characteristics.[7]

In both cases, this means that the "value" of a good (a painting, or an automobile) is obtained by adding the values of all the characteristics embodied in the good (such as composition and drawing for a painter, or speed and number of doors for a car); each value is, in turn, the product of the unit value of the characteristic or its weight β_i, times the number x_i of such units. If the good can be fully described by say, four characteristics, its total value V is simply:

$$V = \beta_1 x_1 + \beta_2 x_2 + \beta_3 x_3 + \beta_4 x_4.$$

If we follow de Piles, the characteristics of a painting (of a painter in his *balance*) are composition, drawing, color, and expression, while the number of units of each characteristic is the score that each painter obtains. If one could determine the unit value of each characteristic, it would be possible to compute V. One way of doing this is intuitive. It consists of adding the four grades to obtain 50 for Rembrandt and 37 for Michelangelo. This implies that one assumes arbitrarily that all the weights β_i of the above formula to be equal to one. (It is worth noting that de Piles was careful enough not to do that.) One could also think that drawing is three times as important as the other parts, and thus set $\beta_2 = 3$, giving Rembrandt and Michelangelo values of 62 and 71, respectively. The previous ordering of the two artists would be reversed, giving the impression that all this is very arbitrary, and that de Piles was right to consider his *balance* as a game.

It is, however, possible to determine the β if the value V of each painter (or painting) is known. Then, one can, using a statistical method known as regression analysis, determine the weights, β_1 to β_4, in an objective way. This raises two issues: what is regression analysis doing and how can one determine the values V.

Regression analysis is concerned with the relation between one variable (say values, V) and a set[8] of other variables (the x_i, here the scores on composition, drawing, etc.), leading to an "equation" which has exactly the same representation as the one used above. The difference is that now the V and the x_i are given, while the β_i (the weights of each characteristic in the total value V) will be determined through a calculation (or, as is often said, will be "estimated"). This is easy to explain if the set of "other variables" consists of a single one, say composition, since in that case, one can give a convenient graphical representation of the problem in which now, the equation is simply $V = \beta_1 x_1$, a special case of the one considered earlier.

In Figures 1a–1c, a painter is represented by a point (an observation). On the vertical axis one can read his "value," on the horizontal one his score on composition. In Figure 1a, the scatter of points leads us to conclude that there

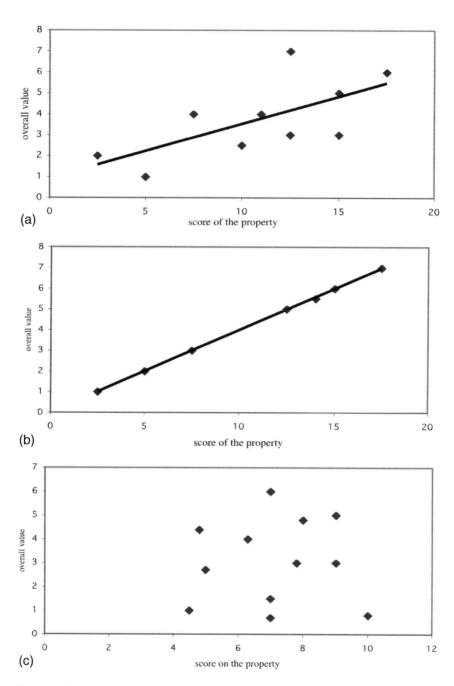

Figure 1 Three cases of adjustment by regression analysis.

On the contemporaneousness of Roger de Piles' Balance des Peintres   115

exists a positive, upward sloping relation between the two variables (the larger the score on composition, the larger the value of the painter), that can approximately be represented by the line which goes through the scatter of points.[9] If all the points were exactly on the line (as in Figure 1b), one could obtain the value of a painter by simply reading his score on composition. This is the ideal case, since, more generally, the relation between the two variables will be more fuzzy, but if the scatter of points is reasonably flat in one direction and elongated in the other direction (as it is in Figure 1a), one can accept that there exists a relation, and compute, using some criterion,[10] the slope of the line. In Figure 1c, we also represent a scatter that does not have the same southwest-northeast pattern, and there is no obvious choice for the slope: it can be anything. This points to two extreme cases, the first in which all points lie on the line (a perfect adjustment) and the second, where any choice of slope is as good, or as bad as any other (almost every line is possible). The case illustrated in Figure 1a is intermediate, and is due to the fact that V is measured with some error or that composition (the x_1 variable) does not explain value in a perfect way so that, instead of $V = \beta_1 x_1$, the relation should be written $V = \beta_1 x_1 + u$, where u is a random disturbance, which originates from elements that we ignore.

These considerations lead us to define a coefficient which will measure the quality of the adjustment of the line to the scatter of points. This coefficient (called R-squared) is defined in such a way that it will vary between one (perfect adjustment, Figure 1b) and zero (any adjustment is possible, Figure 1c), while intermediate values will hold for cases such as the one in Figure 1a.

The slope of the line, β_1, is a number that can be estimated. It will come with two more numbers which describe an "interval" in which the slope can vary, a measure of the relative uncertainty with which the slope is estimated.[11] A narrow interval will correspond to a good adjustment (the slope is equal to 0.20, but it can vary between 0.19 and 0.21, which is pretty accurate). A wide interval is the sign of a poor adjustment. For instance, if the calculated slope is equal to 0.20, but the interval goes from -0.30 to 0.70, then the direction of the line is not determined with much accuracy. It could be downward instead of upward sloping so that even if the estimated coefficient is equal to 0.20, there is some likelihood that it could also be equal to zero (since zero belongs to the interval $[-0.30, 0.70]$). If so, then the variable has little or no influence (a non significant influence) on V, and can thus be ignored.

This reasoning can easily (at least in mathematical terms, not in graphical ones) be extended to the case of a relation between one variable V and a set of variables, $V = \beta_1 x_1 + \beta_2 x_2 + \beta_3 x_3 + \beta_4 x_4 + u$, where again, u is a disturbance term due to non measured variables or to some randomness or measurement errors in V. For each variable of this set, one can determine a coefficient (a slope) together with the interval in which it can vary. If this interval is narrow, the variable has an influence on V. If it is large and contains zero, the variable can be discarded, since it does not contribute to explaining V.

We now discuss how the values V can be determined. It may appear that this turns out to be as "subjective" as what de Piles did in quantifying the characteristics

116   *Victor Ginsburgh and Sheila Weyers*

in which he decomposed a painting, though this is often done by critics for some artistic productions, such as movies[12] but rarely so, if ever, for paintings or painters.

Art philosophers put the burden of the proof of quality (or of value) on specialists; they also believe that some unanimity among specialists, even if subjective, is needed,[13] though they never "quantify" quality. Therefore, values have to be "quantified" in an indirect way. We describe two possible measures, each of which is incomplete and prone to defects. However, if both lead to similar conclusions, one may think that it was worth the effort.

The first measure is the length of the entry that is devoted to each artist in a contemporary encyclopedia, in this case, the 34 volumes of the Grove (1996) *Dictionary of Art*. The length of the entries constitute probably a subjective choice,[14] but this choice was made by a large group of art historians, the editors of the dictionary, according to some reasonably well established (and hopefully) consistent rule.

The second measure is inspired by economists who argue that prices are good indicators of values. And these may indeed be good approximations, at least in the competitive world of auctions—the source of the data used in our paper. In an auction, the price is set by those who bid for the painting: museums curators or collectors who usually rely on specialists before bidding. Moreover, prices obtained at auction are "accepted" since they will serve as yardsticks for future auctions (and transactions by art galleries), and thus have a certain flavor of unanimity, at least among specialists. Even art historians believe that it would be "absurd" (Haskell, 1976) to ignore the information carried by prices, though prices fluctuate too much to be of help in explaining tastes. Junod (1995) goes even farther by claiming that "financial transactions [of artworks] are the expression and the criterion of aesthetic judgments ... the construction of contemporaneous values is more and more resulting from the collusion between dealers, critics, collectors, curators and, sometimes, artists themselves." Finally, though sociologists disagree with economists that "the auction paradigm embodies rational economic man in his purest form," auctions can nevertheless be regarded as "processes for managing the ambiguity and uncertainty of value by establishing social meanings and consensus." (Smith, 1989, pp. 162–163) Thus again, unanimity or at least consensus about values comes at the foreground in the sociological appreciation of auctions. We shall thus also use prices obtained at art auctions (held between 1977 and 1993) to represent values.

Finally, one can also wonder why we choose "values" measured in the late twentieth century—entries in a recent (1996) dictionary and prices obtained at auction between 1977 and 1993—for masters considered by de Piles in 1708, almost three hundred years earlier. There are three reasons for this. First, widening the time span between the date of creation and the date at which the value of a painter (painting) is assessed is a way of taking into account what art philosophers have come to call "the test of time," which makes it possible to separate fashion from art. Second, it makes it possible to test whether the judgment passed by de Piles in the early eighteenth century has itself passed the test of time. Third, data

On the contemporaneousness of Roger de Piles' Balance des Peintres   117

on prices for more recent years are probably less prone to "measurement errors," including cheating.[15]

Estimation of the weight parameters β_i requires observations concerning the values V of painters, and the scores given to each of them by de Piles. The length of the entries in the dictionary are easy to measure. For prices, the situation is more complicated since instead of observing a price for each painter, we can only observe the prices for his paintings when they are sold at auction, but this is easy to circumvent.[16]

The results, shown in Table 1 are based on 41 of the 54 painters[17] scored in de Piles' *balance des peintres.* They lead to the following comments.

The statistical quality of the adjustments is not very good since the R-squared (which can vary between zero for bad fit and one for excellent fit) are hardly larger than 0.30. The results concerned with the characteristics considered by de Piles are nevertheless extremely interesting. One of these, drawing, is never significant (check that 0 is contained in the confidence interval). Color is significant in both cases, while composition and expression contribute to value only when value is represented by prices.

The coefficients can further be interpreted as measuring the impact on value of a small change in the rating given by de Piles. Consider color again. When value is measured by the length of entries in the Grove (1996) dictionary, the number 64.6 means that every additional point given by de Piles in his grading of color adds 64.6 lines to the entry. Likewise, when values are measured by prices, an extra point on color raises the price of the painter by 11.9%.[18] Color is the most important explanation of value, whether value is measured by art historians (in the *Dictionary of Art* 1996) or through prices.

What these calculation imply is that the contemporary valuation of our 41 painters does not fit with de Piles' ratings of drawing, only mildly so for expression, and composition, but very positively for color. One can wonder why de Piles' valuations of characteristics other than color (and, to some extent, expression and composition) are not in line with contemporary views. Rosenberg's (1967, p. 47) comments are very illuminating in this respect. He writes that "if de Piles himself often failed to make adequate judgments of particular artists and their works, again it was due to the restrictive hold classicism still had on him. While his method of analysis was progressive in breaking down the appreciation of painting into the four components of composition, drawing, color and expression, it was only in his judgment of color that he was free from the prevailing prejudices."

Rosenberg's quotation leads us back to the title of our paper. De Piles clearly breaks new ground in (re)introducing the concept of color in painting. In that respect, he is obviously close to contemporaneous views, but was not good enough at guessing how the late twentieth century would view other characteristics, especially drawing, in painting.

Why should one use quantitative methods in a field where they are very uncommon,[19] and where Rosenberg (and probably many others) could reach a similar conclusion without such tools. A possible answer is given by Burke (1987)

118   *Victor Ginsburgh and Sheila Weyers*

Table 1 Estimation results

	Parameter value	Bounds of interval*		Parameter is significant
		Lower	Upper	
Values are lengths of entries in the Dictionary of Art				
Score on				
Composition	45.052	−21.501	111.605	no
Drawing	−6.754	−96.552	83.045	no
Color	64.644	13.285	116.003	yes
Expression	43.792	−14.779	99.479	no
Goodness of fit (R-squared)	0.335			
No. of observations	41			
*Values are prices** obtained at auction*				
Score on				
Composition	0.047	0.004	0.090	yes
Drawing	0.007	−0.048	0.062	no
Color	0.112	0.081	0.143	yes
Expression	0.046	0.015	0.077	yes
*Dimensions****				
Height (100 cm)	0.576	0.186	0.966	yes
Width (100 cm)	0.452	0.017	0.887	yes
Surface (100 sq.cm)	−0.014	−0.037	0.009	no
*Other variables*****				
Years	17 parameters			contribute in a
Salerooms	7 parameters			significant way
Goodness of fit (R-squared)	0.315			
No. of observations	525			

* The bounds of the interval are computed using the usual 5% probability level.

** For statistical reasons, we use the logarithm of prices instead of absolute prices.

*** All three variables have the expected sign. Height and width contribute positively to the price of a work; surface contributes negatively, since a painting loses relative value if it gets too large.

**** The detailed results are not reported. Suffice it to say that the 17 parameters which capture the evolution of prices over time are different from each other, which points to the fact that price movements were important between 1977 and 1993 (recall the surge followed by the large drop of prices before and after 1990). Likewise, the 7 parameters which capture the saleroom effects are not equal: *ceteris paribus,* some salerooms do better than others.

who writes that though one often learns little from quantitative methods that one did not know already, one should use them to confirm previous knowledge. In the same way as does the discovery of fresh documents, they will strengthen our conclusions.

But there are two other, maybe more interesting, concluding comments. First, our approach illustrates what Vermazen (1975, pp. 9–10) refers to as incommensurable properties, which make it impossible "to rank [works] with respect to the degree of two different independently valued properties." In Vermazen's words,

On the contemporaneousness of Roger de Piles' Balance des Peintres

Appendix Table

	Composition	Drawing	Color	Expression	No. of paintings sold	No. of lines in Turner*
Albani	14	14	10	6	11	434
Barocci	14	15	6	10	1	579
Bassano	6	8	17	0	9	628
G. Bellini	4	6	14	0	5	1503
Bourdon	10	8	8	4	16	293
Caravaggio	6	6	16	0	–	2436
The Carracci	15	17	13	13	17	2603
Corregio	13	13	15	12	–	1083
Cortona	16	14	12	6	–	1139
Da Udine	10	8	16	3	2	144
Del Piombo	8	13	16	7	1	676
Del Vaga	15	16	7	6	–	209
Del Sarto	12	16	9	8	–	742
Diepenbeek	11	10	14	6	2	222
Domenichino	15	17	9	17	5	725
Durer	12	16	9	8	–	2165
Giordano	13	12	6	6	72	696
Giorgione	8	9	18	4	–	1392
Guercino	18	10	10	4	10	634
Giulio Romano	15	16	4	14	1	1257
Holbein	9	10	16	13	1	902
Jordaens	10	8	16	6	34	758
Josepin (Arpino)	10	10	6	2	2	249
Lanfranco	14	13	10	5	6	924
Le Brun	16	16	8	16	4	725
Leonardo da Vinci	15	16	4	14	–	2657
Le Sueur	15	15	4	15	7	396
Michelangelo	8	17	4	8	–	3650
Muziano	6	8	15	4	1	205
Palma Giovane	12	9	14	6	22	281
Palma Vecchio	5	6	16	0	4	264
Parmigiano	10	15	6	6	2	601
Penni	0	15	8	0	–	94
Perugino	4	12	10	4	3	982
Polidoro da Caravaggio	10	17	–	15	–	154
Pordenone	8	14	17	5	–	298
Pourbus	4	15	6	6	9	290
Poussin	15	17	6	15	4	1577
Primaticcio	15	14	17	10	–	313
Raphael	17	18	12	18	2	1694
Rembrandt	15	6	17	12	7	3435
Reni	–	13	9	12	19°	1014
Rubens	18	13	17	17	48	1965

Scores attributed by de Piles, number of paintings sold at auction between 1977 and 1993 and length of entry in Turner's *Dictionary of Art*.

120 Victor Ginsburgh and Sheila Weyers

Appendix Table (continued)

	Composition	Drawing	Color	Expression	No. of paintings sold	No. of lines in Turner*
Salviati	13	15	8	8	2	777
Teniers	15	12	13	6	133	359
Testa	11	15	0	6	2	421
Tintoretto	15	14	16	4	25	1610
Titian	12	15	18	6	9	1638
Van Dyck	15	10	17	13	25	1665
Vanius	13	15	12	13	1	88
Van Leyden	8	6	6	4	–	683
Venius (Van Veen)	13	14	10	10	5	186
Veronese	15	10	16	3	13	1414
Volterra	12	15	5	8	1	172
F. Zuccaro	10	13	8	8	1	307
T. Zuccaro	13	14	10	9	1	268

* There are two columns per page, making for 2 times 62 lines per page. Reproductions of works as well as references are taken into account.

° Though 19 of his paintings were sold, Reni is not included in our calculations, since de Piles did not rate him on composition.

the β which translate the degree of one property (or characteristic) into that of an other[20] are not known. Here, we determine the β, which is a solution to the problem raised by Vermazen, since these β make properties or characteristics commensurate: One unit of characteristic 1 has the same influence on value as β_2/β_1 units of characteristic 2. For example, one point given by de Piles to color is worth 0.67 ($= 43.8/64.6$) point given to expression (in terms of the value as measured by the number of lines in the Grove *Dictionary*). Second, our results which use two very different notions of "value" in art, lead to similar views, and are consistent with the views held by art historians. The first is the implicit aesthetic rating by art historians, derived from the length of the entries in a contemporary art dictionary, the second is the one given by markets (prices obtained for the same artists at auction). The parameter values in Table 1 show that the two views are perfectly consistent: the order in which the four properties are rated is identical. Color is rated highest; it is followed by composition and expression, and finally by drawing, which does not seem to matter at all (in none of the two cases is the coefficient or weight picked by "drawing" significantly different from zero).

Notes

* We are grateful to François Mairesse who introduced one of us to de Piles, and to Neil de Marchi and Philippe Junod for their comments and warm support.

1 And even much earlier, according to Junod (1996) who traces it back to ancient times: Plutarch v. Pliny, Vitruvus, etc.

On the contemporaneousness of Roger de Piles' Balance des Peintres 121

2 See Newman (1996).

3 As well as to Raphael, though de Piles' appreciation of Raphael's way of using colors is not very high.

4 For the scores attributed by de Piles, see de Piles (1708). See also the table presented in Appendix. Note that in Studdert-Kennedy and Davenport (1974), Muziano is misnamed as Murillo. See also Mairesse (1999).

5 Thuillier, Préface, in de Piles (1708, p. xxvii).

6 See also Urmson (1950), as well as the discussion in Dickie, (1988, pp. 157–182). See also Dickie (2000, pp. 228–241), who distinguishes between a descriptive and an evaluative sense of art. One can think of the characteristics as describing the work of art, while ratings evaluate it.

7 A car is not bought for itself, but for the services it ensures, at a certain speed, with a certain comfort (number of doors, air conditioning, length, width), at a given cost (miles per gallon), etc.

8 Note that this set may consist of a unique variable.

9 This implies that the equation is written $V = \beta_1 x_1 + u$, where u is the distance between a point and the line.

10 Such as minimizing the sum of distances (or of squared distances) between the line and the points.

11 At a given probability level.

12 See e.g. Maltin (1998) who rates movies between 0 and 4. This is also very common for wines and restaurants.

13 See e.g. Budd (1995, p. 182).

14 It is interesting to note that even art historians may be sensitive to differences in lengths of entries. Blunt (1956, chapter on Vasari), for instance, notes that Vasari devotes only two pages to Duccio (who was from Siena), while Giotto, a Florentine artist, gets 25 pages.

15 As is well known, and more so in the past than nowadays, works of art are sometime "sold" to walls or chandeliers, instead of being sold to real buyers. See Beckett (1995, p. 79).

16 One could think of computing an average price for each painter. The problem with such an approach is that averages would mean little since prices are not constant over time (here, 17 years), vary with the dimensions of the works, and may differ across salerooms. Therefore, it is sensible to remove as much as possible the effects of these heterogeneities, and compute average prices for (hopefully) more homogeneous paintings. This can be obtained by a first stage in which prices of individual paintings are regressed on their dimensions, and sets of categorical variables representing years and salerooms. (For each year between 1977 and 1993 and for each saleroom in which a painting was sold during these years, a categorical variable is defined, which takes a value equal to one or to zero. Assume for instance that we deal with a painting sold in 1989 by Christie's. The categorical variables representing the year 1989 and the one representing Christie's will take the value one, while the values of all the other categorical variables (other years and other salerooms) defining that sale will take the value zero. For further details, see Chanel, Gérard-Varet and Ginsburgh (1996). The price of each painting is then corrected in order to take out the effect of dimensions, year of sale and saleroom. What is left is the price of a painting which includes the value of the painter, and some random unknown effects that are smoothed out, by computing average prices for each painter. It can be shown that the same result can be obtained by including in the regression categorical variables representing painters. One additional and final step is needed and is easy to understand. Instead of representing each painter by a categorical variable, we can as well represent him by the four scores given to him by de Piles. The equation that is finally used looks very much like the one discussed above, except that it includes variables representing dimensions

122 *Victor Ginsburgh and Sheila Weyers*

(height, width and surface), categorical variables for years and salerooms, and a random term:

$$V = \beta_1 x_1 + \beta_2 x_2 + \beta_3 x_3 + \beta_4 x_4 + \gamma_1 \text{ height} + \gamma_2 \text{ width} + \gamma_3 \text{ surface}$$
$$+ \text{ effects of categorical variables representing years and salerooms} + u.$$

The only parameters in which we are really interested are the β representing the effects of the characteristics described by de Piles (composition, drawing, color, expression). We shall also discuss very briefly the effects of dimensions: We expect height and width to have a positive effect on value (γ_1 and γ_2 should be positive), but dimensions should not become too large, so that surface is expected to have a negative effect (γ_3 should be negative). Note that the parameters affecting the categorical variables describing years can be combined to obtain a price index over time, while those affecting salerooms will tell whether, *ceteris paribus*, some salerooms are able to sell at higher prices than others.

17 There are 56 painters in de Piles' balance, but for two of them (Guido Reni and Polidoro da Caravaggio), de Piles gives scores for three characteristics only. There are 14 painters (among whom Polidoro da Caravaggio) of whom no painting was sold at auction between 1977 and 1993, and for comparison purposes, we decided to consider the same 41 painters. See the Appendix for data listing the 56 painters, de Piles' ratings, the number of sales for each of them, and the length of the entry in Grove (1996).

18 Since prices are measured in logarithms, the effect an extra point has on prices is $\exp(0.112) - 1 = 11.9\%$.

19 Note that in his well known book on art history during the seventeenth century in France, Teyssèdre (1964) devotes three chapters (chapters 1 to 3 in part 2) to a quantitative analysis of de Piles' *balance*. See of course also Studdert-Kennedy and Davenport (1974).

20 This is what economists call the "marginal rate of substitution."

References

Beckett, Alice (1995), *Fakes. Forgery and the Art World*, London: Richard Cohen Books.

Blunt, Anthony (1956), *Artistic Theory in Italy 1450–1600*, Oxford: Clarendon Press.

Budd, Malcolm (1995), *Values of Art*, London: Penguin.

Burke, Peter (1987), *The Italian Renaissance: Culture and Society in Italy*, Cambridge: Polity Press.

Chanel, Olivier, Louis-André Gérard-Varet and Victor Ginsburgh (1996), The relevance of hedonic price indices. The case of paintings, *Journal of Cultural Economics* 20, 1–24.

De Piles, Roger (1708), *Cours de peinture par principes*, edited by Jacques Thuillier (1989), Paris: Gallimard.

Dickie, George (1988), *Evaluating Art*, Philadelphia: Temple University Press.

Dickie, George (1997), *Introduction to Aesthetics. An Analytic Approach*, New York and Oxford: Oxford University Press.

Dickie, George (2000), Art and value, *British Journal of Aesthetics* 40, 228–241.

Félibien, André (1686), *Entretiens sur les vies et les ouvrages des plus excellens peintres anciens et modernes*, edited by Sir Anthony Blunt (1967), Farnborough : Gregg Press.

Gombrich, Ernst (1966), *Norm and Form. Studies in the Art of the Renaissance*, London: Phaidon, 1966.

Grove (1996), *The Dictionary of Art*, 34 vol., edited by Jane Turner, New York: Grove.

Haskell, Francis (1976), *Rediscoveries in Art. Some Aspects of Taste, Fashion and Collecting in England and France*, London: Phaidon Press.

On the contemporaneousness of Roger de Piles' Balance des Peintres 123

Junod, Philippe (1995), Comment une oeuvre d'art devient un classique, in Pierre Gisel, ed., *La Sélection*, Lausanne: Payot, 95–108.

Junod Philippe (1996), Critique d'art, in Michel Laclotte et Jean-Pierre Cuzin, eds., *Dictionnaire de la Peinture*, Paris: Larousse.

Lancaster, Kevin (1966), A new approach to consumer theory, *Journal of Political Economy* 74, 132–157.

Mairesse, François (1999), Réflexions sur la balance des peintres de Roger de Piles, *Recherches Poïétiques* 8, 43–49.

Maltin, Leonard (1998), *Movie & Video Guide 1998*, New York: Penguin.

Newman, Geoffrey (1996), Color, in Grove, vol. 7, pp. 626–631.

Puttfarken, Thomas (1985), *Roger de Piles' Theory of Art,* New Haven: Yale University Press.

Rosenberg, Jacob (1967), *On Quality in Art,* London: Phaidon Press Ltd.

Schlosser Julius von (1924), *Die Kunstliteratur. Ein Handbuch zur Quellenkunde der neueren Kunstgeschichte,* Wien: Anton Schroll.

Smith, Charles (1989), *Auctions. The Social Construction of Value*, New York : The Free Press.

Studdert-Kennedy, W. Gerald and Michael Davenport (1974), The balance of Roger de Piles: a statistical analysis, *Journal of Aesthetics and Art Criticism* XXXII, 493–502.

Teyssèdre, Bernard (1964), *L'histoire de l'art vue du Grand Siècle*, Paris: Julliard.

Urmson, J. O. (1950), On grading, *Mind* 59, 145–169.

Vermazen, Bruce (1975), Comparing evaluations of works of art, *Journal of Aesthetics and Art Criticism* XXXIV, 7–14.

6 How aesthetics and economics met in voc ed

Evan Watkins

If you're old enough you're likely to think of vocational education by conjuring up now retro images of shop class greasers, or recovering dim memories of those invidious secondary school tracking mechanisms that doubtless separated most of "us," as fastracked toward college, from "the others" who went—well, who went somewhere else eventually. Of course voc ed has changed over the years, and if you're at all familiar with a wide range of recent initiatives you may instead find yourself thinking of all the current political rhetoric regarding promises of high tech training for everyone for the 21st century. But either way, voc ed seems an unlikely place to explore the obvious themes of this chapter around issues of value, both aesthetic and economic. That is, whether your images of voc ed involve something like metal lathe training, or more currently CNC routing or systems programming, voc ed clearly has to do with work and with money, but not exactly with aesthetics. Nevertheless, for some time versions of voc ed training have trafficked everyday in the most mundane, ordinary forms of direct exchange between beauty and money. There are, for example, well over half a million licensed cosmetologists in the U.S. today, most of whom are women—producing beauty primarily for other women in exchange for relatively small sums of money many times over in the course of a working day. Cosmetology in other words is about beauty and about money and about education, education that is strictly controlled by State licensing procedures.

The *Occupational Outlook Handbook* reports the following about the testing procedure for a license: "After graduating from a training program, students can take the State licensing examination. The examination consists of a written test and, in some cases, a practical test of cosmetology skills. A few States include an oral examination in which the applicant is asked to explain the procedures he or she is following while taking the practical test. In some States, cosmetology training may be credited towards a barbering license, and vice versa. A few States have even combined the two licenses into one hair styling license." Indeed, the *Handbook* specifies that in many States it's possible to obtain a license strictly as an "esthetician": "In most States, a separate examination is given for people who want only a manicurist, esthetician, or electrolysis license" (325).

The *Handbook* goes on to warn would-be cosmetologists, however, that earning a license is hardly the end of the educational process: "For many cosmetologists,"

How aesthetics and economics met in voc ed   125

the *Handbook* continues, "formal training and a license are only the first steps in a career that requires years of continuing education. Because hairstyles are constantly changing, barbers and cosmetologists must keep abreast of the latest fashions and beauty techniques. They do this by attending training in salons, at cosmetology schools, or at product shows. These shows offer workshops and demonstrations of the latest techniques and expose cosmetologists to a wide range of products that they can recommend to clients, an important skill as retail sales become a more important part of the beauty salon industry" (325). As the *Handbook* also details, the qualifications for the job are in fact considerable and remarkably varied. "Successful barbers or cosmetologists usually have finger dexterity and a sense of form and artistry. They should enjoy dealing with the public and be willing to follow patrons' instructions. Some cosmetology schools consider 'people' skills to be such an integral part of the job that they require coursework in this area. Business skills are important for those who plan to operate their own salons, and the ability to be an effective salesperson is becoming vital for nearly all barbers and cosmetologists" (325).

I've quoted these passages from the *Occupational Outlook Handbook* at length because especially for those of us with a background in literary study they almost seem to invite an immediate allegorical interpretation that would in fact foreground some of the obvious themes for this chapter. Or more exactly, rather like a Kafka story, they seem to invite a number of possible allegorical narratives, which often conflict. Surely in one version of possible allegory all this talk of salons and artistry in the *Handbook,* and the implication of continued, heated discussions of the latest and avant-garde developments, could be read like the perfect deflationary parable of a heady early 20th-century European modernism. Perhaps something along the lines of Pierre Bourdieu's famously scathing account of aesthetic value in *Distinction* (1984). After all, who would know better than Gertrude Stein that "business skills are important for those who plan to operate their own salons," while meanwhile of course Ernest Hemingway could be busy lamenting the lack of "finger dexterity" in the new wannabes coming over from the States.

Alternatively, in a very different allegorical frame of interpretation, one might effectively leverage everyday cosmetology practices and training into a means for filling out that most undertheorized portion of Bourdieu's *Distinction,* having to do with what he rather glibly calls a "working class aesthetic." For while certainly the upper reaches of cosmetology might intersect with Hollywood or rock star high fashion, the majority of working cosmetologists ply their trade in the midst of what would surely qualify for Bourdieu as a working class and lower middle class milieu for working class and lower middle class people. Where as Bourdieu anticipates there exists little nonsense about "formal distance" and "aesthetic control" and "ironic detachment" and the like. Nor any woo-woo noises at all about the retro elegance of beehive.

I'm not just spinning out possible allegorical readings only to make fun of them, however. For while such allegory is forced, there are good reasons to register some sense of existing ensembles of connection between what the *Handbook* is describing about cosmetology and its related fields and the issues surrounding

126   *Evan Watkins*

the confluence of economics and aesthetics. As I mentioned a moment ago, cosmetology is about beauty, about money, about education, and about State control of licensing procedures. It's also about a still very gendered division of labor as it affects that constellation of beauty, money, education, and the State. Thus, it seems to me to afford, if not exactly an occasion for leaping immediately to an allegorical frame of interpretation, an angle of entry into the themes of this volume that is worth pursuing further, perhaps even a privileged angle of entry.

State censorship and State funding of the arts, for example, raise obvious issues of power and money in relation to aesthetic value. In another register, questions about the borrowing of an ersatz economic terminology to supply an ostensible materialist ground for cultural analysis, or about how in the world economists get Nobel prizes for recognizing that people don't always make economic decisions rationally, or whatever, also raise crucial issues of power relations. But I take it as one of Foucault's most enduring lessons that one can often learn the most about organizing lines of power within a social formation not by direct approach to what seems an obvious fulcrum of power, but rather by exploring those often so visible as to be overlooked sectors which nevertheless etch distinguishing features clearly into prominence.

In this context, think again about the *Handbook* outline of qualifications for the job of cosmetologist: "finger dexterity," "a sense of form and artistry," "people skills," and "business skills." All must be evident not only in the tests for licensing, but, as the *Handbook* emphasizes, in a continuing process of lifelong education if you will, where what Foucault famously called "governmentality" is strung out along and instantiated within a remarkable series of everyday encounters and interactions in countless numbers of lives, from licensing to taxation policies. In other words, voc ed as I want to explore it here can function as a kind of trace line for following out the configurations of exchange systems that define the working relationships of work in the midst of the everyday selling of beauty.

I mentioned earlier that voc ed has changed considerably over the years, and one of those changes seems to me to have a particular significance for this chapter. The tracking system that many of us might still remember from high school, which divided eventual voc ed participants from college prep students, had its origins very early in the 20th century, most notoriously in the so-called "dual track" theorizing of Charles Prosser (1925). Unlike his near contemporary John Dewey, for example, who advocated some form of vocational training for everyone, Prosser felt it necessary to clearly separate an "academic track" from the vocational training suitable for the majority of students. In Prosser's view, for that vast majority "work" had to be understood as a horizon of necessity that defined their lives. Voc ed students had to learn to adjust their expectations to the levels of actually available jobs, and they had to learn "as habit," Prosser emphasized, both the mental motions and the physical behaviors associated with particular jobs. Work was a necessity, and voc ed was about the daily preparation necessary to accommodate oneself to the world of work.

The particularly significant change I indicated above, however, began roughly with the Career Education movement of the 1970s. By the seventies obviously, both

How aesthetics and economics met in voc ed   127

working conditions and cultural conditions had altered almost beyond recognition from the teens and early twenties when Prosser was formulating his ideas. If it seems fair to summarize that, for Prosser and others voc ed had been a way to constitute a working class for an industrial economy, by the seventies arguably vocational training and certification had become a middle class phenomenon. Even today, with all the statistics about the burgeoning numbers of students entering four-year colleges and universities, it remains the case that slightly less than 25% of any given high school graduating class actually *finish* a four-year degree. For most people most of the time some form of vocational certification, often job required, becomes the last level of educational attainment they achieve. Certainly by the seventies voc ed, by whatever name, was a familiar feature of a putatively middle class range of values and expectations.

At the same time of course, the cultural pressures to get a college degree, with the presumed level of pay and social prestige that came with it in the working world, were already accelerating exponentially. Students who might eventually find themselves in a job situation that would require, let's say, a certificate of competence in doing plasma diffusion for electric etching nevertheless at some earlier point in their lives were likely to have imagined themselves with a college degree in some "upper management" position, however vaguely defined. By the seventies, in other words, the clash between culturally induced pressures on career expectations on the one hand, and vocational education as Prosser's vision of having to accommodate oneself to work as an imposed realm of necessity on the other, had reached a visible pitch of intensity. These, broadly, were the circumstances on which the Career Education movement impinged.

At the theoretical level, for example in the work of Donald Super and John Holland, the Career Education movement involved a profound shift in emphasis from Prosser's instrumental psychology of adapting students to available jobs to the questions of why people choose certain careers in the first place and how they advance (or not) in their chosen direction. The emphasis on a student-centered "total psychology" of motivation and choice seemed much more in accord with the deeply individualistic assumptions of a middle class culture. But far more significantly, it displaced attention away from what had come to seem the top down imposition of specific "habits" of thinking that had occupied most of Prosser's attention. Not only could students be encouraged instead to "think for themselves." Thinking *about* oneself emerged as a crucial imperative in the educational pursuit of an eventual career. That is, the theoretical attention to student psychology in practice flowed over into a refocusing of students' attention on their own interests and capabilities. As vocational training, career education in effect promised a curriculum of self-inquiry.

What interests me particularly, however, in this emphasis on career choice and motivation is the larger and in the seventies still largely implicit shift from conceiving of work as an horizon of necessity as Prosser had imagined it to instead conceiving of work as a realm of freedom where one examined the array of possible options and chose what best accommodated one's desires. In other words, speaking very crudely and schematically here, within the terms of vocational training it

128   *Evan Watkins*

became possible to regard the labor market as remarkably similar to the consumer market of goods and services. At some level, the shift in vocational training initiated by the Career Education movement also marked the emergence of what might be called the consumption of work. I don't mean to imply that the choice of work and career would appear in exactly the same terms as a consumer choice of available toothpaste brands or bedroom suites. Nevertheless, it seems to me impossible to imagine all the current rhetoric of encouraging students to "invest" themselves in their education in hopes of realizing a big-time job payoff, let alone the now almost universal pressures in our culture to get into a good college as a means to that end, without recognizing how behind that rhetoric and those pressures lies the assumption of vocational preparation as in effect consumer training to make good individual choices in a marketplace consumption of work options for the future.

I've of course drastically foreshortened a long and complicated history of vocational education in order to arrive at this point of thinking about voc ed training as involved with the consumption of work. Because it's as we begin to imagine the consumption of work as a distinct and emergent social process that we can return once again to careers like cosmetology and the questions they raise about the role of aesthetics and images of beauty in the daily world of work. As any number of cultural studies theorists for example might remind us, consumption always seems driven by desire, and desire configured in terms of one of the most familiar of current psychoanalytical narratives as lack. That is, crudely, it's assumed that in order to expand consumer culture must continually encourage feelings of lack that can seem to be realized in the purchase and use of an always-proliferating array of consumer goods and services. This is a narrative that offers a relatively easy explanation for the process of what I've called the consumption of work. Rather than Prosser's realm of necessity, in effect the labor market itself has been recreated as if like the world of consumption it offered worker-consumers a fabulous range of choices for the eventual fulfillment of desire as lack.

Further, the labor market understood in this way would help to explain both the persistent feelings of worker dissatisfaction with their jobs and perhaps more importantly the apparent acceptance of job mobility and even temp work over long term job stability. In a current world, that is, where workers on average change jobs every 3.5 years, the process of consuming work seems to make an immediate sense. Like the consumer world where the current purchase is never enough, where it acts instead simply as a spur to seek further purchases, one's current job too might well appear in this light as never really a source for satisfaction. Workers would constantly be on the lookout for something better, something truly able to fulfill their hopes and ambitions. I don't want to suggest in this context that cosmetologists and other beauty operators are in contrast never openly dissatisfied or never yearn for "better" jobs and working conditions. Nevertheless, it does seem to me that cosmetology and related fields offer a means to complicate this largely psychoanalytic account of work as consumption.

Cultural images of beauty, and of fashion generally, seem an obvious example of desire-as-lack driven consumption. Yet cosmetologists are also beauty workers

How aesthetics and economics met in voc ed 129

as it were, engaged in the production of beauty and encouraged by virtue of their training to understand their work as among other things the expression of their own talents and abilities. As even the *Handbook*'s staid language recognizes, the most successful cosmetologists must at the same time understand their work as an active collaboration with their patrons who supply not only much of the raw material of the work as it were, but also a wide range of ideas and assumptions about the outcome. In this context, in other words, work as consumption is simultaneously consumption *as work*, an active and collaborative process.

Consumption as work in this sense is not quite so easy to explain in the familiar psychoanalytical terms of desire as lack. There are of course alternative narratives of desire; feminist reinterpretations of both Freud and Lacan for example have done much to reveal the masculine assumptions coded into such a narrative. But I want to turn attention away from these debates about desire for a moment in order to consider instead the role of value, specifically aesthetic value, in this ensemble of relations marked out by the process of consumption as work. I said at the beginning that cosmetology offers one everyday example of direct exchange between money and beauty, but of course it's not really quite that simple. The beauty shop patron also pays for work, and for particular talents, skills, and knowledges. Further, the aesthetic image at issue in fact functions in a quite complex transaction which as the *Handbook* reminds us implicates nothing less than the apparatus of the State itself by way of licensing procedures, taxation, accreditation for training institutions, and so on.

In larger terms, an attention to this complexity at issue helps to raise another kind of question about what I've noted as the shift in vocational education training that began with the Career Education movement. Prosser's vision of voc ed had an obvious utility relative to the conditions of a burgeoning industrial economy. Much of the large-scale production of durable goods for example involved jobs that were highly routinized and "deskilled." Thus Prosser's attention to the instrumental psychological conditioning that would adapt students to these kind of jobs makes a certain amount of sense. Voc ed training had to emphasize such psychological conditioning even more than actual job-specific skills. In contrast, however, it's far from clear how the kind of reform initiatives that date back to the Career Education movement could be imagined as having a similar utility in the contemporary conditions of the economy.

I've suggested that a career education emphasis on individual motivations and desires seemed much more in line with largely middle class expectations than Prosser's top-down discipline of accommodation. Likewise, the idea of the consumption of work seems to me a convenient shorthand formula for a wide range of reform initiatives through the eighties and nineties that continued to build on the efforts of those who had been involved with career education planning. But while this recognition helps to explain the shifting assumptions of vocational training with respect to an educational clientele of students and their parents, it doesn't yet help much to understand the utility of such training for the economic and political interests at stake in the educational process, from would-be employers to government policy makers. If, crudely, Prosser's vision of voc ed could be seen

130   *Evan Watkins*

as serving well the economics of advanced industrialization, how exactly would today's economic and political interests be served by in effect turning would-be workers into consumer-desiring machines?

I would argue that the aesthetics of cosmetology and related fields supplies one plausible kind of answer. For in these fields, as I argued above, I think it is clear that the consumption of work also and at the same time involves a certain form of the work of consumption. If one then asks, however, what exactly is worked *on* in this cosmetological process, then it seems to me we might twist yet another familiar formula into a significant indicator of what's at stake. Beauty shop patrons and operators typically see the outcome of the process as an expression, respectively, of an image of beauty and of a particular set of skills, talents, and abilities. But ultimately what is worked on in the process to achieve this outcome is nothing less than the subject, the self. That is, the process is also a process of subject formation that implicates both operator and patron insofar as both are collaboratively engaged in reaching an outcome. Thus rather than an aesthetics of self-expression, it might be better to invert this familiar formula to think instead in terms of the process as something like the expressive formation of the aesthetic self or the subject as aesthetic.

The key of course is to remember that this is a *working* subject no less than a consuming subject. For rather than simply a consumer-desiring machine, both operator and patron, again, understand their engagement in the process as a form of work. Further, as I emphasized earlier, the aesthetics of the process are indeed of interest to the State. Licensing exams, for example, are designed to measure among other things the "artistic abilities" of the would-be operator, and shop transactions are governed by tax regulations. Perhaps more to the immediate point, we can see in the process as a whole—from cosmetology training to the shop exchange of money—something that seems to me every bit as much a process of subject formation as that involved in Prosser's early vision of the formation of an industrial working class in vocational education. Of course it's a different subject, and a different self altogether; the student-subject as aesthetic didn't exactly figure much in Prosser's thinking. But it does seem to me plausible to suggest that on a much larger scale the figure of the worker as "aesthetic self" might well have as much real utility for today's range of economic interests as Prosser's vision had for the largely industrial economy of the twenties and thirties.

In the large institutional structures on which Foucault focused our attention, the "discipline" at issue became over time more and more a matter of *self*-management rather than a continual forced imposition of top-down imperatives. Discipline occurred, as it were, to the extent subjects both interiorized normative regularities and learned to think of those regularities as generated "from within." Thus perhaps needless to say, much recent critique in cultural studies and other fields influenced by Foucault, even at the risk of a rather facile simplification of Foucauldian analysis, has concentrated on revealing the illusory characteristics of a process by which structural regularities could appear as if highly individualized desires intrinsic to specific subjects.

How aesthetics and economics met in voc ed   131

Because it now exists at a convenient historical remove, a Prosserized vision of vocational education can now also offer a crude and starkly dramatic instance of such a process. The "best" voc ed students were those who most thoroughly assimilated a "reasonable" set of expectations about their eventual jobs and largely "took responsibility" for their training in accordance with norms that had come to seem a matter of their own deepest desires. Never mind that "from the outside" it might appear obvious enough that such desires were marvelously coincident with the economic imperatives of a burgeoning industrialization.

But contrast for a moment the kind of worker Prosser imagined as the "ideal" voc ed graduate with this passage from editors Lauren Reznick and John Wirt explaining in their introduction to a recent collection of essays, entitled *Linking School and Work: Roles for Standards and Assessment* (1996), the large scale changes they foresee for vocational education in relation to the emergence of a postindustrial economy: "For the first time since the industrial revolution, the demands being made on the educational system from the perspectives of economic productivity, of democratic citizenship, and of personal fulfillment are convergent. Today's high-performance workplace calls for essentially the same kind of person that Horace Mann and John Dewey sought: someone able to analyze a situation, make reasoned judgments, communicate well, engage with others and reason through differences of opinion, and intelligently employ the complex tools and technologies that can liberate or enslave according to use. What is more, the new workplace calls for people who can learn new skills and knowledge as conditions change–lifetime learners, in short. This is, as a result, a moment of extraordinary opportunity in which business, labor, and educational leaders can set a new, common course in which preparation for work and preparation for civic and personal life need no longer be in competition" (10).

The emphasis on the need for workers to be engaged in a lifelong process of education, the emphasis on flexible skills and abilities, and so on, has a clear echo in the *Handbook* language describing cosmetologists specifically. But more importantly, it seems to me the figure of the ideal worker they describe, the subject or self ideally formed to be a worker in today's economy, also arguably has a certain *aesthetic* value and integrity. This is not a worker driven by the contradiction between the rights and responsibilities of citizenship with its putative equality on the one hand, and the obviously unequal and often invidious hierarchies of the working world on the other. This is not a worker who has had to accommodate her or his desires to the routine demands of the available jobs Prosser envisioned. It's not even a worker who might find the job unpleasant or distasteful while still gaining some satisfaction from the knowledge that it's essential at some level to the ongoing productivity of the economy. This is a worker imaged to take a real satisfaction from the very everyday processes and practices of work—the worker as also satisfied consumer of the work she or he does in effect. It's a worker formed in and through the expression of the self as a kind of aesthetic value, and the work is an expression of this aesthetic self-formation.

One must of course contrast this visionary language of Reznick and Wirt to the realities of the actual jobs many people hold in today's labor conditions.

132   *Evan Watkins*

But vocational education training has never been merely about the teaching of whatever job-specific skills. From Prosser's time onward, it's always also been about the formation of worker-subjects. One could of course argue at length whether today's students are really "duped" to a greater or lesser degree by a Reznick–Wirt imaginary than voc ed students in the past were deceived by the promises implicit in Prosser's form of training. But the more immediate issue seems to me less a matter of demystifying false promises than of tracing the utility of such promises in the first place.

Cosmetology again offers a good clue, to the extent that the work largely takes place in a vast number of small shops that often differ dramatically in any number of ways, rather than concentrating large masses of workers in immense institutional structures. At the same time, however, the manufacture and distribution of tools, technologies, and chemical solutions; the intricate publicity circuits of an immense fashion industry; the organization of time intervening in millions of lives; the administration of state licensing examinations, and so on, together offers an image grid of interlocking spheres of commerce that staggers the imagination with its sheer size and volume. And, of course, its remarkable volatilities at any given point of contact between beauty shop operator and patron. It's an image in other words that focuses together a certain maximum of social saturation and spread with an equally maximal intensity of focus on individual encounters, with the whole accelerated into a seemingly perpetual and dizzying motion that is nevertheless as "everyday" as emerging from a shop with a good do.

This is the moment when it becomes possible to recognize with a little more clarity perhaps the doubled value of a certain aesthetics of self and self-formation. For the everydayness of these daily beauty shop encounters is grounded in the "beauty" of the produced self as a kind of still point in the midst of all this swirling complexity. Aesthetic value, that is, lies not only in the perceived beauty that results from the process of work as consumption that has taken place, but also and importantly in the simultaneous presence of that beauty to all the social sectors that in effect have co-operated in the result. "Still point" is then perhaps an inadequate metaphor for a presence of aesthetic value as the self that is "everywhere" as well as "everyday." There's after all nothing "still" about that everywhere/everyday. It's not a hidden center or invisible presence somehow radiating through the whole, but a presence whose presentness is coterminous with all the swirling motion of continually intersecting vectors. The doubling of aesthetic value in other words is possible only insofar as motility is instantiated in the beauty of the result itself changing daily. Motion is all, and the aesthetics of this processual self is the means by which you're always there *because* and not despite the sense in which there's no there there, no stable center to organize this perpetual motion.

Thus the secret of that State licensing exam process described in the *Handbook* where the ostensible goal is the regulation of beauty shop operators, the necessary submission of subjects to a standardized State initiated examination, is that regulation in this sense nevertheless has become redundant in these circumstances. For what the exam produces is not really a relentless parsing of failures from successes among those who submit to the exam, but rather the necessary conditions

How aesthetics and economics met in voc ed   133

for the continued proliferation of aesthetic value. The failures are merely a by-product, which in fact can nearly always be "re-tooled" to succeed in the next performance. Indeed, it is the language of re-tooling that allows this relatively restricted process of State exam administration to join the much larger process of vocational education reform initiatives in general, dedicated precisely to the re-tooling of a U.S. workforce to meet the needs of a 21st-century economy. As I suggested earlier, the tracking mechanisms that had played such a crucial part in the early history of voc ed have largely disappeared in these current reforms. For like the regulatory power of the cosmetology licensing exam, their controlling power to divide success from failure has become redundant. Motion is all, and the ceaseless repetition of always varied performances serves instead to augment the continual production of an endlessly flexible workforce. This takes place, I would add, under the sign of an aesthetics of the self always under formation. The doubling of aesthetic value in consumption as work is also the work of consumption necessary to build the economics of laboring selves in this putatively new 21st-century economy.

The State mandated licensing exam specifically for cosmetologists, however, is a reminder that the State has hardly disappeared or been allowed to "wither away" in a so-called privatization of this economy with its proliferating educational institutions and avenues of training. For if in the register I was describing above it is the aesthetics of a self coterminous with a swirling multiplicity of intersecting social vectors, that register must now be re-inflected as it were to imagine a State that is no less effectively everywhere. Not because it seems to have been inserted into every corner and recess of everyday life, but because that very everydayness, like the good, do from the beauty shop, is constitutively threaded with and through the motility of the State.

That cosmetology specifically, however, yet remains in some sense a deeply gendered image of beauty, of work, and of daily practices must also function as another kind of reminder altogether. So far from being a residual carryover from the terrible rigidities of a hierarchical past, the gendered demographics of beauty shop labor open into a realization of the lump sum accounting of value added so necessary to an aestheticized economy of the working self. What is at stake in such accounting is less the regulation of identity as worker marked by gender or class or racial characteristics than the acceleration of social processes that feed on the waste of identities. Motion is all, and the idea of a "lifelong education" so crucial to both cosmetology in particular and vocational education reform in general suggests how in that continual acceleration of motion identities must always be made and re-made, or "re-tooled," over and over in the course of daily experience even.

It should then be possible to recognize that the process of an aesthetic self-formation I've been describing is also the process of an *educational* self-formation. The aesthetics of self can be sustained in motion only insofar as it is an aesthetics that is also and everywhere educational. For a lifetime. Or, to neatly double the terms in this circumstance, an ideal of aesthetic education that at one point had seemed carefully restricted to a high level university curriculum has now mutated

134   *Evan Watkins*

into a common element throughout the vast multiplicity and range of job training programs of all sorts. I don't mean to imply by such a formulation that, for example, the process of learning CNC routing has somehow come to acquire an "aesthetic" dimension over and above the mechanics of acquiring the necessary skills for the job. Rather, the surplus or value added of the aesthetic has as its subject precisely the subject who does the work. The cosmetologist who in collaboration with the patron engages in this daily process of beautiful working-subject formation can then also serve as a shorthand metonymy for a whole range of educational processes producing aestheticized worker-subjects.

It's no secret that there has been a remarkable chorus of criticism over the last ten years or so regarding the so-called "vocationalizing" of the university, the reduction of "higher" education to the flatline imperatives of the marketplace at the expense, for example, of the training for citizenship ideally informing educational goals. It is a remarkable chorus because it can be heard across a complex ideological spectrum including "left" critics like Stanley Aronowitz and Henry Giroux no less than conservative critics like Allan Bloom. I don't want to minimize the ideological distinctions that inflect these critiques toward quite differently imagined outcomes. Nevertheless, the targeting of marketplace vocational imperatives is surprisingly uniform, and it's in this context that I want to argue in contrast for the recognition of a kind of "universitizing" if you will of vocation and job.

The universitizing not only takes the obvious form of all those manifold pressures to go to college, get a four-year degree, and so on. Equally important, as I implied above, it occurs in and through the aesthetics of worker self-formation no longer by any means restricted to the "aesthetic education" formerly available only in upper level university humanities curricula. In larger terms what this implies is that so-called marketplace imperatives are themselves *already* universitized. Rather than impinging from the outside to deform the realization of idealized educational goals such as the training of an informed democratic citizenry, the imperatives of the labor market in particular have dramatically reconstructed the relations of "inside" and "outside" the university. Like now residual forms of identity politics, the attempt to hold the line against any further reductive vocationalizing of higher education can only waste itself continually against an adversary who simply refuses to stand still and fight. To borrow completely out of context a phrase (perhaps unkindly, as he was himself a late product of an aestheticized education in the extreme) from the late R. P. Blackmur (1967), resistance becomes "a struggle in marmalade," as sticky as it is unsatisfying.

Which is not quite the same, however, as foreclosing on any possibility of collective political action altogether. The incommensurables that mark the accelerated motions of worker-subject formation after all continue to bear, as everywhere in the training of cosmetologists, the visible indicators of social processes of economic *class* divisions in the very motor force of an accelerated economics of work. I know of no emergent aesthetic calculus of value that has as yet succeeded in harmonizing the *direction* of political force exerted in the everyday of production. If perhaps the heavy stabilities of embedded resistances can no longer impede the flow channels of accelerated motion, nevertheless there

How aesthetics and economics met in voc ed   135

remains every reason to think that the invention of new collectivities of political action might yet turn that motor force into an effective politics of counterdirection that will no longer afford the respite of the aesthetic.

For the proliferation and doubling of aesthetic value as its circuits are enlarged from a specific and highly restrictive form of university education to the multiple sectors of newly imagined vocational training also and for the same reasons results in a persistent process of *devaluing* as well. Universitizing in other words must devalue in order to proliferate, in a by now familiar interchange whereby the condition of scarcity necessary to the realization of aesthetic value cannot endure the doubling or valorization of that value beyond itself. Thus what appears in a psychoanalytic frame as the "lack" that functions as the motor force of desire might better be understood in this context as a second order devaluing produced within a process of aesthetic formation rather than simply the hollowing out of lack that continually accelerates its motions.

Or to put it still another way toward the end of a polemical conclusion, *beauty becomes a class process* occurring across the dividing line of conditions of scarcity—directly as jobs and economic resources no less than through the elliptical motions of cultural distinction. We hear daily that class processes are now difficult if not impossible to discern in an economic order where accelerated shifts of social positioning seem the norm rather than an anomaly and where representatives of formerly excluded groups now serve in the President's Cabinet as trusted advisors. I take this to mean, however, that we must learn to look into those motors of acceleration rather than continuing to peer behind them in order to locate some hidden, stable, hierarchical indices of inclusion and exclusion. "Devaluing" after all is only a kind of shorthand for what otherwise can be recognized as indeed a fundamental class process of exploitation, and one that takes place within rather than exogenous to the conditions accelerating the production of the labor of a new economy.

Class processes in other words can no longer be imagined as if a kind of hidden, stubborn reality behind the appearance of a continually shifting, unstable social order. The motility implied by an emphasis on class *processes* must be understood at least literally enough to recognize, again, the inherence of an exploitative devaluing within the constitutive conditions of a 21st-century production of labor power. Cosmetology—and indeed vocational education reform in general—is by no means the only angle of entry into this refocusing of attention on class. But just as vocational education early in the century must open directly onto an analysis of industrial working class formation, there seems to me good reason to think that current reform initiatives offer an equally useful means for grasping how a now nearly ubiquitous middle classing of U.S. labor everywhere depends on a simultaneous devaluative process of working classing that labor. Within this context the beauty in motion produced by cosmetology thus limns the larger contours of an aestheticizing of worker-self formation that, in a familiar Marxian formulation, carries its own contradictory force into the accelerated motions of the social field. Motion is all, but only in that fabulous aesthetics of the moment appearing to recede forever into the past even as the future closes down somewhere

136 *Evan Watkins*

else than where one didn't leave quite quickly enough. Beyond resentment or some apocalyptic hope for a return of the repressed, the work of class politics begins in the refusal to foreclose a future for so many.

References

Blackmur, R. P. 1967. *A Primer of Ignorance*, ed. Joseph Frank. New York: Harcourt.

Bourdieu, Pierre. 1984. *Distinction: A Social Critique of the Judgment of Taste.* Cambridge: Harvard University Press.

Occupational Outlook Handbook, 1998–1999 Edition. Indianapolis: JIST Works, Inc., 1998.

Prosser, Charles. 1925. *Vocational Education in a Democracy*. New York: The Century.

Reznick, Lauren and John Wirt, eds. 1996. *Linking School and Work: Roles for Standards and Assessment.* San Francisco: Jossey-Bass.

7 Economics meets esthetics in the Bloomsbury Group*

Craufurd D. Goodwin

The Bloomsbury Group was a collection of friends who enjoyed each other's company and conversation and interacted and collaborated in various ways over more than half a century. The core members were the artists Vanessa Bell, Dora Carrington, Roger Fry, and Duncan Grant, the art critic Clive Bell, the theatre critic Desmond McCarthy, the novelists E. M. Forster, Virginia Woolf, and David Garnett, the historian and biographer Lytton Strachey, the political theorist Leonard Woolf, and the economist John Maynard Keynes. Despite their frequent disclaimers to the contrary, it does seem possible to discern a coherent "Bloomsbury view" on many important subjects, including the relations of esthetics to economics.

Roger Fry was the member of the Group most committed to a search for a theory of value in the arts. He was trained in science (double first in natural science at Cambridge) and he remained devoted to the scientific method. The distinguished scientist Karl Pearson was a fellow of Kings when Fry was a star science student at the college, and Pearson's *Manual of Science* may have been mentally at Fry's side throughout his career. He seemed always to be engaged in theoretical speculation of some kind to organize his thoughts on a subject. He reflected in 1920 that: "A certain scientific curiosity and a desire for comprehension have impelled me at every stage to make generalizations, to attempt some kind of logical co-ordination of my impressions ..." (Fry, 1909 and 1920, in Goodwin, 1998, 86). Fry was often teased by the other Bloomsburys for the force of his arguments. Quentin Bell, son of Clive and Vanessa, reminisced: "Up to a point Roger Fry's arguments were fair enough, but at a certain time a mixture of charm and what, for want of a better word, I would call 'overwhelmingness' would clinch the victory" (Quentin Bell, [1968] 1990, 108). Nevertheless, all the Bloomsburys treated Fry's views with the greatest respect, and on the subject of esthetic value he was for them the acknowledged authority and their spokesman. They followed Fry in finding that what happens in art markets is fundamentally different from what happens in markets for other goods and services. They constructed a new body of theory for the production and exchange of art and they drew policy implications from this theory.

Fry never provided a single list of thinkers that influenced him most in his attempts to explain the valuation of art. His wide experience in the art world as journalist and all-purpose intellectual exposed him to a broad range of sources.

138   *Craufurd D. Goodwin*

Nor did he ever set forth a definitive body of theory to which he subscribed. Indeed, he insisted that "I have always looked on my system with a certain suspicion. I have recognised that if it ever formed too solid a crust it might stop the inlets of fresh experience ..." (Fry, 1909 and 1920, in Goodwin, 1998, 86).

Fry's most important proposal, set forth first in his "Essay in Aesthetics" (1909) and republished in his first collection of essays *Vision and Design* (1920, in Goodwin, 1998), was that there is a natural division of human affairs into two parts: the "actual life" and the "imaginative life." Sometimes he made a further division of the actual life into an additional two parts, the "biological life" and the "emulative life," for a total of three parts. The biological life, he argued, was governed mainly by instinct and by stimuli that had been honed by evolution to make sure that there was adequate attention devoted to food, shelter, personal safety, procreation etc. Fry was happy to concede explanation in the biological life to the principle of natural selection. The Bloomsburys were far from denigrating the biological life; indeed they rejoiced in it. E. M. Forster wrote: "I believe in aristocracy, though—if that is the right word, and if a democrat may use it. Not an aristocracy of power, based upon rank and influence, but an aristocracy of the sensitive, the considerate and the plucky. ... I am against asceticism myself. I am with the old Scotsman who wanted less chastity and more delicacy. I do not feel that my aristocrats are a real aristocracy if they thwart their bodies, since bodies are the instruments through which we register and enjoy the world" (Forster, 1972, 70–1). But the Bloomsburys concluded that, absent wars and a population explosion, the needs of the biological life would be taken care of very nicely through normal economic growth in a market economy. Sooner or later production would increase to take care of all legitimate biological needs and would be distributed reasonably through the price system. In the judgment of Keynes, the authority on such matters in the Group, "the economic problem," meaning the biological problem, "*may be solved, or be at least within sight of solution, within a hundred years. This means that the economic problem is not—if we look into the future—the permanent problem of the human race*" (Keynes, [1931] 1972, 326). By implication, the "permanent problem" was with the imaginative life. Valuation in the biological life, the Bloomsburys conceded, could be understood adequately through utilitarian principles. There humans responded nicely to calculations of pleasure and pain, and market prices reflected these universal forces. Keynes, of course, knew well the literature of economics where these ideas were developed, and most of the others at least knew John Stuart Mill's works, and they were acquainted, through Cambridge, with Alfred Marshall (Fry even painted the portrait of Mary Paley Marshall, Alfred's wife, that hangs in the Marshall Library).

For an understanding of valuation in the emulative life, Fry and the Bloomsburys turned mainly to Thorstein Veblen, whom Fry may have discovered first during his years as curator at the Metropolitan Museum in New York. It appears that, like Veblen, they found the instinct of emulation to be universal among humans. Fry wrote that through one device or another each human "wishes to express to the outside world that sense of his own importance of which he has continually to remind other people" (Fry, 1926, in Goodwin, 1998, 111). But the Bloomsburys

Economics meets esthetics in the Bloomsbury Group   139

were less cynical than Veblen and more prescriptive about what might be done to make the best of these inevitable characteristics of humankind. They accepted that to be human was to be emulative and, although they agreed that there was need to restrain the waste that is implicit in emulative behavior, they thought it was possible in part to channel emulative instincts into constructive action.

It was in the imaginative life where the things that mattered most to the Bloomsburys took place: art, literature, music, science—activities that they described collectively as "civilization." But what determined the amount of these things produced and the values ascribed to them in society? They concluded that for the most part production and value were socially determined through accidents of history that might be described today as "path dependency." No one could predict the progress of civilization from any timeless equilibrium model. Indeed, a distinctive feature of activities in the imaginative life, Fry argued, was that they did not elicit instinctive responses as did goods in the biological and emulative lives. The precise nature of the response produced in humans by the products of civilization was, in fact, a primary puzzle. The greatest inspiration Fry received on this point came from Leo Tolstoy's essay *What is Art?*. Tolstoy argued that true art was not about "beauty" in the conventional sense but about "esthetic emotion" communicated from artist to audience. But what exactly was this emotion? Fry rejected Tolstoy's claim, made earlier also by Ruskin, that true art implied a deeply moral, or even religious, message. Fry argued that this was confusing the biological life with the imaginative life. "Art, then, is an expression and a stimulus of this imaginative life, which is separated from actual life by the absence of responsive action. Now this responsive action implies in actual life moral responsibility. In art we have no such moral responsibility—it presents a life freed from the binding necessities of our actual existence" (Fry, 1909 and 1920, in Goodwin, 1998, 75).

The strength of Fry's case for a distinctive treatment of valuation in the imaginative life depended on there being a demonstrable difference from value in the actual life. For this he appealed first to introspection and the common consensus, "for most people would, I think, say that the pleasures derived from art were of an altogether different character and more fundamental than merely sensual pleasures, that they did exercise some faculties which are felt to belong to whatever part of us there may be which is not entirely ephemeral and material" (76). For Fry, it seems, the distinctive personal and psychological experience of artists and esthetically sensitive consumers of art was a form of verification of his hypothesis of a tripartite division of human experience. Fry said that the effect of a rich imaginative life on society was salutary even if the content of the art was not specifically moral: "do we not feel that the average business man would be in every way a more admirable, more respectable being if his imaginative life were not so squalid and incoherent? ... this desirability of the imaginative life does distinguish it very sharply from actual life, and is the direct result of that first fundamental difference, its freedom from necessary external conditions. Art, then, is, if I am right, the chief organ of the imaginative life; it is by art that it is stimulated and controlled within us, and, as we have seen, the imaginative life is distinguished

140   *Craufurd D. Goodwin*

by the greater clearness of its perception, and the greater purity and freedom of its emotion" (77).

What were the characteristics of works of art that distinguished them from goods in the actual life? Fry continued: "If, then, an object of any kind is created by man not for use, for its fitness to actual life, but as an object of art, an object subserving the imaginative life, what will its qualities be? It must in the first place be adapted to that disinterested intensity of contemplation, which we have found to be the effect of cutting off the responsive action. It must be suited to that heightened power of perception which we found to result therefrom" (80). For further guidance on this question Fry turned to the young discipline of psychology, and he found there that "the first quality that we demand in our sensations will be order, without which our sensations will be troubled and perplexed, and the other quality will be variety, without which they will not be fully stimulated" (80). These were ideas that he may have taken from the eighteenth-century art critic Roger de Piles. While living in New York Fry traveled to Cambridge to talk at Harvard with the economics-trained psychologist Denman Ross, and he was intrigued by Ross's finding that "a composition is of value in proportion to the number of orderly connections which it displays" (81). He found that "the artist passes from the stage of merely gratifying our demand for sensuous order and variety to that where he arouses our emotions" by attending to the "emotional elements of design": rhythm, mass, space, light and shade, and color (82). These elements became the basis of the Bloomsbury "formalist" esthetics.

Fry was never satisfied that he had adequately understood or fully explained what took place in the imaginative life. He played a little with Tolstoy's suggestion that there might be an analogy to the transmission of infection in disease. He read Freud but rejected Freud's attempt to explain "the whole nature of the artist in a small pamphlet" (Fry, 1939, 3 and Fry, [1924] 1928). Fry was intrigued by the new device of the radio, and he speculated that the artist might be visualized as the transmitter and the audience as the receiver. Fry was sometimes criticized for the vagueness of his notions, most notably by the dyspeptic literary critic I. A. Richards. Richards was particularly angry at the insistence by writers of Fry's ilk that morality was not an issue for true art. He wrote: "That these authorities are sadly incompetent is a minor disadvantage. Their blunderings are as a rule so ridiculous that the effects are brief" (Richards, 1924, 34). Richards also upheld the position with which most economists of the time would have felt comfortable, that activities in the arts are essentially similar to those elsewhere in human life: "they differ chiefly in the connections between their constituents ... our activity is not of a fundamentally different kind. To assume that it is, puts difficulties in the way of describing and explaining it, which are unnecessary and which no one has yet succeeded in overcoming" (16–17). Here was the essential objection to Bloomsbury attempts to modify economics through esthetics—that there was no such thing as the imaginative life; this objection could have come from contemporary economists as well as from a literary theorist, but it did not. Fry replied to Richards at length in his essay "Some Questions in Esthetics," published in his second collection of essays *Transformations* (1926). He argued

Economics meets esthetics in the Bloomsbury Group   141

in clarification of his position that "in all cases our reaction to works of art is a reaction to a relation and not to sensations or objects or persons or events. This, if I am right, affords a distinguishing mark of what I call esthetic experiences, esthetic reactions, or esthetic states of mind" (Fry, 1926, 3). Despite the series of examples he offered to make his point it is doubtful that Richards and Fry's other critics were mollified.

The Bloomsburys were convinced that valuation in the imaginative life could not be understood simply as response to utilitarian stimuli, coordinated through the market mechanism. The differences in the imaginative life from the biological and emulative lives were, to them, very important. On the supply side of the labor market in the imaginative life artists, writers, and scientists did not typically perceive their activities as onerous and a source of disutility that had to be compensated by utility derived from expenditures of income. Quite the contrary, they were driven to action by an irrepressible urge to communicate—something like Veblen's instinct of workmanship. Yet, at the same time, artists, writers, and scientists were human beings that had their own biological needs and emulative desires. These realities, they believed, had to be kept in mind and dealt with when attempting to understand, and form, policy within a society.

Most of the other Bloomsburys took Fry's lead and reflected from time to time on just how the imaginative life is fundamentally different from the biological life and requires, therefore, a different set of analytical constructs. E. M. Forster is a case in point. He too used Tolstoy's notion of art as infection to explain the phenomenon but he went on from there. Employing his own metaphors he examined the three distinct processes called by Fry vision, design, and transformation; the first two the almost mystical moments when an artist first experiences inspiration and converts this revelation into an artistic conception, and the third the process of transformation into a work of art. Forster mused as follows: "What about the creative state? In it a man is taken out of himself. He lets down as it were a bucket into his subconscious. And draws up something which is normally beyond his reach. He mixes this thing with his normal experiences, and out of the mixture he makes a work of art. It may be a good work of art or a bad one—we are not here examining the question of quality—but whether it is good or bad it will have been compounded in this unusual way, and he will wonder afterwards how he did it. Such seems to be the creative process. ... The creative state of mind is akin to a dream" (Forster, 1972, 111 and also 113; that Virginia Woolf too was reflecting on similar questions as early as 1909 can be seen in her essay "Art and Life," a review of a book with that title by Vernon Lee. Virginia Woolf, 1986, 277–80). The art historian Kenneth Clark, for whom Fry was something of a mentor, described the "moment of vision" as "one element of human experience which remains almost identical, in origin and effect, whether it is turned into poetry or into painting" (Clark, 1981, 1).

A short story entitled "The Other Side of the Hedge" by E. M. Forster is an allegory of some of the questions the Bloomsburys were exploring in their search for an explanation of esthetic value. Forster, who was always a mild skeptic in Bloomsbury, believed that, desirable as it might be, it was not easy for humanity

142 *Craufurd D. Goodwin*

to shift its emphasis from biological and emulative objectives to imaginative ones. Forster introduces a long distance runner who comes across as the quintessential utility-seeking economic man that lives only in the biological and emulative lives. In a foot-race that is surely a metaphor for life, this man outpaces his ill-disciplined brother who "wasted his breath on singing, and his strength on helping others." The runner appreciates that he "had traveled more wisely, and now it was only the monotony of the highway that oppressed me—dust under foot and brown crackling hedges on either side, ever since I could remember." The runner tires, lies down, and by chance crawls through the hedge next to the road, away from the race. There he finds himself in another world—in Roger Fry's imaginative life to be sure. "The blue sky was no longer a strip, and beneath it the earth had risen grandly into hills—clean bare buttresses, with beech trees in their folds, and meadows and clear pools at their feet." But the adjustment to these new sights was not easy for the runner, trained as he was to the habits and experiences of biological and emulative goods in the market economy. He exclaims: "I was bewildered at the waste in production, and murmured to myself, 'What does it all mean?' ... Every achievement is worthless unless it is a link in the chain of development." For the first time the runner becomes aware of the futility of emulative competition but experiences difficulty in discovering an alternative economic norm. "This is perfectly terrible. One cannot advance: one cannot progress ... Science and the spirit of emulation—those are the forces that made us what we are." The person who guides the runner through the new land [the imaginative life] regrets its under-population. "For our country fills up slowly, though it was meant for all mankind." The runner, despite the evident attractions of the imaginative life, continues to yearn for the old ways. "Give me life with its struggles and victories, with its failures and hatreds, with its deep moral meaning and its unknown goal!" Ultimately, relieved to be free of the tensions that were created by a brief exposure to the imaginative life, the runner decides to pass back through the hedge, away from the imaginative life and into the rat race once again of the biological and emulative activities on the road. There, at last, utility maximization provides once again a straight-forward guide to life. As he leaves, the gatekeeper of the land beyond the hedge observes: "This is where your road ends, and through this gate humanity—all that is left of it—will come in to us" (Forster, 1947, 39–48).

The nearest things to canonical works of Bloomsbury on precisely how value is determined in the imaginative life are Fry's "Essay in Aesthetics" and his *Art and Commerce* published by the Woolfs' Hogarth Press in 1926. On this topic of valuation in the arts there was substantial unanimity among the Bloomsburys and consistency over time. They conceived of an ideal art market system, somewhat analogous to the perfectly competitive markets of the neoclassical micro-economist; this ideal system, they thought, would yield results they desired for the imaginative life. There the demanders of works of art, literature, and science would purchase abundant and increasing quantities, inspired by the esthetic emotion communicated by artists and writers. Some of these art works would perish quickly; others would be accumulated as a kind of artistic capital. To the extent

Economics meets esthetics in the Bloomsbury Group 143

that a society with such a market system produced and accumulated art works as a substantial proportion of its total output it became "civilized." Here the genuine "esthete" determined both what art would ultimately be produced, and how much. Following Fry's account in his "Essay in Aesthetics" the Bloomsburys denied vociferously that the response to art by the esthete was a search for utility. Utility explained only an instinctive response in the biological life. Reception of esthetic emotion, by contrast, permitted the recipient to achieve an esthetic state of mind, something different in kind from the satisfaction of consumer wants. Confusion of the esthetic emotion with utility, they believed, led to serious misunderstanding of the imaginative life and to mistaken public policy. Keynes went so far as to say in 1938: "I do now regard that [the Benthamite tradition] as the worm which has been gnawing at the insides of modern civilisation and is responsible for its moral decay" (Keynes, 1949, 96). Theirs would be a market system on a higher plane than mere utility, with more exalted norms, and on a grander scale.

The success of any market system for the arts was not, however, automatic; it would depend on the market institutions that had emerged over time and on the social context in which they were embedded. On the supply side there was need for firms that could successfully channel the energies of those free spirits who are the artists and writers. On the demand side there had to be a sophisticated populace willing to pay for the education of the potential customers of the artist, and to tolerate these esthetically sensitive consumers. By implication, moreover, a market for products of the imaginative life sufficiently robust to sustain the numbers of artists and intellectuals required for civilization could exist only in societies where total output of goods and services was large enough to yield some surplus.

The Bloomsburys saw a number of challenges to sustaining a satisfactory set of market institutions for the arts, potential market failures as it were. The first was that the instinct of emulation would eat up the available surplus after the biological needs had been answered. Then, it might appear falsely that the society was too impoverished to afford an imaginative life. This was essentially the message delivered some decades earlier by Thorstein Veblen in *The Theory of the Leisure Class* (1899) and some decades later by John Kenneth Galbraith in *The Affluent Society* (1958). The second challenge was that much of the surplus could disappear into producer rents. This would occur in the arts with sudden shifts of fashion that caused the price of an artistic product to rise above the normal price, the price that permitted wage payments to the artist that covered their biological needs (a concept similar to the economist's minimum average cost). Sometimes shifts in fashion followed the discovery of a new and highly successful way of conveying esthetic emotion; at other times shifts in demand were simply speculative, when purchasers attempted to outguess the market. The deleterious effects of rent payments were two: first, effective demand was drained away from the wider artistic community to successful artists in the form of the producer rents (a term not used by Fry, even though the idea is clear); and second, some exceptionally creative artists were diverted into rent seeking and stultifying repetitive reproduction away from their dynamic and progressive careers. Thus, according to Fry, Guardi in search

144   *Craufurd D. Goodwin*

of rents had wasted a fine talent painting the same scenes of Venetian canals again and again for grand tourists, John Singer Sargent had frittered away his career on portraits of society ladies, and Gainsborough had been led into painting mainly the emulative prizes of the British aristocracy: their houses, their horses, their game parks, their wives, and their dogs.

The third potential market failure identified by Fry and the Bloomsburys was inadequacy of information. They believed that, in part at least, the capacity to receive esthetic emotion, and therefore even to recognize it, was an acquired art and subject to improvement. Since many demanders in the art markets did not have either the experience nor the time to develop fully their esthetic sense prior to a purchase they held back and were in need of guidance. A healthy market, therefore, required a community of sophisticated and responsible critics to guide purchasers. These critics could act like the financial advisors in capital markets and help the purchasers identify "fundamentals."

Because the Bloomsburys believed that something approaching an ideal art market had never in fact existed, and might never exist, rather than speculate very much about such a happy state they concluded they should attempt to understand better art market phenomena in the real world from a study of their surroundings and of history. There they discovered that even with market failures the arts and literature had prospered to a surprising degree in many times and places. They suggested two general explanations for this satisfactory condition. First, goods of the imaginative life had often been combined with, or had in effect piggybacked upon, other goods and activities in the biological and emulative lives of humans. Second, various institutions and classes of individuals had played unexpectedly important roles in advancing the arts. These roles required some explanation.

It was an article of faith with the Bloomsburys that the products of the imaginative life need not always have conventional forms: easel painting, for example, or novels with recognizable plots. They themselves experimented with everything from kinetic scrolls to streams of consciousness, and they were delighted to discover that they had had innumerable predecessors through time: for example armorers for primitive chieftains who had concealed their esthetic emotions on the shields of their patrons; and artists for the Medieval Church who had worked out an implicit pact with their sponsors that permitted them to communicate their emotion through the decoration of sacred objects so long as they avoided blasphemy. Fry observed that the hosts for art as it had hitch-hiked through history were typically a large category of decorative items that he called "opifacts"—"any object made by man for other purposes than the necessities of life" (Fry, 1926, in Goodwin, 1998, 112). These joint goods responded to some instinct in either the biological or emulative lives of humans but in some cases were constructed so that, incidentally, they could also transmit esthetic emotion. This combination of roles was not in Bloomsbury eyes in any way reprehensible. Indeed they thought it should be studied sympathetically and understood because it was likely to remain essential to sustain the imaginative life for some time to come. In fact, new variants of opifacts with artistic potential were always appearing. One that fascinated Fry in his own time was the advertising poster. Posters served the

Economics meets esthetics in the Bloomsbury Group   145

obvious practical purposes of conveying information and drumming up sales of whatever they displayed. But posters could also be works of fine art, as numerous art lovers have found in our own time. Other examples of opifacts with an esthetic dimension were ceramics intended for household use, and clothing that conveyed the emotion of the artist-designer. The problem of valuing separately the art embodied in such joint goods by the stealth artists was not addressed by the Bloomsburys.

Although a vision of a perfect art market shines through quite often in their writings, perhaps because they were so immersed in the day to day complexities of the markets in their own time they preferred to focus much more on the particularities of imperfections in these markets. But here too they generalized. They found that, over time, a few social groups, classes, and institutions had through their patronage on the demand side of the market been overwhelmingly important in the production and exchange of art. The only way to make sense of contemporary market phenomena, therefore, was to understand the market behavior and objectives of these actors. Through most of human history three had been especially critical: the monarchy, the aristocracy, and the church. In their extensive historical writings the Bloomsburys paid close attention to all three. But in the present day, they concluded, they had become largely irrelevant. They had lost their economic power and their market presence, and they had been replaced in the art market by new classes and new institutions. Three of the new ones, at least, deserved close study. The first Fry called "the snobbists," meaning those who purchased art not for its own sake but as speculators in anticipation of future gain. What distinguished a snobbist from a simple speculator in any market was that his intended gain was not in cash but in repute, meaning "exaltation in one way or another of his personal worth either in his own or still more in others' eyes" (Fry, 1926, in Goodwin, 1998, 113). Snobbists were likely to be nouveau riche, a quality nearly unknown before the industrial revolution. For his emulative life the snobbist looked for not only what was currently fashionable but for what was likely to become à la mode before long. The snobbist's demand, Fry found, was driven primarily by the instinct of emulation but it was not therefore necessarily worthless to society. It could assist in the progress of civilization so long as snobbists could be led to the purchase of genuine art and therefore support the genuine artist. If snobbists, perhaps through subtle direction and advice, purchased mainly genuine art and not other merely inconsequential opifacts their demands could be added to those of the genuine esthete and the purchaser of joint goods to sustain vigorous art markets.

The second social class, after the snobbists, that had gained a prominent place in contemporary art markets Fry called variously "the classicists" or "the plutocrats." These were the new men of great wealth, with many of whom the Bloomsburys had close relations: Pierpont Morgan, Isabella Stewart Gardner, Samuel Courtauld, and Lord Lever, to mention only some of the most prominent. These collectors bought the works only of highly reputable and fully certified dead artists. Like the snobbists in buying art they were making a public statement and seeking to gain repute. They did not trust their own taste and were by nature risk averse. Typically they insisted

146 *Craufurd D. Goodwin*

on scholarly approval of their prizes. Unlike Thorstein Veblen and the American muckrakers the Bloomsburys were not deeply cynical about or condemnatory of the plutocrats. Indeed, they saw them as welcome custodians of the artistic capital of society, and they observed that for the most part they performed this function rather well, especially when guided by such skilled consultants as the Bloomsburys themselves. Fry advised Mrs. Gardner and Pierpont Morgan, and participated in the cataloging of the great Lever collection (Fry, 1928). Fry and Keynes were instrumental in steering the Courtauld wealth toward the Courtauld Gallery and Courtauld Institute. Indeed, Fry, Keynes, and Clive Bell were among the first of their generation in the arts community to recognize and treat the plutocrats not as predators in the art market but as prized cash cows accessible to the private sector for the support of functions for which others, including the state, were neither enthusiastic nor well equipped to sustain.

A well-functioning market for the work of dead artists, Fry believed, would be dominated by plutocrats advised by shrewd and well-informed critics. It would settle quickly at relative prices reflecting the relative merits of the artists. The price level in the markets for old masters would be socially determined, influenced on the supply side by the degree of destitution of the social classes that felt compelled to sell, in his day the aristocracy facing death duties, and on the demand side by the new found wealth of the demanders, currently the plutocrats, as well as the strength of their instinct of emulation. In these markets neither utility nor cost of production, the conventional determinants of value for economists in the Bloomsburys' day, had much relevance.

The final new institution in the contemporary art markets that Fry believed deserved close study was the modern manufacturing corporation. On the one hand corporations had the power to stultify the arts by constraining their designers from expressing esthetic emotion. New designs reflecting genuine artistic creation were expensive, and all novelty was notoriously risky. Safety lay in pandering to the execrable taste of the "herd" of common people and to endless repetitive production. But the corporations had exhibited some exciting exceptions to this policy, and with the potential of new materials and under the pressure of international competition there was reason for hope that the corporation could become a positive force in society. Fry was particularly intrigued by the possibility of establishing high-tech design laboratories that he recommended to government be created through a novel public–private partnership.

The Bloomsburys took their combination of esthetics and economic theory seriously, and it gave them policy directions that were at times divergent from those that flowed from neo-classical economics. For them the overriding policy question to be addressed was "what should be done to insure that a substantial number of the best workers in the imaginative life remained engaged at their highest and best use so that civilization could be advanced?" The most obvious possibility was for the state to support and control the community of artists, writers, and scientists. But in Bloomsbury such a policy was anathema. Roger Fry had watched closely as the government had misused the "Chantrey Bequest" (Fry, 1903), an endowment left by a philanthropist to the state for the support of British art, and all of the

Economics meets esthetics in the Bloomsbury Group 147

Bloomsburys developed deep suspicions of a government that had botched the prosecution of World War I. Virginia Woolf personified their views in the lazy and incompetent bureaucrat Hugh Whitbread in *Mrs. Dalloway* ([1925] 1992). As World War II loomed E. M. Forster compared the British cultural achievement to date through minimal involvement by the state with the German dependence on government. "Now, Germany is not against culture. She does believe in literature and art. But she has made a disastrous mistake: she has allowed her culture to become governmental, and from this mistake proceed all kinds of evils. In England our culture is not governmental. It is national: it springs naturally out of our way of looking at things, and out of the way we have looked at things in the past" (Forster, 1972, 31).

The alternative to public intervention on the supply side of markets in the imaginative life was for society to nurture a large enough private demand for the products of the imaginative life for suppliers to cover their biological needs, at least, from market sales of their wares. But where could this demand come from? The Bloomsburys explored a range of possibilities. Clive Bell argued in his polemical book *Civilization* ([1928] 1973) that society should arrange for the sustenance of a community of sensitive demanders of the products of the imaginative life. Members of this community would develop both artistic standards and techniques of enforcing quality control that would require their full attention; they would have an important responsibility and needed total "leisure" to fulfill it: "The existence of a leisured class, absolutely independent and without obligations, is the prime condition, not of civilization only, but of any sort of decent society" (152). Bell made it clear that the maintenance of a class of leisured demanders of the elements of civilization was not costless and might require an inequitable distribution of the social product. Using a politically incorrect metaphor he suggested that this amounted to a form of economic slavery (as in "wage slavery"). "Civilization requires the existence of a leisured class, and a leisured class requires the existence of slaves—of people, I mean, who give some part of their surplus time and energy to the support of others. If you feel that such inequality is intolerable, have the courage to admit that you can dispense with civilization and that equality, not good, is what you want" (146). At the time Bell's notion was derided by critics as nothing more than disgusting snobbery and elitism. On reflection, and with the inflammatory language put aside, Clive Bell's scheme sounds today rather like the system of liberal education in the United States that has, in fact, been heavily subsidized by society and has undoubtedly become a major source of support for the arts and humanities at the grass roots by educating and inspiring a growing element within the population of sympathetic readers, viewers, and listeners.

The only three times and places in history when, the Bloomsburys believed, societies had autonomously and voluntarily arranged themselves in the way prescribed by Bell, so as to stimulate the imaginative life and the progress of civilization from the demand side, were ancient Athens, Renaissance Italy, and nineteenth-century France. The Bloomsburys attempted to learn as much as they could from the histories of these experiences, but it became clear to them quite quickly that to make progress in their own time and place they needed to understand

148   *Craufurd D. Goodwin*

better the peculiarities of the markets that were around them. Here they drew upon the market theory that had been developed mainly by Fry.

Many of the specific policy proposals the Bloomsburys made were designed to deal with the various potential failures in the art market that Fry had identified analytically. They found that there were problems on both sides of the market but probably fewer on the supply side. For the most part artists and intellectuals were self-starters and needed only reasonable coverage of their biological needs to take on their artistic labors with a will. But artists were also free spirits, impatient with the conventional discipline of the work place. It was necessary, therefore, to experiment with new kinds of firms in the modern market economy that would preserve artistic freedom and the social environment in which artistic creation was possible while at the same time remaining profitable and viable. To this end they established the Omega Workshops, the Hogarth Press, the London Artists Association, and other experimental organizations.

Another source of potential market failure that the Bloomsburys addressed was lack of reliable information throughout art markets. In particular potential demanders, including snobbists, classicists, esthetes, government leaders, and even the working class "herd," needed guidance about what was genuine art. These demanders insisted upon assurance that they would not lose money or face before they made an artistic purchase. Often the basic esthetic sense of potential demanders was entirely sound, if it had not been corrupted by the institutions and practices of modern society. But still they needed confirmation—and this the Bloomsburys set out to provide over their extensive careers as journalists, historians, and critics. In this role they were similar to the competent financial analyst that Keynes applauded as a stabilizer of capital markets and a source of comfort to hesitant investors. An especially creative device the Bloomsburys developed for improving art market information on the demand side was the Contemporary Art Society that gave a kind of Good Housekeeping Seal of Approval for hesitant purchasers to works of art by emerging artists. Coming in the 1920s just before the formation of the Book of the Month Club that had the same objective for literature, the Contemporary Art Society was a genuine innovation.

Closely related to their concern for improvement in the quality of information in the art market the Bloomsburys were committed to arts education. Here they saw a need on the supply side of the market, and shortly before he died Fry made a plea for the first university-based "arts studies" tripos (curriculum) at Cambridge (Fry, 1939, chap. 1). But they also saw arts education as a means to sustain the demand for the arts over time, the weakness of which had always been one of the greatest obstacles to the progress of civilization. The Bloomsburys were conscious of the mistakes that could be made in arts education and they called for experiments with new methods as the first step in reform. They formulated an interesting point about arts education that they put to the economist Arthur Pigou through the Cambridge historian Goldsworthy Lowes Dickinson. Since education was thought of as bringing about technological progress by making labor and production more efficient, why could education not be seen also as making consumption more

Economics meets esthetics in the Bloomsbury Group 149

efficient? If education could raise the production function, why could it not also raise the utility function? There was no satisfactory response from Pigou.

On the problem of rent seeking in art markets that Fry found could be a serious drag on the progress of civilization the Bloomsburys came up with a creative solution that happened to be consistent with their esthetic theory as well— anonymity for the artist. The esthetic significance of anonymity was explored by several Bloomsburys. For example, E.M. Forster argued that great literature became an entity on its own and no longer had any meaningful relationship with its author. "As it came from the depths, so it soars to the heights, out of local questionings; as it is general to all men, so the works it inspires have something general about them, namely beauty. The poet wrote the poem, no doubt, but he forgot himself while he wrote it, and we forget him while we read. What is so wonderful about great literature is that it transforms the man who reads it towards the condition of the man who wrote, and brings to birth in us also the creative impulse. Lost in the beauty where he was lost, we find more than we ever threw away, we reach what seems to be our spiritual home, and remember that it was not the speaker who was in the beginning but the Word" (Forster, 1972, 83). Fry thought the economic benefits of anonymity could be even more pronounced than the esthetic ones. If the works of one anonymous artist suddenly gained fashion, the increased revenues received through higher market prices could be spread among the less favored artists in the firm where the successful artist worked. Moreover, since the rents would no longer follow fashion artists would no longer be distracted from career paths and would respond as they should to artistic criteria only. The commitment to anonymity was implemented at the Omega Workshops where the only identifying mark was the symbol of the last letter of the Greek alphabet. Fry also held a celebrated "no-name exhibition" at Omega that enraged the critics who thought this must be one of those inside Bloomsbury practical jokes. The Omega experiment came to an end in part because the artists who were favored by fashion (including Bell and Grant themselves) became increasingly weary of seeing their rents distributed to the fellow artists who were not so favored.

The final aspect of Bloomsbury economic policy toward the arts that may be noted is their attitude toward the various players they encountered there. They were often outspoken and harsh in their criticism but they were seldom doctrinaire or dismissive. All sinners, they implied, might be redeemed: government, plutocrats, snobbists, esthetes, even the working-class herd. Moreover, there was no single road to virtue. That they themselves would not accept any final solution but insisted on remaining open for suggestion did not endear them to many of their more authoritarian contemporaries. But it makes them seem appealing in our own day.

The Bloomsburys constructed their esthetic and micro-economic theories mainly because these tools promised to enlighten problems that intrigued them and to answer some of the questions that puzzled them most: in particular they wanted to know what actually takes place in the imaginative life and how civilization can be promoted. That Roger Fry was trained in natural science undoubtedly helps to explain why he, and they, moved so often from the particular to the

150   *Craufurd D. Goodwin*

general. Their lives as wide-ranging public intellectuals help to explain their eclecticism.

Bloomsbury esthetics, for a while at least, had wide impact. Formalism is now part of our vocabulary, and Roger Fry's first essay has been in print for almost a century. But Bloomsbury micro-economics has left a much smaller footprint. Its influence can be seen directly in the work of a few second generation Bloomsburys, such as Kenneth Clark, whose enormously popular book and TV series *Civilization* reads like a Bloomsbury manifesto. But little progress was made in extending the promising approaches taken by Fry. Why? The answer would seem to be that such an extension would have meant a head-on confrontation with modern micro-economics. To have pursued Fry's speculations about the act of creation and transmission of an esthetic emotion threatened the notion of utility maximization and would have required close collaboration of economics with psychology, dangerous heresy then and now. To have extended Fry's price theory based on the behaviors of various changing social groups would have required cooperation of economists with the discipline of sociology and experiments with very complex modeling. This too would have meant swimming upstream through rough waters, an exercise the Bloomsburys but not too many others have enjoyed.

Note

* A discussion of this topic directed more toward the interests of historians of economics is contained in Goodwin (2001).

References

Bell, Clive. [1928] 1973. *Civilization*. Chicago: University of Chicago Press.
Bell, Quentin. [1968] 1990. *Bloomsbury*. London: Weidenfeld and Nicholson.
Clark, Kenneth. 1981. *Moments of Vision and other Essays*. New York: Harper and Row.
Forster, E. M. 1947. *The Collected Tales of E. M. Forster*. New York: Knopf.
Forster, E. M. [1951] 1972. *Two Cheers for Democracy*. London: Edward Arnold.
Fry, Roger. 1903. "The Chantrey Bequest." *Athenaeum*, 7 November, 621.
Fry, Roger. [1920] 1924. *Vision and Design*. London: Chatto and Windus.
Fry, Roger. [1924] 1928. *The Artist and Psycho-Analysis*. New York: Doubleday Doran.
Fry, Roger. 1926. *Transformations: Critical and Speculative Essays on Art*. London: Chatto and Windus.
Fry, Roger. 1928. Introduction to *A Record of the Collections in the Lady Lever Art Gallery*. London: R. T. Batsford.
Fry, Roger. 1939. *Last Lectures*, with an introduction by Kenneth Clark. Cambridge: Cambridge University Press.
Galbraith, John Kenneth. 1958. *The Affluent Society*. Boston: Houghton Mifflin.
Goodwin, Craufurd D. 1998. *Art and the Market: Roger Fry on Commerce in Art*. Ann Arbor: University of Michigan Press.
Goodwin, Craufurd D. 2001. "The Value of Things in the Imaginative Life: Microeconomics in the Bloomsbury group," *Review of the History of Economic Thought*, No. 34, 56–73.
Keynes, John Maynard. 1949. *Two Memoirs*. London: Rupert Hart-Davis.

Keynes, John Maynard. [1931] 1972. *Essays in Persuasion*, Volume IX of *The Collected Writings of John Maynard Keynes*. London: Macmillan.

Richards, I. A. 1924. *Principles of Literary Criticism*. New York: Harcourt Brace.

Veblen, Thorstein. [1899] 1979. *Theory of the Leisure Class.* New York: Penguin Books.

Woolf, Virginia. [1925] 1992. *Mrs. Dalloway*. New York: Harcourt Brace Jovanovich.

Woolf, Virginia. 1986. *The Essays of Virginia Woolf.* Volume I (1904–12), edited by Andrew McNeillie. New York: Harcourt Brace Jovanovich.

8 Individualism, civilization, and national character in market democracies

Regenia Gagnier

This chapter on competing models of Individualism in theories of Progress, Civilization, and Taste is motivated by a general concern with the term *market democracy*: the idea that we express our democratic "voice" not by way of our democratic vote but by way of our economic choice. The political system of "social democracy" and the economic system of the "market" have collapsed into one, so that, whether our choices are "free" or the product of multiple constraints, what we buy reveals all the preferences we are allowed to express. Although the essay primarily considers historical models, it will conclude with some discussion of biotechnology and the consumer-citizen that marks the dominant conception of the individual in market democracies today. Inevitably, this is a study of national stereotypes, the ways that Britain, the United States, and Europe have modelled ideal types with competing national inflections. If "recombinance" can be seen as postmodernity's contribution to such models, the components of ideal models of individualism in art, literature, and philosophy provide an index of possibilities.[1]

The fear of mass society was perhaps best expressed by F.G. Masterman in *From the Abyss* (1902) and taken up in Eliot's *Wasteland* (1922) and Orwell's *1984* (1949). It may be called the sublime shock—in the Kantian mathematical sense—of urban numbers and the implicit obliteration of the individual within them. As Masterman put it,

> This, then, is the first thing to note of us, not our virtue or vices, beauty, apathy, or knowledge, but our overwhelming, inconceivable, number. ... Our streets have suddenly become congested with a weird and uncanny people. They have poured in as dense black masses from the eastern railways; they have streamed across the bridges from the marshes and desolate places beyond the river, they have been hurried up in incredible number through tubes sunk in the bowels of the earth, emerging like rats from a drain, blinking in the sunshine.
>
> (Keating, 1976)

Individualism, civilization, and national character in market democracies 153

Masterman's fears increased with his recognition of the democratic power of the multitude:

> Through the action of benevolent Government it has now been invited to contemplate its strength. It has crept out into the daylight. At first it has moved painfully in the unaccustomed glare, as a cave bear emerging from his dark den. Now it is straightening itself and learning to gambol with heavy and grotesque antics in the sunshine. It finds the exercise pleasant; it uproots a small tree, displaces a rock, laughing with pleased good-humour. How long before, in a fit of ill-temper, it suddenly realizes its tremendous unconquerable might? (Ibid.)

This image of the masses as genial infant Pantagruel, with its polymorphous, immature pleasures, gives way to that of total abjection—all loss of boundary and distinction—in a South American rain forest, whose noble trees are overwhelmed by lush, infinitely varied parasites. Ultimately the competition among life forms is suicidal, and in Masterman's metaphor of decadent tropical forest a literal wasteland prevails:

> Some inexplicable change; slowly, imperceptibly, the torrent of life has overreached itself; the struggle has become too terrific; the vitality is gradually dying. And then, as the whole mass festers in all the gorgeous, wonderful beauty of decay, comes the mangrove ... symbol of the inevitable end. And with the mangrove the black-marsh and the reeking, pestilential mud. Until at length all the glory and life and struggle of tropical forest has passed away for ever; and in its place stretch the ... silence of stagnant, scum-coated pools, and the salt, interminable, tideless sea. (Ibid.)

To this expressed fear of the mass's obliteration of the individual I add my second concern: the nature of female autonomy, which I have explored in the contrast between the men of taste at the *fin de siècle* who asserted their individuality through their active choice and the women of the period who rejected choice. As I put it in a chapter on the so-called New Women of the 1890s and male leisure:[2]

> The question is, was there something profoundly contradictory between the freedom that the male Aesthetes wanted in the aesthetic life—the consuming life of Paterian aestheticism—and the embodied self-control of reproductive powers linked to New Womanism? The Aesthetic men wished to unravel and wear away their bodies in the pursuit of pleasure, while the New Women shored up theirs as productive vessels ... When Grand, Schreiner, and other New Women rejected sex for pleasure in favor of pronatalism, were they choosing biological sex as a higher destiny, or a Kantian freedom in perfect service to the State? Were they choosing a kind of Kantian autonomy in the face of the apparent heteronomy, the being buffed about by desire, of

154   *Regenia Gagnier*

male Aesthetes and consumer society? Or were they choosing something else altogether?

(Gagnier, 2000)

The third strand I shall explore has to do with variant forms of Individualism in contestation from the *fin de siècle* to the Second World War, especially competitive "market" Individualism, drawn from contemporary social science and often associated with the United States; psychological individualism, a category promoted by culturalists such as Matthew Arnold and typically associated with Civilization outside the US; and post-Darwinian theories of biology and instinct, typically associated with the rise of mass society. In the first model, tastes are exogenous, pushpin is as good as poetry; in the second, tastes are hierarchical; and in the third, tastes are biological and instinctive. In political economy progressive individualism was manifest in the division of labour, in evolutionary biology in the origins of species, in physiology in racial differentiation, in literature and the arts in psychological realism, and so forth. Herbert Spencer's influential idea that all Progress was progress toward individualism implied at the broadest cultural levels fears of anomie, isolation, and egoism. Arnold had argued for a strong State to counteract the excesses of competitive individualism, only to deplore the diminishment of the individual when it lost its deep psychological "character" that seemed to be particularly threatened by market developments in the Americas. The political theory of Individualism, promoted by Spencer's followers, countered *both* the fears of mass society and those of a homogenous paternalistic State by proposing the evolution of individual "character," of a character that would regulate itself for the social good and would thereby not need State control. Other, specifically national, inflections of "character"—"national character"—will be discussed below.

I. Autonomy and independence

Women were both active shapers of individualist ideology and the object of theories of instinct. In her famous treatise on marriage as a social institution (1897), Mona Caird first followed Spencer in seeing monogamy as a condition of Progress, but went on to consider the lack of individuation in inseparable couples not just "irritating" but "an index of united *degeneration*" (Caird, 1998). In the debates Caird's essay generated, popular science writer Grant Allen argued for progressive individualism through sexual selection:

> It is a mark of disease to have too frequent and too universal sexual impulses. It is a mark of health and of high development to have them relatively seldom, relatively strong, and powerfully specialised upon particular individuals. The higher types are the most selective. ... Unchastity ... in the highest sense is the impulse to sexuality, without a strong and selective individual preference. ... That advance in discriminativeness is a leading feature in evolutionary progress.

(In Heilmann, Part III of vol. I, p. 344)

Individualism, civilization, and national character in market democracies 155

Caird's and Allen's respective emphases on individual distinctiveness may be analysed by way of the distinction between autonomy and independence. Feminist theory of the last 25 years has held that for both nation-states and individuals the pursuit of independence tends to eliminate all values but self-affirmation thus gives rise to irreducible differences that in turn, in both nation-states and individuals, increase the likelihood of conflict. Autonomy, on the other hand, is relational, and compatible with submission to a common need or even common law. New Women were certainly individuals with diverse interests and goals; yet if there is anything common to the many women who wrote under that name it would be their assertion not of independence but of autonomy. It is still rare for women to assert independence, Hobbes's or Nietzsche's "pure differentiation" or radical difference. (See Nietzsche's dictum in *Will to Power* (1888): "One desires freedom so long as one does not possess power. Once one does possess it, one desires to overpower" (Nietzsche, 1968).) Having rarely possessed power, women have rarely desired to overpower. What New Women wanted, collectively, was freedom, autonomy, not "power over" but "power to," empowerment. Their focus on individuation was particularly *findesiècle*, acting on Spencer's dictum that all Progress was progress toward Individualism through increasing differentiation. They perfected a psychological type and there were attempts to make that type the bearer of Progress. This type took the individual, rather than the group or class, as the primary social unit, thereby differing from the social models of mid-century. Yet the difference between independence and autonomy comes out in New Woman literature.

This difference distinguishes New Woman writing from that of men writing about new women, from the suggestive Hubert Crackanthorpe to the assertive Grant Allen. Hubert Crackanthorpe's collection *Wreckage* (1893) was called "little documents of hell" because they crystallized the conflicts of independence between competitive male and female egos.[3] This competition between the sexes—their struggles for independence—made Crackanthorpe's stories particularly attractive to the British School of psychoanalysis, in its early stages more concerned with masculine struggles of independence than feminine quests for relational autonomy.

The most famous New Woman novel by a man, Grant Allen's *The Woman Who Did* (1895), like Crackanthorpe published in John Lane's Keynote Series, represents a woman negating all relations. Herminia Barton refuses all help from her family, declines an offer of marriage from a Fabian socialist, and determines to bring up a daughter entirely independent of social constraint. When her daughter rejects independence and seeks relationships, Herminia drinks prussic acid. The narrator concludes, with Nietzschean purity, "Herminia Barton's stainless soul had ceased to exist forever."

Women-created New Women were not so rigidly independent. They wanted autonomy, individual development, but they wanted it through *relationship*. New Woman literature primarily analyses feelings in relationships. There are hundreds of stories, but the themes are relatively few and constant: relationships between wives and the husbands they do not love; between wives, husbands, and the wife's

156   *Regenia Gagnier*

object of desire, who typically inspires extended fantasy; a relationship between an aspiring woman author and male Jamesian master who exploits and casts her off, often stealing her work or objectifying her self for his own art; a relationship between a woman who wants autonomy and a man who therefore cannot recognize her as a woman. These relationships are scrutinized self-consciously as if with thermometers of pleasure and pain.

The New Women were testing the limits of autonomy and emotion, constraint and freedom, at the level of the individual person and body. Within a few years Freud would offer a theory of affect in his Lecture on "Anxiety" (*Introductory Lectures on Psychoanalysis*, 1916–17), in which affect is a triple "combination" of bodily discharge, perception of that motor action, and a qualitative assessment of pleasure or pain, held together by an indefinable "core" experience (Freud, 1961). We note that to describe the "combination" the term Freud chose was "keynote"— not only the title of the George Egerton volume that for many epitomized New Womanism but also the title of John Lane's series so identified with its authors and themes of gender relations. We shall not follow Freud in pinpointing the nature of that core experience. The point here is to show how this female (and in this case bourgeois) self-analysis of "the perception of the feelings that have occurred and the direct feelings of pleasure and pain" appears as tension between autonomy and emotion or constraint and freedom in the literature. In Egerton's story "Now Spring has Come," published in *Keynotes*, the protagonist sees her lover after a year's absence. "I was touched by glowing shivers; that sounds nonsense, but it expresses the feeling. Why? I don't know why. I was analysing, being analysed, criticising, being criticised" (Nelson, 2001). When George Egerton's *Keynotes* was satirized by "Borgia Smudgiton" (Owen Seaman) as "She-Notes" in *Punch* (17 March 1894), it was precisely this intense self-analysis that he mocked (see Showalter, 1993). Many more examples could be cited from Victoria Cross, George Fleming, Vernon Lee, Netta Syrett, Edith Wharton, and Olive Schreiner.

Nancy Armstrong argued in *Desire and Domestic Fiction* (1987) that the female subject in mid-Victorian fiction became central to the modern idea of the self-regulating individual. The previous discussion marks a later stage of that development, in which the modern psychological individual that became the subject of psychoanalysis began its self-analysis through the meticulous calculation of pain and pleasure aestheticized in New Woman fiction. This self-analysis, the continuous alternation between expression and constraint of emotion, was figured in Alice Meynell's "A Woman in Grey" (*The Colour of Life*, 1896) by the woman on her bicycle. She is poised between freedom and constraint, temper and judgment, danger and security: "She used gravitation to balance the slight burden of her wariness and her confidence. … She put aside all the pride and vanity of terror, and leapt into an unsure condition of liberty and content" (Meynell, 1947).

There were attempts to place this self-analysing, self-regulating, balanced New Woman at the forefront of Progress and Civilization. In *Eugenia*, Sarah Grand writes of her protagonist: "She was … essentially a modern maiden,

Individualism, civilization, and national character in market democracies 157

richly endowed with all womanly attributes, whose value is further enhanced by the strength which comes of liberty to think, and of the education out of which is made the material for thought. With such women for the mothers of men, the English-speaking races should rule the world" (Grand, 1894). After having toyed with his ideas and emotions for the fiction's duration, Eugenia rejects the decadent male (otherwise known as a sophisticated man of the world). Her disgust with him provides a new model—as we shall see, a chilling new model—for the twentieth century—eugenic youth's innate good taste: "I object to his opinions; his mind is a rotten conglomerate of worn-out prejudices. And I object to his debility; he has to substitute alcohol for good nerve and muscle, and there is a general suspicion of taint in him that I have no word for, but feel, and it repels me. His husk is attractive, I allow, but I am not going to marry the husk of a man" (168). She also rejects his city, London, with "its wealth and its squalor and its teeming population" that stifles "the better feeling" (161): "It is all haste and crowding and no hope. Individuality is lost in the mass, and with individual traits go the recognition of individual joys and sorrows, those items of emotion of which we are always so intensely conscious in ourselves" (162).

Yet female autonomy did not come without a cost. In Victoria Cross's *Six Chapters of a Man's Life* (1903), Cross imagines a male perspective on the autonomous woman, here called (after her earlier sketch in *The Yellow Book*) Theodora. Like Cross's *Self and Other*, the novel opposes the selfish pleasures of sex to care of the beloved for itself. The narrator Cecil Ray is a confirmed bachelor of 28 who is bored by women. Through the generosity of a friend, he meets the captivating Theodora, an epicene figure with the body of a boy and an undisguised moustache. Throughout their courtship, Cecil is obsessed with her lack of "will," her "absolute submission" to him (Cross, 1903: 33,80,106, and passim).[4] Yet while he is obsessed with his domination of Theodora, she herself and the reader rather see her actions as autonomous. She cross-dresses freely, overtly detests children, and has no desire for a traditional relationship with Cecil.

Cecil's vague job is something of a surveyor on the site of Ninevah, and he is eager to return to "the East," where (in familiar Decadent mythology) death can come quickly and one is therefore encouraged to seize the pleasures of the moment. In England, on the other hand, one falls into habits of ambition for the morrow (a well-known political economic theory of climate). Theodora opts to accompany him to the East despite the dangers, disguising herself as his male companion. Toward the end of their stay in Port Said, Theodora persuades Cecil to enter a strange house where dances are performed for male spectators. She and Cecil are so aroused by an exquisite dancing "figure in the carpet" (207) that he kisses her on the mouth in view of the Egyptians of the house. They thereby comprehend her femininity and inform Cecil that while he must go they will keep Theodora in the house for a week before returning her to him. Although they give their word, which Cecil does not doubt, that she will be returned alive after seven days, Cecil's immediate proposition is that he should shoot her to save her from the shame.

158 *Regenia Gagnier*

Theodora sensibly argues that she would prefer to live and begs him not to shoot her. It has taken me some time to understand the violence of the character's response:

> I longed to destroy her now, as I had once longed to possess her, to shatter and burst those eyeballs and blot out their light for ever, to lay open the temples and transform them into a shapeless bleeding mass, to keep her mine now as I had made her mine then. To check those quick heart-beats, to see the veins drain out their blood, and the whole malleable body grow damp and pulseless, would have been to me now the keenest supremest pleasure, surpassing even the ultimate moment of possession. ... Those lips that I had known I would rather see mutilated and blackened, streaming with blood from my own hand, than know they had been pressed, smiling, by another. (216–17)

In the event, he does not kill her but she is returned to him degraded and disfigured by disease, and he duly learns to love her "unselfishly, for herself" (230). On their way back to England, however, Theodora throws herself overboard and Cecil renounces egoism, thus concluding the paradigm of will as domination (Cecil), autonomy (Theodora), and consent (a union of egoless love), all played out against the backdrop of "Eastern" pursuit of pleasure and British self-control. One needs to return to Klaus Theweleit on the men who wanted to strangle women with their bare hands before the Mongolians (i.e., Russians or communists) had the chance to do so, to reduce them (in the same terms) to a "bloody mass" or dead nature rather than give them up to the enemy. The reduction of women to "bloody mass" or dead nature was a theme that was to run through Freikorps literature (see below, section IV) (Theweleit, 1987). Cecil and Theodora's relationship (even their explicit rejection of parenthood) does not contravene current evolutionary psychology on the male modules for jealousy, male rage against women having sex with others, and male domination. What is more interesting to the cultural critic is Victoria Cross (née Vivian Cory) herself in light of Theweleit's findings, for she is a woman who presumes to write six chapters of a man's life and to express male ego-domination in order to draw the moral of unselfish love. Yet there is an eerie English poster from the First World War (Theweleit, p. 135) entitled "Red Cross or Iron Cross?" advertising the unselfish love of English nurses; while the "Victoria Cross" was the highest British military honour for "acts of conspicuous bravery in the presence of the enemy." Even among women writers, there was clearly ambivalence with respect to autonomy and independence.

II. Psychological individualism

The New Woman's focus on the individual's feelings and emotions in intimate relationships opposed Civilization to massification, psychological realism to social realism, and gave birth to the elite preciosity of Modernism. In bourgeois British culture, the refined emotions in intimate relationship that characterize civilized taste were opposed to the mass *national* emotion that absorbed the individual

Individualism, civilization, and national character in market democracies   159

under the State in fascism. When Clive Bell wrote *Civilization: An Essay* (1928) as an "investigation into the nature of our leading war-aim," he saw the individual threatened on all sides by fascism, Philistinism, and trade unions (Bell, 1938). England, Bell points out, "has cherished … a respect for privacy far superior to anything enjoyed by Continental countries. The English eccentric, the crank, the genius, driven by the prevailing atmosphere into odd holes and corners" (85), is now under threat from mass society, "the season-ticket holders on the one hand, and the trade unions on the other" (86). If they "succeed in doing their worst, it is probable that within a few decades England, disgarlanded of genius, character, and originality, will appear naked in her normal barbarity … She will have eliminated her individualism" (86). Between the alleged barbarism of the United States, to which we shall turn below, and the consummate civilization of France, the British had forced themselves into a unique state of individualism:

> The life of a first-rate English man or woman is one long assertion of his or her personality in the face of unsympathetic or actively hostile circumstances. An English boy born with fine sensibility, a peculiar feeling for art or an absolutely first-rate intelligence, finds himself from the outset at loggerheads with the world in which he is to live. For him there can be no question of accepting those national conventions which express what is meanest in a distasteful society. … English youth is likely to become more and more aware of himself and his own isolation. (80)

In his resistance to Philistinism, which Bell, following Matthew Arnold, sees as the pursuit of wealth and work as ends in themselves, à la the Americans, the English youth grows more and more individualistic: "Daily he becomes … more of 'a character'" (81).

Yet Civilization at its highest requires not polarized independence but fraternal autonomy, which is why France is more "civilized" (81). The more hostile the British environment is to beauty, humour, social amenities, the more the British youth is driven to combative independence (82). Bell's notion of Cosmopolitanism, the rejection of prejudicial notions of difference, which is central to the concept of Civilization developed by his mentor Roger Fry and his popular descendant Kenneth Clark of the television series *Civilization* (see in this volume Craufurd D. Goodwin, "Economics meets Esthetics in the Bloomsbury Group"), is based in individualism. At this point class and taste replace race and nation altogether: "a civilized man sympathizes with other civilized men no matter where they were born or to what race they belong and feels uneasy with brutes and philistines though they be his blood-relations living in the same parish" (97). These men will recognize each other across race and nation through their correction of instinct by reason and their "deliberate rejection of immediate satisfactions with a view to obtaining subtler" (142). Their defining characteristic will be "the acquisition of self-consciousness and a habit of reflection. … Self-consciousness, which leads to examination and comparison of states of mind" (58–9). Bell concludes that Civilization is artificial and unnatural, and he stunningly turns the Victorians on

160   *Regenia Gagnier*

their head with the realization that: "Progress and Decadence are interchangeable terms" (142). This progressive, decadent man "will discriminate. He will have peculiar wants and particular desires" (156). Progress is increasing refinement of choice; and such individuation leads to the Decadent inward turn away from the mass.

For Bell, civilization requires the existence of a leisured class (see Goodwin, op. cit.), and a leisured class requires the existence of slaves, "of people, I mean, who give some part of their surplus time and energy to the support of others. If you feel that such inequality is intolerable, have the courage to admit that you can dispense with civilization and that equality, not good, is what you want" (175). He concludes that, "It is amongst the receivers of unearned income that you must seek that leisured class which uses money as a means to good" (183). For Bell, British individualism has led to the autonomy of a small group but denial of social autonomy altogether; the independence of what he calls the "Civilized nucleus" or "Civilized core" depends on the receipt of unearned income. Deploring the atomistic, competitive individualism of the United States and the massification of fascism, Bell appealed to his own rentier class for the refinements of Civilization.

Bell's distinction between individual and mass had roots in the highest cultural authority. In the last essay he ever wrote, "Civilization in the United States" (*Nineteenth Century*, April 1888), Matthew Arnold uncannily said that he had waited long enough (he died the year it was published) to pronounce on the much publicized American "character" and "the success of the Americans in solving the human problem" (Arnold, 1986). Granting that the United States seemed to have solved "the political and social problem" of "freedom and equality, power, energy, and wealth" (489), Arnold praises US institutions at the forefront of modernity and democracy, particularly in contrast to British class and hierarchy; he praises the US for providing access to more of the comforts and conveniences of life; he praises them for dispensing with invidious titles like Esquire, whose only function was to distinguish gentlemen from working men; he praises American women for their freedom and self-confidence that make them a source of pleasure to "almost everyone" (494). But he rejects wealth and wider access to a rising standard of living—that is, he rejects purely economic notions of Progress, which he calls mere "development"—as the measures of "Civilization":

> Do not tell me only, says human nature, of the magnitude of your industry and commerce, of the beneficence of your institutions, your freedom, your equality; of the great and growing number of your churches and schools, libraries and newspapers; tell me also if your civilisation—which is the grand name you give to all this development—tell me if your civilisation is *interesting*. (495)

Arnold proceeds to define the sources of interestingness as distinction and beauty, "that which is elevated and that which is beautiful"—both of which are associated precisely with the kinds of hierarchy and distinction that the greatest

Individualism, civilization, and national character in market democracies 161

happiness of the greatest number in America had ostensibly compromised. Due to its constitutional ethos "glorifying the average man" and to an irreverent press, the Americans to Arnold lacked a sense for distinction, for awe, and for respect. Arnold concludes his last published work with a stark contrast pointing out that America's genius—its democracy and equality—was also its tragedy. Calling the British malady its social distinctions, its "upper class materialised, middle class vulgarised, and lower class brutalised" (503–4), he concluded that the American "predominance of the common and ignoble, born of the predominance of the average man," was a malady, too, in that it threatened Distinction (see Gagnier, "Law of Progress", 2000).

The proponents of "Civilization" outside the US typically feared what Freud called "the psychological poverty of groups," in which "individuals of the leader type do not acquire the importance that should fall to them and the bonds of society are chiefly constituted by the identification of its members with one another" (Freud, 1961). "The present state of America would give us a good opportunity for studying the damage to civilization which is thus to be feared," writes Freud. In considering the United States, Arnold also feared for psychological complexity. The idea, iterated from Arnold and Dostoevsky through Nietzsche to Bell and Freud, was that *réssentiment* leads to a rich inner life and that pleasure and indulgence led to formlessness and shallowness. Americans seemed short on internal life and psychological depth, largely because, due to their democracy, knowledge, technology, and wealth, they were effectively satisfied with external reality or superficies.[5] Europeans, on the other hand, dealing with all the complexity of shame, guilt, resentment, envy, desire, etc. arising from the class system and social hierarchy, seemed much more lively inside themselves.[6]

Henry James put it negatively in his book on Hawthorne. "The absent things in American life that an English or French imagination would find appalling," he mused, were "No state, in the European sense of the word, and indeed barely a specific national name. No sovereign, no court, no personal loyalty, no aristocracy, no church, no army, no diplomatic service, no country gentlemen, no palaces, no castles, nor manors, nor old country houses, nor parsonages ... no sporting class" (James, 1967). While the Old World novelist would think that "if these things are left out everything is left out ... The American knows that a good deal remains; what it is that remains," concludes James, "is his secret, his joke, as one may say" (ibid.). The deep psychology of the Anglo-European was thus opposed to the smooth materialism of the Americans.

III. Biology and the masses

Probably the most famous essay on Civilization, Freud's "Civilization and Its Discontents" (1930), was published within a year of Bell's. In Freud's essay, Civilization or what Freud calls the "cultural super-ego" literally takes over the individual's powers, regulating the unruly id-like social body until the individual, which Freud equates with instinct, is obliterated altogether. Figuratively, Freud displaces the structures of mental life onto the social body. Freud defined

162   Regenia Gagnier

"the decisive step of Civilization" as "the replacement of the powers of the individual by the power of a community" (Freud, 1961a: 95). But Freud's individual is not the product of British refinement, or US competition, but German instinct. Civilization can only be achieved by 1) "character formation," or the turning of a correction of an instinct into a "character trait," e.g., correcting or redirecting the anal eroticism of children into the "anal character" of the civilized adult; 2) the sublimation of instinct, as in the turning of sexual love into Christian love; and 3) the renunciation of instinct (97). And Freud does not think that these corrections, sublimations, and renunciations will ultimately triumph except in the cases of a few "leaders." For one thing, women, representing as they do the interests of the family and sex life, are allied with instinct (193), whereas "the work of civilization has become increasingly the business of men" (103). For Freud, the happiness of the individual is directly opposed to the creation of a great human community (140): "The two urges, the one towards personal happiness and the other towards union with other human beings, must struggle with each other in every individual; and so, also, the two processes of individual and of cultural development must stand in hostile opposition to each other ... [T]his struggle between the individual and society is a dispute between the economics of the libido, comparable to the contest concerning the distribution of libido between ego and objects" (141). He criticizes the communists not because of their attack on property, but because they naively believe that property is the source of aggression. Rather, aggression is innate to the organism, and a group of organisms can only overcome their respective aggressions by turning them toward another group, the proverbial Others (113–14). Ultimately for Freud, despite its becoming the business of men, Civilization, or "the ethical demands of the cultural super-ego," may fail:

> [E]ven in what are known as normal people the id cannot be controlled beyond certain limits. If more is demanded of a man, a revolt will be produced in him or a neurosis, or he will be made unhappy. The commandment, "Love thy neighbour as thyself," ... is impossible to fulfil; such an enormous inflation of love can only lower its value, not get rid of the difficulty. Civilization pays no attention to all this; it merely admonishes us that the harder it is to obey the precept the more meritorious it is to do so. But anyone who follows such a precept in present-day civilization only puts himself at a disadvantage *vis-à-vis* the person who disregards it ... At this point the ethics based on religion introduces its promises of a better after-life. But so long as virtue is not rewarded here on earth, ethics will, I fancy, preach in vain. (143)

Freud concludes his great critique of Progress and Civilization with the individual's resistance to the cultural super-ego: "when one surveys the aims of cultural endeavour and the means it employs, one is bound to come to the conclusion that the whole effort is not worth the trouble, and that the outcome of it can only be a state of affairs which the individual will be unable to tolerate" (145). Thus Freud inverts Spencer's idea that all Progress is progress toward individualism: for Freud, all progress and civilization are away from individualism

Individualism, civilization, and national character in market democracies   163

toward the herd or mass. Freud's human species made up of instinctual aggressions, the control of which he calls "the economic task of our lives" (96), is chained by biology. In his *The World as Will and Idea* (1818) Schopenhauer had written, "I call the body the objectivity of the will" (Schopenhauer, 1883). The body's will to live, its sexual and aggressive instincts, were like the force of gravitation, the force that germinates and vegetates plant life. Nietzsche, who regarded himself as Schopenhauer's successor, modified Schopenhauer's will to live via Darwinism into a conception of the will to power.[7] Each of them saw the individual's life-force in aggressive competition, as in Masterman's rain forest, with others and with the demands of civilization, the herd, slave morality, and so forth. Autonomy was herdlike; independence was all that mattered. In fact one knowedgeable writer on Individualism sees all of them exemplary of "bourgeois thinking" in their uniform conception of individuals as "isolated, self-sufficient monads in opposition to culture" (Morris, 1991).

Yet in this light we should recall that in 1930, the year of Freud's essay, the same language of conscious, unconscious, instinct, and affect was used to other effect to describe the synergy of the revolution of 1917: "Marxism considers itself the conscious expression of the unconscious historical process. But the 'unconscious' process, in the historico-philosophical sense of the term ... coincides with its conscious expression only at its highest point, when the masses, by sheer elemental pressure, break through the social routine and give victorious expression to the deepest needs of historical development. And at such moments the highest theoretical consciousness of the epoch merges with the immediate action of those oppressed masses who are farthest away from theory. The creative union of the conscious with the unconscious is what one usually calls 'inspiration.' Revolution is the inspired frenzy of history" (Trotsky, 1970). Such shifting recombinance of the categories of individual/mass/gender/communism were illuminated brilliantly by Theweleit's studies of the Freikorps cited above.

Freud indicts the communists for their naïve faith in Eros's ability to triumph over Destruction, once property has ceased to divide humankind. At the end of "Civilization and Its Discontents" Freud mocks the socialists for their "fresh idealistic misconception of human nature"—never better expressed than in the quote above from Trotsky—but Freud adds offhandedly "I do think it quite certain that a real change in the relations of human beings to possessions would be of more help [in furthering civilization] than any ethical commands" (143). Having clarified the reality of psychic life, Freud abandons the empire of biology and concedes to culture.

Thus in the period up to the Second World War, individualism meant market competition in the US, psychological complexity and refinement for the Anglo-European, and biology for German science.[8] The masses meant something different to each as well. Market competition recognized only competing individual interests; it did not recognize the idea of individual v. Civilization. Indeed in the US the development of the individual competitor was tantamount to the progress of Civilization. The Anglo-Europeans, on the other hand, saw all masses as threats. The German scientists saw them as not threat enough to tame the animal bundle of

164   *Regenia Gagnier*

instinct that each individual member could not rise above. Only the communists, and only at the moment of revolution, saw the masses as the creative union of the conscious with the unconscious, the inspired frenzy of history.

Enter *Der Führer*. In the 1930s, in "The Psychological Structure of Fascism," Georges Bataille analysed the split between the communists and the fascists, both of whom were "heterogeneous" to the "homogeneous" Establishment, in terms of the fascists' affective identification with the leader (Bataille, 1985). Twenty years later, Adorno wrote an essay called "Freudian Theory and the Pattern of Fascist Propaganda" (1951) asking how individuals turned into the masses. Freud had claimed that the bond that integrated individuals into a mass was of a libidinal nature. In a group one could throw off the repression of unconscious instincts, and it was but a short cut from violent emotions to violent actions. Adorno followed Freud in seeing fascism as a rebellion against the repressiveness of civilization, but it was "postpsychological" in that it took Civilization's standardized mass culture, robbed of autonomy and spontaneity, and simply *reproduced* it for fascism's own purposes. "Fascists fail to develop an independent autonomous conscience and substitute for it an identification with collective authority which is … irrational, heteronomous, rigidly oppressive. … The phenomenon is adequately expressed in the Nazi formula that what serves the German people is good. The pattern reoccurs in the speeches of American fascist demagogues who never appeal to their prospective followers' own conscience but incessantly invoke external, conventional and stereotyped values which are taken for granted and treated as authoritatively valid without ever being subject to a process of living experience or discursive examination" (Adorno, 1985). Adorno continues that prejudiced persons generally display belief in conventional values instead of making moral decisions of their own. Through identification with the great little man, they submit to a group ego at the expense of their own ego ideal that becomes virtually merged with external values. The psychological liquidation of the subject that surrenders itself to the group anticipates "the postpsychological de-individualized social atoms which form the fascist collectivities" (136). One of the basic devices of fascist propaganda is the concept of the "great little man, a person who suggests both omnipotence and the idea that he is just one of the folks, a plain, red-blooded American" (127). This leads to a society of repressive egalitarianism, the transformation of individuals into members of a psychological "brother horde."

The politicizing of the psychological as understood by Freud and Adorno, the emancipation of humankind from the heteronomous rule of the Unconscious once and for all, was tantamount to the abolition of psychology (136) as the great bourgeoisie of the nineteenth century knew it. It is where the early critiques of US market society's shallow psychology, later epitomized in economic theories of revealed preference and rational choice, led: a mass consumption society ruled by great little men controlled by slogans such as what serves the American economy is good (see Garnier, 200a). Politically, it was the assertion of national independence over autonomy with other states: when you have power, you want to overpower. This absence of a rich internal life and capacity to make complex moral decisions—the absence of sympathy and understanding, the foundations

Individualism, civilization, and national character in market democracies 165

of successful democracy—is what Santayana pointed to when he said that the
United States had passed from barbarism to decadence without the intervening
Civilization.

IV. Biotechnology and the consumer-citizen

Although it is always dangerous to write history while it is being lived, the
current consensus is that in the last quarter of the twentieth century we entered a
third stage of modern technocracy. The first was the industrial revolution, which
is now developing globally; the second was the mass transmission of cinema,
television, and radio, which fulfilled the traditional bourgeois's worst nightmares
of mass society; and the most recent is called the Information Age. The first
produced beautiful bourgeois individuals with deep subjectivities (on the backs,
as Bloomsbury knew, of the workers). The second produced masses, fascism,
socialism, and the sublime hopes of democracy. The third is in the process of
producing biotechnological individuals.

Many of us from Foucault's biopolitics onward have explored dimensions
of this third phase. In *Redesigning Life? The Worldwide Challenge to Genetic
Engineering* (2001) Chaia Heller situated biotechnology within the new forms
of production that emerged as capital reached the limits of industrial production
and began to target the reproductive dimensions of cultural and biological life for
intensified commodification (Heller, 2001). As noncompetitive US firms moved
their industry to the third world, capital-intensive service industries increasingly
began to commodify dimensions of everyday life, reducing the reproductive
dimensions of social life to mass-produced informational product (everything we
associate with "lifestyle": childcare, leisure, personal fitness and cosmetics, and
so forth). This further diminished the distance between commercial marketplace
and the realm of home and neighbourhood that had appeared in the industrial
revolution, massively invading the realm of everyday life, tearing apart and
reconstructing our patterns of consciousness, will, and desire. The commodities
manufactured by the informational market system increasingly took the form of
services that shaped taste and expectations: restaurants, fashion, leisure, childcare,
healthcare and fitness, welfare and financial services. One familiar effect of the
process is what Heller calls

> enchainment, or the strangling of a local economy by a ring of chain stores
> and businesses. These chain stores owe their economic and cultural potency
> to their ability to reproduce a set of patented symbols, images, texts, building
> design and production protocols dispersed in the form of franchised service
> factoryettes. For reproductive cultural practice to become capital intensive,
> both the service product and the process must be transformed into intellectual
> property. McDonalds's success lies in its ability to transform hamburgers into
> a patented semiotic field of information signs, symbols, images and texts. We
> see ... service commodities whose value is linked not necessarily to their
> general *content*, but to their *form*, or informational value. (409)

166   *Regenia Gagnier*

"It's the golden arch," writes Heller, "not the beef, that makes McDonalds a world power" (409).

As service industries have proven, the production of practice is often more lucrative than the production of product, or, as Keynes said with reference to Information, it is better to transport recipes than cakes (see Keynes, 2000: 73). Informational capital as a form of flexible production appropriates the attentiveness and situational orientation of the domestic sphere—it panders to the individual maximizing her pleasure/tastes. The Burger King jingle says it:

> Hold the pickles, hold the lettuce
> Special orders don't upset us
> All we ask is that you let us
> Have it your way. (410)

In a section called "The Rise of Recombinant USA," Heller says that, if rationalization and homogenization were the hallmarks of industrial capitalism, then recombinance—the effect of customizing or personalizing—is the emblem of informational capital (410). As the keywords of the industrial revolution were commodification, reification, and fetishism, the keywords of the Information Age are flexibility and recombinance. The dissolution of the idea of citizen into the idea of consumer, with the new notion of consumer-citizen (or "stake-holder"), signals for Heller the final collapse of humankind into *homo economicus*. Yet it is different from earlier forms of *homo economicus* precisely because its matrix is Information, which is not scarce, rather than the world of scarcity that has been the domain of traditional economists and Marxists alike. The eclipse of scarcity in the Information Age may mean that economists of both the Right and the Left will be superseded by culturalists.

The consumer-citizen is the role the individual takes in market democracies. Market democracy is the idea that we express our democratic "voice" not by way of our democratic vote but by way of our economic choice. The political system of "social democracy" and the economic system of the "market" have collapsed into one, so that, whether our choices are "free" or the product of multiple constraints, what we buy reveals all the preferences we are allowed to express. Nor do I think that, at least at this stage of the Information Age, all the talk of post-human cyborgs adds anything to that analysis. What is the relation, we might ask, of the human individual as maximizer of self-interest, centre of consciousness, will, and critique to the so-called post-human cyborg? So far, the post-human cyborg simply uses technology to further augment its function as consumer-citizen. It may pursue happiness faster or with more information, but this is an extension of individual will to power and knowledge, not its antithesis. Furthermore, while the post-human cyborg has provided images helping to liberate us from gender and other stereotypes, as in Donna Haraway, Ira Livingston, Judith Halberstam, Neil Badmington, and others' work, the economic analysis does not differ.[9] Readers familiar with Benjamin Disraeli's Victorian version of the Two Nations, the rich and the poor with no contact between them, will

Individualism, civilization, and national character in market democracies   167

appreciate the genetic twist in the following respected scientist's techno-eugenic vision.[10]

> As time passes, the mixing of the classes will become less and less frequent for reasons of both environment and genetics. ... If the accumulation of genetic knowledge and advance in genetic enhancement technology continue ... the GenRich class and the Natural class will become the GenRich humans and the Natural humans—entirely separate species with no ability to cross-breed, and with as much romantic interest in each other as a current human would have for a chimpanzee. Anyone who accepts the right of affluent parents to provide their children with an expensive private school education cannot use "unfairness" as a reason for rejecting the use of reprogenetic technologies ... There is no doubt about it ... whether we like it or not, the global marketplace will reign supreme.
>
> *(Redesigning Life*, p. 137)

In the same volume as Heller's essay, David King, the editor of London-based *GenEthics News*, reminds us of the history of biotechnology in eugenics, which, at its root, is the managerial urge to tidy up the accidents and messes that arise from sexual reproduction. The eugenicists of the early twentieth century often contrasted the care taken over the genetics of crops and domestic animals with the casualness of human reproduction. This desire to bring human reproduction under scientific control was the common factor between the right wing and the socialist eugenicists, who saw eugenics as a progressive and humane aspect of modernization. In essence, King writes, "eugenics is a form of technocracy, an attempt at social management based on the knowledge of a scientifically qualified elite. It is no surprise that Henry Ford was a key devotee of eugenics ... summarized in 1913 by Harry Laughlin, the linchpin of the US eugenics movement, as simply the application of big business methods in human reproduction" (*Redesigning Life*, p. 172).

This invasion of the most minute and, as it were, private parts of the individual, the gene, by big business will doubtless produce momentous change in the way we conceive individuals. King reminds us of earlier attempts "to tidy up the accidents and messes that arise from sexual reproduction," of other human engineers "appalled" that "human reproduction was out of rational control and left to chance" (ibid.), and we may conclude with a comparison that, while extreme, delineates the fantasy of control. Theweleit's *Male Fantasies I: Women, Floods, Bodies, History*, on the literature of the Freikorps 1918–45, was translated into English in 1987. It described the worldview of men who were first soldiers in WWI, then irregulars serving domestic repression, especially of socialists, and finally Nazis. In the literature by and about them, the soldier males ceaselessly bespoke their love for the German people and fatherland; the homeland soil, native village or city; their uniform; other men, inclusive of comrades, superiors, and subordinates; the troops, parish, or community-of-blood; weapons, hunting, and fishing; and animals, especially horses. They infrequently

168   *Regenia Gagnier*

mention women as objects of love, though mother and what Theweleit calls the "white nurse," or the lady wife or sister devoted to the Corps, may be briefly mentioned.

Most women are threatening, enervating, indecent, and aggressive—and allied in the men's minds with communism. The "male fantasies" that Theweleit collected systematically reduced the hated working-class women and communists to "a bloody mass," but they also reduced the women the soldier males tolerated to *dead nature* by processes of idealization that de-vivified, also a kind of killing. Theweleit believed that these men meant not only to dissolve the object (women) but also themselves, and he claimed that we see in the Freikorps men the failure of ego-development or individuation. In traditional psychoanalytic theory, this failure to individuate, the basis of psychosis, arises in the pre-Oedipal relation with the mother. Unable to differentiate himself, the soldier-male *screens* himself against wives, "white" mothers, and sisters, but he *destroys* proletarian women, "rifle-women," and erotic women. All of whom—all life in fact—are threats to the soldier male's carapace of a self. Hence his goal is always to de-vivify, to transform life into death.

Unlike Freud, however, who posited a "death Drive" according to which human aggressiveness is a biological given of the species, Theweleit following object relations theory sees the Freikorps' murderousness as a specific effect of gender relations. When the Freikorps robbed women and the masses of their autonomous life, by reducing them to "bloody masses," they reshaped reality anew into the large, englobing blocks that would serve as the building material for the Third Reich. As Theweleit shows with the support of hundreds of illustrations, the monumentalism of fascism would seem to be a safety mechanism against the bewildering multiplicity of the masses. In his chapter on "Floods, Bodies, History," Theweleit shows how the soldier males perceived themselves as "steely individuality" holding out against the tides of communism threatening Germany" (they liked to call themselves "Prussian"); but Theweleit sees them rather as carapaces of steel with nothing inside—no egos, but walled fortresses with no inhabitants. Rather than their stated goal of "rekindling the fire of enthusiasm for national honour and national feeling in each individual" (390 and passim), the carapaces that formed the Nazi columns in the Entry March of the Banners or the Standards of Victory at Nuremberg rallies had merely dammed the flood of disorderly life, channelled the mess into orderly columns. It was reported that in those rallies "You couldn't see the individual people," only the columns themselves in service to the state (429–30).[11] The men without egos threatened on all sides finally found union with others in that armoured millipede. As Auden wrote in a poem about the armoured male, without individuality, affect, or expression, "The Shield of Achilles":

> Congregated in its blankness stood
> An unintelligible multitude.
> A million eyes, a million boots in line,
> Without expression, waiting for a sign.

Individualism, civilization, and national character in market democracies 169

Whether or not Theweleit was right about the aetiology of fascism, the Freikorps soldier males wrote repeatedly of their "steely individuality" and had a conception of masculine independence that somehow was transformed into those anonymous columns. Biotechnologists today also seem obsessed with the dream of *individual* perfection, of the idea that each individual can be all that it can and they want it to be, independent of environment and of others. Readers may know the reference: the most popular logo of the US Army in recent years has been "Be all that you can be," using the brand of individualism to sell military corporatism to young people without economic alternatives: "Be all that you can be / In the Army." In all cases—Freikorps, biotechnologists, and the Army—the fact that the images of individuality were deluded does not make them less powerful or threatening.

Here I have selected three national stereotypes of individualism, the recombinant consumer-citizen pursuing happiness and maximizing self-interest, the fascist individual in service to the state, and the reflective, often female, subject of Arnoldian liberalism. I could have chosen other images, equally true or false, but also equally potent in the course of history. Theweleit's contribution was not only his collection of data, which corroborates much cultural study of the psychology of gender, but also his fundamental critique of a psychoanalysis that opposes a Real to an Unreal, or a Rational to an Irrational. He thought in 1977 that we should not take our basic analytic categories from Enlightenment models but rather study life models against death and killing models. This aspect of his work has rarely been picked up by critics, either by psychoanalytic critics or gender theorists, probably because it is explicitly ethical and value-defining. Poststructuralists and postmodernists still play the same deconstructive games with Reality and Illusion, Reason and Irrationality, confined within the idealist categories of the Enlightenment. For Theweleit the fact that the Freikorps soldiers were deluded about women and communists and about themselves did not make their murderousness less real. If Baudrillard has taught us anything about the postmodern condition, it is that fantasies like Disneyland exist in part to distract citizens from the illusory, aspects of everyday life. In itself, however, the fact that politics is illusory, or that a government's self-image bears no correspondence to the way the rest of the world perceive it, is uninteresting, merely a postmodern fact. What is interesting to the cultural critic or symbolic analyst is whether there is any correspondence between the extreme phantasies of the Freikorps and our contemporary genetic engineers "appalled that human reproduction is out of rational control." As the individual's patterns of consciousness, desire, and will are increasingly colonized by "informational product," the politics of labour and the economics of scarcity will continue to be rethought.

Notes

1 Recombinance is a figure taken from genetics emphasizing rearrangement of parts rather than mutational change. Biotechnologists design new forms by recombining DNA.
2 The New Woman was the term applied to self-consciously modern women at the *fin de siècle.* It was contested, not least by the women themselves, but it has come to indicate

170 *Regenia Gagnier*

a public representation in literature, art, and the media generally of self-conscious female modernity. Modernity may be taken to mean the pursuit of material well-being and economic independence, scientific knowledge, and political emancipation. For extended discussions of the New Woman, see Ann Ardis (1990), Ledger (1997), and Richardson and Willis (2002).

3 I analyse Crackanthorpe's "A Conflict of Egoisms" in *The Insatiability of Human Wants* (Gagnier, 2000a), pp. 170–1.

4 I am grateful to Virginia Blain for drawing my attention to *Six Chapters*. See Blain (1990).

5 It is arguably the historical commitment to such materialism that made cultural theory in the United States so receptive to postmodernism.

6 In his most Arnoldian mode, Terry Eagleton has referred to the "ironically titled United States." See Eagleton (1999) and Gagnier (2002).

7 For the most concise statement, see Nietzsche (1980).

8 Of course there were exceptional counter-movements to these broad national characterizations, and I have discussed them elsewhere. These are "ideal types" in Weber's sense that were exaggerated in twentieth-century national cultures.

9 The locus classicus is Haraway (1985). See also Halberstam and Livingston, (1995) and Badmington (2000).

10 This is Lee Silver, a molecular geneticist and developmental biologist at Princeton.

11 See also Georges Bataille, "The Psychological Structure of Fascism": "*Human beings* incorporated into the army are but negated elements, negated with a kind of rage (a sadism) manifest in the tone of each command, negated by the parade, by the uniform, and by the geometric regularity of cadenced movements .... In fact, the mass that constitutes the army passes from a depleted and ruined existence to a purified geometric order, from formlessness to aggressive rigidity ... thus the implied infamy of the soldiers is only a basic infamy which, in uniform, is transformed into its opposite: order and glamour" (1985: 150–1).

References

Adorno, Theodora W. 1985. "Freudian Theory and the Pattern of Fascist Propaganda," in *The Essential Frankfurt School Reader*, eds. Andrew Arato and Eike Gebhardt (New York: Continuum): 118–37.

Ardis, Ann. 1990. *New Women, New Novels: Feminism and Early Modernism* (Brunswick, New Jersey: Rutgers University Press).

Badmington, Neil. ed. 2000. *Posthumanism* (Basingstoke: Palgrave).

Bataille, Georges. 1985. "The Psychological Structure of Fascism," in *Visions of Excess: Selected Writings 1927–39* (Manchester: Manchester University Press): 137–60.

Bell, Clive. 1938. *Civilization: An Essay* (London: Pelican).

Blain, Virginia. 1990. "Cross-Dressing in Fiction: Literary History and the Cultural Construction of Sexuality," in *Feminine, Masculine, and Representation*, eds. Terry Threadgold and Anne Cranny-Francis (Sydney: Allen and Unwin): 140–53.

Caird, Mona. 1998. *The Morality of Marriage* in *The Late-Victorian Marriage Question: A Collection of Key New Woman Texts*, ed. and introduced by Ann Heilmann, 5 vols. (London: Routledge), Vol. 1.

Cross, Victoria. No date. *Six Chapters of A Man's Life* (London: Pearson).

Eagleton, Terry. 1999. *The Idea of Culture* (Oxford: Blackwell).

Freud, Sigmund. 1961a. *Civilization and Its Discontents*, vol. XXI (1927–31) of *The Standard Edition of the Complete Psychological Works*, trans. James Strachey (London: Hogarth).

Individualism, civilization, and national character in market democracies 171

Freud, Sigmund. 1961b. *The Standard Edition of the Complete Psychological Works*, trans. James Strachey (London: Hogarth): vols. 15–16.

Gagnier, Regenia. 2000a. *The Insatiability of Human Wants: Economics and Aesthetics in Market Society* (Chicago: University of Chicago Press).

Gagnier, Regenia. 2000b. "The Law of Progress and the Ironies of Individualism in the Nineteenth Century," *New Literary History*: Special Issue on Economics and Culture 31:2 (Spring): 315–36.

Gagnier, Regenia. 2002. "Oxford Occidentalism, or the Idea of America," in *Kenyon Review*, Winter, 179–88.

Grand, Sarah. 1894. "Eugenia, a Modern Maiden and a Man Amazed," in *Our Manifold Nature* (London: Heinemann): 139–40.

Halberstam, Judith, and Ira Livingston. eds. 1995. *Posthuman Bodies* (Bloomington: Indiana University Press).

Haraway, Donna. 1985. "A Cyborg Manifesto," in *The Socialist Review*, repub. in *Simians, Cyborgs, and Women: The Reinvention of Nature* (New York: Routledge, 1991): 149–82.

Heller, Chaia. 2001. "McDonalds, MTV and Monsanto: Resisting Biotechnology in the Age of Information Capital," in *Redesigning Life? The Worldwide Challenge to Genetic Engineering*, ed. Brian Tokar (London: Zed Books): 405–19.

James, Henry. 1967 [1883]. *Hawthorne* (London: Macmillan).

Keating, Peter. ed. 1976. *Into Unknown England 1866–1913: Selections from the Social Explorers* (Manchester: Manchester University Press).

Keynes, John Maynard. 2000. *Global Futures: Shaping Globalization*, ed. Jan Nederveen Pierterse (London: Zed Books).

Ledger, Sally. 1997. *The New Woman: Fiction and Feminism at the Fin de Siecle* (Manchester: Manchester University Press).

Meynell, Alice. 1947 [1896]. "A Woman in Grey," in *Prose and Poetry: Centenary Volume* (London: Jonathan Cape), eds. Fredrick Parr, Viola Meynell, Olivia Sowerby, and Frances Meynell. Intro by Vita Sackville-West. In Angelique Richardson, ed. *Women Who Did: Stories by Men and Women 1890–1914* (London: Penguin, 2002), pp. 179–80.

Morris, Brian. 1991. *Western Conceptions of the Individual* (Oxford: Berg).

Nietzsche, Friedrich. 1968. *The Will to Power*, ed. Walter Kaufman, tr. Kaufman and Hollingdale (New York: Vintage).

Nietzsche, Friedrich. 1980. "What is Noble?," in *Beyond Good and Evil* (London: Penguin).

Richardson, Angelique, and Chris Willis. eds. 2002. *The New Woman in Fact and Fiction* (London: Macmillan).

Schopenhauer, Arthur. 1883. *The World as Will and Idea*. Trans. R.B. Haldane and J. Kemp, 3 vols. (London: Trubner).

Theweleit, Klaus. 1987. *Male Fantasies I: Women, Floods, Bodies, History*, trans. Stephen Conway et al. (Minneapolis: University of Minnesota Press).

Trotsky, Leon. 1970. *My Life* (New York: Pathfinder Press).

A New Woman Reader, ed. Carolyn Christensen Nelson (Canada: Broadview, 2001), p. 30.

Daughters of Decadence: Women Writers of the Fin-de-Siecle, ed. and introduced by Elaine Showalter (London: Virago, 1993).

Matthew Arnold in the Oxford Authors Series, eds. Miriam Allott and Robert H. Super (Oxford University Press, 1986), pp. 489–504.

9 Art, fleeing from capitalism

A slightly disputatious interview/
conversation

Deirdre McCloskey (and Jack Amariglio)

The original interview/conversation, since added to and edited, took place on November 22, 2002 at Deirdre McCloskey's magnificent apartment in Chicago. In sending me directions to her home Deirdre included the following instructions: "You come out on Congress Expressway, and walk away from the brown building over the street called The Chicago Stock Exchange. Think 'Fleeing from Capitalism'!" Deirdre, of course, would rather have me slouching toward this icon of rampant accumulation and speculation, though not as a way to find her home. Ruminating later on Deirdre's instructions alongside her views about what she regards as the mostly irresponsible bolt of artists since the 19th century away from capitalism and their own bourgeois roots, it occurred to me that she had, indeed, not only given me righteous directions, but also an affable affirmation and gentle acknowledgment of my own lifelong line of flight. Not to mention a title for this piece. JA

JA: I've heard you quite vehemently criticize artists and others who "bite the hand that feeds them." Could you say more about this, especially your concerns about the criticism of capitalism put forward in much 20th-century art and culture?

DM: To put it simply, which is all I can manage, around 1848 European artists and intellectuals turned against markets and capitalism. One sees it in painting and poetry and novels and drama. And later I think even in music. The treason of the artists came just after they had turned to the market. Earlier—with the important exception of painters in bourgeois Holland during the Golden Age—the arts had been dependent on patrons, such as the Church or the nobility. The novel had from its inception in Defoe been a bourgeois form, depending on markets. Even its precursors in writers like Dekker were pro-bourgeois. By the early 19th century all manner of other art forms had abandoned patronage in favor of the market. What is important about Holland in the Golden Age is exactly that it showed what an art market could do when tied to bourgeois buyers and to bourgeois attitudes among the artists (no Romantics, they). As Tyler Cowen has argued in a brilliant series of books, capitalism is good for art, not bad. The aged Haydn showed what could be done for musical art on the frontier of capitalism, moving in

Art, fleeing from capitalism   173

1791 from the livery of Prince Miklós Esterházy of Hungary to popular acclaim and commercial success in London. Beethoven was the first to support himself by selling his compositions to the public rather than to a noble patron. For reasons I do not fully understand, the arts turned in the 19th century against capitalism, and kept turning. By the 20th century, as Paul Delany showed recently in Woodmansee and Osteen's, *The New Economic Criticism*, modernism in art was again dependent on patrons, such as museums, universities, foundations. The academic turn in the arts after 1945 has made things even worse. A professor of poetry need not write for anyone, much less the bourgeois masses who bought Scott and Browning and Hugo.

JA: What is it that disturbs you about this?

DM: Lots of things. Mainly, as an enthusiast for capitalism I am irritated by the anti-capitalist line in high art since 1948. Cowen, as I say, has worked this out most fully. But you can put it in other terms. For instance, the arts after 1848 display an anti-Daddy prejudice that I find distasteful. So should you! Marx and Engels are not the only instances of sophomoric rebellion against bourgeois fathers. The English poet Arthur Clough, for instance, was the son of a cotton manufacturer, and we are treated therefore to such effusions as:

> Thou shalt not steal; an empty feat,
> When it's so lucrative to cheat. …
> Thou shalt not covet, but tradition
> Approves all forms of competition.

How different from Dr. Johnson a century before: "There are few ways in which a man can be more innocently employed than in getting money."

JA: There are numerous things that are of issue in your response, and some things, of course, I'm sure I don't agree with, which shouldn't surprise you. One of the things I'm interested in is your take on whether or not you think art *should* represent any particular political and/or class position. It seems to me that you're disturbed by these artists coming from bourgeois families and who represent the bourgeoisie in unfair ways. I'm interested in two aspects of your disturbance. First, what is an "unfair" representation of the bourgeoisie?

DM: "Unfair" isn't quite the word I would use. Dickens in his early novels is amused by everyone: by lawyers, by politicians, by wives, by husbands, by everyone. Beginning with *Dombey and Son* in 1847–48, however, he stops being amused by businessmen. His novels become more and more harshly anti-bourgeois. He is part of the treason of the clerisy I am worried about. And as is rather typical, he really had little idea of what he was talking about. He understood the business of publishing and the theatre, but took no trouble to grasp a wider economics. In common with a good many literary people, he could not see exchange as voluntary or beneficial, unless it was payments for his books and his theatrical performances. And in common with even

174 *Deirdre McCloskey (and Jack Amariglio)*

many economists at the time, Dickens did not grasp the astonishing creativity of capitalism. Marx and Engels of course did, and said so in *The Communist Manifesto*. The conservative critics (Dickens being one) could see only the ugliness of industrial cities. They said, "Isn't it awful that people don't live in rose-covered cottages any more?" The progressive critics, though, were often trapped in a zero-sum view of the economy. Even the last edition of Mill's *Principles* (1871; he was by then very much a progressive) sees the future as one of tiny gains, from free trade for example, and minor improvements from education. He and other socialists did not see that the working class would be *enriched* by capitalism, because capitalism was *so* creative. In the century after 1871 the places that adopted capitalism would grow in income per head by a factor of twenty. In short, capitalism was the salvation of the poor. It is unhappy, though understandable, that artists in the 19th century didn't grasp such a big truth. But it is scandalous that artists and intellectuals still in the 21st century haven't yet grasped it. It's like getting Stalinism wrong.

JA: Why do you think it is the responsibility of artists, or aesthetics in general, to somehow represent this view (or any other)? Here, again, I am interested in the issue of representation in and through art itself. Part of what this book is about is the interchange or interaction between aesthetics and economics, economic ideas, and economic representations. So, there are many ways to talk about the forms of interchange between art and economics. When I hear you critical of this anti-capitalist representation, I'm interested, first, in figuring out how you think the art "works" to be anti-capitalist and, second, if you think there's some obligation on the part of artists because of their class background, etc. to represent what you consider to be a "truer" or "fairer" vision.

DM: Yes, I do think there is an obligation. The artist is in charge of innovation in our imaginations, and if she is irresponsible, as most artists have been about the economy for the past century and a half, we are impoverished. One is put in a false position by not speaking up for the known virtues of one's *own* class. Yes, the vices, too. Both. The point is that one has more reliable insights into one's own class than into someone else's. The artistic projects of William Dean Howells or of Robert Frost or of the English novelist Arnold Bennett, or in our own time John Updike, is to represent people as engaging in business as people, not as cardboard cutouts of The Evil Capitalist. Artists have an ideological responsibility to be truthful about the society around them. The avant-garde in art since the middle of the 19th century, though, has been persuaded that being truthful means to attack, attack, attack. The attack would be less unbalanced and adolescent if the avant-garde knew a thing or two about economics. It commonly doesn't. Consider for instance the monetary crankiness of Ezra Pound (who especially attacked Arnold Bennett for being, of all horrible things, financially *successful*). Art has an ethical role. We would hardly be having this conversation if we both didn't think it did. If an artist, even a historian, tells fairy tales about the racial

Art, fleeing from capitalism 175

history of the Aryans, the outcome is ethically bad, no matter how pretty the fairy tales may be. If we tell stories again and again about how corrupting it is to participate in an economy, we're going to undermine the ethical foundations of capitalism. In fact, we have. The ethical responsibilities of artists was not in doubt, incidentally, until the aesthetic movement of the late 19th century. No one before then thought art was anything else than a carrier of values for society. It's a peculiarly modernist idea that you can, and indeed should, do art in an ethical vacuum, with no constraint of justice or truth. "There is no such thing as a moral or an immoral book," declared Oscar Wilde in 1891. "Books are well written, or badly written. That is all." Well, no.

JA: Don't you think there's a tension here between two things, both of which you value? One is the idea of the artist having the freedom to represent in whatever ways they want to represent, not being forced by the state. The other is that you feel strongly that they ought to represent according to particular moral strictures. How do you make sense of this conflict?

DM: That's what I meant by saying I have no non-contextual criticism of socialist realism, or of the Ashcan School, or of social criticism in art. If people are *persuaded non-coercively* that it's a fine thing for Diane Arbus to turn the people she photographs into pathetic and hateful objects, I wish to try to counter-persuade them they are mistaken. Keep the state out of it. I have no wish to bring government censors in to stop Arbus' photographs from being shown, say. I merely want people to stop liking her stuff. People are often confused on this point. Criticism and persuasion and railing-against are not "censorship." Censorship involves the cops.

JA: How about the idea of the abolition of art? If art is so decidedly anti-bourgeois or anti-capitalist, would you like to see its demise? Or what's the value of art for you?

DM: No, that's Plato's view. Because the artists in his view can't be trusted to tell people the right things, we should abolish or exclude them from the ideal state. It's the communist model and it's the fascist model. It's an awful idea. As a gentle anarchist, I cannot approve. No I don't want to abolish the arts. I want them to flourish. And in fact they have under capitalism, to an extraordinary and gratifying extent. I have in mind all the range from high brow to low, film and pop music, country music and vernacular architecture—all the ornamental and story-telling arts. But they all have ethical content. Here I follow Wayne Booth, who was not always a fashionable critic but was a very good one, who wrote on ethical criticism, among many other things. Art has consequences. If you place the Marquis de Sade in the hands of a twelve-year-old boy, as Booth notes, you may do damage.

JM: I'm interested in knowing what kind of damage. We might disagree on what the damage is that might be done.

DM: Yes, we might disagree, though we could agree I think on how to find out. If Junior starts killing pets in the neighborhood and develops into a serial

176 *Deirdre McCloskey (and Jack Amariglio)*

killer of people later on, and he had Sade at age 12, and his brothers did not ... there'd be evidence of an influence, I suppose. You've put your finger on the problem in my way of thinking, though. I want artists to be ideologically correct, on my side, but I don't want to push them around. I'm a pro-capitalist, but an anarchist. Not a conservative or a Republican. But, there's a problem, too, on the "art for art's sake" side. It says that the artist must be, above all, autonomous and free, free, free—though, by the way, supported by state taxes and given jobs at the state university and allowed to use public resources for free, free, free. The problem is that either art has influence, or it doesn't. If it doesn't have any influence, then we needn't bother to inquire into the connection between art and political ideology. Art would be pure froth, socially speaking, spume on the waves of social causation. This would make a good deal of leftish art criticism of the *Rethinking Marxism* brand irrelevant. If art doesn't influence anything, then I suppose we can forget about it. But if it *does* have influence, then the influence can be good or evil, and it's not irrelevant to look into its evil effects.

JA: It strikes me that you place incredible responsibility in the hands of the artist, and you present the idea that the canvases or the texts can be read fairly straight-forwardly. Yet, in your own work, especially as you worked with the ideas of people like Rorty, the idea that language mirrors a reality so that there's a transparency is very much called into question. It seems to me that you have a strong sense of the representations of the anti-capitalists or anti-bourgeois, and there aren't many places yet where you are talking about seeing contradictions, or doubling-back, or aporias, or so forth.

DM: I've been surprised sometimes when I've read with care supposedly anti-capitalist texts. I'm often surprised to find that they aren't as anti-capitalist as I had remembered them as, or as I expected them to be from their reputations. And that's not terribly surprising—I shouldn't have been surprised—because if you're John Steinbeck you are a good novelist or if you're Arthur Miller you're a good playwright, and you are comfortable with the complexities in life. *The Grapes of Wrath* or *The Death of a Salesman* are not anti-capitalist in any simple sense. They are not the "tractors are good, capitalism is bad" kind of art. When I read, to go back to the 19th century, William Dean Howells' *The Rise of Silas Lapham*, I was expecting an anti-capitalist tirade. Instead I got a pretty sophisticated picture of what happens in the business world. When you read the first successful book by Thomas Mann, *Buddenbrooks* ...

JA: Yes, I was going to ask you about that.

DM: The same point. It's not just an anti-capitalist tirade. The closest to a straight-forward anti-capitalist tirade is Sinclair Lewis's *Babbitt*. What really bothers me—and this comes to your point about reading and audience—is how these texts are read. Perhaps you are right—it's more a matter of reader response than "what's in the text," whatever exactly that would mean. Perhaps I should make my appeal more to people who see literary art as straight-forwardly

Art, fleeing from capitalism   177

anti-capitalist or pro-capitalist instead of to the people who produce the images. A good example is Grant Wood's painting, *American Gothic,* held by the Art Institute of Chicago, and for which by the way he was paid four hundred dollars—another issue about capitalism in art! It is commonly read as a savage criticism of the middle class in the mid-West. Well, look again. I agree there's no such thing as a correct reading of a work of art. It's an object that we use for whatever task we have in mind. I suppose what I'm objecting to is not so much the artists as the users of the art.

JA: This shift is an important one, because use is also a complicated process, how they're read.

DM: One can't control how you're used or how you read. One can try, but ideas and images have a way of shifting away from authorial intention. As Marx famously said, "I am not a Marxist."

JA: So, reading, therefore, is a very important component of your concern.

DM: Yes. You've helped me clarify my currently muddy thinking on the issue. There's a *rhetoric* of art in capitalism which is the responsibility of the speaker, but the *hermeneutics* is the responsibility of the critic or the reader.

JA: One criticism that's been made of modernism and its connection to capitalism, rightly or wrongly, is that there's a link between realist strategies in representations and a transparency of the capitalist economy. Capitalism has often been portrayed as naturalistic, a force of nature.

DM: Yes. It's real.

JA: It's real. That's exactly right. That capitalism is real. And anti- or postmodernist criticism observes this on many different levels. One is the critique of capitalism "in-itself" as an economic system, though this is not a special preserve (if at all) of postmodernism. But certainly there's been an attack on representation and the notion of the real: naturalistic or realistic conceptions of representation. So, is it possible that some avant-garde art, which is in some ways anti-capitalist, but is at the same time promoting more complicated notions of reading, has some value to people like yourself?

DM: Well, I think you've got your chronology wrong. I think the anti-realism is a late move in Post-Impressionism or Literary Modernism—think of Picasso c. 1910 or Pound c. 1920. In music, the attachment to conventional harmonies—at least in academic or avant-garde music—is first attacked harshly by Stravinsky and some others, and then in the 1920s by more. As Virginia Woolf said, "on or about December, 1910, human character changed." But I agree with anyone who says that representation is phony in itself. What does it mean to say that a prose paragraph "represents" something standing there in the Real? Prose is prose and a pipe is a pipe. Describing a chair in words does not present it. Even in painting it does not: "Ceci n'est pas une pipe." Music is the extreme case. The twittering of birds aside, when does music ever "represent" something in the world? The ambition of all art to attain the condition of music, though, is an early

178   *Deirdre McCloskey (and Jack Amariglio)*

20th-century obsession, and is not commonly associated with pro-capitalism, but instead with anti-capitalism. Picasso, for example, was all his life a socialist.

JA: But, I'm agreeing with you here. I'm saying that a lot of the critique of representation and the movement toward anti- or non-representational art— I'm thinking about Russian Constructivists and Suprematists and even Italian Futurism …

DM: Yes, Italian Futurism was the first one. The Italians don't get enough credit!

JA: … that in some ways, there was a double or interwoven project. There was a sense that the world—the capitalist world—had to be rethought. That many of the commonplace and seemingly natural, obvious ways in which capitalism was seen to work, according to ideologies that promoted those ideas, needed to be aborted or at least confronted. And one way that some of these early revolutionary or avant-garde artists thought was to call into question representation, to call into question the smoothness of language, the continuity of language, the continuity of images. To break up images. Part of it was to mirror—some of them thought they were mirroring transformations that were occurring in capitalism, capturing notions of speed, capturing notions of movement, fragmentation, disruption.

DM: As in Cubism.

JA: Yes, Duchamp's *Nude Descending a Staircase*. But others, or even some of the same people, also thought they were making a rupture in the realm of image, language, text, with earlier or traditional forms of representation, and they saw themselves engaged in that project alongside the anti-capitalist project. Now, some of that disruption, I assume, is important to you. When we first started, I wondered if you wanted to go back to still life, to the Dutch golden age. How do you want to rescue that?

DM: I don't think that free verse makes free societies. I don't think that realism is bourgeois. I don't think that styles in art have any necessary or even convenient connection with political programs. Here I am following my colleagues in English at the University of Illinois at Chicago, Gerald Graff, for example, or Stan Fish, who say this all the time. For example, let's take Hopper, to speak of another painting in the Art Institute, *Nighthawks*, which, oddly, is these days starting to edge out *American Gothic* as the cliché piece of art that everyone has to have.

JA: But, you understand that.

DM: No, I don't.

JA: Part of it is that the rural ethic and image, compared to the urban diner, seems remote—the fifties are closer to us, and not just in time, than the twenties or thirties.

DM: Good point. Are we getting over The Pastoral? Environmentalism argues, not. Anyway, one could take the Ashcan School of American art, of which Hopper, I think, is a part, as having a politics. An anti-capitalist politics. It's awful in the cities, one would say: these people are so sad; there is not even an entrance or an exit to the diner. It hasn't got a door.

Art, fleeing from capitalism   179

JA: (laughing) *No Exit.*

DM: Yes. But you can also appropriate that image in a more positive way, or as a pro-urban statement. A more image-sophisticated person than I am would I am sure have no trouble. We are back to the reader's role.

JA: Do you think the same thing is true of Dutch art in the golden age?

DM: Yes.

JA: That is, that it can be read against the way you read it? For example, I reviewed an article for *Rethinking Marxism* in which the author, Iona Singh, makes the argument, that the nature of what Vermeer was doing, that his particular use of material "ground" was decidedly anti-bourgeois. Her argument is that there have been attempts to make Vermeer this great icon of art, and to see in Vermeer notions of spirituality, light, and so forth. In her view, Vermeer disrupts the whole bourgeois language and imagery of the time, just by virtue of the way in which she describes the actual paint that Vermeer used and how he used it. She traces his use of paint through Vermeer's connection to the craft guilds of the time, the fact that he had real knowledge of the ground he was using, and that the ground he used produces certain effects; she argues that the effect that this ground produces is a much more distancing and critical effect than that which was used by de Hooch, and others.

DM: I can agree with the technical point, which seems plausible, and I must say I do not get an especially pro-bourgeois feeling from *A View of Delft*, say. But, I think Singh's argument as you describe it is a perfect illustration of the hermeneutic responsibilities of our times. Dutch art of the Golden Age was grotesquely misunderstood in the 19th century because critics had forgotten the semiotics that contemporaries took for granted. Dutch artists, it is claimed by many 20th-century critics, had an elaborate code in which they said things. For one thing they were all believing Christians. For another their heads were filled with Dutch proverbs—Dutch is to this day an exceptionally proverb-rich language. They said: "Greed is bad." Yes. They said that a lot, though not as much as we would if we were to make a similar art. But as Simon Schama shows the point was not to attack capitalism but to moralize it, to overcome the embarrassment of riches, "*overvloed*," which means "abundance" but contains in it the worry about flooding, as the water-constrained Dutch said. They said: "You're all going to die." This was prominent in a highly Christian and plague-ridden age. "You may think the surface of this glass or this apple—these surfaces beautifully rendered through the improved possibilities of oil paint—is oh, so nice, but, look here, it merely shows that you, too, are going to die." And so forth. But as you and I agree, it's not a slam-bang argument. The artist's intent at the time is not a decisive argument for our appropriation of the art. Now, there I agree. But Singh I am sure realizes that she's *appropriating* Vermeer. Good. But she's not necessarily *uncovering* his intentions, although there may be some fact of the matter to be revealed on that happy day when we find an autobiography of the painter. I can see in any case what she means: there's an odd lack of sympathy in

180 *Deirdre McCloskey (and Jack Amariglio)*

his paintings, unsettling. He's a cool, distanced painter. Contrast Franz Hals, who regardless of whom he's painting is amused. Early Dickens. Vermeer is more like Flaubert, the cold eye.

JA: Yes, by contrast there's something very defamiliarized about Vermeer. Something like an alienation.

DM: Exactly. The woman getting the letter from her servant. On one level, in view of her rich clothing, we're to take her as a bourgeoisie. She is planning an assignation, perhaps, or her lover has died in the wars. But we are put one step away from being sympathetic. And you can call it anti-bourgeois if you want, though I think that's a stretch. But a quite different way of putting my vexation with how art is read is: I'm distressed that there isn't as much discussion as there ought to be about the economy in art. Middle-class life is not on the agenda, which strikes me as a bad thing, since we are all middle class.

JA: This is exactly where I wanted to turn. To what extent is art a place where economic discourse arises and/or economic discourse is itself furthered? I wonder if maybe some of our difference in vision—if there is one, is the question of what constitutes economy, about economy in a text, etc. What exactly you are looking for?

DM: I think I'm looking for talk about people at work. And I see too little of it. Whereas you and David Ruccio, taking a broader view of the economy, see that any representation of place in the economy would count. Van Gogh has a very nice painting of a bridge he saw in the south of France. It reminded him of lift-bridges at home in Holland. You can say, "Aha, this is part of the transportation system. Van Gogh is talking about the economy." Well, no. I think not. He's talking about an artifact. That doesn't make it about economic activity, as I see it.

JA: How about representations of money? Do you see that as economic?

DM: I do. If in some Dutch painting of the 17th century there is shown a money-changer, if there are some coins on his table—and there are in fact quite a few such paintings—that indeed is "about" economic activity. Often the wife is the active changer. It was certainly intended as so, in the highly moralistic style of the 17th century. And if you had a novel about a banker, that'd be the kind of thing I'd be looking for. Here's a fault with my way of looking at the project: how to handle housework?

JA: I was going to ask you about things that signify economy to you, and those that don't.

DM: I certainly view housework as part of the economy. There's that wonderful Vermeer painting—since he only did 35 paintings, so one can be fairly exact without actually being, as I am certainly not, a serious student of these matters!—it's his only painting of an exterior of a building, where the maids are sweeping the sidewalk. It surely counts as a representation of the economy. But then you have to ask of bucolic art—*Orfeo*, the originating opera by Monteverdi, for example—whether it is "about" imaginary shepherds and their economy? My answer is no. It's "about" song,

Art, fleeing from capitalism   181

about panpipes, about sexuality, much more than about being a shepherd. (I am by the way very uneasy about the word "about," since the apparent subject of any moderately good piece of art is such a small part of its full meaning to a competent reader. Much art, for example, is in large part "about" the artistic technique itself.) So, I don't want to draw the boundary too generously. And you can ask why. Why draw it the way I want to draw it? Where one draws it has ideological effects. I can pick an easy one, where we completely agree: if all that counts as economics and the economy is what comes into the marketplace, then housework is set aside, and as an economic historian I will point out that one is thereby ignoring about half of national product before, say, 1800 even in advanced England or Holland or Japan or North China. Such accounting would misunderstand what people do, what Marshall called the "ordinary business of life." But an extreme postmodern sensibility would say, as I take it you and David would say, that nearly everything's about the economy.

JA: Here's a problem I have on this point. It has to do with whether things can be read literally. One thing you've said is that you want to keep bounded in a particular way what constitutes representations of economy or not. Your examples are quite literal. Yet, you also recognize codes. You recognize that something stands in for other things. Since you've written on metaphor, you understand this better than all of us. So, I'm interested in whether you can expand your notion of how to read texts, artworks, etc. in terms of economy even when there aren't the obvious signs of economy. Part of this has to do with the question of what's meant by economy, but also what would be the translation practices—like any metaphorical practice, how do you move from, for example, seeing two people holding hands to some comment on factory production? I don't know how you would do such a thing, but I'm interested.

DM: I'm not sure I am at present equipped for it. It seems to be best at least for someone of my modest abilities to move cautiously out into that space, in a disciplined way, so that I know what I'm talking about. I've tried to read and do some of it in a course I teach at UIC called "Economics for Advanced Students in the Humanities." The "new economic criticism" is what's at stake—Martha Woodmansee at Case Western has skillfully advocated it for a long time, and I was involved to a degree early on, and Susan Feiner, and you and David Ruccio. I see it now as a branch of what the English professors call the New Historicism. My colleague at UIC (yes, we do have now one of the best English departments in the world!), Walter Benn Michaels, wrote a brilliant book of the New Historicism called *The Gold Standard and the Logic of Naturalism* (1987). As Walter shows, one could do an economic criticism that goes beyond the usual suspects. For example, consider Jane Austen's novels. If you think about the economy the way I do, and I take it the way you do, you notice that there are no domestic servants in the novels. Someone has to be cleaning the houses and serving the food. But there is no ordinary servant who's given voice—governesses, yes; maids, no.

182   *Deirdre McCloskey (and Jack Amariglio)*

It's quite striking. And that is a downgrading of domestic production. This is by contrast with, say, Hardy, later, or even Fielding, earlier. It's of course an occlusion of a whole social class. Part of the structure of society is being ignored. From a neoclassical point of view, in an Austen novel national income is being measured incorrectly, so to speak. From a Marxist point of view, the class structure of society is being ignored. Even though her novels are not "about" the economy, the *way* they are not about the economy is a representation.

JA: That's a very important point. In many ways, some critics—certainly some postmodern critics—have taught us to read absences, and the presences in the absences, and also the absences in presence.

DM: In the old vocabulary, "in between the lines."

JA: Yes. A lot of the precedent for that is Freudian. There is an incredibly developed and sophisticated psychoanalytic literature about culture. People read paintings, texts, etc., and out of a table sitting in the middle of the room they'll describe the entire psychical make-up of the owners or the people who inhabit the room, and so forth. I'm interested in how or even if this can be done for economics. Some people have asked me why I want to do this. They've said that this kind of move—analogous to the Freudian one—is very imperialistic; it reduces everything (in this case, to the determinations of the economic content). I'm not interested in producing this reduction in the form of the economic reading, or to say that economic content is dominant, but I am concerned, like you are, about the invisibility, or the presumed invisibility, of the economy.

DM: That's my main complaint about modern art since 1848, the occlusion of men-at-work, and most particularly middle-class men-at-work. The novel since then hasn't occluded the women as much. In fact, it's given them a voice that they didn't have before. Largely because women started to be allowed to participate as artists, the middle-class women and their work have been brought into the light. Look at the paintings of Mary Cassatt. Some people are brought into the light, yet others have been cast into the shadow. The attempts in the last century and a half to bring the proletariat into the light of art are impressive and good. But you can almost say there's an economy of this—there's an opportunity cost of casting the bosses and managers into the dark.

JA: It sounds like what you value is a connection between what I'll call the politics of representation and representation as it works in the texts. There's a sense in what you've said that there is an importance of representing middle-class men and women because there's a politics of representation. You want them represented in the consciousness and the politics of the time. It's the same thing as people saying, let's bring housework into the light, or the proletariat into the light. You understand that there's also questioning about whether it works quite that way; that is, what the connection is between political representation and also representation in and through art, texts, and so forth.

Art, fleeing from capitalism 183

DM: My view, of course, is a standard liberal view, in the European sense of the word "liberal." It's pluralism. Let's hear all the voices. And it's the same view I have of all politics. I admit that it's a wishy-washy, "let's hear what he has to say" view. But we've tried being *non*-wishy-washy in this sense in the 20th century, 1914–89, and it didn't work out very well. On that evidence I favor wishy-washy. What I don't like about the politics of art in the last century and a half is the way it has cast into the dark the lives of people whom I regard as forces for good, namely, the bourgeoisie.

JA: So, you do have the sense that artistic or aesthetic representations really have an effect on constituting people as political subjects.

DM: Yes, and you people of the left agree with me on this. If there aren't any blacks in novels, if the servants vanish, if the proletariat is not personalized, you say, oh my, what in heaven's name is going on here?

JA: It's an interesting problem. On the one hand, sometimes I think it's important to call up what those silence or absences "mean"—how you can read them as reflections of a way of portraying an activity or sphere of life in which all of the blood is let out by virtue of there being no servants, nobody takes out the garbage, nobody shits, nobody does any of the things that go on in daily life. And this gives us a certain conception. So you can read about the nobility or landed gentry as though, somehow, magically, everything happens, and that it has no connection to these lives. On the other hand, there's the problem of what these representations actually do when they do occur. Your comment reflects it. Other than counting skin color or gender, what exactly has this achieved, what are its political effects? Sometimes, as you know, being represented can be far worse than not being represented.

DM: There's no question. In Hollywood, before the 1960s, blacks in the United States were represented like that famous servant in *Gone With the Wind*.

JA: Butterfly McQueen. Or Stepandfetchit.

DM: Or Topsy, in *Uncle Tom's Cabin*. But in *Uncle Tom's Cabin* there's enough time to develop the characters some, and redeem their humanity, while in films they are only quick clichés, and that's it.

JA: Which is why sometimes representation is a terrible thing. You know: *please* don't represent me.

DM: That's right. "Please keep me out of this." And, once again, that's my complaint about art during the last century and a half, this anti-capitalist art. That is, it *has* represented the rich, or business people, or the bourgeoisie, but puh-leaze stop representing them that way. If the only way you can think about a realtor is in terms of George Babbitt, you are missing a good side of capitalism. I admit that there might be lots of people who are not too far from that harsh parody. But on balance I wish Sinclair Lewis hadn't written *Babbitt*. It's a good piece of art—A-minus, maybe B-plus on a tougher cosmopolitan standard, just as art. But it has had a terrible effect on people.

JA: It does allow, though, people to have a counterdiscourse.

DM: If there is a discourse. And if the discourse doesn't take over the minds of the educated, as it has. I guess that's where I'm locating my complaints, as

184   *Deirdre McCloskey (and Jack Amariglio)*

we've figured out. I'm not actually complaining about the artist, though I think I have a few artist-specific complaints. I think there's a problem in the Romantic vision of the artist, which has persisted down to the present. A late-Romantic elevation of the Artist to The Coolest Guy Around has in the 20th century reduced some arts to a purpose of loftily insulting the viewer or reader: Hey, it says, this stuff is *complicated*, and you, oh dummy, are probably not up to it. Virginia Woolf was this way in her attitudes and in her work, at least in her experimental fiction, and certainly the Joyce of *Ulysses* and above all *Finnegan's Wake* was. Footnotes in *The Waste Land*. Serial composition in music. Jazz after Charlie Parker. Painting after Braque. Well, I say Valley-Girl style, *huh*? Why should *that* be the purpose of art? The notion is that Art is meant to shock. It's certainly not how artists before the Romantic Movement thought of what they did. It's not in the nature of Art— capital A—that it has to be insulting to the main class that supports it. But we agree that the real problem occurs in the popularization of these views, in their newspaperization. When anti-bourgeois feelings are newspaperized and naturalized, that's the dangerous point. When it becomes an insult to be called middle class—"oh, you're so middle class"—that's where thinking has stopped. And it's not that people are objecting to the middle class on any sensible, thought-out, principled, scientific, evidentiary grounds. Or so I say. It is merely that they have been told, they think, by Picasso that they should sneer at the middle class.

JA: Are you ever nervous about art exhibitions or bookshows, or any kind of connection between corporations, money, or any aspect of what you consider capitalism and art? Are you ever concerned?

DM: Not particularly. The first Impressionist exhibition took place in a strikingly modern industrial/commercial building in Paris, close to where they had the Academic show. A couple of floors of this building were loaned to the Impressionists (they did not call themselves that yet) by a commercial photographer. So it was a commercial building, a bourgeois enterprise, that subsidized the beginning of Impressionism. I don't see any problem with that. Art has always had patrons of some sort. As I say, paying for art was dramatically democratized in the 19th century, and had been earlier in Holland.

JA: This is one area where you and I agree. I don't have the view that art is degraded by its connection with capitalism. I also don't view, in the other direction, that art is degraded by its connection with the socialist state. That's where you and I may disagree.

DM: It depends on what you mean by a "connection." The problem with states is that they have, or claim, a monopoly of violence. So, when art is connected, say, with the Mafia, and the Mafia goes around enforcing some kinds of art by aiming shotguns at people, that's where I draw the line. That violence. I do not accept the common left view that persuasion or exchange is "another form of violence." Violence is violence, torture in Iraq, whether by "our" enemies or by the CIA, and very different from offers of arguments or money. I realize that "violence" can be defined more broadly as reduction of people to a thing,

Art, fleeing from capitalism 185

and that in this sense violence exists in markets. But I prefer that "violent" reduction to the Gulag or to Room 101.

JA: What about the artistic practice itself? The fact that it is art, that art is constructed in a particular way, the fact that its meanings are not contained within itself? As you said earlier, you write a text and you are not in control of the effects of the text. I understand that you might object to the state and state intervention in art, but then there are the products of that art, the artifacts. Yes, one could treat them disdainfully, one could see them as crap because they are produced under the Stalinist regime, or one can treat them as texts as any texts that have certain political connections and ideological connections, but that also have possibilities within them, so then not all one meaning.

DM: I actually heard someone at the School of Criticism and Theory at Cornell a couple of summers ago make a similar point about the "recuperation," as she put it, of Soviet-era art. I found her plea shocking and even embarrassing. I'm a little bit inclined to say, ok, how about the ...

JA: Yes, I understand: how about the "recuperation" of Nazi art ....

DM: You get the point. So one starts wondering, well, all right, maybe there's something in Pound's anti-Semitic works that comes up to the standard of his early imagist poems. But, but, but. Still, a lot of art was created under hideous patronage. We look at the Coliseum, and admire it, say, oh what a lovely, wonderful building. But of course its purpose was the staged killing of human beings. Yet still we look at it with admiration.

JA: Definitely. Think about the kind of patrons who made possible Italian Renaissance art, tyrants and evil priests. But a differentiation can be made. I'm really not interested in recuperating Nazi art. But the art itself is not a simple reflection of the politics of the period. It's not that it's divorced. Postmodern philosophy has done a lot to recuperate the work of Heidegger and Nietzsche.

DM: Particularly Heidegger. I am less clear that Nietzsche is to be blamed for the way he was used by fascism. Everything bears the traces of its political origins. Yeats, whom I admire as a poet very much, was essentially a conservative and was hostile to the errors of 1916, and was questionable in all kinds of other ways, believing literally in fairies, and wanting to revive mythology as a living force in Irish politics. So it bears the trace. But what does one conclude? You ought to watch out for it, I guess. You oughtn't to be naïve about what it intends or means (the two are different)—"the Jew squats on the windowsill, the owner," says Eliot, and we properly worry. But the line doesn't have stable meanings, slam, bang, and so: exclude Eliot from one's English course. It may be that we come to a point where it doesn't matter to us, in ten or a hundred or a thousand years. We don't care that a twelve-foot lion sculpted in Mesopotamia three millennia ago was in aid of an appalling tyranny. In Chicago's Oriental Institute we stand and admire its suppleness and grandeur. Or we find in it other thoughts: "My name is Ozymandius, king of kings:/ Look on my works, ye mighty, and despair."

186 *Deirdre McCloskey (and Jack Amariglio)*

JA: I'm interested in the word you used: the idea of the "trace." The trace of a time, a politics, whatever. Works can carry the trace of an economy. How does one read traces? That is why I said earlier that what seems obvious as a representation can be very different from tracing representations. I bring up this issue because I often find it very disconcerting to think of the opposition between art produced under conditions of freedom, which bears the trace of ... I don't know what ... freedom perhaps, and art produced under conditions of tyranny, which bears the trace of tyranny. There's something very disturbing about claiming that it's so clear-cut—that one can read freedom from the conditions of its production. Because the conditions of its production, as you know in economics, aren't the product. The product is different from its conditions of production. They're not entirely separated, but the product is something that has its own dynamic and life.

DM: I completely agree, and admire non-orthodox Marxism for emphasizing this. The main example that I'm emphasizing in my book published in 2006 on bourgeois virtue and elsewhere is indeed the free choice of extremely free men—especially men—in France in the 19th century, and in England especially in the 20th century, and in the United States in the 20th century, and so forth—to oppose capitalism. There's a long discussion—you can find it in Schumpeter, and in Daniel Bell, and maybe before—about the cultural contradictions of capitalism. It may well be that free countries, and capitalist countries—and I accept that these may not be one and the same thing—produce the art that undermines them. That would be tragic, or at least very sad, in my way of thinking. But anyway it is an instance of art being powerful. I don't think it's just amusement or ornament.

JA: We don't have the same view of capitalists, though I don't think what matters to me are the people called capitalists as much as the process itself. I'm not interested in the vilification of capitalists as people. I find that living in a culture of personification and individuality, too much is attributed to the person, for good or evil. If you were a Marxist today ...

DM: Perish the thought!

JA: ... you might think of capitalism in terms of its class process, as one in which what Marxists have always called exploitation takes place. So, you wouldn't be concerned with the representations of middle-class men qua men, but you might be very concerned with what you consider the effects of an exploitative production process. Sometimes those juxtapositions are more interesting, which is the juxtaposition of the perfectly well-meaning, well-living bourgeois with the possibility that the people who exist in their workplaces experience something we can call exploitation.

DM: But, there's a deep problem here: that is we don't have the artistic means to make the points about unintended consequences. Suppose you take a Marxist view, for example, in which the unintended consequences of perfectly nice behavior is the reproduction of class relationships and exploitation. Or suppose you take the cheerful capitalist view, that the unintended

Art, fleeing from capitalism 187

consequence of perfectly nasty behavior is that the workers are well-paid, that national income goes up, and everyone's happy …

JA: … There could even be profit sharing!

DM: … Indeed: that's what the capitalist promise is! In the end, and the "end" comes quickly if you let markets rip, all profit is shared. That's one of the big failures of prediction in Classical Economics, of which Marx is an example. They believed that the rentiers would engorge the national income, when in fact almost from the moment they started to make the assertion the share in national income of land rent (including mineral rights and urban properties) has been falling, so that by now it's extremely small. It fell from 15 percent in England in, say, 1817 to under 3 percent now. But regardless of what the facts are, there is an artistic problem. You have to personalize the unintended consequences to make them interesting. A nice example of this is *The Grapes of Wrath*. I reread it a few years ago on my way out to a term-long visit to that hive of Marxist economists at the University of California at Riverside. I started listening to the tapes in Oklahoma. A thrilling moment was unintended, crossing into California at Needles at the *same time on the tape* the Joads were! Steinbeck tries to do two things in the book, in alternating chapters. He'll have a chapter of the story of the Joads—and that's what a novelist can do—and then he tries to be, interspersed with this, a social scientific character, as though he's looking from a great height down at the American economy, seeing the great movement from the Dust Bowl to California. The most effective parts of the book are the ones that are personal, and the less effective parts are the ones that try to do social science. It's a problem in a painting or in a movie to get the abstractions across. I suppose that what I'm saying is that art is emblematic. Have you ever seen the movie of Ayn Rand's *The Fountainhead*? Gary Cooper is the architect hero. It's very well done as a film. Rand was in control of it artistically, which is very unusual in Hollywood. She insisted on putting in all the abstract speech-making. You may recall that Cooper gives a very long speech at the end of the film, something like 5 minutes, which is long in movie time. So they had to handle the abstraction because she forced them to. But it's not what movies are naturally good at, any more than novels are. So, there's a problem. Anti- or pro-capitalist points of any subtlety, beyond Bad Capitalist/Good Capitalist, are hard to make through art.

JA: Here's a problem. When I watch a movie, most movies, about Nazis in Germany, Nazis are evil, vile—every human failing in the bourgeois imagination exists in the Nazis. Everyone is such a personification of evil that it's overwhelming. It makes it very easy to think that one could always tell a Nazi, and it absolves you from ever seeing your own actions as part of a movement. That one could, in fact, flip a switch for an electric chair, or open up the gas, *and* that one could also at the same be a good father or husband, or so forth.

DM: And, alas, we "know" that's untrue. The banality of evil.

188 *Deirdre McCloskey (and Jack Amariglio)*

JA: But I find these representations extremely problematic—your notion that personification is necessary or useful has an ideological effect. It allows one to detach oneself. There's no complicity.

DM: I agree. I've written on that very point in the early chapters of *The Bourgeois Virtues*. I've written about the word evil. If evil is just about a parody—Dr. Jekyll and Mr. Hyde—then it's very simple. Then, of course, *we* are not evil.

JA: Yeah, it just can be read. It's a mirror. A transparency.

DM: Whereas if you drive carelessly and heroically on the highway, you don't intend any bad, but you may still cause a terrible accident. You don't see your own suburban evil. We agree on that. But, I'm making also a technical point. Perhaps I'm wrong. What the arts are skilled at, I am claiming, is precisely what we economists often say "oh that's just an anecdote" as though anecdotes don't have any power over us, or relevance as science. They do: after all, the history of the world is an "anecdote," sample size $= 1$.

JA: Sometimes it's possible—it has been possible in 20th-century art and theatre, for example—to produce what Brecht called "alienation effects." It's exactly the opposite of your notion. One doesn't identify with character or personality, but one maintains a kind of distance, and this distance has a certain pedagogical purpose.

DM: Yeah, but he's a bad example, since he was so relentlessly anti-capitalist. You know, the big, fat capitalist with a sign on him that says "Fat Capitalist" is how he does it. There's a point that my former dean Stanley Fish makes about *Paradise Lost* which is to the point here. We are invited to be sympathetic with Satan, and the Romantics all said, from Blake on, "Oh, Satan is such a wonderful character! The most attractive personality in his book is the devil." "Milton," as Blake actually said, "must be of Satan's party. Here's this guy who thought he was a Puritan, but actually was a devil-worshipper." But, as Stan points out, and other scholars do, too, that's part of the game. The game is to get you to like the devil, and then see through the devil. So that you have the experience of being fooled by precisely the superficial nonsense that Satan is fooled by. That's why Stan's old book on this was called *Surprised by Sin*. You as the reader of the poem are surprised that you are participating in the sin of pride, that is the chief sin, the only sin, of Satan.

JA: I would want to hold on to that kind of reading for capitalists. I'm comfortable with your criticism because as I said I'm not moved by demonizations of capitalists, or of middle-class life. I am however much more interested in the effects of capitalism, in what it is as a process, what its effects are, and how these play out. I don't think that the effects are all one way. No simple story can tell what these effects are. I'm not much disturbed—some of my colleagues may be disturbed by—sympathetic portrayals of capitalists. It even intensifies my point.

DM: Yes, then it's ironic. A horrible example of this is the complicity of the Dutch people in the extermination of Dutch Jews. It was precisely because, unlike

Art, fleeing from capitalism 189

the Belgians, they had regular bourgeois habits, whereas the Belgians to this day are very disorganized, seen as impulsive—there are a whole lot of jokes regarding this difference, about Southern Dutch and Northern Dutch. And that North Holland tendency to be obedient, punctual, careful resulted in the extermination of two-thirds of the Jewish population of Holland, whereas the sloppy, anti-statist—because they'd been in the Spanish or Austrian empire for so long—traditions of the South Netherlands *saved* two-thirds of their Jews.

JA: Yeah, I like my representations to have this kind of irony. I also like the complicity. I like the fact that I can both detach, but also that there's not sufficient distance. I can't think that these are evil people and I'm not capable of this. Sometimes I'm much more persuaded, and feel more passionately, about my politics and art, or my views of economics and art, when I think that, sure, I'm capable of that. When I think I'm not outside, on the one hand, and on the other hand, I am outside and can see through.

DM: You know, there's an interesting point that you make. That sensibility—the emphasis on irony—is very modern, and in some ways, very postmodern. It's against the naïve view, as we regard it now—we being belated, being late in the history of this art. There's a famous statement by Umberto Eco describing postmodernism in which he says, "a man who says to his girlfriend a sentence that could come out of a Barbara Cartland novel, like 'I love you madly,' will not be appreciated. Whereas, if he says, 'as Barbara Cartland says, "'I love you madly"'—that works in a postmodern sense." Quotation does work in a belated age, and is very open to irony—a point that the Blessed Wayne Booth made long ago.

JA: This calls attention to the different levels of representation. There are always displacements that keep occurring in representation. Irony is one form of displacement.

DM: Yes, surely, there are all kinds of displacement. There were some displacements into the realms of utopia, common in poetry and painting, in which you clean up what happens. There are displacements into the world of symbol. And so forth. I find it tiresome sometime, but it goes with the territory. I do like for example the Harold Washington Library up the street here in Chicago, which has quotations of—quote, quote—Gothic, and—quote, quote—rustication circa 1900—quote, quote—and you see them nudging you. My architect friends mainly hate the building. I, and most Chicagoans, love it.

JA: Deirdre, let me move to another topic. You and I were both trained, though very differently, as economists. One thing I've been concerned about is the idea that a discipline contains its own inventions. And that's the only place to look at new ideas.

DM: There, we completely agree. This inward-looking has been a catastrophe.

JA: Do you have examples, from your own life experience, where new ideas have come to you about economics through art, aesthetics, etc.? I want to be careful here. I'm not talking about reaffirmations of ideas that you have,

190 *Deirdre McCloskey (and Jack Amariglio)*

or reflections of your economic views. But, do you ever experience art as a place where economic discourse is created?

DM: Absolutely. I became a socialist in part because of *The Grapes of Wrath*, which I read when I was sixteen. That and Cisco Huston singing Woody Guthrie songs. I was already something of an anarchist. I had read Prince Kropotkin. And, Emma Goldman. Goldman was my childhood hero. Then I read *The Grapes of Wrath* and became a sort of Joan Baez socialist. I read the first few pages of the Communist Manifesto and thought I was a socialist. So, there in a naïve way is an example from my personal history of an idea coming from art. For a long time, though, I was learning to be a professional economist, and I had my hands full with Keynes and Marshall and so forth. But, in the last 20 years, and especially in the last 10, art has become more and more an important source for me of economic thinking. Again, literary art mainly: I'm not a very visual person. For instance, I read *Buddenbrooks* about 1990 from a sense of shame that I hadn't read it. The only Thomas Mann I had read was *Death in Venice*, because it's short. I saw suddenly in *Buddenbrooks* the force of speech in bourgeois life, at least as perceived through Mann, a child of the high bourgeoisie. It's one of the main themes of the novel. The grandfather is a North-German merchant in the Napoleonic Wars, and he makes the fortune of the family going around making deals, talking, talking. There's an important scene where Tom, his son, is out strolling with his wife in the countryside, and because he's a grain merchant and has to keep up good relations with farmers, he stops by a farmer's house and talks to him. And he makes a deal, for some rye. Mann waxes eloquent about this particular speech act. The novel is filled with speech acts in aid of business—that's one of the things that makes the novel very unusual, in treating bourgeois men at work with a certain respect. And politics, too. Tom, who's now an older man in 1848, and the rest of the town council are held by the mob—the proletarian mob—in the council chambers and aren't allowed to come out. Night fall, the street lanterns, and Tom says, "I've had enough of this." And he goes out and confronts the mob, and with his voice is able to assert his class position. It started me thinking about the role of speech in bourgeois life, not always for the good, and indeed in economic life in general. I was made ready for such an obvious insight through my obsession with rhetoric in economic science. Language and the economy, as I've told you, will be the subject of my next big project, after (so to speak) bourgeois virtue. At the two ends of my economic life I was open to art. In the middle it wasn't that important because I was preoccupied with becoming a competent economist, not thinking anew.

JA: Like the households without servants in Jane Austen, I know how easy it is to think invisibly about art, about what's on your walls, on your table, and the effects that the stuff is having. It is a point that Arjo Klamer and you have long made. This culture is working on you whether or not your self-ideology is one of autonomy.

Art, fleeing from capitalism 191

DM: Indeed. For instance, modernist architecture teaches us constantly that humans, as Isaiah Berlin put it, though not in this context, can do "anything they rationally propose to do." So there's a kind of Enlightenment optimism about rationality and the capabilities of rationality that shows in the modernist skyscraper. It's the intended statement, and indeed, as you say, has a subliminal effect on us. Like downtown Dallas: you think, "Well, we can plunk down 30 of these big glass buildings and we'll have a modern city."

JA: I read *Buddenbrooks* when I was 18. I read it when I was taking a course, I believe it was in history. I was an undergraduate history major.

DM: I was too, until I actually had to take a history course, and found that it required gigantic amounts of *reading*! This would not fit well with my social life, so I switched to economics.

JA: I believe it was a 19th/20th-century European history course. That was one of the texts in the course.

DM: *Buddenbrooks* is a great text as history. It's not of course a photograph of what actually happened, but an imagination of it, an inscription. It perhaps tells more about 1900 than about 1800.

JA: Up to that point growing up, I don't have a recollection of knowing what the middle class was. That is, I have images of it, but there's no texture to it. Because I didn't know people who were doing that for a living—not really; maybe a couple of relatives, but I didn't have much contact with them. So, in some ways I learned the outline of a class perception, coming from particular experiences and discourses about those experiences, from a book like *Buddenbrooks*. It created for me what the middle class was. It wasn't that it was an addition for me, but it was the basis of my "knowledge" of the middle class. I think that's true for many people. There isn't a true dichotomy between all of these objects we call art, and something called reality. It is our real life.

DM: That's a terribly important point. Again Wayne Booth makes it, and Stanley Fish, and all my heroes. We humans live in a world of imagination. Marvell put it this way:

> The mind, that ocean where each kind
> Does straight its own resemblance find;
> Yet it creates, transcending these,
> Far other worlds and other seas,
> Annihilating all that's made
> To a green thought in a green shade.

And Edwin Muir, of our inarticulate cousins the animals:

> [they] are not in time and space
> From birth to death hurled.
> No word do they have, not one

192　*Deirdre McCloskey (and Jack Amariglio)*

> To plant a foot upon,
> Were never in any place.
>
> For with names the world was called,
> Out of the empty air,
> With names was built and walled,
> Line and circle and square …

Since the invention of art, which appears to have been about 50,000 B. C., which also appears to be the time of the invention of full language, our world has been, in part, a world created by art, and our experience of life is seen through. I knew a lot of members of the proletariat as a kid, though upper middle class myself. But I didn't for instance know anything about the agricultural working class when I first started reading about them, though later briefly I worked a summer with them (compare Frost, "The Death of the Hired Man"). It's a great materialist mistake that we have a life, and then there's this ornamental stuff we call art. I think you and I agree that such a notion is false. And it's that which makes art important. After the invention of the printing press, the photograph, film, the amount of re-presentation that we invite into our lives is amazing.

JA: It's hard to read the traces of these things in our work, in our ideas. But, I'm very opposed to the idea that we have the autonomy from the creative processes that our disciplinarity imposes upon us. The problem is how to then create discourses of translations. They can sometimes be extremely clumsy. You know, "he saw that painting, and then he wrote this." It's so easily transposed, that there's nothing that mediates. As you say about abstraction, how do you tell a story in which there are many mediations?

DM: I think it's often helpful to keep the example of music in mind. In music there's no issue of representation, usually. Yes, you can do a thunderstorm, in Beethoven's *Pastorale* symphony—and say, oh yeah, how quaint: a thunderstorm. But that's not what most music is. I'm very suspicious— even contemptuous—of the idea of a realism positing a view from nowhere. It's crazy. Most particularly, the idea that there are "realistic" novels in this special sense seems to me absurd. Or that there are realistic films. I've only become fully aware of the point about movies in the last year or so—which shows how exceptionally stupid I am on the whole about such matters. Not just because there are camera angles and so on, but because in film you can't do what you can do in a novel. In the novel you can do a tremendous amount of internal dialogue. You can make it the whole novel, if you want to. That was the experiment of Faulkner, for example. It's all the thoughts of his characters. An entire 100-page riff in *The Sound and the Fury* is Benji perceiving the world—you're inside his mind. You can't do that in a film because photography is about externals. And, likewise, in a novel you can't do externals, only chat about them. Margaret Mitchell wouldn't *show* the Battle of Atlanta in the novel, but one could in the film of *Gone with the Wind*. One could witness the famous scene of the Confederate wounded,

Art, fleeing from capitalism   193

rank on rank. The whole idea of art as a mirror of nature, to borrow Rorty's title, is a piece of romantic nonsense, *because one or the other part of life, the thought or the external*, is missing.

JA: Let me shift again. A good deal of contemporary criticism of art's complicity with capitalism—maybe for the last hundred years, actually—has been over the issue of commodification—the idea that when art becomes a commodity, it signifies as a commodity. And that its main purpose or meaning is to be a commodity, to be sold. And that therefore that it loses its aesthetic value, or that its aesthetic value is identified now with economic value.

DM: So the first thing the newspapers report about a painting is its value, its price.

JA: Do you have any similar concerns? Arjo Klamer, for example, has such concerns. When art becomes a commodity it gets seen only an object of consumption, where consumption is understood as satisfying material needs. And we lose the non-consumption qualities of art, as a different kind of experience—or, rather, there are some experiences that cannot be reduced to consumption, so that when art becomes a commodity, it is now a matter of consumption, and that these other experiences are either developed in terms of consumption, or just neglected. What's your take on this?

DM: I don't know why art should be exempt from the general commodification of society. But more importantly, as an economic historian I would point out that we've always had commodification. The idea that there's a rise of commodification is I think false, although it is very common in the thinking of the left and the right about economic history. There's a myth, which we sometimes don't make explicit, that there was a time when art and faith and work and love were all non-commodified. And then, this terrible thing happened. Sometime during the 16th century or the 19th all these things came to be bought and sold. But as history it's a fairy-tale. *Everything* was for sale in the Middle Ages. Kingdoms were for sale. Wives and husbands were for sale. Marketplaces were for sale. Eternal salvation was for sale. Everything had a price in Europe in 1400 or 1300, and no one objected. On the contrary, it's in the modern world—in the 19th century especially—that we developed this notion that there are spheres that are sacred and not-to-be-mixed with the profane. The separate sphere of the bourgeois woman as a sacred place, in which she specializes in the virtues of faith, hope, and love while her husband goes out into the harsh world where he must exercise only courage and prudence—not even justice—is something we made up. The idea that art is *not* a commodity is a shockingly modern invention. Phideas, in 5th-century Athens, Michaelangelo, and so forth were businessmen. There are wonderful passages in the autobiography of Benvenuto Cellini where he brags about how much the Pope paid for this silver or gold goblet that he, Cellini, did. Cellini never thought of himself as an Artist, with a capital A. He just said, I am the best craftsman, absolutely the best, and the best *seller* of my crafts around, and I can beat all you other guys, and if they don't like it, I'll be glad to take out my sword and attack you, as he often did. It's a piece of modern sentimentality, a post-Romantic illusion, to think

194 *Deirdre McCloskey (and Jack Amariglio)*

of the Artist with that capital A. The posture of modern Artists is very annoying: almost as annoying as modern Scholars or Scientists. It reminds me of the attitude of modern astronomers, astrophysicists. They want lots of money from the NSF and NASA to build telescopes, and they want you and me to pay. Now: talk about useless! Why does the public need to know about the origin of the universe, or the composition of planets? It's of less value than poetry. You can make a case for a national poetry foundation much more plausibly than an argument for a national science foundation paying for telescopes. And, yet when they're challenged on this point, they'll either take the prudence view, which I call the "Tang defense." That is, you have a space program to develop powdered orange juice. Or, they take the "high frontier" defense. "Oh, the future of humankind is to look into the universe," and they get all weepy. Some artists do exactly the same thing. They are hard-nosed careerists—and I have no objection to that, and the artists I know are all like that. They want to sell their paintings. Commodification is *exactly* what they have in mind. They don't care if it's an art collector who's going to hide it away in his mansion, or some public-spirited person who's going to let the proletariat see the painting. They could care less. (Art dealers, "gallerists" as they call themselves, do care, as Olav Velthuis has shown.) They want us to think of them as priests, and we ourselves especially want them to be priests. But they're priests who sell indulgences.

JA: I hope you see the irony in your position. We *do* have a National Poetry Foundation. It's the National Science Foundation! That's our modern poetry.

DM: Good point. These are all substitutes for an established religion. We don't have an established religion. We created instead a raft of other establishments, academic life for instance. You and I may complain about our colleges, but we're paid more than we're worth! If we had to earn an honest living, if we had to go work, we'd be paid less.

JA: On some points you make, I find myself in agreement. I thought the point you were going to make about artists is that many do—not all—want to sell their paintings, and then they often treat their consumers as philistines. This is an interesting dynamic. On the one hand, they participate in the market since they say they have no choice: they have to earn a living. The very fact that they commodify their art implies that the consumer may be king. But they mock their consumers. Precisely because they see the consumption of their work as consumption. There's something about consuming their work—this person wants my work just to consume it and not for other reasons.

DM: I'm not so sure that artists have that attitude. I suppose some do. But others view their customers with respect. And that I think is the healthy relationship between artists and customers. When you're engaged in sneering at your customers, I think you do bad work as a capitalist.

JA: But don't you think there's a transformation in the very terminology? That they endow their customers with non-customer characteristics, which then enables them to treat them with respect? As "patrons," say. Analogously, if

Art, fleeing from capitalism   195

you treat the artist just as a "producer," that might bother the artist, but if you have a different way of thinking about the term artist, you can buy from this person much easier.

DM: Yes, I think this is quite generally true in capitalism—that you bring the sacred into relationships because you can't stand it to be all profane. The classic example is when you buy a house. You imagine yourself to have a relationship with the realtor. Some realtors have more integrity than others but on the whole—I don't mean to offend anyone—they're not your friends. Or you go and buy a dress: "Oh, it's you, dear," says the saleswoman. I don't think we should be excessively critical of this. It's the people like college professors, who don't have to face the marketplace, who urge a stony, hard-nosed realism on everyone. The professors say, "You *must* know that it's an exploitative relationship you're in, and this person you deal with is out to take advantage of you. Don't you know that, you fool!?" Well, actual business people and actual customers can't live that way. No one can. Wouldn't you agree, Jack? That we have to sweeten our lives?

JA: Yes, but it's not just that. This is a point that you and Arjo and I and others have often made, in somewhat different ways. There is something questionable about the cardboard reductionist views of what it means to be a seller or a buyer, which is why I object so often to the neoclassical theory. There are so many things that go into buying something—so many emotions, feelings, and so forth.

DM: I'm slowly, year by year, coming to agree with you. I'm a slow learner.

JA: The same thing is true with the seller. There are many things going on with the seller.

DM: I agree. I just bought a painting that you can see on the other side of that post from a friend from church. It's a painting of clouds. Small. It's small because it cost a lot of money, at least by my modest standards for spending on visual art. I felt that I should buy it, as a patron. And I bought that painting there—that one with an Iowa scene—from a student artist in Iowa City. I like the painting, but I didn't buy it entirely on consumptionistic grounds. And that painting there I bought as a patron from an amateur—she was a square-dancing friend of mine in Iowa. It was the only painting in the exhibition of hers I could stand; all the others were sentimental, and then in this one, she hit it just right. So, that's why I bought it. It's not that I'm a virtuous person. But, that's what we do, as you said.

JA: Do we need to ennoble—use a language of ennoblement of—the actions of capitalist daily business? I understand that artists may have a lot of respect for people who buy their art, but sometimes they endow these buyers with certain characteristics and qualities, good qualities if they are well-disposed. Sometimes that language of endowment may be that of "the consumer," but sometimes the language shifts to treat such people as "people of taste," for example.

DM: What I'm concerned about is that we shouldn't keep reinventing the aristocracy. The great accomplishment of the bourgeois political movements of the late 18th and 19th centuries was to cut the power of the aristocracy. And in places where that failed, like the German empire, it had bad consequences. We've got to stop looking back on the aristocracy as the model always for the sacred, or for "high stuff," or for the best—that's what the very word "aristocracy" means, of course, "the rule of the best." Academics and artists view themselves as the new aristocracy. They say it often. D. H. Lawrence, who is a reliable source of fatuous remarks of all kinds—fatuous, fascistic remarks—said just this in 1905. That's the purpose of my book, to criticize a particular form of fascism, namely, that which reinvents an aristocracy and sneers at the people. We need a bourgeois identity that's stable, instead of always slipping back into being a cowboy, or being a patron of the arts, aristocratically. The cowboy, or the Duke exhibiting "my last duchess, there upon the wall, looking as if she were alive," are the imaginative models that are presented to us. To go back to the very beginning of our conversation, I'd like to see more models for a satisfactory bourgeois life. We have beautiful images of heroes and saints. Vivid, beautiful, with a thousand years of art behind them. In some cases three thousand. But heroes and saints are not what we need. We need people who are prepared to treat others as equals, who are prepared to make deals, prepared to respect each other. Those are the bourgeois virtues. Put it this way. The universal class into which we are gradually sinking—well, not "sinking": the class we're all becoming—is not the proletariat. This was a big, big mistake by Marx, to suppose that the proletariat was our future. And it's not just in Marx. It's a Classical Economics mistake. If art and society are going to function well together, aren't going to kill each other off, then we have to have an art that comports with this fact and stops denying it. I have a lot of evidence early in my book of how hardy the courageous cowboy, hardboiled detective, knight, the Seven Samurai/High Noon/Shane kind of figure is in the imaginary of the American bourgeois male. It's bad for the soul, and it's bad for business.

JA: It's an interesting point, that the very notions that we have—that the representations that we have of what constitutes what we think of as individuality may be an individualized lord.

DM: Exactly. It's dangerous because it's anti-female, it's anti-gay, it's anti-black. It's about the dream world of bourgeois white, American men and how grand such people are. How they should decide things with their fists. Look at Bush II, strutting around. There's a very interesting scene in *The Sun Also Rises*, where the hero and narrator comes into a Parisian dance hall with his girlfriend, and sees a bunch of gays, in this case effeminate homosexuals. The hero is almost overcome with a desire to hit them—as he puts it, "to swing on them."

JA: But I wonder in your own imagery about individuality, and so forth, whether one can find traces of a similar sort. When you are forced to state what are the virtues of the individual in the economy, since you endow this individual with a certain mastery, and orderliness, and …

Art, fleeing from capitalism   197

DM: I understand. A perfect example of this is Ayn Rand, who, as Arjo pointed out to me a long time ago, is a romantic. She's romantic about heroes: they're Arthurian knights. The danger is of modern American businessmen thinking of themselves in terms of Sun Tzu's *Art of War*. (By the way, the translation is the Princeton University Press's cash cow, selling gigantic numbers, supporting a whole library of scholarly books!) If you think of being a manager as exercising the "art of war" then you are going to do a lot of unjust and nasty things, because that's what tough guys do. When the going gets tough, Nixon used to say, the tough get going. Have you ever noticed that John Wayne is always manhandling women? He's always grabbing them by the arm.

JA: Yeah, placing them somewhere. He "relocates" them.

DM: There was of course in our father's generation, that was the expected role. Even very sweet types—Gary Cooper does this. In *The Fountainhead*, Gary Cooper rapes the heroine.

JA: So, if that's our conception of what it means to be an individual or a hero …

DM: A disaster. There's a mistaken, ahistorical claim that individualism springs out of European civilization in the 16th century, and before that we were collectivist. Well, try telling that to people in the middle ages. They'd say, "What do you mean collectivist? Are you nuts? We can't be collectivist. We've got to watch out for ourselves and we're individualists, you can be sure of that." But there's a version of individualism which is not "individualism" of the comic book sort, that is, it is a *moral* individualism. The country club version of the Adam Smith/*Art-of-War* folks says, "Being selfish is all that's necessary." I was coming home last night from Northwestern on the subway. As I was standing on the platform a young woman next to me took the plastic cap off a water bottle and threw it on the platform. In a grandmotherly way, I said, "Dear. You've dropped that." I didn't want her to throw it on the pavement. And instead of catching the point, she said, "Oh, no, I was just throwing it away." And I said—and it just came out of me—"What kind of citizen are you throwing this on the platform?" And then some guy got into the act on the other side, and he said, "Do you know how long it takes plastic to biodegrade?" She was out of it. She didn't know what we were talking about. We didn't carry it on, but we were indignant at her violation of the rules of civilized behavior. And I think that's what art should be telling us. Not just that we're isolates, and the world is a lonely place, and how awful it is, and every woman for herself. But: that we're part of a community, that we should care about other people. Chagall, not Picasso.

JA: This conception of individualism is not usual. It allows for us to see that the individual hero, as feminists have long said, also gets his shirts ironed. When he goes out into the street, somebody has ironed his shirts, somebody has fed him, and so forth. So, we're seeing him at a moment, and that moment is glorified, and the rest of the conditions that allowed him to go out that way are completely obliterated. Marx had a term for this notion of the individual, which you may not like: the social individual.

198   *Deirdre McCloskey (and Jack Amariglio)*

DM: No, I don't object to that. I think the social individual is exactly what we ought to be. He approved of that, right?

JA: Well, he's describing it at a particular historical moment.

DM: He's making the point that we're all in a society that we think that we're individuals.

JA: Yes, but he also had a value that he placed on this notion of the individual.

DM: By the way, that point that you make that someone has to do the washing up is something that's become a lot clearer to me as a woman than as a man. Then, it was, oh well, it's tough. Now, I'm sharply aware that someone has to clean the toilets—because I'm cleaning them. The new "virtue ethicists," who are disproportionately women, are always making the point that an Aristotelian ethics cannot forget—as utilitarianism or Kantianism or reversed Hegelianism always is forgetting—that everyone was once a child, being taken care of. Another of my heroes, Alasdair MacIntyre, has come to see that we are "dependent rational animals." All three.

JA: This is what I was trying to discuss earlier when we were talking about economic representations, and when you might "see" maximizing behavior. What would characterize that sight, and how would you go about talking about it? Sometimes I think that our images—our imaginary—are very much connected with such notions as the individual; that is, the isolated individual, or the hero. That's not a company in which the people have talked to one another to come up with a decision about how to make a profit. So, we can have this image of someone who makes this dramatic, individualist decision to make profit (maximizing behavior). But this is very different from a company in which people sit down to make decisions to make profits.

DM: Actual people. With egos. Who were once children, and speak this or that language.

JA: For example, our mutual friend Bregje is working on a project on ideas, and one of the aspects she's investigating is the question of intellectual proprietorship, when and how it is that people adopt languages of "this is my idea," or when it is "your idea," or when do you know it's "your idea." When you talk about the exchange of ideas, as I said to you, this is one way to talk about it. We can see each other as proprietors of ideas. Another is that we're collaborators.

DM: Yes, indeed. I've always favored the collaboration, at least theoretically. I'm a socialist at heart, I suppose.

JA: So, these imaginaries are really important. What's the language we're going to use to describe such processes? Same thing with profit maximization. Even if you accepted it, you could have a language that makes it very different from the heroic or isolated individual.

DM: Here's how I argue. There are virtues. You can make a good case for there being 7 virtues—the 7 principal virtues. I don't care too much about it being exactly 7, though they work well and have 2500 years of European thought behind each of them. Anyway there are virtues and they cannot all

Art, fleeing from capitalism 199

be collapsed into the virtue of Prudence, as Bentham wished, or the virtue of Justice, as Kant wished. The extreme types of the hero who has only courage, or the saint who has only love, supplemented by faith, or the merchant who has only prudence, supplemented by commercial courage—these are dangerous models for human beings. If you're an artist who adopts the attitude "I'm going to paint anything that will sell, I don't care, I don't have any artistic ideas or principles, I'm just going to paint commodities," then you make yourself into a lousy artist. If you're a businessperson whose only virtue is the bottom line, you end up as an Enron executive serving time in prison, or just extremely wealthy and extremely corrupt. And so forth. It is vice. In fact, a classic analysis of evil and vice is that it's the extreme exercise of *one* virtue, unbalanced by the other six. So, the prisons are filled with courageous people, and that's how they justify their lives: "At least I'm a man, I'm tough, I'm brave." Yeah they're brave, but they're unjust, and unloving, and intemperate. So, it's in terms of the classical virtues that I want art to proceed.

JA: So, do you think that aesthetic representations are, for you, expressions of a moral economy? Do you really want it to be that much of a project?

DM: Yes. There's nothing historically unprecedented about what I'm saying. Before 1848 all art was this way, all art was an improvement project. That didn't mean that Bach didn't compose on aesthetic principles that did not themselves derive from ethical thinking. He certainly did. And what distinguishes him from others not so good is that he was very good at it. But his project was to glorify God. He said so. And he didn't just say so—it's obvious in his oratorios. It's not just because he was the paid church organist that he did so, though that was one reason, a commercial, non-Artist motive. It was because he believed in God. In fact, a change occurs in the moralization of art when advanced intellectuals stop believing in God, stopped justifying God's ways to man. I think that's where the modern artistic problem comes. On the one hand the artist gets elevated to a priesthood; before they didn't think of themselves as being priests. But these new "priests" become scornful of their flock, and stop preaching to them. The museum becomes a church, especially in the 19th century, and then develops in the late 20th century into a site from which to mount assaults on the bourgeoisie that paid for it. And science and art together become substitutes for religion. The Science section of *The New York Times* is like a Religion page. As you said before, the astronomers sound like artists. Art and science acquire an elevated position because we've got a hole in the sacred in our society, filled with art and science. But the people so elevated let their new aristocratic position go to their heads. In fact, you know that I think we should all go back to believing in God. She's a better bet than Science or Art.

JA: Do you think you have a better chance of converting people to bourgeois virtues through belief in God?

DM: Yes. Many middle-class people want a purpose in life, and don't have it. They need to be told that the work they do is worthwhile. It's a scandal

200 *Deirdre McCloskey (and Jack Amariglio)*

that so much of our art is contemptuous of what most people do. There's nothing wrong with being the manager of a grocery store. It's not evil. It's not bad. It's good. It makes me weep to think of people who regard their lives as meaningless because artists and intellectuals have failed so signally in the last century and a half to carry on the project of developing the art for a commercial society. They have devalued all manner of work, proletarian and bourgeois.

JA: The irony here is that there are critics who argue that all art is so tied to capitalist commodification that it is a sign for commercial society. And your point is that art for commercial society doesn't exist!

DM: In its content, it hardly exists. Though there are contrary tendencies. American black music was highly commercial from the beginning, and is a gigantic artistic achievement. It was on the radio right from the beginning commercial, understandable. When Charlie Parker initiated an exclusive way of playing jazz, which eventually becomes highly academic, then it stops being as bourgeois as it ought to be. When jazz artists start thinking of themselves as Jazz Artists, capital J, capital A, and stop trying to please ordinary people in a juke joint, then it loses its popular juices. Here I follow the English poet, Philip Larkin, who was also in the 1930s and 1940s a jazz critic. He spoke of the Three Ps as the great curse of modern art in the 20th century, the Three Ps who made art difficult, who made it an elite activity, instead of something that could be bought and sold with pleasure. Instead of being commodified. The Three Ps in his view were Pound, Picasso, and Charlie Parker. To which I would add, for the economists listening, Paul Anthony Samuelson.

JA: I think we should end on that note.

Part III
Name your price

10 Imaginary currencies

Contemporary art on the market—critique, confirmation, or play

Olav Velthuis

Introduction

On the 4th of January 1997, the Russian artist Aleksandr Brener visits the Stedelijk Museum of Amsterdam and fixes a large dollar sign with green spray paint on Kazimir Malevich's white canvas *Suprematism* (1922–27). Afterwards he turns himself in voluntarily to a guard of the museum. More than a month later, Brener explains in a written statement that the sign was no crime but a political act, directed against the cultural elite and the atmosphere of amorality which prevails in the art world.[1] The dollar sign was a proof of truly democratic art, the forebode of a revolution that would put an end to the economic, political, and cultural corruption of our times. It was meant to lay bare how corrupt the "money trade" of the art world is, and how subversive the play of market forces. The fact that the media coverage of the incident was most of all interested in the economic value of *Suprematism* (over six million euros according to the insurance policy) went to show.

Brener's political motives notwithstanding, the art world was outraged; at court the artist got sentenced to imprisonment for ten months and a fine of about $7,000 for the restoration of the painting. Only a small number of individual artists, along with the international art magazine *Flash Art*, were sensitive to the radical avant-gardist background of his iconoclastic act. As Brener himself maintained, artistic movements such as Dada, Surrealism, Russian Futurism, and, more recently, Situationism had preceded and inspired him. In other words, the painting-turned-into-currency carried on the legacy of the avant-garde, which had always been critical of the official institutions that constitute the art world (see Bürger, 1974 [1996]). For symbolic reasons, the art market was an appropriate target for the political statement Brener wanted to make. Although other artists have expressed their interest and concern about the economy in less radical formats, Brener's act does not stand on its own. In fact, the contemporary art world has seen a resurgent interest in economic topics such as the creation of economic value, the constitution of money, or the commercial character of the art world. Artists started issuing their own bonds or money, marketed seemingly non-commodifiable goods such as air or sea water, infiltrated in businesses or started their own, and created their own alternative economies, in which gift rather than market exchange comes

204   *Olav Velthuis*

to dominate. "Imaginary economics," to twist a term by the literary scholar Kurt Heinzelman, is in other words booming (Heinzelman, 1980).

The reasons for this strong interest in economic topics among contemporary artists are diverse. To name a few: the hierarchy of high and low art has been questioned since the 1960s; the relationship between art and commerce, which partially coincided with this hierarchy, changed accordingly (Huyssen, 1986). Also, the notion of an artwork as a two-dimensional canvas or three-dimensional sculpture was questioned by new art forms such as conceptual art, performance, and installations and the "dematerialization" of the art object (see Lippard, 1997); for imaginary economics, this "dematerialized" art object was a welcome medium, since it provided many more means of expression than the flat, painted canvas of the past. Moreover, due to the renewed interest in modern artists like Marcel Duchamp and Joseph Beuys, contemporary artists have become reflexive about the different roles artists can play in society, about the interdependency of the artistic and other societal fields, and about notions of what art is (see Danto, 1997; Kaprow, 1993). Thus, many contributions to imaginary economics take the form of what Beuys called "social sculpture": they are interdisciplinary, participative interventions in everyday life, which actively question the boundaries of the art world.

Strong as it is in the last decades of the 20th and the first decade of the 21st century, interest in economic issues is certainly not new to the field of art. A sheer endless list of modern artists has been concerned with the economy in general and the art market in particular in interviews, autobiographies, letters, or other recorded statements, mostly in negative terms.[2] Some, most notably Marxist, art historians have made the more radical claim that modern art can be read as a structural critique on capitalism; artistic movements such as futurism and cubism would for instance represent the fragmentation, alienation, and disruption of everyday life caused by capitalist markets (Brettell, 1999, p. 60). Finally, Duchamp, Beuys, and other well known artists such as Andy Warhol, Yves Klein, and Marcel Broodthaers have addressed the intersection of art and economics in their work more explicitly: they fabricated their own checks and bonds (Duchamp), exchanged air for gold (Klein), converted gold into art (Broodthaers), printed dollar bills in edition on silk-screens (Warhol), or wrote texts about the identity of art and economy on banknotes and blackboards (Beuys).[3]

Production of knowledge

In this paper I consider such artistic creations of money, constructions of firms, and convolutions of value as attempts to reflect on, investigate, or comment on economic processes (see Velthuis, 2004, for a more elaborate statement). The focus of this paper is on work made in the late 20th and early 21st centuries. One reason for this focus is that work made in this period may have been well represented in a series of exhibitions which have put the interrelationship between art and economy firmly on the agenda of the art world, but it hardly attracted any scholarly attention. This work merits the attention of social scientists since

Imaginary currencies 205

the artists involved, intentionally or not, produce knowledge about the economy. Their body of work can be seen as a discourse which presents substitutes as well as complements to other economic discourses, whether those of academics or of laymen (see Amariglio, this volume; Amariglio, and Ruccio, 1999).

Knowledge production with artistic or poetic means obviously has its shortcomings. If only because of its non-verbal character, imaginary economics is hardly systematic, precise, or encompassing. Its focus tends to be on the particular rather than the universal, on commentary rather than analysis. Therefore, if academic economists have systematically ignored laymen's everyday discourses on the economy, which they refer to pejoratively as *ersatz* economics and which they treat as "a less organized, inchoate version of the knowledge produced by academic economists," imaginary economics is even less likely to be taken seriously (see Amariglio and Ruccio, 1999). Nevertheless, the case for art as a source of knowledge is far from novel (see e.g. Young, 2001). Indeed, the claim of this paper is that contemporary art enhances our understanding of the economy. Just as other non-academic discourses continuously challenge what is considered to be "economic," and how the economy should be understood, artists have done so as well. Imaginary economics, to put it in the words of Jack Amariglio and David Ruccio, has a discursive structure and an integrity of its own (Amariglio and Ruccio, 1999).

As will become clear from this paper, the contributions made by artists engaged in imaginary economics vary widely in terms of style, medium, and strategy. Indeed, it has been noted that, while modern science has increasingly specialized in the course of the 20th century, visual art underwent the opposite process of "despecialization" (Bierens, 1999). This has led to a situation in which artists can legitimately make work in media as different as theater, video, dance, and poetry. Some, for instance, like the American artist Mark Lombardi, stay relatively close to academic representational means by depicting the global economy as a complex network between politicians, business firms, rogue states; in order to do so, Lombardi meticulously makes large-scale pencil drawings on which numerous nodes are connected through ties of different sorts. Others opt for a strategy of mimicry and parody, which puts them at a much further remove from academic means: artists such as SERVAAS, Nobuki Tochi, or eToy, for instance, have started their own business enterprises, albeit with tongue in cheek. In doing so, they have drawn attention to the symbolic apparatus of the modern business firm, which may go unrecognized in daily economic life, but which bestows legitimacy upon the firm nonetheless.

The strength of some contributions to imaginary economics, such as Sylvie Fleury's ready-made sculptures of empty shopping bags with the names and logos of luxury brands, is that they are evocative at a single glance. Other works, however, such as Michael Landy's meticulous process of first archiving, then decomposing, and finally destroying all his belongings, are captivating because they slowly unfold in time.[4] Some works within imaginary economics, such as Beuys' statement *Kunst=Kapital* ("art=capital"), written on banknotes as well as blackboards, are so ambivalent as to raise different questions simultaneously.

206   *Olav Velthuis*

Other works, such as the installations by the critical artist Hans Haacke, present the viewer with a strong, politically informed commentary that seems to allow for a single reading only.

In substantive respects, the variety of knowledge produced by imaginary economics contrasts with the relative uniformity of the academic discipline of economics, dominated as it is by neoclassical thinking. In the remainder of this paper, I will distinguish three substantively different moments in imaginary economics: the critical moment of the 1970s, the affirmative moment of the 1980s, and the playful moment of the turn of the 21st century. Before elaborating on this threefold classification, let me point out that this classification is doubtlessly equivocal. First of all, although my characterization of the 1970s as a critical moment and the 1980s as affirmative is not new (see e.g. Lippard, 1997; Ardenne, 1992 [1995]; Foster, 1996), their fit is far from perfect. Critical imaginary economics is hardly limited to the 1970s. For instance, embedded in movements like "activist art" and "community art" (Lippard, 1984), and thanks in part to the negative impulses provided by Reagonomics and Thatcherism in the 1980s and neo-liberalism and globalization in the 1990s, critique has been carried on to the 21st century. Conversely, during the critical days of the 1970s, pop-art, considered to be affirmative and commodifiable by many art critics, art historians and artists, maintained a strong presence in the art world.

Secondly, rather than *being* critical, affirmative, or playful, imaginary economics can at most be said to *inspire* or *suggest* one reading rather than another. In many cases different, often opposite, readings are possible. The work of artists as different as Andy Warhol and Marcel Duchamp, for instance, have both received critical as well as affirmative interpretations (see e.g. Jones, 1994; Huyssen, 1986). Or take the example of Landy, the artist who destroyed all his possessions. According to some, his work should be seen as a critique of the dominant role that property plays in postmodern consumer society; by destroying his possessions, Landy suggests that a different economic reality is possible in which purchasing power does not reign and the intimate tie between identity and property is cut through. Others, however, may point at the affirmative implications of Landy's work: with his project the artist may have destroyed his own possessions, but for doing so he was compensated handsomely. In the currency of attention, for instance, 40,000 people came to see his show, the British press wrote about it abundantly, while curators invited him to participate in other, future shows. Also, the entire process was registered in a documentary as well as a book that was published afterwards. To put it in the words of the French sociologist Pierre Bourdieu, Landy profitably exchanged economic capital (material possessions) for a form of capital of another, symbolic or reputational kind (Bourdieu, 1992 [1996]; Cumming, 2002; King, 2002).

Jacques Derrida has recognized the very multiplicity of meanings of such projects, the indeterminacy of signifiers that any text, including works of art, set in motion, as a form of play in itself (Derrida, 1970; see Sutton-Smith, 1997). In this paper I will use the word "play" in a more restricted way: as a free activity on the part of artists, which takes place in isolation from the wider economy,

Imaginary currencies   207

is unproductive as well as uncertain, obeys to its own rules rather than the "laws of the market," and revolves around make-belief and imagination.

From criticism to complicity

In the 1970s, contemporary artists by and large tried to bypass the market by making non-commodifiable work such as performances, happenings, conceptual art, or printed matter that could be reproduced easily and cheaply. By doing so, these artists presented a political-economic critique of the art world and its focus on originality and uniqueness, its fetishization of the art object, and the alienation that commodification caused among artists.[5] As Lucy Lippard, an activist and one of their key spokespersons, characterized their political-economic strategy: "since dealers cannot sell art-as-idea, economic materialism is denied along with physical materialism" (Kwon, 2003, p. 84; Lippard, 1997; Rosler, 1984, p. 325). The aim of many was, in the words of Peter Bürger, to eliminate art as an institution, to bring art back into life, or at least to subject the reigning economy of the art world to critique (Bürger, 1974 [1996]).

Out of this political-economic context, a high-profile, successful group of artists emerged which would commonly be referred to as appropriation artists, including Barbara Kruger, Sherrie Levine, Jenny Holzer, Cindy Sherman, Robert Longo, and Louise Lawler. Many of them "appropriated" images that were readily available in either low or high culture; they combined these appropriations in a collage-like fashion, which subverted their original meanings, and supplied them with critical, allegorical overtones. Apart from addressing issues of representation and feminism, these appropriation artists scrutinized the functioning of the art market in the Western art world.

Kruger's collage "When I hear the word culture I take out my checkbook," for instance, questions the motives that drive collectors in their acquisition of art (the *oneliner* was "appropriated" from Jean-Luc Godard's 1963 movie "Le Mépris"; see Linker, 1990). Lawler unmasked the modernist notion of the autonomy of art by photographing works of art, often made by well-known artists, in their everyday habitats. These habitats included auction houses (either before or during the actual sale), the so-called neutral white boxes of art galleries, the bedrooms or living rooms of private collectors, entrances of corporate offices, and storage spaces of art dealers. By doing so, Lawler questioned the neutral, decontextualized presentation of artworks in museums and art catalogues. Her work suggests that art circulates in a commodified regime like any other commodity; works of art serve to enhance the status of corporations, to decorate a living room, or, simply, to make a nice profit for its owner (Lawler, 2000; Elger and Weski, 1994). Levine became known for photographs she made of books depicting works by modern masters such as Vincent van Gogh, Claude Monet, or Egon Schiele; with these copies of copies, she pointed at the fetishist connotation of the masterpiece, or, to put it in terms of art historian Benjamin Buchloh, she "depletes the current commodity status" of these artworks (Bochloh, 1982). What is it about these works that we exactly value, her work urges us to ask. To what extent does the name of the artist

208 *Olav Velthuis*

function here, as in the capitalist economy, as a brand name? Why is the art world so keen on distinguishing originals from copies, fakes, and forgeries?

If appropriation art was diachronically related to the 1970s and its economy of the non-commodity, its synchronic context was a different one: the 1980s saw a "come back" of the art market and the two-dimensional, commodifiable painting, headed by German neo-expressionist painters (e.g. Georg Baselitz, Rainer Fetting, Jörg Immendorff), Italian trans avant-garde painters (most noticeably Francesco Clémente, Sandro Chia, and Enzo Cucci, nicknamed as the three Cs), and American post-modernist painters such as David Salle, Eric Fischl, and Julian Schnabel.[6] These were the days that the art market boomed in capitals around the world, that works of art fetched record prices which subsequently made headlines in the newspapers, and that artists were treated as celebrities in the popular press. At the end of the decade, the curators of the prestigious 1989 Biennial Exhibition at the Whitney Museum in New York noted in the introduction to the catalogue that "[w]e have moved into a situation where wealth is the only agreed upon arbiter of value. Capitalism has overtaken contemporary art, quantifying and reducing it to the status of a commodity. Ours is a system adrift in mortgaged goods and obsessed with accumulation, where the spectacle of art consumption has been played out in a public forum geared to journalistic hyperbole" (Armstrong, Marshall et al., 1989, p. 10).

In the eyes of some, this reinforced the validity of the critique developed by appropriation artists, but others responded with an affirmative type of imaginary economics. At the time, one of these artists, Haim Steinbach, characterized this shift adequately in a forum discussion titled "From Criticism to Complicity": "There has been a shift in the activities of the new group of artists in that there is a renewed interest in locating one's desire, by which I mean one's own taking pleasure in objects and commodities, which includes what we call works of art. There is a stronger sense of being complicit with the production of desire, what we traditionally call beautiful seductive objects, than being positioned somewhere outside of it (Steinbach, 1986)."

The affirmative moment of the 1980s used similar citational techniques as appropriation artists; going further back in the history of modern art, they made use of the Duchampian readymade, albeit without its initial critical and radical implications. Steinbach himself, for instance, arranged series of aesthetic consumer objects as different as trash cans, pans, teapots, shoes, often in series, on triangular pedestals attached to museum walls; in one idiosyncratic work, Steinbach made his affirmative intentions more explicit by incorporating one of his own bank statements in his work (Ardenne, 1992 [1995], p. 113). His colleague Ashley Bickerton put a digital counter in one of the so-called commodity-sculptures he made. At a gallery show the counter displayed the acquisition price of the work; afterwards it advanced with two dollar cents per minute. "It corresponded roughly to how much pieces were going up at that point," the artist explained (Haden-Guest, 1996, p. 205). Jeff Koons, like Steinbach, displayed series of everyday commodities such as vacuum cleaners and basket balls in showcases and aquariums, which he sophisticatedly lit with neon lights. In all their sublimity,

Imaginary currencies   209

these objects seem to suggest that no world exists outside of the economy of permanent desire in which they circulate.

Art historian Hal Foster argued in *The Return of the Real* that these and other commodity artists did not resist "the manic marketing of the time," but instead identified with "the spectacle of the market" (Foster, 1996, p. 99). They reduced Duchamp's notion of the readymade to an empty sign, deconstruction to complicity, and ideology critique to contempt: "Engagement of the dominant culture became a near embrace, and identification with patrons seemed all but total. Artists and patron alike tended to regard art in terms of prestige signs and investment portfolios, and both tended to operate under a conventionalist ethos that treats almost everything as a commodity-sign for exchange" (Foster, 1996, p. 122). The conclusion of this type of imaginary economics work is that the logic of art and economy coincide and that artistic and economic value are fully commensurable.

The market is the medium

The mold of imaginary economics of the 1970s and the 1980s was the binary mold of critique versus affirmation. Imaginary economics of the 1990s and onwards has questioned this mold in a number of respects. When it comes to critique, for instance, artists do not necessarily position themselves outside of the political economy they are criticizing; instead, they are implicated in the system that their work addresses. In doing so, some of these artists do not resist the market, but deploy it as one of their artistic tools. Their critique does not aim at the values underlying the art market such as originality, autonomy, and uniqueness, but at the elitism of the art world, its social exclusivity, and the power position that gatekeepers such as critics and curators occupy in this political-cultural constellation. For instance, the Belgian artist Guillame Bijl, the Danish artist Jens Haaning, or the Thai artist Rirkrit Tiravanija all seduce outsiders into the art world by using the (super-)market as a democratic institution. As a result, the critique-affirmation dichotomy is overturned in their work. In 1999 Haaning opened a supermarket called *Super Discount* in the art museum of a Swiss town. There he offered necessities as well as luxury items for sale against discount prices. Haaning was able to do so by importing these items from France, and circumvented various import duties by labeling them as pieces of art. In the Migros Museum of Zurich, Tiravanija organized a supermarket titled "Social Capital." Among a select range of supermarket goods that could actually be sold, Tiravanija exhibited his own work as well as works by among others Dan Flavin, Thomas Schütte, and Gilbert & George out of the collection of the museum. On various occasions, Bijl installed entire supermarkets in a museum context, without the possibility, however, of visitors actually buying these goods (Larsen, 1999).

The Swiss artists Christoph Büchel and Gianni Motti likewise tried to involve outsiders in the art world with the help of the budget for an exhibition that they were granted by the Zurich art institution Helmhaus. The intention of their project, which they called *Capital Affair*, was to leave the museum space entirely empty,

210 *Olav Velthuis*

and to invite visitors to the exhibition to look for a certificate, which they would hide somewhere in the museum with the help of a notary. The first person to find the certificate would be entitled to the entire budget of 50,000 Swiss francs. This would have turned the exhibition combination of a Buddhist contemplation of the void, and a vulgar treasure hunt; it would have forced visitors to museums to look with their own eyes rather than following the instructions of an audio guide or information board, but at the same time it would lay bare the fetishist desires that the museum instigates; it exposes the spectacle of economic value that museums harbor. In doing so, the project moreover had a striking anti-elitist connotation: high art may only draw an elite; the chance to win a large sum of money draws the masses. However, after the Zurich city president heard about the project, he forced the museum to decrease the budget to 20,000 Swiss francs shortly before the opening of the show. Upon this decision, Motti and Büchel decided to cancel the exhibition in its entirety.

Büchel also made use of economic means when he was invited to participate in the international exhibition *Manifesta 4* in Frankfurt, Germany. He decided to sell his right to participate in the exhibition to the highest bidder in an *eBay* internet auction. With this project, which he called *Invite yourself*, Büchel questioned the monopoly that curators have in the allocation of museum space and institutional recognition. The highest bidder, and *de facto* invitee to the Manifesta, was the New York artist Sal Randolph. She paid $15,099 for her right to participate. Randolph, herself a notorious opponent of the market as well as the elitism of the art world, invited artists of the whole world to participate in her own project, which she called *Free Manifesta* (in the same year Randolph also organized a *Free Biennial* in Venice). As opposed to the actual Manifesta, with its opaque selection process of artists, Randolph allowed anybody to participate if they wanted to: "Any artist who wishes may participate with such works as ephemeral installations, guerilla performances, interactions, dérives, situations, giveaways, ambulatory declamations, parties, neo-happenings, apartment shows, guided experiences, screenings, projections, mail art, downloadable music, web-based work," she wrote in her invitation.

Or take, finally, the case of John Freyer, an American artist who sold all his belongings, including intimate objects like the braces that he wore as a child, on the internet through the auction website *eBay* (see Cohen, 2002; Mirapaul, 2001).[7] The work raises critical questions about the market, and about the dominance of commerce on the once Utopian medium of the internet in particular, by actually making use of it. And by buying Freyer's possessions on the electronic market, "ordinary" people, sometimes without even knowing it, participated in his art project; in an attempt to further democratize the project, Freyer later visited the new owners of his possessions in order to find out how the biography of these possessions, to use a term of the anthropologist Igor Kopytoff (1986), had been continued after the sale.

In all these cases, artists do not see the market solely as an instrument of exploitation and alienation, but also of liberation and democratization. They deploy the market as a provocation directed at a snobbish art world whose official, albeit

Imaginary currencies   211

false, stance it has long been to keep commerce at bay. Indeed, Marx had already recognized the market's positive, but destructive, side when he argued that the market would eliminate the pre-modern feudal power structures that serfs were implicated in.

Reversed imperialism

The critique-affirmation mold has not only been hollowed out by this new generation of critical artists, but also by a new type of affirmative imaginary economics which emerged in the 1990s. The artists involved no longer bought into the economic imperialism which Steinbach, Bickerton, or Koons seemed to propagate, but instead claimed a form of cultural imperialism: art and economy would not be congruent because the logic of the art world is deep down a quantitative logic, but because the economy would be increasingly dependent on the qualitative logic of the arts, including cultural values like creativity, identity, and originality. As Jeremy Rifkin puts it in *The Age of Access*: "Machine images like efficiency, productivity, utility, deliverability, and computability are falling by the wayside, replaced by theatrical images of cultural production" (Rifkin, 2000).

The Dutch artist collective Orgacom put this reversed imperialism in practice when they started scrutinizing economic processes in detail and complicating mainstream economic conceptions of these. As *artists in residence*, they study business firms and other organizations. Subsequently, they try to visualize the corporate culture or communicative processes within these organizations, highlighting which values the organization revolves around. Within one of the organizations that were their "clients," Orgacom organized election campaigns for all employees, including those who had previously not been able to voice their concerns. After interviewing these employees, Orgacom designed campaign material such as posters for them.

Likewise the British artist Rachel Baker stressed the need for cultural values within the commercial domain by organizing a temp agency for artists within an exhibition she was invited to participate in. Artists could register with the agency, after which Baker would look for a suitable employer. She motivated the project as follows: "Artists are an underexploited human resource for the modern workplace and the workplace is an underexploited resource for the modern artist. (…) Managers are realising the need to cultivate creativity and conviviality to maximise profits since hard labour and long hours are no longer guarantees of results."[8]

The playful economy

The third and last element that distinguishes post-1980s imaginary economics from previous moments is its playful character. Contrary to both critical and affirmative economics of the 1970s and 1980s, a new generation of artists refuses to take either the economy or art world seriously. Instead, these artists create their own, isolated commercial universes, in which fake money circulates, mimicry

212 _Olav Velthuis_

companies produce objects that nobody wants, and economic decision making gravitates around parody. These universes are organized according to the often idiosyncratic rules of the artist's own making. Cherishing the non-utilitarian and the unproductive, playful imaginary economics proposes a radically different mode of thinking about the economy. Without fixing an alternative, the suggestion is that economies cannot be analyzed in terms of critique vs. affirmation or other modernist dichotomies like market vs. gift, price vs. value, production vs. creation, or self-interest vs. altruism.

Surely this playful element is not new to imaginary economics. Take the check that Duchamp wrote in 1919 to pay for the services of his Parisian dentist, Daniel Tzanck. Duchamp fabricated the check by hand; worth 115 dollars, it was drawn on the "Teeth's Loan and Trust Company, Consolidated," located on Wall Street. The status of the Tzanck Check, as the work has come to be referred to, has always been ambiguous, taking the identity as a copycat work of art and counterfeit money at one and the same time. Also, in spite of being constructed as legal tender, it was part of a reciprocal exchange relationship rather than a quid-pro-quo market exchange. As Heinzelman remarked about the Tzanck Check: "Because the check is both an artistic imitation of a monetary draft and an economic imitation of an artistic creation, the question of 'value' is thrown into hopeless confusion (...) Duchamp's check, like the surrealist's readymade object or _object trouvé_, purposefully distorts the question of value by raising it in an inappropriate or surprising context. Here, economic and aesthetic signifiers cross, disrupting each other. The check is found to be a 'sign' only as a given individual is willing to bestow significance upon it" (Heinzelman, 1980, p. 4). Or as Dalia Judovitz noted in relation to the check: "[v]alue is created through exchange, through the display, circulation, and consumption of the work, in a game where worth has no meaning in and of itself" (Judovitz, 1995, p. 163).

Such confusions of value, incidental as they have been throughout the 20th century, have become a returning feature of imaginary economics after the 1980s. The American artist J.S.G. Boggs for instance fabricates his own currency, like Duchamp.[9] Boggs' hand drawn bills are readily distinguished from actual money; the backside of the bills is left blank and accidental puns are added to the front. Instead of "In God we trust," an orange 50 dollar bill reads "Red gold we trust"; a Swiss 100 Francs bill depicts Boggs himself as an "angry young man"; on a 10 dollar bill the building of the American treasury is replaced by the supreme court accompanied by the text "Please give me a fair trial"; "United States of America" is modified into "Unit of State of America."

The playfulness of Boggs' bills is also underscored by the various rules he makes up for his own artistic endeavor. The most important one is that he only parts with his money in an actual economic transaction, against the face value of the bill he has drawn. In fact, Boggs managed to spend his bills in several million dollars, worth of economic transactions. He paid for a Harley Davidson motorbike, for hotel and restaurant bills, for airplane tickets, for artworks, rare old bills, and for many other goods. In Portland, Boggs bought a hamburger with a 1,000-dollar bill, and received 997 real dollars in exchange. He will not sell his work directly

Imaginary currencies   213

to collectors, however, in spite of the demand which has emerged for his bills throughout the years.

Another rule is that collectors can buy a tip to find out where Boggs spent his bills a day after the transaction. Subsequently, they can try to buy back the bill from the shopkeeper who was so brave to accept it; in almost all cases, the resale value of his work is many times higher than the face value of the bill, thereby exemplifying the so-called endowment effect. Both from an economic and from a legal perspective, this raises confusion, as is illustrated by the transcripts of a court case which followed after the American secret service raided Boggs' studio:

> JUDGE GINSBURGH: So if they were in circulation, they would have a purchasing power of $100,000 if some people accepted them as currency?
> MR. YALOWITZ: Right, although they don't, and they don't go into circulation, because they are actually works worth much more than face value. Only a fool would attempt to pass it on as genuine, because they are worth substantially more than their face value.
> JUDGE TAFEL: But Mr. Boggs passes them on for no more than their face value.
> MR. YALOWITZ: Well, – – [uproarious laughter, including from Boggs] well, that is part of the transaction, you see. That is part of the challenge of the performance."[10]

Like Boggs, the French artist Matthieu Laurette pokes fun at economic rationality and the neoclassical notion of utility maximization. For his project "El gran trueque" ("The big exchange"), Laurette bought a car with the budget of an exhibition in the Spanish town of Bilbao. Subsequently he invited people to offer him an object for sale during a TV show. Laurette accepted the highest offer, for which the bidder received the car in exchange. This loss making loop was repeated a number of times, after which the artist finally ended up with a set of cheap glasses, which he offered for sale on *eBay*. For another project, Laurette put himself to writing slogans, cutting out coupons, requesting free samples, and all kinds of other arrangements that are used in capitalist economies to transform "innocent" people into money spending machines. Laurette, however, used these commercial schemes parasitically in order to make a living. With the products he acquired, he almost managed to survive. Subsequently, he presented this subversive strategy in different talk shows in France, thereby playfully promoting his own type of consumerism.

Other artists opted for a strategy of mimicry rather than subversion. The Swiss electronic art collective eToy, for instance, presented itself as the equivalent of a successful new media company, with its own corporate culture, business plan, and advisory board. The stocks they issued had as a disclaimer: "etoy.SHARE is a revolutionary art product of the etoy.CORPORATION. This product does not follow the rules of ordinary financial markets. Investing in etoy is a high risk art operation. (…) experts do not recommend the etoy.SHARE as safe investment for

214   *Olav Velthuis*

retirement pensions (…) etoy.SHARE is a high risk investment with prospect of profit in cultural values." In that capacity eToy waged a war against the online toy merchant eToys, one of the internet companies whose market value exploded during the internet hype of the late 1990s, and plummeted subsequently when the bubble unexpectedly burst. The reason for the war was that the toy company (with "s") had sued the art collective (without "s") for confusing and misleading potential customers and investors who accidentally arrived on the website of eToy rather than eToys.

Like eToy, the Japanese brothers Nobumichi and Masamichi Tosa started a company called Maywa Denki. The company specialized in product demonstrations of retail articles such as its "Nonsense Machines." The German artist Res Ingold has for decades been the president of Ingold Airlines – *a pleasure to fly*. The company has a professional website, which lists the company history, its annual reports, a description of its fleet, an account of its initial public offering, as well as a list of supporters. What remains unclear, however, is what the company has to offer. Booking a flight is impossible at least. The late Dutch artist Servaas, finally, established a company called Int.Fi\$h-handel Servaas & Zn. The mission of the company was "to use marketing strategies to produce and sell fish, fish air and fish accessories." For instance, the company sold hectoliters of seawater for about 25 dollars, as well as ten liter cans of fish air. Also, Servaas sold herring, and was eligible for a lower VAT rate while doing so because his herring was marketed as pieces of art.

Conclusion

Kunst=Kapital, art equals capital, the German artist Joseph Beuys once wrote on a banknote of ten German Mark. This essay can be read as an attempt to provide different interpretations of Beuys' statement; to be more precise, I have suggested that artists from the 1970s onwards have implicitly interpreted Beuys in different ways. First of all, his statement could be seen as a critical comment on an art world that is slowly endorsing by a capitalist logic of commensuration, quantification, and commodification. That interpretation prevailed in the critical moment of the 1970s, in which artists tried to circumvent the market by making work that could not be commodified. Two decades later, this interpretation sounds again, but the media of critique have changed radically. Rather than being outsiders, artists like Büchel or Freyer explicitly position themselves within the commercial forces they aim at criticizing; this choice may have partially been inspired by the inconsistency of previous generations of critical artists, whose work questioned the market, while at the same time commanding high prices in their overtly commercial New York galleries as well as at auction. The result was that institutional critique was institutionalized in itself, and supplied with the questionable predicate of official, high art. Unwilling or unable to distance themselves from such practices, a new generation of critical artists explicitly chooses to make use of capitalist markets, either for provocative purposes, or to exploit the democratic meanings that markets at times carry with them.

Imaginary currencies 215

A second moment within imaginary economics does not conceive of Beuys' identity in critical, but in affirmative, terms. When artists like Jeff Koons put a series of *Hoover* vacuum cleaners in a perfectly enlightened showcase, they celebrate rather than unmask the commodity character of art in contemporary society. Within their analysis, the logic of the arts is fully congruent with a capitalist logic, and there is no reason to be disconcerted about that. This affirmative stance has far from disappeared; after the booming art market of the 1980s, the natural habitat of artists like Koons, Steinbach, or Vaisman collapsed. But just as the terms of critical imaginary economics have changed, so have those of the affirmative moment. Post-1980s affirmation, retrieved in the work of artists such as Swetlana Heger, Plamen Dejanov, or Orgacom, have reversed the terms of debate. Rather than the arts adopting a quantitative capitalist logic, capitalist markets have adopted the qualitative logic of the arts, their work suggests. The postmodern economy would evolve around cultural values as diverse as creativity, innovation, identity, and inspiration. Looking for new societal roles outside of the world of art, artists would therefore be able to contribute to economic life.

The third moment that I have discussed leaves binary categories that have inspired modern thinking about the relationship between economy and culture, such as production/creation, price/value, market/gift, self-interest/altruism, behind it (cf. Smith, 1988). Playful imaginary economics does not let itself be seduced into making one-dimensional, normative statements about the economy. Their interpretation of Beuys' *Kunst=Kapital* is that both terms are fundamentally social constructs. Using strategies of mimicry and parody, artists like Matthieu Laurette and art collectives like eToy suggest that the economy is based on arbitrary rules and symbolic games that are no more and no less rational than those of primitive economies discussed so poetically in classical anthropological literature. By changing the rules of the game, these artists claim that the seriousness with which society treats its sublime economy may well be reconsidered.

Whatever interpretation of Beuys' statement is privileged, the variety of images and ideas that imaginary economics has generated throughout the last decades presents a sharp contrast to the relative dominance of neoclassical thinking within academic economics. All things considered, the market for academic ideas hardly accords with the ideology of free trade that reigns among neoclassical economists. For those who seek an alternative to that monopoly of ideas, imaginary economics may be a fruitful alternative.

Notes

1 http://utopia.knoware.nl/users/like_art/b_verkb.htm, "Verklaring Alexandr Brener," 19.2.1997. More than two decades before, New York performance artist Tony Shafrazi had written "Kill All Lies" with red paint on another monumental work in the history of art, Picasso's *Guernica*. At the time, 1973, the work was on view in the New York Museum of Modern Art. Shafrazi made sure the press was present at the event (Haden-Guest, 1996, p. 48); the event therefore fits better in then flourishing practices of performance art than in Brener's radical avant-garde tradition. Shafrazi would later open a commercial gallery in SoHo, the main gallery district of New York in the 1980s.

216   *Olav Velthuis*

2 The *topos* in their comments is that art and commerce are mutually exclusive. The 19th-century British artist and, later in his life, social critic John Ruskin insisted for instance that an artist can only make a good painting if he is intrinsically motivated. Conversely, "no good work in this world was ever done for money, nor while the slightest thought of money affected the painter's mind. Whatever idea of pecuniary value enters into his thoughts as he works, will, in proportion to the distinctness of its presence, shorten his power" (Ruskin, 1904, p. 115). The French impressionist painter Degas barred collectors from his studio, shouting "here we don't sell; we work" (Brown, 1993, p. 275). Degas' contemporary Vincent van Gogh compared the art market in a letter to his brother Theo with the tulipomania of the Dutch 17th century, infamous as it was for its speculation and vulgar money grubbing; the other *topos* among modern artists was to equal the art market to the stock exchange (Coppet and Jones, 1984, p. 15). With similar intent, other artists compared the art market to the stock exchange. Duchamp, for instance, wrote in a letter to the American photographer and short-lived art dealer Alfred Stieglitz that "[t]he feeling of the market here is so disgusting. Painters and paintings go up and down like Wall Street Stock" (cited by Tomkins, 1996, p. 285). Pablo Picasso, in many ways Duchamp's direct opposite, seemingly shared his contempt of the market. About one of his Parisian art dealers, he said bluntly: "le marchand, voilà l'ennemi"—the dealer, that's the enemy (Fitzgerald, 1995, p. 3; see also Haskell and Teichgraeber, 1993; Jensen, 1994).

3 About Duchamp's checks, see Velthuis, 2000; about Klein's exchange, see Duve, 1989; about.

4 For his project, Landy made an inventory of the 7,006 objects he owned, put them in a plastic bag, and transported them to a vacant retail space in the London city center. There, Landy and ten uniformed assistants put the objects on a conveyor belt and disassembled them. At the end of the conveyer belt, a grinder was running which would transform the parts into powder, and separate into different materials such as plastic, metal, wood, paper, or fabric. Apart from relatively neutral possessions, Landy also destroyed letters, his own passport and birth certificate, artworks that had been given to him by well-known artist friends, and a coat that belonged to his deceased father.

5 Their attempt ultimately failed, however; even in the 1970s, some galleries became interested in hosting performance art and inviting conceptual artists, whose work seemed impossible to commodify, to exhibit in their galleries on a regular basis. One of them, Vito Acconci, realized with hindsight that "we might not have provided things to sell, but we provided something that every business needs. We provided advertising, window dressing. If anything, I think we made the art gallery system stronger. They could say, 'look, we can even deal with *this*!'" (Haden-Guest, 1996, p. 40). Art critic Thomas Crow noted likewise that the desire of artists to challenge "modernist complicity with the marketplace" ended up enhancing it, because they needed the gallery space and curatorial activity in order to perform their work (Crow, 1996, p. 82); and if the art of the seventies itself was difficult to sell, its documentation was not.

6 The Italian artist Sandro Chia, whose work was bought in large quantities in the early 1980s by the British advertising agent Charles Saatchi, and "dumped on the market" a number of years later, commented with hindsight: "Today, works of art imitate and are inspired by the economy. The economy has itself become the work of art, acquiring all the qualities a work of art should have: pitilessness, ruthlessness, cynicism, grandiosity, communicativeness, abstraction. Economic systems and economic values rule the art world, especially in New York" Chia, (1990).

7 A list of all the objects available on Freyer's website, www.allmylifeforsale.com.

8 See www.irational.org/tm/art_of_work/management.html.

Imaginary currencies 217

9 For a detailed history, see Weschler, 1999.
10 Transcripts of court hearings of Boggs' lawyer Kent A. Yalowitz and judges Ginsburgh and Tafel, 1995.

References

Amariglio, Jack and David F. Ruccio, "The Transgressive Knowledge of 'Ersatz' Economics," in: R. F. Garnett (Ed.), *What Do Economists Know?*, London: Routledge, 1999, pp. 19–36.

Ardenne, Paul, "The Art Market in the 1980s," *International Journal of Political Economy*, 25(2), (1992 [1995]), pp. 100–28.

Armstrong, Richard, Richard Marshall, et al., *Catalogue 1989 Biennial Exhibition. Whitney Museum of American Art*, New York: W.W. Norton, 1989.

Bierens, Cornel, "Sculpture of a Particle Accelerator," in: *Formule 2.1*, Berlin: Künstlerhaus Bethanien, 1999, pp. 110–16.

Bourdieu, Pierre, *The Rules of Art*, Stanford: Stanford University Press, 1992 [1996].

Brettell, Richard R., *Modern Art 1851–1929. Capitalism and Representation*, Oxford: Oxford University Press, 1999.

Brown, Marily R., "An Entrepreneur In Spite of Himself: Edgar Degas and the Market," in: T. L. Haskell and R. F. Teichgraeber (Eds), *The Culture of the Market. Historical Essays*, Cambridge: Cambridge University Press, 1993, pp. 261–92.

Buchloh, Benjamin, H.D., "Allegorical Procedures: Appropriation and Montage in Contemporary Art," *Artforum* (September 1982), pp. 43–56.

Bürger, Peter, *Theory of the Avant-Garde*, Minneapolis: University of Minnesota Press, 1974 [1996].

Chia, Sandro, interview with, "Making Art, Making Money," *Art in America*, July 1990.

Cohen, Adam, *The Perfect Store. Inside Ebay*, Boston: Little, Brown and Company, 2002.

Coppet, Laura de and Alan Jones, *The Art Dealers. The Powers Behind the Scene Tell How the Art World Really Works*, New York: Cooper Square Press, 1984.

Crow, Thomas, *Modern Art in the Common Culture*, New Haven: Yale University Press, 1996.

Cumming, Tim, "Stuff and nonsense," *The Guardian*, 13.2.2002.

Danto, Arthur C., *After the End of Art. Contemporary Art and the Pale of History*, Princeton: Princeton University Press, 1997.

Derrida, Jacques, "Structure, Sign and Play in the Discourse of the Human Sciences," in: E. Macksey and E. Donato (Eds), *The Structuralist Controversy*, Baltimore: Johns Hopkins University Press, 1970.

Duve, Thierry de, "Yves Klein, or The Dead Dealer," *October*, 49(Summer), (1989), pp. 72–90.

Elger, Dietmar and Thomas Weski, *Louise Lawler. For Sale*, Ofstfildern: Cantz, 1994.

Fitzgerald, Michael C., *Making Modernism. Picasso and the Creation of the Market for Twentieth-Century Art*, New York: Farrar, Straus and Giroux, 1995.

Foster, Hal, *The Return of the Real. The Avant-Garde at the End of the Century*, Cambridge: MIT Press, 1996.

Haden-Guest, Anthony, *True Colors. The Real Life of the Art World*, New York: Atlantic Monthly Press, 1996.

Haskell, Thomas L. and Richard F. Teichgraeber, Eds, *The Culture of the Market. Historical Essays*, Cambridge: Cambridge University Press, 1993.

218   *Olav Velthuis*

Heinzelman, Kurt, *The Economics of the Imagination*, Amherst: University of Massachusetts Press, 1980.

Huyssen, Andreas, *After the Great Divide. Modernism, Mass Culture and Postmodernism*, Basingstoke: Macmillan, 1986.

Jensen, Robert, *Marketing Modernism in Fin-de-Siècle Europe*, Princeton: Princeton University Press, 1994.

Jones, Amelia, *Postmodernism and the En-gendering of Marcel Duchamp*, Cambridge: Cambridge University Press, 1994.

Judovitz, Dalia, *Unpacking Duchamp: Art in Transit*, Berkeley: University of California Press, 1995.

Kaprow, Alan, *Essays on the Blurring of Art and Life*, Berkeley: University of California Press, 1993.

King, Jamie, "Opruiming. Michael Landy's (mislukte) gebaar," *Metropolis M*, no. 5, okt/nov 2002, pp. 28–31.

Kopytoff, Igor, "The Cultural Biography of Things: Commoditization as Process," in: A. Appadurai (Ed.), *The Social Life of Things. Commodities in Cultural Perspective*, Cambridge: Cambridge University Press, 1986, pp. 64–91.

Kwon, Miwon, "Exchange Rate: On Obligation and Reciprocity in Some Art of the 1960s and After," in: H. Molesworth (Ed.), *Work Ethic*, Baltimore: Baltimore Museum of Art, 2003, pp. 82–97.

Larsen, LarsBang, "25 Swiss francs and a coconut," *Art/Text*, nr. 66, August/October, 1999, pp. 57–9.

Lawler, Louise, *An Arrangement of Pictures*, New York: Assouline, 2000.

Linker, Kate, *Love for Sale. The Words and Pictures of Barbara Kruger*, New York: Harry N. Abrams, 1990.

Lippard, Lucy, *Six Years: The Dematerialization of the Art Object from 1966 to 1972*, University of California Press, 1997.

Lippard, Lucy R., "Trojan Horses: Activist Art and Power," in: B. Wallis (Ed.), *Art After Modernism. Rethinking Representation*, New York: New Museum of Contemporary Art, 1984, pp. 340–58.

Mirapaul, Matthew, "The New Canvas: Artists Use Online Auctions for Art Projects," *The New York Times*, 5.2.2001.

Owens, Craig, Scott Bryson, et al., *Beyond Recognition: Representation, Power, and Culture*, Berkeley: University of California Press, 1994.

Rifkin, Jeremy, *The Age of Access*, London: Penguin, 2000.

Rosler, Martha, "Lookers, Buyers, Dealers and Makers: Thoughts on Audience," in: B. Wallis (Ed.), *Art After Modernism: Rethinking Representation*, New York: New Museum of Contemporary Art, 1984, pp. 311–40.

Ruskin, John, *A Joy For Ever*, London: George Allen, 1904.

Smith, Barbara Herrstein, *Contingencies of Value. Alternative Perspectives for Critical Theory*, Cambridge: Harvard University Press, 1988.

Steinbach, Haim, In: Peter Nagy (moderator), "From Criticism to Complicity," *Flash Art*, Summer 1986 (no. 129), pp. 46–9.

Sutton-Smith, Brian, *The Ambiguity of Play*, Cambridge: Harvard University Press, 1997.

Tomkins, Calvin, *Duchamp. A Biography*, New York: Henry Holt, 1996.

Velthuis, Olav, "Duchamp's Financial Documents: Exchange as a Source of Value," *Toutfait. The Marcel Duchamp Studies Online Journal*, 1(2), (2000), www.toutfait.com/issues/issue_2/Articles/velthuis.html.

Velthuis, Olav, *Imaginary Economics*, Rotterdam: NAi Publishers, 2004.

Imaginary currencies   219

Wallis, Brian, Ed. *Art after Modernism. Rethinking Representation*, New York: New Museum of Contemporary Art, 1984.

Weschler, Lawrence, *Boggs. A Comedy of Values*, Chicago: University of Chicago Press, 1999.

Young, James O., *Art and Knowledge*, London: Routledge, 2001.

11 The sociology of the new art gallery scene in Chelsea, Manhattan

David Halle and Elisabeth Tiso

Overview: the debate over the commercial market and its dominance

Chelsea, on Manhattan's Far West Side, has with stunning speed become the center of Contemporary Art in New York City and the United States. Between 1998 and February 2008, the number of commercial galleries in Chelsea grew from 71 to at least 268, dwarfing other art districts in the United States and supplanting SoHo, once the most dynamic gallery neighborhood in New York City. The number of SoHo galleries has now fallen to 44 from its 1990 peak of 262. (See Figures 1 and 2.)[1]

This mega-concentration of commercial galleries in Chelsea represents an opportunity to engage the long debate over the impact of the rise of the market and the decline of patronage as the major way that art is produced. Our five-year study suggests that the current situation is pluralistic and far more interesting than allowed by perspectives that just stress the dominance of commercialism in a one-dimensional way, or conversely by approaches that simply ignore the market's role. "Economics," in the language of the editors of this volume, is important but definitely not "everywhere" in Chelsea.[2]

The contours of the debate over the role of the market and commercial forces in art have long been drawn. On the one hand, an important line of twentieth and now twenty-first century thinkers decry the growth of market forces whose impact, they argue, has been huge, and lament the commercialization of art as, for example, it is processed through the modern corporation. These thinkers include F.R. Leavis and the "mass culture" school as early as the 1920s and 1930s, the (Marxist) Frankfurt School such as Adorno and Horkheimer in the 1930s, and, later, Western and Central European intellectuals such as Baudrillard and Václav Havel in the 1970s as they contemplated the penetration of their societies by Western capitalist culture (with Hollywood movies as paradigmatic). A recent statement is by the curators of the New Museum of Contemporary Art which opened, with great anticipation, in December 2007 in the Bowery in New York City. For example, curator Richard Flood complained that "Making art in the early twenty-first century is just the same as making art in any other century, except for the money that coats everything like ash.

The sociology of the new art gallery scene in Chelsea, Manhattan 221

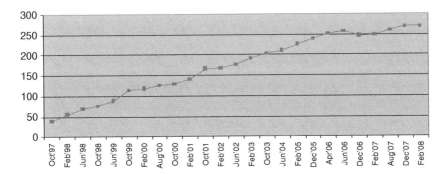

Figure 1 Growth of galleries in Chelsea, 1997–2008.

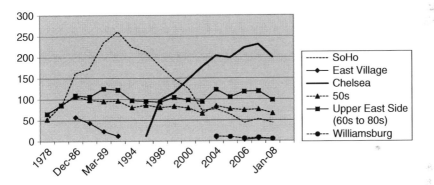

Figure 2 Art gallery areas, Manhattan and Brooklyn, 1978–2008.

… Nowadays there are masterpieces everywhere, racing into the marketplace like sperm to the womb. … In an age of maximal distraction … there is no time wasted waiting for a masterpiece to achieve connoisseurial consensus. Some blowhard just pronounces it so, and that's all. Well, maybe it helps if there is a carefully choreographed auction where a manipulated record is set and an art riff on bad history commences, as dollars, euros, yen and rupees confirm the status of a masterpiece. But, really the appellation has replaced the reality."

Although there are differences of emphasis and degree among these theorists, they all tend to believe that this commercial, market system imposes products onto a largely passive, mass public that this public would not otherwise purchase, and that it flattens out the tastes and critical sensibilities of the public. These theorists also often argue that the system "contaminates" the works by forcing the artists to produce what the market will sell, not what the artists would like to produce. Adherents of this perspective often refer to the whole process as the "commodification" of art.[3]

222   David Halle and Elisabeth Tiso

On the other hand, such views have been repeatedly criticized as, at the least, exaggerated. For example, it has been said that it is simplistic and condescending to imply that, for the audience, art and culture has just one set of meanings (or one "basic" set of meanings) that are somehow attached to commodified cultural products and that the audience simply absorb. Why should cultural products have just one set of (basic) meanings and even if they do where is the evidence that people more or less passively accept these meanings?[4]

The evidence from Chelsea's commercial gallery system suggests a current situation that is fascinatingly complex, in sometimes unexpected ways. There are, for sure, several ways in which the market is important and even dominant in Chelsea.

First, Chelsea does represent the triumph of the commercial gallery system as a mode of showing and distributing art. Unlike SoHo, which was initially colonized by artists and which represented, in its early days at least, an attempt by artists to short-circuit the market (e.g. by selling directly from their studios to customers), Chelsea was developed primarily by commercial galleries. Few artists live in Chelsea. They could not afford to even a few years ago when Chelsea first began to develop as an art gallery area, still less now. Nor is Chelsea like the East Village of the 80s, which was the first major attempt in New York City to create a new art district for contemporary art distinct from SoHo. The East Village's grass-roots, artist-based movement fizzled after a few years, partly because it lacked the commercial muscle of Chelsea's dealer driven move.

Further, several international gallery giants such as Gagosian or Pace-Wildenstein are active in Chelsea. These galleries are trans-atlantic operations with outlets in European cities too, and they have the economic resources to attract artists from smaller galleries. Such international corporations, long dominant in other economic spheres, are still fairly new in the gallery world. Their importance is likely to grow.

Also, every Chelsea gallery must deal with New York City's ferocious real estate market. Indeed, SoHo's decline and Chelsea's rise were above all real estate-driven. Rents soared in SoHo from 1995–1999, driven by an influx of clothing boutiques, and forcing a mass migration to Chelsea of galleries that could not afford the new rents. Learning the lesson of SoHo, many of those galleries that came early to Chelsea (with sufficient capital) bought their spaces, so as to insulate themselves from the commercial rental market. The other galleries signed leases and many were concerned about what would happen to their rents when those leases expired. Actually, by 2005 the main threat to Chelsea art galleries, to those who rented and even to those who owned their space, was not boutiques but the voracious demand for condominiums in Manhattan, with developers willing to pay enormous sums for condominium development on land now occupied by galleries. The heart of Chelsea's art gallery district is currently zoned to prohibit condominiums, but in 2005 the surrounding area, which includes many galleries too, was rezoned to permit condominiums. No-one knows how all this will play out, but in Chelsea's art district, real estate is, if not King, then probably Queen.

The sociology of the new art gallery scene in Chelsea, Manhattan   223

On the other hand, several Chelsea developments offset, or modify, an image of the world of Contemporary Art as dominated by the commercial market juggernaut.

First, Chelsea's gallery system offers an enormous free "show" of Contemporary Art. Very few of the audience come with the slightest intention of purchasing works. Further, in terms of its openness, continuity, size, and the range and quality of works displayed, Chelsea's free show has few parallels in the history of art, though it intensifies a trend begun in SoHo. Whether this is a trivial development, or a significant counter-trend to the modern tendency to commercialize leisure life (e.g. via the imposition of entry/access charges), remains to be determined.

Also, the overwhelming majority of galleries in Chelsea are neither global nor just "star," but small, and often not hugely profitable, shops that offer a plethora of uniquely crafted products whose collective effect amounts to a crucible of creativity. In many ways this is the opposite of commodification, and echoes an earlier, artisan structure, though in a modern market context.

Related to the previous point, the artists we interviewed, both the successful and the struggling, tend to embrace the commercial gallery system. They do not, on the whole, see it as a structure of dominance or oppression. Rather, they believe that it offers them a range of market venues for displaying their work that is to their advantage and that contrasts with the more restricted opportunities available through the museum world. Most artists consider that museum directors and curators—at MoMA, the Whitney, the Metropolitan, and so on—tend to be more conservative than commercial galleries, more focused on established art and less open to new art and artists.

Nor, as privately funded institutions, are the commercial galleries subject to the morality spats that periodically roil the U.S. art scene. Such spats focus on publicly funded institutions since they involve a debate over whether public funds should finance certain topics (e.g. pornographic art, gay art, "anti-Catholic art," "political" art). Commercial galleries, by contrast, are free to show almost all forms of art, and artists know and appreciate this.

Finally, and perhaps most important of all, is the evidence from a content-analysis of the art displayed in Chelsea, and from interviews with the audience that attend the galleries there. We identified five major, and three minor, themes that dominate the content of the art and also pervade the meaning of the art for the spectators who view it. For example, there is (in the works and among the audience) a concern about the destruction of the modern landscape, and there is an interest in depictions of inter-personal life that either avoid the romantic image of the nuclear family, or present it in a highly critical light. It is not plausible to analyze such themes as being pre-packaged and imposed by commercial forces. Rather, they are often intimately connected with central themes and issues in the audience's lives and are, in many ways, about the artistic depiction of modern life. Critics who argue that the audience are not well-understood if represented as basically passive receptacles for art are certainly correct, and the same considerations suggest problems for those who talk about the "commodification" of art.

224   *David Halle and Elisabeth Tiso*

In what follows we first discuss those factors that affirm the importance of the market. We then turn to the developments that either run counter, or are unrelated, to this.

Data

Our research in Chelsea began in 2000. To make the study systematic, we organized it around the galleries, and did so in two main ways. First, we drew a sample of 40 galleries selected at random from all those in Chelsea. We refer to this as the "general" sample. Second, we studied all of the most famous and economically successful galleries. We identified 16 such galleries, which we refer to as the "star" list. They include Gagosian, Paula Cooper, Metro Pictures, Matthew Marks, Pace Wildenstein, and Luhring Augustine. (Table 1, note a, contains the full list.) In this way, we were able to study both what is going on throughout Chelsea generally and also to focus on the famous galleries that attract the best-known artists and are often international leaders in the art world.

Commercialism/the market

The gallery system

Chelsea does reflect the dominance of the commercial gallery system as a way of presenting and distributing art. This is a crucial difference from SoHo, which was first turned into an art district by artists. Chelsea was developed primarily by commercial galleries, although the not-for-profit DIA Foundation was a key initial pioneer in 1986. (DIA was founded and funded by the De Menil family, much of whose huge fortune comes from Texas oil.) Then in 1993 DIA's director, Lynne Cooke, found space near the DIA for the young gallery owner Matthew Marks, who purchased it. Matthew Marks quickly encouraged his friends Pat Hearn and Paul Morris to move their galleries from SoHo to Chelsea, and the growth of commercial galleries in Chelsea had begun. For example, Paula Cooper, who had opened the first SoHo gallery in 1968, purchased a run-down Chelsea garage in 1995 and left SoHo.

Few artists live in Chelsea. They could not afford it even when Chelsea began to develop as an art gallery area, still less now. (The reasons why SoHo was affordable for artists but Chelsea was not are discussed later.)

International galleries

Several international gallery giants such as Gagosian, Marlborough, and Lelong have moved to Chelsea. These are trans-atlantic operations, some originating in the United States and others in European cities. It is tempting to call them "global" (a term often used very loosely these days) but in truth even the largest rarely have galleries in more than a handful of countries. Still, they have the economic resources to attract (or poach) artists from smaller galleries, and from "star" but not

Photo 1 Matthew Marks Gallery, Chelsea. *This was built from a former garage, which is a typical form of Chelsea conversion. Unlike SoHo, which was founded by artists (with galleries coming later), Chelsea as an art district was developed primarily by commercial galleries (after the DIA Foundation's pioneering move).* Photo by Elisabeth Tiso.

Photo 2 Gagosian Gallery, Chelsea. *This gallery, whose one-story structure covers 10,000 square feet and almost a third of a city block, approaches, in size, a small museum. Gagosian has several galleries in the United States and abroad. There are just a handful of such global galleries in Chelsea, but they represent a new direction for the art world.* Photo by Elisabeth Tiso.

Photo 3 Gagosian Gallery, Interior (section). *This cavernous space parallels the height of many museum interiors.* Photo by Elisabeth Tiso.

international galleries too. The United States dealer Gagosian, for example, has two galleries in Los Angeles, two in New York City, two in London, one in Rome, and a Paris office and is looking for space in Hong Kong. The French gallery Lelong, which has outlets in Paris and Switzerland, recently opened a branch in Chelsea, as did another large French gallery, Yvon Lambert. Such international corporations are a fairly new, but growing presence in the gallery world and are bringing the latter more in line with other spheres of the economy. Still, the overwhelming majority of galleries in Chelsea are neither international nor just "star" but are often struggling boutique operations, as we discuss later.

Andrea Rosen, a "star" list Chelsea gallerist who owned just one gallery, complained about Gagosian's business model:

> Gagosian has a different agenda from 99% of the other galleries. He's not interested in recording the place of his artists in history or in long-term relationships or in preserving the archives of his artists. For Gagosian, it's all about money. It's really about the business model that didn't exist before. He's instilled a sense of competition. Still, it's not all bad. He does bring art to a wider audience, and he's had many fabulous shows.

Paula Cooper was less critical of the internationalists:

> It's a huge world now, the art world is enormous. It's completely intertwined, e.g. there are shows all over the world of everybody. The American-European

The sociology of the new art gallery scene in Chelsea, Manhattan 227

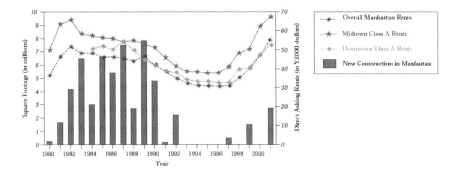

Figure 3 Trends in direct asking rents and new construction completions in Manhattan, 1980–2001.

Source: Charles Schumer and Robert Rubin (co-chairs), *Preparing for the Future: A Commercial Development Strategy for New York City*, June, 2001.

thing has exploded. Artists are coming from all over the world. There are so many big international shows.

The Manhattan real estate market

Manhattan's daunting real estate market is an ever-present force with which galleries must deal. Real-estate drove SoHo's decline and Chelsea's ascendancy as art gallery districts. Figure 3 shows how commercial rents in Manhattan basically doubled from 1995–2000, and Figure 2 depicts the associated decline of SoHo galleries, gradual until 1995, steep thereafter, and the highly correlated rise of Chelsea.

The havoc wreaked by rising commercial rents in the late 1990s on those SoHo galleries—the majority—that were on commercial leases and did not own their spaces is affirmed in interviews with Chelsea gallery owners and managers (both those on the "general" gallery list and the "stars") who fled Soho in search of affordable space. The interviews are replete with references to "greedy landlords/developers" who do not care about art.

Miles Manning, now director of the Elizabeth Harris gallery in Chelsea, worked for the Danish Contemporary Art gallery (DCA) in SoHo in the early 90s. The DCA rented the ground floor of 420 Broadway, SoHo's most famous art gallery building. The building had a star cast of gallery owners—John Weber, Leo Castelli, Ileana Sonnabend. Manning explained what then happened:

> The DCA had a two year lease (in SoHo) with a three year option beyond. Our landlords, two Dutch businessmen, started coming to us in the 2nd year [1997] to get us up to the 4th floor, but they really wanted to get us out. Meanwhile most of the ground floors in other buildings were closing or moving, because the fashion stores were moving in. We saw the handwriting on the wall.

228   David Halle and Elisabeth Tiso

Mary Boone was across the street. She had the same landlord as we did. Her lease came due, they had a fight, and Rene Lazard, the German fashion designer, moved in.

There were 28–30 galleries here (in Chelsea) then. Finally the landlord said (to us) "We want you to get out. What will it take?" We said: "If you find us comparable space in Chelsea." They offered us $250,000 plus they found this space. Here we have 5,000 square feet and we're paying 1/3 less than we paid in SoHo. November '97 we opened our doors and since then, all around us, more and more galleries have moved in.

Moving early was our luck. Otherwise our lease would have played out last year [2000] and the gallery would have ended. We would have been priced out of the market and unable to afford to move here. Survival stories in the art world are about knowing when to act and leave. Those who don't make it right end up as footnotes in history!

Most of the gallery owners who fled SoHo commented on a change in the composition of the SoHo audience in the mid-90s and beyond. High-end shoppers now largely replaced those who came to view art. The new audience was despised by most of the gallerists. For example, Barbara Gladstone (star list), who rented space for her gallery in SoHo from 1983 to 1996 until high rents drove her to Chelsea, commented:

When I first moved to SoHo it was very quiet. Then, once rents got so high [her landlord wanted to triple her rent], the crowds were now a detriment. The real collectors couldn't get into the gallery. The new crowd didn't know the difference between a gallery and a furniture store. There'd be fifty people in the gallery, and no collectors, because they'd [the crowds] be going down the street to shop, from one shop to the next. Anything is better than that.

Seeming to affirm these judgments, a recent (March 26, 2006) feature article in the *New York Times* Real Estate section described SoHo as a "shopping nirvana. Bloomingdale's arrived last year, and it would be hard to find a major designer or upscale retail outlet that hasn't."

The East Village of the 80s was a brief offshoot of SoHo and primarily an artist-based movement interested in expanding the content of contemporary art (e.g. to make room for political art and for figurative art especially depicting sex including gay sex). When landlords in SoHo lowered rents in the early 1990s recession, many of the East Village's new galleries returned to SoHo.[5]

Will Chelsea go the way of SoHo?

Not surprisingly, a much debated topic among Chelsea gallery owners and other observers is whether real estate developments will eventually cause a similar debacle for the art galleries as happened in SoHo. Several of the earliest, large galleries to move to Chelsea bought their spaces, partly because prime, first floor rental locations were not readily available and partly as protection from the commercial rental market. The other galleries in Chelsea signed leases and

The sociology of the new art gallery scene in Chelsea, Manhattan   229

were keenly aware of what Chelsea insiders called the "2005" factor, a reference to the year when leases expired for the cluster of galleries that had moved to Chelsea around 1996 and had signed the typical ten-year lease. Many of these galleries worried that an influx of boutiques would eventually drive them from Chelsea too.

Barbara Gladstone, who co-owns her Chelsea building—a converted warehouse—with Matthew Marks (his second Chelsea gallery) and Metro Pictures, commented:

> I have mixed feelings about Chelsea. I moved here four years ago [1996] because my rent in SoHo was going to triple. I was looking for a place where I could buy something in order to be protected from landlords.
>
> What I like about Chelsea is there's nothing to do here. So if you come, you come to look at the art. But the neighborhood here is changing. The way it happens is first you have galleries, then restaurants because the rich people who buy the art want somewhere to eat and someone figures out there are rich people around. And they [the rich people] want to buy things, and then you get the boutiques, and "that's the end of the neighborhood." SoHo went like that.
>
> Still, I feel protected here because I've bought my space. Most of the gallery owners that moved here early bought. There weren't that many Chelsea spaces to rent. This building was a warehouse. Now they're building an apartment house across the street. It's a rental building. "There goes the neighborhood."

Gallery owner Clement Glasser was less sanguine, commenting (in 2002):

> Chelsea will go the way of SoHo surely in fifteen years. I'm 100% sure. There'll be a lot of boutiques. The main difference is there are no high buildings here. The only fixed point in New York is the Upper East Side—that's always the right place to show secondary artists, Vermeer to Balthus. The super-rich people live there.

A member of the audience for a show by Claes Oldenburg and Coosje van Bruggen commented:

> It's a real estate play. I've seen the same thing in New York for 30 years. They (i.e. the real estate industry) bring in the art. Then the real estate prices go up, the real estate people bring in the fancy shops, then they build fancy apt buildings, then the rent goes up so the galleries will have to leave.

Still, 2005 came and went without a cataclysm. Indeed, the number of galleries in Chelsea continued to rise that year, from 226 in January to 239 in December. (See Figure 1.) Further, the global and star galleries were in expansionist mode. By 2005 Matthew Marks owned four Chelsea galleries, Paul Cooper had opened a second, and Marianne Boesky's new space was in construction.

230   *David Halle and Elisabeth Tiso*

Yet major change was in the air. A key factor that had limited the rise of rents in the art gallery area of Chelsea was the fact that, zoned as manufacturing, it had no resident population of artists who could give the district a special caché. By contrast the process of SoHo becoming an art neighborhood began with artists moving into the neighborhood to live from 1959 onwards.[6] SoHo's cast-iron industrial buildings were ideal for the space artists needed. Artists were able to afford to move there because landlords could charge only very low rents because almost no-one else wanted to live in SoHo. This was because the neighborhood seemed doomed after Robert Moses, in 1959, announced plans for a ten-lane Lower Manhattan Expressway, which would have wiped out SoHo. To much surprise, after an epic struggle, the Lower Manhattan Expressway was finally defeated in 1969. The ensuing promise of stability, and the presence of artists, created a demand for bars and restaurants and then galleries, and then tourists came including art buyers.

The artists' industrial lofts in SoHo were, at first, illegal residences, since the area was zoned M1-5 which permitted light industry and commercial establishments such as galleries and retail stores, but precluded residential. After the defeat of the Lower Manhattan Expressway, the Department of City Planning legalized residences in 1971, but only for artists, changing the zoning to M1-5A and M1-5B, with the A and B designations permitting artists to live there so long as they were certified as such by the DCP.[7] Actually, the certification of residents as artists was, and still is, widely ignored (by the DCP too), so SoHo lofts traded freely on the residential market. This created an on-the-spot coterie of wealthy residents/shoppers to help support the clothing and later furniture stores too, both small boutiques and large chains, to attract tourists (shoppers), and to add to the upward pressure on commercial rents that eventually displaced most of the galleries. By the mid-1990s SoHo was a "hot" neighborhood.

Chelsea's zoning was also M1-5, which is why the art galleries were able to move there. But Chelsea never came under the rent reducing apparent death sentence of a project like the Lower Manhattan Expressway, so even from the start few artists could afford to live there. Chelsea also lacked SoHo's multitude of attractive, cast iron buildings, although it did have some very large warehouse and industrial buildings into which artists could have moved had they been able to afford to.

The heart of the Chelsea gallery district is concentrated on the midblocks between W. 20th and W. 27th Streets and 10th and 11th Avenues, in converted warehouse buildings and garages. The wealthier galleries tend to occupy first floor converted garages in expensive remodelings designed by architectural minimalist gurus like Richard Gluckman. The ordinary galleries more often occupy a small, upper floor, section of one of the large warehouse buildings.

Without a resident artist population willing to live there illegally in exchange for tiny rents, there was little demand for services such as restaurants and stores to open in Chelsea's art gallery district. Nor, under existing (M1-5) zoning, was there an opportunity for owners of the buildings in which the galleries were located to sell to a developer who would build condominiums or residential rental buildings on the site, an enormously profitable proposition in Manhattan's current (to 2006) real estate market. Thus Chelsea's art gallery district lacked condominium residents to provide wealthy, on-the-spot shoppers. As a result most of the upward pressure on the rents paid by galleries in Chelsea in 2005 came from other galleries seeking to move to prime space there, although a handful of boutiques had moved in by 2005 (e.g. Comme les Garçons was an early pioneer).

This, however, was not a stable, market equilibrium. In 2005 the Department of City Planning ushered through the approval process a West Chelsea rezoning plan, which created a special purpose zoning district. The crux of the plan, which was supported by the local Community Board (CB4), rezoned much of the manufacturing area around the art gallery section, but not the art gallery section itself, to a Commercial (C) designation which allowed residential development. (See Figure 4. The zones C6-2, C6-2A, C6-3, C6-3A, and C6-4 replaced manufacturing zones.) The DCP kept the original manufacturing zoning for the core of the gallery section, with the intention of protecting the galleries from the commercial pressures that would be unleashed in the surrounding areas by the ability to build residential buildings (condominiums).

The 2005 West Chelsea rezoning had actually been triggered by another intricate dance between ferocious commercial considerations and other concerns, revolving around the High Line, a long disused elevated railway that ran through the art gallery area. A local group, including some architects, had come up with a plan (first mooted in the late 1990s) to turn the High Line into a public park along the

Photo 4 High Line railroad. In the background is the Frank Gehry-designed IAC headquarters (opened 2007), which was built under the pre-2005, manufacturing zoning. The new zoning is unleashing a wave of condominiums. Photo by Elisabeth Tiso.

Figure 4 West Chelsea rezoning, 2005.

The sociology of the new art gallery scene in Chelsea, Manhattan   233

model of the Promenade Plantée in Paris. A crucial part of this plan, which by 2002 had the strong support of Mayor Bloomberg and the DCP, involved finding a way to compensate the property owners who owned land under, and adjoining, the High Line and who had long sought to demolish the High Line so that they could develop their properties. Organized as the Chelsea Property Owners, they had threatened to hold up the High Line project indefinitely with legal and political action unless they were financially compensated for being unable to develop their properties when the High Line was turned into a park rather than demolished.[8]

The compensating mechanism that City Planning settled upon was to allow the High Line property owners[9] to sell their air rights to owners/developers in a special transfer zone composed of "receiving sites." This special transfer zone did not immediately adjoin the High Line, so the visibility of the High Line for its park mode would be somewhat preserved from the encroachment of tall buildings. The zone's value as a development site (whose owners would be willing to pay for air rights so they could construct taller buildings) was assured by its having been rezoned from manufacturing (M1-5) to commercial (C), which allowed residential, as well as art galleries.

As well as providing a mechanism to satisfy the Chelsea Property Owners, the whole West Chelsea rezoning suited one of City Planning's broader goals, namely fostering residential development in West Chelsea and throughout the city. Thus DCP planned to encourage the creation of 65,000 new residential units throughout the city over the next few years, on the reasonable grounds that this allowed more people to live in the city and also increased the city's tax revenue.

In short, the 2005 rezoning is strikingly ambiguous. It is unclear if retaining the art gallery section zoning as manufacturing, while rezoning the area around the art gallery section to allow profitable residential development (C), will have the desired effect of insulating the galleries. The DCP said, bluntly, that the large galleries' current protection consisted mainly of the fact that they were already commercially strong enough to afford high rents. As it wrote:

> The proposed action is not anticipated to diminish the viability of the art gallery industry in West Chelsea. Most of the larger art galleries, which represent the bulk of the industry, are not vulnerable, as they currently pay premium rents, particularly ground floor establishments (\$45 to \$60 psf).

Actually, the fact that many of the large galleries owned their own spaces certainly provided better protection than their sheer commercial power. Gagosian, in a typical attempt to combine art with the latest economic developments, in 2007 applied for permission to build a condominium tower on top of his art gallery in Chelsea!

City Planning said nothing about how the many smaller galleries in Chelsea would fare beyond its ambiguous assertion that the large galleries constituted the "bulk of the industry." This might have been true as a statement of the proportionate value of Chelsea art sales attributable to the large galleries, but it was not true as a statement of the relative number of small and large galleries.

234   *David Halle and Elisabeth Tiso*

Still, retaining the manufacturing designation did provide some insulation for the small galleries.

Overall, the ability of galleries to occupy a niche position in the real estate market was critical to the original establishment of Chelsea as an art district and will be critical to its survival. Under the prevailing manufacturing zoning, galleries were able to move to Chelsea because they could compete with such uses as garages, and yet were protected from the hopeless task of competing with condominiums. Whether commercial considerations will eventually lead to Chelsea's demise as an art gallery area, as they did with SoHo, is uncertain, but the possibility will always be there.

Non-commercial forces

While the previous points are consistent with a perspective that stresses the importance, and sometimes the dominance, of the commercial market, there are several other developments that offset, or modify, an image of the world of Contemporary Art as ruled by the commercial market Behemoth.

"The best free show in town" and the general audience as creators of "buzz"

Chelsea galleries represent a strikingly new role for the audience. In the traditional gallery there was an expectation that most of those who entered did so with at least some thought of buying. By contrast, very few of the audience for Chelsea galleries have any intention of buying the art. We refer to these non-buyers, who constitute at least 95% of the audience, as the "general audience."

The Chelsea gallery audience is not, of course, a cross-section of the general public, but it is reasonably representative of the public who are interested in Contemporary Art. As such, it includes a sizeable proportion (about half) of art professionals (artists, curators, designers, critics etc.). It is a plausible assumption that the rest of the public (i.e. those who do not attend galleries that display Contemporary Art) do not on the whole have clearly defined views on the subject and indeed probably have only a hazy notion of what "Contemporary Art" is.

This "general audience" freely admit that they have come just to look, not to buy, usually because they cannot come anywhere close to affording the works. They are, therefore, viewers but arguably not "consumers" if the latter refers to people whose role is to purchase goods in the market.

Chelsea galleries impose no entry charge, do not pressure the onlookers to buy, and are open and welcoming. This shift in the function of the gallery is institutionalized in current gallery practices. On not one occasion during our research did a gallery employee make the classic "can I help you?" sales approach. The typical Chelsea gallery has an unobtrusive reception desk well to the side of the entry so that viewers can walk straight into the gallery without feeling any need to interact with the person at the desk.

The sociology of the new art gallery scene in Chelsea, Manhattan   235

Chelsea gallery owner Barbara Gladstone ("star list") referred to the Chelsea scene as "one of the best free shows in town," and the spirit of this comment was repeated by many owners and viewers. Further, this free show in many ways surpasses in quality and quantity that provided by New York's museums, almost all of which charge an entrance fee. Entry to the recently re-opened MoMA is $20. This absence of an admission charge runs counter to the strong tendency in the modern world towards the "commercialization of leisure life," whereby a growing proportion of spare time consists of events for which admission is paid (see, for example, Clark, 2004).

The gallerist Andrea Rosen ("star list") argued, plausibly, that this constituted a radically new relationship between gallery and audience:

> The wonderful thing about Chelsea is that there has been a change in the public's attitude to the art. The spaces are accessible. Galleries are free, unlike most museums. On a typical Saturday 1,000 people come through the gallery. Sometimes I say to friends who haven't been here before, "Why not come by the gallery?" Often they're hesitant, they're thinking of the older galleries where they're expected to buy.

Hence Chelsea galleries have a dual role. To the traditional role of the gallery as a place where art is sold has been added the role of the gallery as a place where huge numbers of people can come to just view contemporary art, including the latest work by the stars of the field, without feeling the slightest obligation to buy or even to pretend that they might buy.

Of course some people, i.e. the "collectors," do buy the art. Often these come to private showings and pre-views. For sure they are also part of the general audience (though less than 5%).

But our research suggests that the "general audience" —those who come to look with absolutely no intention of buying—may perform a crucial function, that of validating the art for the collectors, of helping to create and to support the "buzz" without which collectors are unlikely to have the confidence to buy, or to continue to buy, the works. This was suggested to us as a hypothesis by several audience members we interviewed, and several gallery owners said it was plausible. This "filtering" or validating mechanism may be a new and interesting way in which the market works. In the language of economics, it helps create an upward shift in the demand curve for the works of particular artists. Still, it is too soon in the development of the "free show" phenomenon to be sure what is going on.

Illustrative are a random sample of twenty-five of the spectators who came to an exhibition of drawings by Claes Oldenburg and Coosje van Bruggen at the Paula Cooper Gallery, in May 2004. The show consisted mostly of small drawings, watercolors done on lined paper depicting standard restaurant food items—shrimp cocktail, banana split, and so on. Being small drawings, these were selling for about $15,000, far less than art usually sells for in "star list" Chelsea galleries. So assuming that the demand for art is inversely related to its price—the standard economic assumption—the audience for this show could be expected to

236   *David Halle and Elisabeth Tiso*

be somewhat more inclined to purchase the art than the audience for the average "star list" show.

Still, only one person in this sample had even a thought of buying anything in this show. He was a man in his mid-40s, dressed in a smart yellow jacket, who identified himself as a "collector" of "modern and contemporary art." He was with a woman who identified herself as his "art adviser." She explained she was taking him around to "see as many galleries as we can fit into the next forty-five minutes." A chauffeur waited outside so they would waste no time.

The rest of the audience had no intention of buying. Indeed, for about half, the question whether they came to buy elicited satirical comments on their financial condition. Consider the following examples:

- A female professor of speech pathology at Lehman College, who had come with her husband and another male friend: "No we're not here to buy; unless the price is in the two digits." [The group laughs heartily.]
- A married couple, a photographer and a designer, who live in Greenpoint, Brooklyn: "We come to look, not to buy. We're living in Brooklyn!" [They laugh at the point that if they could afford to buy this art they would not be living in Brooklyn.]

Galleries versus museums

Almost half (46%) of the audience members interviewed during the study preferred going to Chelsea galleries over going to museums. Only 10% preferred museums. The rest liked museums and galleries equally. Those who preferred galleries did so partly because galleries are free and partly because they perceived Chelsea galleries as more open and innovative in their choice of artists, and generally less intimidating, than museums. For example, a female in her 40s from the upper east side of Manhattan who worked as a secretary said she felt uncomfortable in museums and found galleries more inviting. Two recent unemployed male grads from Yale University, asked if they frequented galleries or museums more often, laughed and said: "It's easier to go to galleries because they don't cost $20." A museum curator from Utah felt that New York museums (MoMA, Whitney, Met) tended to show over and over again the same canonical contemporary artists to the detriment of the younger and off-beat artists. Chelsea offered her an opportunity to see what was new and different.

The gallery system as opportunity for the artist

The artists that we interviewed rarely see the commercial gallery system as oppressive. Instead, they believe that it offers them a broad range of market opportunities for displaying their work, far broader than those offered by the museum world where the official gatekeepers are more likely to make cautious judgments favoring artists who have already established reputations elsewhere, especially in the commercial galleries. These views are generally shared by more successful artists showing in star Chelsea galleries (e.g. Mike Bidlo, Dan Graham, or Bill Owens) as well as by artists who are struggling, many of whom were part of the audience that we sampled.

While no artist that we interviewed would refuse patronage work (a commission from a museum or private person), none see this as a viable alternative to the main system, the operation of the commercial market through the gallery system. Thus the call, in the writings of some of the "commodification of art" school, for a return to private patronage as the main way of funding art seems hopelessly distant and foreign.

The multiplication and persistence of small galleries

Despite the presence of a handful of global galleries, Chelsea would not be the dense art gallery neighborhood that it is without the plethora of small, boutique-size galleries, owned by individuals not corporations, that make up by far the majority of the gallery scene. In this sense the Chelsea gallery world is still a far cry from, and seems to refuse to conform to, the oligopolistic concentrations (Gaps, Starbucks, and so on) that mark so much of the rest of the economy including the leisure and entertainment sector. This is, of course, a central reason why the gallery system offers, for most artists, a far more open system than the museums.

Art historian Thomas Crow has commented on this peculiarity of the gallery system, with so much of it existing at the "artisanal level" (Crow, 1996a, 1996b). Crow theorizes that what underpins this system is that the art sold in the galleries constitutes a form of unique intellectual property, a highly creative product akin to some of the unique software programs that permeate the "continually beta" world of high technology. The Contemporary Art world too requires continual novelty. This analogy between art/art galleries and artisanal shops selling unique products in a "continually beta" world suggests a complex situation that does not fit simply into a model of market dominance.[10]

Many of these small galleries appear to be economically marginal operations, and while often these are excused as tax right-offs, this answer seems too simple. The owners/dealers often say they view their activity as not just commercial but as philanthropic, almost akin to a calling or a religion, where they believe that it is important to display their artists' works not only to sell but as providing a message or knowledge-based service to the public, much like a museum. Interestingly, as large galleries come to see their roles as similar to museums, museums are starting more and more to function like galleries. The Los Angeles County Museum has an Art Sales and Rental Department representing "dynamic and cutting edge Southern California Artists." This convergence of museums and galleries raises interesting and as yet unresolved questions about "commodification" of art in the twenty-first century.

The content of the art displayed in Chelsea

Analysis of the content of the art in Chelsea's shows, and interviews with the audience, further undermines a "commodification" perspective. Five topics dominated the content of the art, to the point of being arguably obsessions.

238 *David Halle and Elisabeth Tiso*

Each of these topics constituted at least 13% of all the works in the sample. See Table 1.

Depictions of landscapes/nature constituted 25% of all the topics. These landscapes divide into two main kinds. There is the classic "good stretch of countryside/water/sky" (13% of all the topics). Here human figures, animals, and other items are either absent or small enough to avoid detracting from the view. This vision featured prominently in Western landscape art over the last 200 years, and clearly remains immensely popular (see Andrews, 1999).

The second type of landscape, 9% of all topics and almost as common among Chelsea landscapes as the first, is "radical environmental." These landscapes foreground concern, and often alarm, about the deterioration of the natural environment. This world is depicted as threatened by human development in numerous ways. It is variously shown as shriveled by suburban growth, criss-crossed by freeways and other transportation devices such as power lines, littered with garbage, polluted by devices that ruin the atmosphere, and subject to apocalyptic nuclear and other holocaust-style shocks. This "environmental art" is, in many ways, a new genre that has appeared since the 1960s. An interesting example is Nigel Cooke's *Silva Morosa*. See Photo 5.[11]

Sex, as a theme, is just as popular as landscapes, constituting 25% of all the topics of the art displayed in Chelsea. About half of these images go beyond nakedness to depict sexual activity—most often intercourse between male and female, sometimes same-sex intercourse, and sometimes male or female masturbation. (Counted here are a few cases where the image focuses primarily on the sex organs, though without showing sexual activity.)

The other half of the images classified as "sex" here depict people (usually women) naked or semi-naked, but not engaged in sexual activity. These are, therefore, more akin to the classic nude of art history. Often these naked images shade into feminism as the artist and audience use them to muse on the role of women in modern society. In some cases in the Chelsea sample, where the people naked are men, the images trigger musings on homosexuality.

Like "radical environmental art," sexual intercourse has not been a mainstream topic of Western art until Contemporary Art. Naked or semi-naked men and women pervade the history of Western art, but they have rarely been depicted as engaged in sexual activity. Nor have sexual organs usually been the image's primary/exclusive focus, rather than just an important part of the overall composition. This is one reason why in art history, even in the twentieth century, such naked or semi-naked figures have basically been classified as "the nude," not sex. The term "sex" is not even indexed in the two classic histories of art, Gardner (2005) and Janson *et al.* (2006). From time to time the adjective "erotic" occurs in histories of Western art, but this is always attached to descriptions of particular works, rather than to an entire genre that is prominent in a particular epoch.

There are a few possible exceptions. Indian art has a well known "tradition of eroticism" which, for example, depicts pairs of men and women (mithunas) embracing or engaged in sexual intercourse in an extraordinary range of positions. Still, Indian art is "Asian" not Western art. Further, this tradition is usually

The sociology of the new art gallery scene in Chelsea, Manhattan 239

Table 1 Subject matter of the art shows in the sixteen most important ("star") Chelsea galleries[a]

% of all shows (n = 32)[b]	
	MAJOR TOPICS[c,d]
25%	LANDSCAPES
	Classic landscapes (Beautiful views) (13%)
	Environmentalist landscapes (Landscape is threatened) (9%)
	Political (3%)
25%	SEX
	Sexual activity and/or focus on sex organs (12%)
	Nudes or semi-nudes (without sexual activity or focus on sex organs) (13%)
16%	DECORATIVE/ABSTRACT
16%	TROUBLED NUCLEAR FAMILY
16%	NATURAL FORMS/MAN-MADE BASIC MATERIALS
	MINOR TOPICS
9%	POOR, THOSE IN TROUBLE (Poor, addicts, etc.)
6%	MASS PRODUCTION/COMMODITIES
6%	POLITICAL
3%	RELIGION

[a] *The galleries include: Paula Cooper, Matthew Marks, Barbara Gladstone, Larry Gagosian, Metro Pictures, Robert Miller, Marlborough, Mary Boone, Andrea Rosen, Luhring Augustine, James Cohan, Pace Wildenstein, Cheim and Read, Galerie Lelong, Sonnabend, Marianne Boesky. A different group of experts would probably not pick an exactly similar list of "star" galleries, but we believe there would be agreement on the vast majority in the list.*

[b] *The research is still in progress, with n = 32 so far.*

[c] *Classifying the content of the art is not straightforward. For example, a depiction of a naked female could, in theory, be about at least one or several of the following—classic mythology, anatomy of the nude, eroticism, or feminism. The depiction might, on scrutiny, not even be unequivocably a female. This objective ambiguity is obviously one reason why artists usually title their work, to endow it with, and narrow it down to, particular meaning(s). So, in classifying the works we supplemented this "objective" look with a second perspective that considers the artist's intentions. We derived these intentions from the written materials that accompany most shows, since these typically have the artist's approval. These materials include the title of the works, any other wall text, and any catalogue and press release. These two perspectives—the "objective," supplemented by the artist's intention/commentary—are the basis for the classifications in Table 1.*

[d] *Multi-topic works/shows. Several of the works/shows covered more than one topic. If the topic constituted a third or more of the show (or if it had some other prominence, e.g. the first room in the gallery as with Warhol's movie "Blow Job") it was assigned 1 point. Thus some shows could count for up to 3 points. For example, Cecily Brown's images depict landscapes and sex and are decorative.*

These "multi-topic" works/shows therefore have more weight in the overall table than single topic works/shows. We did this because our aim is to understand which topics are most widespread in Contemporary Art, so if a show has three topics that should be recorded. Hence the percentages in Table 1 sum to over 100. An alternative way of handling "multi-topic" shows/works would have been to assign to each topic a fraction of a point that corresponded to the importance of the topic in the show. For example, Cecily Brown's work/show could receive half a point for landscape, a quarter for sex, and a quarter for decorative. As it turned out, this counting procedure did not give especially different results, in terms of determining the main topics of the art, than the procedure that we used in Table 1.

Photo 5 **Nigel Cooke**
Silva Morosa
2003
Oil on canvas
72 × 96 inches (183 × 244 cm)
Image courtesy of Andrea Rosen Gallery, NY
Photo by Oren Slor.

classified as a basically religious, not secular, phenomenon, with the figures seen as deriving from the Hindu and Buddhist religion and rooted in the symbolization of fertility and the propagation of life. Another interesting case are the rooms in ancient Pompeii, which contained depictions of mortals in sexual intercourse with mythological figures. Still, these rooms were hidden at the time—art historians call them the "secret rooms." They were also apparently linked to mystical religious cults—the rites of the Greek god Dionysius (Roman Bacchus). They are now housed in the Archaeological Museum of Naples, viewable only by adults. Sexual intercourse was sometimes depicted on ancient Greek pottery, but that was over two millennia ago.

This handful of possible exceptions underlines the point that sexual intercourse has, at least for the last two millennia, been unusual in Western art. Clearly in depicting sexual intercourse Contemporary Art is influenced by other widely available components of modern culture such as pornographic magazines and web sites.

The sociology of the new art gallery scene in Chelsea, Manhattan   241

A third topic is the nuclear family, but typically depicted with a critical or satirical edge as a troubled institution (16% of all topics). Serenely confident families and individual family members, of the kind depicted by Norman Rockwell, are so rare as to be almost taboo. This topic—the problematic family—also seems a new genre in art history. While troubled families have obviously existed in actuality throughout history, in the past periods artists or patrons have not wished to depict them in a sufficiently systematic way so as to make them a recognizable genre.

The fourth topic (16% of all topics) is the decorative/mostly pure design. Grouped under the umbrella of "abstract" art, this topic was seen by an "avant-garde" in the twentieth century as the apogee of art, superior in almost every way to other specific topics depicted in representative or figurative art. The anthropologist Franz Boas even argued that the aesthetic core of "primitive art" too was formalistic abstraction. These claims are now widely seen as not only exaggerated, but as having alienated much of the broader public.[12] Thus in Contemporary Art nowadays as it is displayed in Chelsea the abstract/decorative has settled into a more modest, though still important, position as (just) one of five themes.

A fifth topic is raw/basic materials, either of nature (wood, stone, etc.) or man-made (steel I beams, plastic structures), along with a related interest in the basic constituents of our world. This topic also clearly has affinities with the first topic of landscapes as well as with discoveries in modern science, especially molecular biology.[13]

These five topics suggest a general picture that is far more interesting and complex than could be derived from some view that the art is imposed on people. On the contrary the topics are mostly rooted in modern life and in the complex and varied ways that people (artists and audience) experience today's world. For example, environmental landscapes seem rooted in post-1960s alarm about the deteriorating natural environment. Landscapes as "beautiful views" gained a massive fillip from the suburbanization of life that has been ongoing now for two hundred years. Sexual intercourse seems to mimic current interest in pornography and modern feminist themes. The troubled nuclear family is a basically new art genre that is certainly related to (historically) high divorce rates. The decorative, downgraded now to a more realistic place as one among several motifs and currents, is a perennially popular genre in art. The interest in basic materials (natural and fabricated) and in the constituents of the world seems to derive from the stunning advances made by molecular biology, mixed with interest in the landscape environment.

What the audience see in the works[14]

Interviews with samples of the audience for particular shows likewise suggest that these themes flourish because they resonate with the audience's lives in an ongoing, creative, and interactive way. This is the best interpretation of the main reasons that the audience offer when asked why they like a particular work. It undercuts

242   *David Halle and Elisabeth Tiso*

the idea that the dominance of market forces and commercialism has led to a homogenization of the audience's views, which mechanically reproduce a set of meanings somehow attached to the works.

Robert Adams

Consider two case studies. First, Robert Adams's photos in a show at the Matthew Marks Gallery (January 2006). In the show Adams continues the theme—his life work—of how humans have ravaged the natural landscape. "Turning Back" revisits states such as Oregon and Washington and notes how sadly deteriorated are their forests as compared with when explorers Lewis and Clark encountered them. The wall text explains:

> Two hundred years ago, Lewis and Clark recorded finding in the American Northwest a landscape of monumental trees. Most of this ancient forest has since been clearcut, as has later growth. We travel now to confront these facts and look for hope.

The photographs in the show focus on the mutilation of the trees to make way for development. Examples include a tree stump in a cemetery alongside tombstones (titled "A cemetery, Bandon, Oregon"); a road cut through a forest (titled e.g. "A stump next to Oregon Highway, 47, Columbia County"); mature trees lying cut down to make way for development; spindly, immature trees likewise felled for development (titled "Stacking the de-limbed trunks of an immature harvest"); a huge cross-section of a tree trunk showing many rings to stress its age but also cracked in half; and birds flying (forlornly?) over tree-less fields (nowhere to nest?).

Of the audience interviewed (a sample of 20), half liked the show without reservation. In almost all cases this was because they resonated with Adams's concern about the fate of forests, and of the environment in general. A female in her early twenties, who had come to New York from Texas in order to study teaching English as a second language:

> I really like the idea, i.e. the exploitation of nature, what we've done to it. We're slowly starting to take over nature, but you can't live without it.

A female curator who works at the Museum of Contemporary Photography in Chicago:

> I think it's a very interesting show. I'll probably include his work in an exhibition I'm doing dealing with the contemporary landscape. He [Adams] started in the 70s with environmental landscape … it's not like Gursky with big large flashy color photos. The show (I'm curating) is "Landscape and Trauma." It's about how you can document trauma to the landscape with a camera … For example, there will be photos of Siberia work camps, and concentration

The sociology of the new art gallery scene in Chelsea, Manhattan 243

camps in Germany long after the camp has been taken down, and you still see a rough disturbance in the landscape ….

On the other hand, almost half the audience found the show unappealing, either because they found Adams's treatment of a potentially interesting topic to be dull, or because they were not that interested in seeing the subject depicted in art. Many of these spoke about an excess of trees, tree overload, tree fatigue.

For example a female lawyer in her fifties who bought art frequently and lives in the affluent New York suburb of Rye:

I'm disappointed with this show. This is "pure trees," "too many trees," its like taking a long walk in the woods. I own a tree or two myself. How can you object to someone who's objecting to the destruction of nature? But I go for the visually interesting.

A female in her early forties whose profession was art adviser (instead of Adams's work, she was looking for some "very large-scale abstract canvases" for her clients):

The subject of trees, deforestation, I blanked out. I've just seen 15 shows in Chelsea and I've been spoiled by large scale. The scale [smallish photographs] here is boring. And it's traditional, black and white.

Some trite little art show isn't going to do much. You might as well fall asleep here. Artists' political statements are pathetic and pointless. I'm looking for very large-scale abstract canvases.

Mary Ellen Mark

"Sex" with a feminist perspective is the topic of documentary photographer Mary Ellen Mark's show, "Falkland Road" (November 2005, the Marianne Boesky Gallery). The setting is the brothels of Bombay (Falkland Road). Shots included the prostitutes waiting for business, applying makeup, having sex with customers (the latter were slightly secluded in a rear room of the gallery), napping, bathing, and crying (Photos 6–7). Young children of the prostitutes were in some of the photographs, giving the impression that this was often a generational business into which women were born. The prostitutes themselves were often aged around 13–15.

For the audience sampled, this was the best-liked show, by far, of those where we interviewed. The reaction to this show was more uniform than to any other. Everyone praised it, citing one or both of two reasons. First the commentary about the plight of the women, exploited and mistreated, cited by 90% of respondents. There was a uniform sympathy with, and objection to, the suffering and exploitation of the female prostitutes. (The show included a few photos of transvestites, but no-one mentioned them.) Moreover, the line between these feminist issues about the exploitation of women, so prominent in the minds of the audience, and eroticism was clearly drawn. Although there were several images of women frontally naked,

Photo 6 **Mary Ellen Mark**
Putla with a Gold Necklace, Bombay, India (from Falkland Road Series)
1978
C-print
16 × 20 inches.
Image courtesy of Mary Ellen Mark Library, New York Studio.

including the first, and most prominently displayed as viewers entered the show (Photo 6), no-one, when asked generally about what they liked in the images, volunteered that they found them erotic. This contrasts with other artists (e.g. Lisa Yuskavage) where some in the audience could empathize with the women (feminism) while others saw the same women in erotic terms. Again, this underlines the critical importance of the audience interviews as the only way of determining whether images are or are not actually erotic.

The second reason for liking the show was the technical merit of the photos—their colors and the thoughtfulness of their staging. This was mentioned by 60% of respondents.

The following comments are illustrative. A male in his 30s, also a documentary photographer:

> It's wonderful, amazing. Artistically it's really great, but it's all about the content, the despair and tragic situation in which they live. It's heartbreaking to see these women, they're exploited, some by their own choice and some are brought from Nepal. And it's a rarity to have this in Chelsea. Documentary is very hard to show and to sell at the galleries—of course the galleries have

The sociology of the new art gallery scene in Chelsea, Manhattan 245

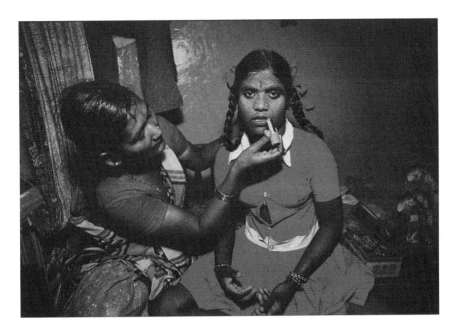

Photo 7 **Mary Ellen Mark**
A New Girl Being Made-up for the First Time, Bombay, India (from Falkland Road Series)
1978
C-print
16 × 20 inches.
Image courtesy of Mary Ellen Mark Library, New York Studio.

to sell, though this may sell now. I hope it does, though these pictures are not pleasant in someone's living room.

I know her work from before, this is some of her earliest work. I'm happy she's being re-released, it deserves to be. Things didn't change much in India, it's always relevant to communicate stories like this. And the fact that it was shot in slides and color chrome makes it so unique, you don't find that these days.

An Asian male in his 40s, born in Hong Kong, who works as an artist in Toronto where he also teaches Chinese calligraphy:

It's powerful! I can see the suffering of life, it goes on generation by generation. The people don't know what they're doing, just like the animals, maybe it's the rhythm of nature. But it's reality.

We are in North America here, so people here are surprised, but in India and Africa and all round the world these things are happening all the time. Here you are so sheltered.

246   David Halle and Elisabeth Tiso

About a third of the audience also commented on how, beyond the suffering of the prostitutes, there was an issue of the exploitation of the children (the male quoted above had this in mind when he referred to "generation by generation"). A female photographer in her 40s who lives in New York:

> Some of the images are positively scary, feral [animal] like. I assume she took 100s of photos and selected these with the feral quality because they were more powerful. These were done more than twenty years ago, but there's a recent documentary "Born into Brothels" about the same topic done by a woman who went into this same area and tried to rescue the children from all this. Things haven't changed.

In short, these photographs managed to evoke feminist sympathy while basically shuttering out an erotic component. Thus the audience for Mark's show, like that for Adams's work, demonstrates the active way the audience typically react to the works.

Conclusion

Approaches that stress the commercialization and (in stronger versions) the commodification of art are consistent with some features of Chelsea such as the agglomeration of commercial galleries, the rise of the international gallery, and the threat that the commercial real estate market may replace galleries with residential condominiums and/or stores selling more profitable merchandise. Yet some of Chelsea's most interesting features do not fit this model. These include Chelsea's role as providing a giant free art show for people, few of whom are "consumers" (i.e. purchasers) of art, its place as a flexible and open structure of opportunity for artists that far surpasses the opportunities offered by museums, and the fact that the vast majority of galleries are not international (let along "global") or star but small, boutique-like operations selling unique products, each one of which proclaims its individuality and the creativity of the artist who produced it. Above all, a commodification theory fails to jibe with the active way the audience attributes meaning to the art and with the way the audience often scrutinizes the art for ways in which it may be significant for their lives. In a complex way much of the art in Chelsea, like Impressionism in its day, relates to the visual depiction of contemporary social and economic life, albeit a mediated and selected version of that life.

Notes

1 *The Art in America Gallery Guide for Chelsea*, the source of the data in Figure 1, appears every two months as a fold-out map. Galleries must pay an annual fee of $175 to be included in the guide, so the actual number of galleries in Chelsea is higher (by about 40% based on actual counts in selected buildings) than in Figure 1. The data in Figure 2 are based on another guide, *Gallery Guide* (which has comparative data), which is why

The sociology of the new art gallery scene in Chelsea, Manhattan   247

they differ a little from the Chelsea numbers in Figure 1. *Gallery Guide* also charges a fee to be included and so also underestimates the actual numbers.

2 There have been a number of empirically based studies of the role of the market, at other stages in its development, in the art world. A broadly historical study of the evolution of the commercial art market is Getty Research Institute (2004). A study of the art market in France is Moulin (1967). A recent study of how art Galleries in New York and Amsterdam set prices is Velthuis (2005).

Theorists who have called for the open-minded, empirical study of art markets include Fredric Jameson who considers the market to be "the most crucial terrain of ideological struggle in our time" and calls for examining the market not just as an ideological or rhetorical trope but as a "real market just as much as about metaphysics, psychology, advertising, culture, representations, and libidinal apparatuses." See Jameson (1998).

3 For Leavis see Leavis and Thompson (1937). For the formulations of theorists of "mass culture," see Rosenberg and White (1957). The formalist art critic Clement Greenberg also believed that the market system often encouraged mass-produced products of low aesthetic quality ("kitsch") that were largely passively absorbed by an uncritical audience. See Greenberg (1939). For some of the original Frankfurt-School formulations see Horkheimer and Adorno (1994) and Adorno (1983). More recent Western theorists in a similar tradition include Baudrillard (2004a,b) and Jameson (1979). See also Havel (1979) and the New Museum of Contemporary Art 2007; Curator Flood's quoted remark is p. 12.

4 For some of the critics see Bauer and Bauer (1960), Gans (1974), Frith (1981), Miller (1987), Halle (1994), and Roseler (1979).

5 On the East Village move and real estate see Deutsche and Ryan (1984).

6 The main study of SoHo as an art neighborhood is Simpson (1981). For some artists SoHo also represented an attempt to escape the commercial art gallery market by showing their work directly to the public in alternative spaces—e.g. artist co-operatives or private lofts. There is no such movement in Chelsea.

7 For a lucid guide to these zoning designations see the Department of City Planning's, *Zoning Handbook* (2006). M1-5 is a manufacturing designation with the 5 indicating a permitted floor area ratio (FAR) of 5. FAR is the ratio of total building floor area to the area of its zoning lot.

8 In 1992 the Chelsea Property Owners obtained a court order requiring CSX, the railroad that owned the High Line, to demolish it. But demolition had been held up because not all the owners of property under the High Line had signed the agreement that specified how the demolition costs would be shared. Meanwhile, in 1999 a group of neighborhood residents, businesses, design professionals, and civic organizations joined forces to form Friends of the High Line, a not-for-profit hoping to turn the High Line into an elevated park. The mechanism that they identified to convert the High Line to a public open space was called rail-banking. As part of the 1983 National Trail Systems Act, the U.S. Congress passed legislation that allowed out-of-use rail corridors to be utilized as trails while being "banked" for future transportation needs. Then in December 2001, in the final week of his administration, Mayor Giuliani signed a Demolition Agreement with the Chelsea Property Owners seeking to compel CSX to demolish the railroad.

The new Bloomberg administration supported the plan to preserve the High Line, though only after an economic feasibility study that showed that over a 20 year period the revenue generated in taxes for the city would be about 140m and the cost to the city only about 65m. (The High Line had long been a favored project of DCP's Director Amanda Burden, who lived in the West Village, just to the south of Chelsea.) As a result, the city on Dec 17, 2002 filed an application to the federal Surface Transportation Board (STB) requesting that negotiations begin to transform the High Line into an elevated public walkway. But the STB made it clear to the city that it would not give final approval

248 *David Halle and Elisabeth Tiso*

for the rail-banking unless a majority of the Chelsea property owners were supportive, at which point the DCP came up with the rezoning and special air-rights transfer plan.

9   Those in a High Line Transfer Corridor, 100 feet wide, encompassing lots occupied by the High Line or immediately to its west.

10 Thus it would be impossible for 300 shoe stores, selling products of varying styles, to exist in a single neighborhood.

11 The "classic landscape," which basically presented a "beautiful view," did of course sometimes hint at such environmental themes. For example, certain artists and patrons of the Hudson River school of landscape were motivated by concern about the harmful impact of the railroad on the landscape and by a related desire to document still unspoiled natural scenery. As early as 1836 Thomas Cole, one of the most important Hudson River school artists, after extolling the American wilderness, lamented that:

> … the beauty of such landscapes is quickly passing away—the ravages of the axe are daily increasing, [leading to] … desecration by what is called improvement … which generally destroys Nature's bounty without substituting that of Art …. I hope the importance of cultivating a taste for scenery will not be forgotten. Cole, (1836).

Such anxiety was, too, a background motif in some Impressionist paintings, where for instance a railroad sometimes popped up in a corner of the picture. Still, the Impressionists for the most part viewed technology positively where it became a metaphor for modernity and modern life.

But these environmental concerns rarely, if ever, intruded center-stage in these classic landscapes, as they do in the radical environmentalist landscapes of Contemporary Art in Chelsea. In his paintings Cole depicted the still beautiful scenery, not the "ravages of the axe." Hence art historians have noted the emergence in the 1960s of a basically new genre, "environmental art."

12 Gardner's standard art history comments that "The prevalence of abstraction and the formal experimentation in much of postwar art had alienated the public".

13 The concern with raw materials also represents a "modernist" formalist interest in the material of art and expands the discourse on "process art" that began in the 60s and that rejected the traditional academic material of art like marble and bronze and sought to examine materials more relevant to life.

14 In order to study systematically the views of the audience, we started with the sample of shows selected for the study of the content of the art (Table 1) and then focused on a sub-group of these, 14 so far. For each show in this sub-group we interviewed 20 audience members chosen at random. Our criterion for selecting shows for this sub-group was to ensure that the topics (content) of the shows were representative of the topics that our content-analysis had revealed as typical of Chelsea art (Table 1).

References

Adorno, Theodor. 1983. "Perennial Fashion: Jazz," in *Prisms*, trans. by Samuel and Shierry Weber (Cambridge: M.I.T. Press).

Andrews, Malcolm. 1999. *Landscape and Western Art* (Oxford).

Baudrillard, Jean. 2004a. "Hypermarket and Hypercommodity," in *"Simulacra and Simulation* (Ann Arbor: University of Michigan Press).

Baudrillard, Jean. 2004b. "The Beaubourg Effect," in *"Simulacra and Simulation* (Ann Arbor: University of Michigan Press).

The sociology of the new art gallery scene in Chelsea, Manhattan   249

Bauer, Raymond, and Alice Bauer. 1960. "America, 'Mass Society' and Mass Media," *Journal of Social Issues* 16, no 3.

Clark, Terry Nichols. 2004. *The City as an Entertainment Machine* (Elsevier).

Cole, Thomas. 1836. "Essay on American Scenery," *The American Monthly Magazine* (January).

Crow, Thomas. 1996a. "Modernism and Mass Culture in the Visual Arts," in *Modern Art in the Common Culture* (New Haven and London: Yale University Press).

Crow, Thomas. 1996b. "The Return of Hank Heron: Simulated Abstraction and the Service of Economy of Art," in *Modern Art in the Common Culture* (New Haven and London: Yale University Press).

Deutsche, Roslayn, and Cara Gendel Ryan. 1984. "The Fine Art of Gentrification," *October*, 31. (Winter).

Frith, Simon. 1981. *Sound Effects: Youth, Leisure and the Politics of rock 'n Roll* (New York: Pantheon).

Gans, Herbert. 1974. *Popular Culture and High Culture: An Analysis and Evaluation of Taste* (New York: Basic Books).

Gardner. 2005. *Art Through the Ages*, Fred Kleiner and Christin Mamiya (Wadsworth, 12th edition).

Getty Research Institute. 2004. *The Business of Art: Evidence from the Art Market* (Los Angeles: Getty Research Institute).

Greenberg, Clement. 1939. "Avant-Garde and Kitsch," reprinted in *Art and Culture: Critical Essays* (Boston: Beacon Press).

Halle, David. 1994. *Inside Culture* (Chicago: University of Chicago Press).

Havel, Václav. 1979. "The Power of the Powerless," in John Keane, ed., *The Power of the Powerless* (London: Hutchinson, 1985).

Horkheimer, Max, and Theodor Adorno. 1944. "The Culture Industry: Enlightenment as Mass Deception," in *Dialectic of Enlightenment*, trans. by John Cummings (New York: Herder and Herder, 1972).

Jameson, Fredric. 1979. "Reification and Utopia in Mass Culture," *Social Text* 1, pp. 130–48.

Jameson, Fredric. 1998. "Postmodernism and Consumer Society," in Hal Foster, ed., *The Anti-Aesthetic Essays on Postmodern Culture* (New York: The New Press).

Janson, H.W., *et al.* 2006. *History of Art* (Pearson, 2006).

Leavis, F.R., and Denys Thompson. 1937. *Culture and Environment* (London: Chatto and Windus).

Miller, Daniel. 1987. *Material Culture and Mass Consumption* (Oxford: Basil Blackwell).

Moulin, Raymond. 1967. *The French Art Market: A Sociological View* (New Brunswick: Rutgers University Press).

New Museum of Contemporary Art. 2007. *Unmonumental: The Object in the 21st Century* (New York: Phaidon).

Roseler, Martha. 1979. "Lookers, Buyers, Dealers, and Makers: Thoughts on Audience, in Brian Wallis" ed., *Art After Modernism: Rethinking Representation.* (New York and Boston: New Museum of Contemporary Art and David R. Godine).

Rosenberg, Bernard, and David White, eds. 1957. *Mass Culture: The Popular Arts in America* (Glencoe, Ill: The Free Press).

Simpson, Charles. 1981. *The Artist in the City* (Chicago: University of Chicago Press).

Velthuis, Olav. 2005. *Talking Prices: Symbolic Meaning of Prices on the Market for Contemporary Art* (Princeton: Princeton University Press).

12 The lives of cultural goods[1]

Arjo Klamer

Let me state my conclusion up front: cultural goods are exceptional and therefore easier to distinguish from other goods. They are not exceptional because they have an intrinsic value that sets them apart. They are exceptional because of the "conversations" that make them "cultural goods." They are "discursive constructs." That is, goods become "cultural" when people treat them as such: in the way they talk about them and in the processes of "valuation, evaluation, and valorization."[2] For instance, the Dutch will experience the sale of Rembrandt's *Nightwatch* to a Chinese businessman dramatically differently from the sale of a container company to that very same businessman. Selling *Nightwatch* is inconceivable, no matter how dire the circumstances. The sale of the container company is a mundane business deal that actually took place.

With this conclusion I deviate from the position that cultural goods are like any other good, as economists typically assume. Even though they may be bought and sold like other commodities, may serve as investments and sources of revenue, they are more than commodities, at least if the adjective "cultural" applies. I do not want to suggest that cultural goods are in essence different from other goods, and therefore that the economist is fundamentally mistaken. Rather, my position is a pragmatic one. In order to make sense of what is going on in the art world, it helps to focus on the distinctive characteristics of the deliberations in which the values of cultural goods are realized. In doing so, it is clear that normal economic arguments play a subordinate role in such deliberations; their contributions do not have a notable effect on outcomes. In an attempt to decipher the exceptionality of cultural goods, I will offer what I shall call a cultural-economic perspective and with it a re-evaluation of notions like value, culture, and valorization, as it mediates between the "culturalist" and "economistic" positions vying for attention in deliberations concerning cultural goods. The key to my approach is the notion of the conversation.

"Conversation" as a heuristic

Consider the painting stored in my attic, rediscovered and remembered during a recent cleanup. My wife and I discussed whether we would throw it out. I doubt

The lives of cultural goods 251

anyone else, including the artist, gives it any thought. Although it is physically there in that attic, it might just as well not exist, and labeling it "art" has no meaning. How differently we would value it, if it turned out to be an early Mondrian. It would end up in some gallery or at least in a prominent place in our house. Newspapers would report the find, art historians would want to see it and write about it, students would use it as a topic for research papers, insurance agents would fret about its value, and, if put up for auction, numerous people would contemplate buying it and wonder about its cost. As a cast off in my attic, the painting is not art because it has no existence in the conversation on art. As a lost Mondrian, its very existence is defined by the conversation of art. To say, therefore, that goods are "discursive constructs" is to assert that their characteristics, their values, are established in such conversations. Just as when a car is at the garage, its discursive construct is that of a machine of transportation because it functions in the talk about nuts and bolts, electronic mechanisms, tuning, lubricating, and so on, but when it is displayed at the museum of modern art, it is art because then its design, its lines and curvatures, become the topic of conversation.

I am using the concept "conversation" with emphasis and insistence. It denotes a distinct way of interacting. Focusing on conversation invites us to look beyond a good, a result, a proposition, or a statement and always to consider such things in their discursive context. Economics, my discipline, is a conversation, or rather a collection of conversations (economists, after all, subscribe to different schools of thought and each school can be said to constitute a distinct conversation). Likewise any set of utterances that acknowledge a shared set of principles of noticeability and relevance is a conversation: soccer, cooking, house building, medicine, horse racing, and, of course, art are all examples of conversations in this sense. It is in conversation that things acquire their meanings and values, their cultural lives.[3]

Despite its commonplace and seemingly simple connotation, I want to retain the term—and the concept—of "conversation" precisely because of its complexity and flexibility. Its root, *conversatio*, means "intercourse," "manner of life." "Conversation" has been used to connote the action of living or dwelling in a place and, more interestingly, the "action of associating or having dealings with others." I want to hold on to "conversation" for this sense. Further, I want to use it because a conversation is fluid and, if it is bounded, the boundaries are often indistinct. A conversation may be a practice or it may not. And it is possible to be in different conversations simultaneously. "Conversation" also denotes "occupation or association with an object of study, in the sense of close acquaintance," making it possible for Francis Bacon to write of the "conversation in books," a reference that extends beyond spoken to written words as well. Thus, "conversation" as I am using the term comprises more than a dialogue or a verbal exchange, referring instead to something like the discourses of economists, or of cultural theorists, or of the arts. Conversation defines all the exchanges, the chatter, the publications, the literature, the conferences, the meetings that constitute these communities, and participation in these conversations establishes who is counted as a member of these communities. Thus, if persons want to be involved in the arts, they can

252   *Arjo Klamer*

attempt to enter into that conversation—an activity, by the way, that is easier said than done.

Economists versus culturalists

The "natural" place to enter into a conversation on cultural goods is in the company of art historians, art critics, art lovers, directors, actors, curators, conservationists, cultural scholars, and others who have a manifest affinity for the topic. These are the culturalists.[4] Presumably, they know how to appreciate the historical, artistic, and aesthetic values of the Elgin Marbles, a new musical composition, or a Rembrandt. Entering their discourse requires one to know about artistic and religious traditions, cultural contexts and histories, while money—or rather "price"—is rarely a topic in these conversations. In contradistinction are the economists who are also willing to discuss the subject of art, music, etc., but whose conversation is dramatically different. Economists usually discuss typical economic issues such as the prices of cultural goods, the costs of procuring them, the economic impact of investment in cultural heritage, jobs, tourism, efficiency, demand, (contingent) valuations, government subsidies, and other topics that have relatively little purchase in the discussions among culturalists.

To most economists, the market is a superior instrument for the allocation of scarce resources. Assume the economic perspective and you will look at the world with a demand-supply diagram engraved on your glasses, or contact lenses. You will view everything in terms of demand, supply, product, and price. You will like markets because they do a superior job pricing goods (cf. Grampp, 1989; Cowen, 1998). You will think that pricing equals valuing the good: subjective (artistic, cultural, and historical) values may diverge, but the moment of exchange enforces one single value, the exchange value. The great attraction of the market is that in a market exchange the party that pays is also the party that benefits. The good gets to the correct party, that is, the party that is willing to pay most for it. Look through these glasses, and you will regret the need for governmental intervention in case of market failures because in that case those who pay, the taxpayers, are usually not the same people as those who benefit.

The discussions of economists and culturalists are so distinct that it makes sense to speak of two discrete discursive practices, conversations, even cultures,[5] which interact very little.[6] Attempts at forging a new conversation between them and their practices inevitably create frictions and frustrations. Whereas economists have made inroads in the public discussions on the arts, culturalists have dominated the academic discourse on cultural goods. Attempts of economists to highlight the economic dimensions appear to have made little impact (cf. Peacock, 1994; Frey, 1989; Throsby *et al.* 1994). One reason for this may be a lack of familiarity with economics on the part of most culturalists. Another reason may be their resistance, or suspicion, towards the "imperialistic" inclinations of economics as a discipline and the particular, if not peculiar, vocabulary with which economists analyze everything human. The ultimate concern of culturalists is that economists insufficiently appreciate the special values of cultural

The lives of cultural goods   253

heritage, and may be less than helpful in preserving and fortifying the cultural sector. Economists, on the other hand, complain about the failure of culturalists to acknowledge the economics of cultural heritage even as they foreground their own perspectives on the value of cultural artifacts. A "cultural-economic" perspective, such as the one proposed here, attempts a middle ground and a new conversation, one that pays attention to the variety of values in play but also attempts to account for economic factors that contribute to our reception of those artifacts.

The cultural-economic perspective presents another possible conversation on art, culture, and economy. Like the culturalist discourse, it pays attention to the variety of values in play, but it also wants to account for economic factors. At the heart of such a conversation is a consideration of value(s).

It's all about values even (especially) if they seem hidden

In the cultural-economics conversation, concepts of value must range widely. The problem with *value* as a term is that it can refer to so many things: beliefs, suppositions, goals, price, etc. At bottom, however, it means distinctions, hierarchies of worth, whatever those *valuations* may be based upon. Indeed, we can think of valuation as the means by which we make certain choices— rational or otherwise. Thus, when I buy a painting rather than a car, I am expressing certain predilections, prejudices, desires, *values* that are weighed in any number of ways—consciously and unconsciously—against others. In buying the painting, I hope to realize certain benefits from it such as having something beautiful in my home, or maintaining a reputation as an art lover, or even acquiring a good investment. Further, because a work of art *qua* art exists in a conversation about its values, it accretes (or loses) value as the conversation continues.

The next illustration presents an actual case in which an artwork is at the center of a process of valuation in which a wide variety of values are in play, with different weights, even if they are not immediately discernible.

An issue of moral ownership

Early in 1999 a retired Jewish banker, Mr. Eberstadt, submitted a request to the board of a foundation connected with the art museum Boymans-van Beuningen in Rotterdam, for the return of the drawing by an early twentieth-century Dutch artist, named Charles van Toorop. He claimed that the drawing belonged to his grandparents and had come to the Foundation illegitimately. At first, the Foundation rejected the claim. Later, however, after a long controversy involving the American ambassador, the Dutch secretary of culture, the city council of Rotterdam, the press, sponsors of the museum, lawyers, and a host of others, it offered the drawing to Mr. Eberstadt in exchange for a symbolic payment of 800 euros, the sum that was paid for it in 1942

254 *Arjo Klamer*

when it came into the collection of the Foundation. Mr. Eberstadt only had to agree not to sell the drawing.[7]

During extensive deliberations in boardrooms, in telephone conversations, in hallways, in newspapers, on television, and in bedrooms, those involved figured out what they wanted and what they valued. When the claim was presented to the board the overall opinion leaned to rejection. Only a few dissented. The ensuing discussions were intense and sometimes emotional. When the dialogue started, the drawing was in storage. During a showing for the board, a curator explained its importance for the collection, informing the board that it was characteristic for van Toorop and should be considered part of the Dutch cultural heritage. Money was never a significant topic of conversation either in terms of the cost of the dispute or the worth of the drawing. Only once did the director note that the piece was valued at about 35,000 euros.

Mr. Eberstadt clearly attached great emotional significance to possessing the drawing. He would not accept the Foundation's initial refusal. He hired a law firm to represent him, and contacted government authorities in the US, the Dutch authorities, and various private parties in order to secure support for his claim. In a report on Dutch national television, he was visibly moved. At one point, he offered to pay for the drawing. Later he withdrew the offer because of his dismay over the reactions of the chairperson of the Foundation. He and his supporters, including the American ambassador to the Netherlands, became morally outraged over what they perceived as the insensitivities of the Foundation concerning the victims of the Holocaust. To his supporters, Eberstadt had a moral claim to the drawing.

The decisions on the part of members of the board had more to do with social and cultural factors. First, an investigation was ordered to determine the legal grounds for the claim. The report stated that the drawing was bought during the war from a trader in The Hague. This trader supposedly had bought it from a person with a German name. It was established that the drawing had been in the possession of the family Flersheim, Eberstadt's grandparents, before they fled from the Nazis to the Netherlands; almost certainly, they had acquired it from the artist himself, whom they had befriended. Anything else is mere speculation. The Flersheims may have felt compelled to sell the drawing before 1937 when they fled to Holland. They may have done so freely. There is some evidence that they auctioned off part of their art possessions, but whether the van Toorop was among those is unknown. The Gestapo may have stolen it. Who knows? We also know that in 1942 the Flersheims were abducted and imprisoned, and that they were murdered in 1944 in Bergen-Belsen.

As for the acquisition of the drawing by the Foundation, two benefactors had paid for the purchase and subsequently donated the drawing to the Foundation of the Boymans-van Beuningen Museum. An earlier court case in the fifties had awarded the drawing to the heirs of the Flersheims, but the Foundation had rejected that claim because a German court had reached this decision. Beyond that, there were no legal grounds for the claim of Mr. Eberstadt. His claim stood no chance in a Dutch court of law. Even if he could have established the improper alienation of

The question was whether Mr. Eberstadt had a moral claim. The board thought not and declared as much in the media. Among the board's stronger arguments were its responsibility of protecting the collection and its responsibility towards those who had donated the drawing to the Foundation. Some members of the board felt strongly about these responsibilities. After all, they insisted, the very reason for having an autonomous Foundation was to be able to resist political pressure to sell, or, as in this case, to give up a piece. It was furthermore mentioned that the drawing had larger significance because it is part of the "Dutch collection." This would justify almost any action to prevent the drawing from leaving the country. It would be the patriotic thing to do. Dissenters on the board argued that Dutch society is morally indebted to the victims of the Holocaust. To them the stance of the Foundation was emblematic of the unconscionable way the Dutch had dealt with the property of Jews murdered during WW II; they argued that the Foundation had the moral obligation to return the painting to Mr. Eberstadt if there is even the slightest doubt about the legitimacy of its being in the collection. The latter position also came to dominate the opinions expressed in the media.

Why not sell the drawing? The issue came up when Eberstadt offered to pay, but the possibility was not given serious thought. One reason is the taboo on selling ("deaccessioning") items from the collection in a museum. When the mission is to collect and conserve, you do not sell.[8] Another important reason was that the drawing had been a gift to the Foundation. Two businessmen had financed the sum of the purchase (about 2000 guilders) and subsequently donated the drawing to the Foundation. The general rule is that a gift cannot be sold. The issue was especially sensitive as descendants of these businessmen are still members of the board.

The dispute became public. It received extensive coverage in the national media and international arts magazines. The American ambassador stated publicly her dismay with the position of the Foundation. The Dutch secretary of culture mediated and so did an alderman of Rotterdam. There were fears about the reputation of the museum—a major sponsor of an important exhibition had already become nervous— local politicians expressed concerns about negative publicity that the case caused for the city of Rotterdam, and it was argued that the case only reinforced the Dutch's reputation for the maltreatment of survivors of the Holocaust in the Netherlands after the war. Added pressure came from a climate in which museums in the US and UK had been forthcoming in the restoration of possessions of Jewish victims as well as other illegally acquired pieces.

In the Summer of 2001 the case came to a conclusion. The Foundation offered Mr. Eberstadt the drawing for the price that the benefactors had paid for it—the sum of 2000 guilders, not even 3 percent of its estimated value. In that way it did not really *give* the drawing back. It gave up its earlier demands for certain conditions such as Mr. Eberstadt giving the museum, or any other Dutch institution, the first right to buy in case he were to offer the piece for sale. In the Fall, Mr. Eberstadt received the van Toorop from the chairperson of the board. The reception was cool.[9]

256   *Arjo Klamer*

Valuation, evaluation, and valorization

The controversy about the drawing revolves around values. For Mr. Eberstadt, the van Toorop is a tribute to his grandparents. It has emotional value to him. Implied is a valuation of kinship and the horror of the Holocaust. For the Foundation, the main value is expressed in its mission of conserving and strengthening its collection. Individual board members may struggle with their sense of obligation towards the Jewish victims of the Holocaust, but the first value overrules the latter, at least initially. Another value that the Foundation could call upon was that of the "Dutch cultural heritage." In identifying van Toorop as part of that heritage, the Foundation had yet another argument to justify its rejection of Eberstadt's claim. With the focus on values, the deliberations are over valuations: the various parties are negotiating the relevant values and in their dialogue are trying to weigh and rank them. The conversations that took place, which revolved around issues ranging from national identity (and pride) to collective guilt and responsibility for Holocaust victims (and their progeny), often held up competing and conflicting claims, assumptions, desires. In the end, however, through what seemed an interminable amount of "talking," decisions were made, compromises were reached, resolutions were formed, rationales were issued.

Economists typically are less concerned with how such decisions are reached than with the effect of those decisions. For them, the most important value coalesces in the moment of exchange, and that value is revealed as price. However, David Throsby, a cultural economist, has come to recognize the importance of identifying multiple values in play in such processes. In his most recent book *Economics and Culture* (2001) Throsby argues that economists need to take the culturalists' perspective seriously. To that end he draws attention to cultural values, such as the aesthetic, spiritual, social, symbolic, and historical (Throsby, 2001, p. 29). Yet, just as an economist is wont to do, he subsequently treats those values as given, as inputs in an economic valuation process. Cultural values become like preferences that people hold—as if they know those and they are inflexible. In reality, people always need to sort through values and establish their hierarchy, as the van Toorop case illustrates.

In such instances, values often change as those involved adopt or develop new ones, discard old ones. They may, as Elizabeth Anderson has written, establish "a complex of positive attitudes toward [a thing], governed by distinct standards for perception, emotion, deliberation, desire" (Anderson, 1993, p. 2). In the language of economists, we would say that they acquire their taste (see Throsby, 1994). This process of valorization is particularly important when cultural goods are the objects of interest. Thus westerners, who dislike Arabic music when they hear it for the first time, may learn to appreciate it when immersed in the Arabic world and inundated with it. The chances for such appreciation increase if they become knowledgeable about it and learn to distinguish different variants. Similarly, people who walk into a museum of modern art for the first time often have difficulties appreciating the abstract works of Mondrian, Newman, Twombly, and others. If they are going to participate in the conversations surrounding

The lives of cultural goods   257

the appreciation of modern art, they must learn to value it. Indeed, context matters. When immersed in an academic setting, even the most practical students ("I'd like to make some money, you know") may learn to appreciate the value of reading and "studying" texts. One hopes that the academic setting affirms and intensifies the importance of reflection, critical inquiry, and other such academic values.

Noting the role of different, sometimes competing, values in cultural disputes helps us to see the complexity of various positions as well as the dynamics as values are negotiated, weighed, and evaluated. In the process of deliberation values change. Indeed, even the process of valorization, when these competing value claims are being sorted out, can have an effect on the ultimate value of a cultural good. Certainly the van Toorop drawing has become more valuable because of all the turmoil. It has gained a history. Merely noting that these different values exist and are working for (and against) each other does little more than give us a sketchy idea of the overall picture of how valorization comes about. In order to speak more precisely, it may be useful to think of values as operating most effectively within certain categories.

Economic, social, and cultural values

Economic values usually refer to the prices of things, or their exchange value. When economists speak of valuing a good, they mean the *pricing* of the good. It is a special kind of valuation as it focuses on the moment of exchange. So much so that, even when exchange does not actually take place, the economist will proceed as if it had and then figure out the price that would have been paid. Economic values can take a number of forms of expression. The GDP (gross domestic product) is a measure of the flow of economic values that a national economy generates. The economic value of a cultural good is what people are willing to pay for it. The economic value of knowledge is the income that can be earned by applying it. Economists speak of human capital to indicate that knowledge is a stock of value that generates a flow of value. In general, economic capital is a stock that will generate a flow of economic values.

Sometimes economic value is the center of attention. In such a climate, profits are primary, and people are valued by their income, or wealth. During these times, cultural producers justify a new theatre, the expansion of a museum, or the conservation of an archeological site most effectively by pointing to the income an investment will generate: jobs, tourism, etc. Because justifications of this sort require economic argumentation, a number of conversational "tropes" have been developed: "economic impact" analyses, contingent valuation methods, and willingness to pay studies (cf. Throsby, 1994; Klamer and Throsby, 2000)—all of which are intended to determine the economic value of a good. According to conventional economic reasoning, all values are embodied in the price of a good. A demand-supply analysis brings together values in the production process, such as technology, the price of labor, real assets, and financial capital: the values on the demand side which are expressed in the

258　*Arjo Klamer*

form of preferences. As a result, someone like William Grampp can consistently argue that the price of a good is its value. For him, the story of value and the good stops there.

Yet, it does not. Even if we were to remain in the sphere of the economic, a wide range of other values arise.[10] (Usually) positive attributes such as "commercial," "business like," "result oriented," "ambitious," "entrepreneurial," "markets," and "freedom," and (typically) negative characteristics such as "cold," "ruthless," "unjust," "immoral," and "constraining" become attached to the good. "Freedom" as a value emerges when people associate the economic with "markets," leading us to think of "freedom of choice." Yet all these values are not economic values *per se*, since they are not prices that can be attached to things. One might say, instead, that they are spillovers of the engagement in exchange relations; what economists might call externalities, and are much more appropriately (and usefully) grouped in the separate category of "social values."[11]

Social values are those closely held positive attributes that work in the context of interpersonal relationships, groups, communities, and societies. People appeal to them in negotiating relationships with others and with associations of people. Social values include notions of belonging, identity, social distinction, freedom, solidarity, trust, tolerance, responsibility, love, friendship, and so on.[12] In everyday conversations, these values preoccupy people far more than economic values. People are constantly deliberating their relationships with others, weighing the values that are important to them, and assessing relationships in the light of those. "Should I care for my children, when I feel responsible to finish this article?" "Can I trust those people to be sympathetic and caring?" "Is she friendly out of friendship or because she expects to gain from knowing me?" "Shall we eat out or make our own dinner?" We are constantly working our social values. In comparison, we spend little time determining and evaluating economic values.

The capacity to deal with social values and adhere to social norms is nowadays called *social capital*.[13] The assumption here is that some people, organizations, or societies have more of it than others. At least that is how Robert Putnam *et al.* (1994) apply the concept in their study of the vitality of democracies: people with a stronger sense of belonging and responsibility, and with a greater ability to trust, do better in making a democracy than those with fewer of these qualities.[14] Poignantly, in a world where economic values and economic capital dominate the political domain, social capital is easily conceived to be subservient to economic capital. Politicians and businesspeople will argue that investments in social capital will be good for economic growth and profit. At school students presumably need to learn social skills so that they will do better in their jobs later. After all, the goal of all things social is economic gain. But is it? Would it not make more sense to think of economic values as being instrumental towards social values? Why else would people seek more income and more profit than to do better in their relationships with others? Even if people have a royal income, the question is always what they will do with it. Whether they go out for sumptuous meals, buy a nice car, a yacht, a new house, or go on trips far away, the issue is always with, and possibly for, whom and

The lives of cultural goods   259

in what way. Sitting in your own luxurious house with pool and a couple of cars can be quite depressing without meaningful relations. The good life must be evaluated in large part in terms of social values. *Economic values are instrumental at best.*[15]

In the case of cultural goods, satisfaction comes more from their social than economic significance. While a cultural attraction may bring economic benefits to hundreds or thousands of people, its special value is linked much more closely to its social functions, how it contributes to issues of identity, heritage, culture, pride, and so on. *Cultural values*, then, are the values that evoke a quality over and beyond the economic and the social. Throsby includes in this category aesthetic, spiritual, social, historical, symbolic, and authenticity values (2000, p. 28). For instance, a temple has cultural value insofar as it connects with a religious practice and invokes the ideals of that tradition. Because of its architectonic properties, it can appeal to an aesthetic sense; it may have historical value and symbolic value as well when it represents something of importance to a group of people. A cultural good may also have social values—the temple may be a meeting place and may function as a national heritage—or economic values— when it generates income. But these are distinct from the cultural values that inhere in it.

According to Kant the quintessential cultural value of a good is its ability to evoke an experience of the sublime. It is the quality that causes awe and "stirs the soul." Kant purports that this quality is disinterested; it does not serve a social or economic goal. Such a characterization of cultural values leads to the understanding of cultural capital *as the power to inspire or to be inspired*, the ability to experience the sublime in a good, to see its beauty or its sacred character, to recognize its place in the history of the arts. Cultural capital, then, is the capacity to realize a meaningful life over and beyond its economic and social dimensions. It is one thing to have good social relationships, yet another to be awed when walking through a museum, attending a religious ceremony, or walking across a ridge in the mountains. In this sense, cultural capital is more than the symbolic knowledge that Bourdieu takes it to be, yet less than Throsby's definition of it as inclusive of all tangible and intangible cultural goods, generating both cultural and economic values. In my definition cultural capital is the "simple" ability to deal with cultural values, regardless of the possible economic returns.

By claiming a separate category for cultural values and capital, not only do I argue that they are separate and distinct from economic values, but that they also require special skills and operate in a distinct sphere—as the culturalists are ready to demonstrate. Although certain disadvantages inhere in the use of the metaphor of "capital" to discuss these qualities, it does retain the advantage of reminding us of the need to invest in social and cultural capabilities. Like economic capital, they require attention and a great deal of work. People usually "build up" cultural capital by participating in cultural activities; discipline, study, and all sorts of sacrifice in order to achieve insight, wisdom, enlightenment, piety, or the ability to experience the sublime may be necessary. Further, people not only acquire cultural capital, they may also lose it; for instance, they may leave their country,

260   *Arjo Klamer*

shift religion, or neglect some cultural practice. Unlike economic capital, however, cultural capital (as well as social capital) does not depreciate in usage; rather it tends to increase in value. When I visit a museum, I use my cultural capital in order to make sense of what I am seeing and experiencing, and by doing so I add to my cultural capital, creating the possibility of an even more intense experience at some later time.[16]

Goods in general and cultural goods in particular

In the standard economic treatment, goods become commodities and as a consequence their economic value stands out. Such a perspective begins already with Karl Marx who starts *Capital* as follows: "The wealth of societies in which the capitalist mode of production prevails appears as an 'immense collection of commodities'; the individual commodity appears as its elementary form" (Marx, 1867, 1977, p. 126; the quotation marks are his). He continues with a few remarks on the use value of a commodity ("use values are only realized in consumption") and then focuses on the exchange value by means of which a commodity becomes a quantity. The latter value subsequently gets his undivided attention as he tries to figure out its relationship with the value of embodied labor power.[17] Not long after Marx, standard economic analysis would dispense with the labor theory of value, but would keep the focus on goods as commodities, that is, goods to be exchanged. Goods are to be produced for exchange, exchanged, and consumed. Their value equals their price in exchange. When actual exchange is impossible, as in the case of public goods (think of national defence), a price is lacking and economists are compelled to derive a price by means of contingent valuation studies and the like. In any case, the analysis begins and ends with the moment of exchange as the critical moment of valuation.[18]

In defiance of the discipline of economics, I propose to think of goods more broadly as they function in—and outside—a market situation: in our fantasies, conversations, personal and social lives, and so on. Goods represent values; they are good for something. Goods can be, and often are, intangible. Knowledge is a good and so is friendship, a view, a landscape. These are goods because they are all good for something, and we have to do something in order to "possess" them. Goods function mostly outside a market situation. For instance, I live in and with my house, value it, positively and negatively, on a great variety of grounds without giving much thought to its market value (even if the mortgage interest is taken out of the bank account each month). While sitting in the yard and admiring the incredible beech outside the window, I am weighing values that have nothing to do with the monetary value of the house. Thinking of the latter might actually devalue the experience.

Goods have a great variety of meanings. They are their meanings. As Douglas and Isherwood observe: "In the protracted dialogue about value that is embedded in consumption, goods in their assemblage present a set of meanings, more or less coherent, more or less intentional. They are read by those who know the code and scan them for information" (Douglas and Iserwood, 1979, p. 5). Consumption is

The lives of cultural goods   261

about those meanings. "[C]onsumption is a system of meaning, like language, or like the kinship system in primitive societies" (Baudrillard, 1988, p. 46). The watch that I just bought at the local market from a traveling salesman has meanings that are distinct from those I attribute to my lover's watch. They give the time just the same, may even look alike, but they are totally different goods anyway. One I associate with my lover and the other is not much more than an instrument of measurement. Having either is different, and losing either is even more different.

Baudrillard would say that goods communicate: "Consumption is a system which assures the regulation of signs and the integration of the group: it is simultaneously a morality (a system of ideological values) and a system of communication, a structure of exchange" (Baudrillard, (1970) 1988, p. 46). Goods will be topics of conversation or at least play a role in conversations ("That is the screwdriver that I once used to scare away that intruder"). In these conversations people negotiate about their meanings and their values. Consequently goods convey, represent, or serve to realize economic, social, and cultural values. A car is an asset and can be sold to realize its economic value. It can be used to travel to a grandmother, or for an intimate conversation, and is then an instrument to realize social values (like love, responsibility, care, and friendship). And to some a car, like the Mini or a Ferrari, may have special meanings over and beyond its social and economic values. In such a case we might speak of the car as a cultural good.

Cultural goods represent, or serve to realize, cultural values. Not only do they comprise things like temples, bridges, paintings, but also intangible goods such as rituals, shared histories, music, traditions. They share the ability potentially to inspire awe, wonderment, or to convey a sense of the sublime. Their value is that they mean something over and beyond whatever economic and social values they have, like cows in the experience of Hindus, an aboriginal painting in an aboriginal context, or an icon for a Rumanian Roman-Catholic. "Cultural" connotes the spiritual, sacred, symbolic, aesthetic, and artistic, the inclination to bring in the social dimension and consider the value of cultural goods in terms of what they mean for a certain group of people. Cultural goods often appear to have social functions. The Greeks view the Elgin Marbles to be Greek and want them back from the Brits to bolster Greek culture. The French are adamant on an exception for cultural goods in the GATT, arguing that countries should be able to protect their cultural heritage. In such arguments, social values are emphasized; cultural values are implicit.

Some cultural goods are viewed as such the world over, like a Rembrandt, a Venetian palazzo, or an ancient Buddha statue. A number of them show up on the world heritage list of UNESCO. Most cultural goods operate as such within a culture, defining, bolstering, and representing that culture; examples are statues commemorating local or national heroes, national buildings, churches, icons, and so on. The evaluation of these goods is a social matter. Interestingly, it is often the appreciation by the outsider that initiates or escalates "local" evaluations. The Dutch, for instance, valued "their" Rembrandt certainly, but became much more

262 *Arjo Klamer*

seriously interested in his works as a national icon only after Americans and Russians had bought many of his paintings during the nineteenth century. The fact that cultural goods can claim such appreciations is in part due to cultural goods' tendency to have "lives" quite different from those of other goods. They do not figure easily in the market. Without doubt, plays, paintings, and music are now produced for the market, but that is because of their entertainment values. A Rembrandt is not for sale. A monument is the business of the government, and a great deal of new art production, especially the art for art's sake, defies the market sphere. Another reason for this exceptional status of cultural goods is that their ownership is often difficult to pin down. Even if a group of people were to claim the ownership of a temple, that temple most likely derives its cultural meanings by virtue of a religion shared with others. Similarly, the Japanese businessman Sato could buy a Van Gogh for a record price to discover that he did not fully own the painting. Van Gogh is common property valued and maintained by many around the world. One need only look back to the Eberstadt case narrated above to note that the Foundation of the Dutch museum, Boymans, found it has no moral claim on a drawing even though it has legal ownership. The shared memory of the Holocaust, another cultural good, proved to be more valuable than the value of keeping the drawing as part of the Dutch collection.

The realization of values

When goods become candidates for exchange, they become commodities (Appadurai, 1986). It is a phase in their life, possibly an important one, but a phase nonetheless. It is then their economic value is being realized. You might not hear this from economists, but goods have a life beyond that phase. Their being a commodity is just one moment in their biography (Appadurai, 1986; Kopytoff, 1986). Things have a life and pass various stages in which their values are being realized, sustained, affirmed, questioned, and so on in characteristic ways. During their gestation, goods are the subject of conversations dealing with their production. A painting comes about in conversations about techniques, art in general, and the world of artists. In those conversations the producer and others involved assess the painting's qualities and appraise the values that are being applied. ("I want to paint again as an antidote to all the technique." "But why in this way? This is really cliché." "No it is not; I just take off on the work I have done earlier," etc.), When the good enters the phase of exchange, in a store or wherever, it becomes the subject of completely different conversations, like those of the marketeers, sales people, and consumers of course. Now its price as well as its use will be a major subject. ("It is a pretty large painting and, given the track record of the artist, I'll price it at 10,000 euro." "But don't you run the risk of missing the buyer who looks for interesting art above the couch?" "Yeah, but why would my work be priced less than that of my friend? Maybe I should take it to another gallery that can appreciate it better." "Listen, it has nothing to do with that. We just assess where the market is. We can

The lives of cultural goods   263

do no better than this. In the end the buyer determines whether the price is right."[19])

The consuming of the good constitutes yet another stage in its "life." In the conventional economic account, consumption is it; as soon as the good ends up in the hands of the consumer the story ends, and so does the analysis. For quite a few goods, consuming is a timely process that involves various people and comprises all kinds of experiences, valuations, evaluations, and so on. When people pay a visit to a museum, they are said to consume the services of the museum, that is, the exhibitions. Yet, what actually happens? They may visit the museum with their family, so the outing may actually have import in that discourse. They may have used the visit to have a nice lunch in the museum or to enjoy being in the building itself. They may have gone to the museum in the hope of meeting certain people. They may experience something in the museum that has a lasting impact. They may have conversations about their experiences afterwards so that the museum visit may have a longer life than the mere visit. People may have learned something; and they may have to account for what they did. So, it is not immediately obvious what the consumption is all about, or, indeed, what precisely is being consumed. It is obvious, however, that the valuation of the museum visit, that is, its consumption, is an entirely different matter, and the subject of conversations far different from those concerning its economic valuation.

Accordingly, the notion of "the life of things" alerts us to the valuations and valorizations that occur before or beyond the commodity phase. Indians realize the cultural value of a cow when they refuse to remove it from the road or slaughter it when they are in need of food. The cow has significant value yet no market has a role in determining that value. Daily religious practices bring out the cultural value of a temple or church; critical discursive practices as well as institutions like museums account for the cultural value of Van Gogh. And the value of a flag may prove itself in the heat of the battle or at a funeral. Thus, we would not do justice to the life of any good, and its values, if we were to focus solely on its commodity phase.

The mode of financing matters: different valuations are possible

Valuations and evaluations take place in different settings, and in distinct spheres, and the exceptional character of cultural goods may be related to the nature of the conversation in which its cultural values come about. Their valuation, therefore, may call for conversations that are incongruent with those that constitute the market. Subject it to the discipline of the market, and its values may be affected, possibly altered for the duration of its life. Price something like friendship, love, courage, truth, or, who knows, art, and you alter the value the good has. Realize its value by means of a market exchange, and it will be a different good from the case in which its value has been realized in the form of a gift or as part of a collective program.

In this line of argument, I deviate once again from the standard economic approach in which the value of a good is ideally realized in a market; an alternative

264   Arjo Klamer

approach is realization by means of a grant from the government or a foundation. Whatever the method, the economic value of the good is presumed to remain the same. Yet, when we take into account the full range of values, this presumption becomes dubious. As Anderson argues: "To realize a good as a particular *kind* of good we place it in a particular matrix of social relations ... [G]oods differ in kind if people properly enter into different sorts of social relations governed by distinct norms in relation to these goods." The context in which a good is placed to realize its value(s) may matter.

Thus, when we submit a cultural good for sale in the market in order to realize its economic value, we subject it to conversations that are characteristic of markets. The good must be priced and therefore will be compared with other goods; its economic value may be stressed; anonymous buyers may enter the bidding. Measuring, pricing, discussing the good, like any other commodity, may well affect the subsequent evaluation of the good. If the price was exceptionally high, the valuation may increase accordingly. We call this the *crowding in effect*.[20] Alternatively, the good may be branded "commercial" because of the sale, and lose some or all of its cultural value in the eyes of those who care. This is the *crowding out effect*. In either case, the fact that the economic value got realized has an effect on the value of the good, a case of (de-)*valorization* in which certain values are enhanced, or diminished.

Valorization can also concern the social values associated with the market, such as "freedom of choice," "consumer sovereignty," "efficiency," "commercial," "greed," and "cold." Once a good becomes a commodity, that is once it "enters" the market, it also contributes to the affirmation of those values that are held in common by all who participate in the market. The effect on a cultural good, like a work of art, is such that not only is its cultural valuation influenced, but the very presence of the good in the market fortifies the "common." And, while the effects of an individual good may be small, as more artists participate in the market as a means of establishing both an economic and cultural value for their goods, the very culture of the world in which they operate—and the conversations they participate in—may change.

Because of what may become of a good in its avatar as a commodity, some goods are kept away from that phase. This is precisely the phenomenon Michael Walzer speaks of when he refers to "blocked exchange" (1983, pp. 100–103). One way of effecting this blockage is to realize the values of cultural goods by means of government subsidies, thus preventing them from becoming a subject of conversations in markets. Rather, they become an item in bureaucratic and political discussions. As a consequence, they are connected with other values like political expediency, national interest, justice and fairness, and bureaucratic discipline. Cultural entrepreneurs who seek the support of the government must adjust their rhetoric and play to whatever values dominate in the political realm. Thus, when politicians are concerned about national identity, accessibility, sustainability, or the integration of minorities, cultural entrepreneurs often profess to cater to such interests in order to garner subsidies. Valorization in such a case addresses the values of the collective, public accessibility, national identity,

The lives of cultural goods 265

sustainability, and integration over and beyond the cultural values a director may have had in mind. Accordingly, entering a good into a stage involving the government implies supporting the common that constitutes the governmental sphere.

Ideally, a good financed in this way attains the status of a public or collective good and is appreciated accordingly: the subsidized temple becoming common property free from the imposition of the market. Neither consumers nor clients but government officials and their consultants determine its value. In practice, certain valuations that governmental financing imposes are suspiciously similar to those of the market. The government strives to be objective in adjudicating between competing claims and is often compelled to support in accordance with well specified rules. After all, civil servants want standards. Consequently, museum directors who are dependent on government money will count the number of visitors and point at the value of additional tourist spending and the number of jobs the museum creates. These measurements, all economic in kind, will help them to stake their claims in the next round of subsidies.

Goods may also function primarily in the social sphere (Klamer, 1996; Klamer and Zuidhof, 1999). This of course applies to goods like friendship, but it is also important to remember that a great deal of artistic value arises from personal and informal interactions that take place without contracts, explicit measurements, rules, and accounts. Many artists paint, draw, compose, or perform without any financial compensation. Parents, partners, spouses, or friends often support them. The value of what they do they gain in social settings, by sharing their art with others. Their art is then a form of a gift. It will make for a different conversation from the ones people conduct in the spheres of the government and the market, with appeals to different values. In the social sphere people may talk about "loyalty," "responsibility," "solidarity," "care," but also about "dependency," "charity," "sacrifice."

By placing the good in a social setting, we ask for negotiations in social terms and prevent associations with market, political, and bureaucratic values. By barring a good like friendship, or a religious ceremony, from the commodity phase, we lock out the values that are associated with that phase and thus create a different life of that good. Such goods are exceptional in that they are not to be used as a commodity and in their incommensurability with commodities: there is no way to establish a quantitative equivalent like a price (cf. Anderson, 1993; Radin).

So what?

The cultural economic perspective breaks the hold that the economic has on public discussions concerning the role of cultural goods. It embraces the culturalist view with its emphasis on the various values that constitute such goods. By no means does this imply that analysis of economic values is beside the point. Especially when the climate is biased towards economic argumentation, the determination of economic value will be persuasive. Apart from rhetorical aspects, economic studies are helpful, as they sort out and define the costs and benefits to the parties involved.

266 *Arjo Klamer*

Yet as helpful as such a framework may be, it is limiting when we want to make sense of the functioning of cultural goods.

The cultural economic viewpoint compels us to distinguish social and cultural values from economic values. It furthermore compels us to consider the various spheres in which the values of cultural goods emerge. Cultural goods are exceptional because they often resist the commodity phase and for good reason. When cultural values are involved, actors require an arena in which the relevant values can surface without suffering from the strictures of the market or governmental control. We need only point to religious institutions as examples. Only rarely is their value established through government programs or market exchange. Such cultural institutions rely mainly on the informally constituted social value and its main instrument, the gift, or donation. Reciprocity in such instances is ill defined, not stipulated in a contract, and requiring an enduring relationship.

The cultural economic perspective has several consequences for cultural policy. As cultural goods come about and attain their value in conversations among people who know and care, their sustenance requires the support of such groups of people. The problem with the Buddha statues in Afghanistan was that they were an affront for the locals, yet were cherished by groups of people far removed from the scene. The latter failed, for all kinds of good reasons, to engage the local people and persuade them of the cultural, and possibly economic, significance of the statues. This is a reason why cultural policy needs to be focused, at least partially, on education and ongoing discussions in the media. Controversies like the van Toorop case can provide great impetus to the (re)valuation of a cultural good.

Ultimately, many cultural goods are financed markets and governments. Performance companies sell tickets and apply for government grants (especially in continental Europe); auction houses and galleries sell visual art. However, they need to thrive in other value spheres as well in order to establish and sustain their cultural values. Therefore, a cultural policy that is geared to the market on one hand, or the government on the other, will always miss the point.

Notes

1 The cases 2, 3, 4, and 5 have been provided by Dr. Ellen Bal. I am very grateful for her material and for various other suggestions she has made for this article.
2 The quotation marks indicate that I use these words with particular meanings that I will have to clarify in the following.
3 It is important to note that by "conversation" I do not mean purposeless chatter or merely an exchange of words. Rather, I intend my use of it to be more akin to the notion of "discursive practices," now so common among theorists. Yet, following John Dewey and, more recently, Richard Rorty, I want to cling to the term "conversation," in part because of its etymology. See the OED.
4 See David Throsby (2000); another possible label might be humanist. Hannerz (1980) considers culturalists as those who view culture in the anthropological sense as the explanatory factor. I use the term to include those who stress the aesthetic, artistic, and emotional dimensions of goods.

The lives of cultural goods   267

5 To be more precise, policymakers actually constitute a third type of player. It suffices to see them as specific combinations of the economist or culturalist characters. Although their role is significant, for analytical purposes we confine our account to discussing only the former two.

6 C.P. Snow observes a similar cultural divide between the sciences and the humanities in his well-known little book *The Two Cultures* (1959).

7 I am a member of the board of the Foundation. This account is mostly based on public information since as a board member I am held to a code of honor that prevents me from revealing internal discussions. In the press I have been noted as an early advocate for the return of the drawing on moral grounds.

8 In practice museums do sell, especially American museums, but always limited quantities of pieces that have lost their value for the collection. A major obstacle for selling a piece is when it has been the gift to the museum.

9 Being a participant in the case, I am self-conscious of the simplifications and distortions in this brief account. Some of the distortions are inevitable as I am not at liberty to disclose all details—deliberations within the board are to be kept secret, for example. And then there is so much more in play, such as individual characters, local context, political factors, miscommunications, emotions (like when people felt hurt, insulted, ignored, bullied).

10 See for example Lane (*) Anderson (1993).

11 Cf. van Staveren (2000).

12 Cf. Waltzer (1983), Chapter 2.

13 see James S. Coleman (1988) who introduces the concept: "Unlike other forms of capital, social capital inheres in the structure of relations between actors and among actors" (p. S98).

14 Other important sources are Coleman (1988) and Portes (1998).

15 When people argue that their goal in life is making money, the researcher may notice that they actually spend a great deal of their time negotiating and maintaining relationships. Money seems a topos to indicate desire and ambition.

16 Such a brief exposition of the role of values and different notions of capital surely provokes more questions than it answers. Let me anticipate a few of them surrounding the three categories I describe. For instance, concerns with the ephemeral character of notions like "values" and "social and cultural capital" arise. Deficient measurements stand in the way of making the roles of these concepts more explicit. Perhaps economic values and capital so dominate contemporary public discourse, at least in the western world, because they are so much easier to quantify. During the previous century or so, economists have worked hard on statistical measures of economic values, such as Gross National Product, profit, income, and wealth. The accounting for economic value has become quite sophisticated, although it has not been without its problems. It has generated an entire industry of statistical offices and accounting firms. Measurements of social capital are in the process of being developed, but they are still in the pioneering stage. Measurements of cultural capital, if possible at all, are far off. UNESCO has been gathering a range of cultural indicators but its compilation of data on all kinds of cultural activities does not yet add up to a meaningful measurement of cultural capital (UNESCO, 2000). Additional subjective measures are called for that can account for the experiences and perceptions of various stakeholders such as local people, visitors, experts, politicians. Deficient and lacking measurements make it difficult to take these values into account when developing policy or considering action. It does not make them less relevant.

17 With his notion of commodity fetishism he criticizes the focus on the commodity phase; in no way does he call attention that the values of a good can be realized outside the situation of exchange.

18 "Economic goods are goods that are properly valued as commodities and properly produced and exchanged in accordance with market norms. [...] I call the mode of

268 *Arjo Klamer*

valuation appropriate to pure commodities 'use.' Use is a lower, impersonal, and exclusive mode of valuation" (Anderson, 1993, pp. 143–144).

19 See Velthuis, forthcoming. Some goods, however, will never enter this phase, for they are "blocked from exchange" (cf. Walzer, 1983, p. 100). A good like friendship is one example, freedom of speech another, divine grace, and, in the western world, marriage and political office. The valuations of such goods take place in conversations that are distinct from others. ("You are not going to risk imprisonment/your life to defend your freedom of speech! I don't want to lose you." "Yes, I will." "So that freedom is worth more to you than our relationship?" etc.)

20 Cf. Frey (1997b).

References

Allison, Gerald, Susan Ball, Paul Cheshire, Alan Evans, and Mike Stabler. 1996. "The Value of Conservation? A Literature Review of the Economic and Social Value of the Cultural Built Heritage." English Heritage; The Department of National Heritage; The Royal Institute of Chartered Surveyors.

Anderson, Elizabeth. 1993. *Value in Ethics and Economics*. Cambridge: Harvard University Press.

Appadurai, Arjun. 1986. *The Social Life of Things: Commodities in Cultural Perspective*. Cambridge: Cambridge University Press.

Becker, Gary S. and George J. Stigler. 1977. "De Gustibus non est Disputandum." *American Economic Review*, 67(March): 76–90.

Benhamou, Francoise. 1996. "Is Increased Public Spending for the Preservation of Historic Monuments Inevitable? The French Case." *Journal of Cultural Economics*, 20(2): 115–131.

Benhamou, Francoise. 1997. "Conserving Historic Monuments in France: A Critique of Official Policies." Pp. 196–210 in *Economic Perspectives on Cultural Heritage*, edited by M. Hutter and I. E. Rizzo. London: Macmillan.

Bianca, Stefano. 1997. "Direct Government Involvement in Architectural Heritage Management." Pp. 13–31 in *Preserving the Built Heritage: Tools for Implementation*, edited by J. M. Schuster, J. D. Moncheaux, and C. A. E. Riley. Hanover: University Press of New England.

Bille Hansen, Trine, Henrik Christofferson, and Stephen Wanhill. 1998. "The Economic Evaluation of Cultural and Heritage Projects: Conflicting Methodologies." *Tourism, Culture, and Communication*, 1(1): 27–48.

Bourdieu, Pierre. 1984. *Distinction. A Social Critique of the Judgment of Taste*. Trans. Richard Nice. London: Routledge.

Bourdieu, Pierre. 1986. "The Forms of Capital" In J.G. Richardson (ed.) Handbook of Theory and Research for the Sociology of Education: 241–258. New York: Greenwood.

Bourdieu, Pierre. 1993. "The Market of Symbolic Goods." In The Field of Cultural Production. New York. Columbia University Press.

Bracewell-Milnes, Barry. 1982. *Land and Heritage: The Public Interest in Personal Ownership*. London: Economic Institute of Economic Affairs.

Carrier, James. 1995. *Gifts and Commodities. Exchange and Western Capitalism since 1700*. London and New York: Routledge.

Clifford, James. 1985. "Histories of the Tribal and the Modern." *Art in America*, 73(4): 164–177.

The lives of cultural goods   269

Clifford, James. 1988. *The Predicament of Culture: Twentieth-Century Ethnography, Literature, and Art*, Cambridge, MA: Harward University Press.

Coase, R. H. 1988. *The Firm, the Market, and the Law*. Chicago: University of Chicago Press.

Coleman, James. 1998. "Social Capital in the Creation of Human Capital." The American Journal of Sociology, 94 (Supplement): s95–s120.

Commission on Preservation and Access. 1993. *Preserving the Intellectual Heritage: A Report of the Bellagio Conference, June 7–10, 1993, Held at the Rockefeller Foundation Study and Conference Center in Bellagio, Italy*. Washington, DC (1400 16th St., NW, Suite 740, Washington 20036–2217): Commission on Preservation and Access.

Cordes, Joseph J. and Robert S. Goldfarb. 1996. "The Value of Public Art as Public Culture." Pp. 77–95 in *The Value of Culture: On the Relationship between Economics and Arts*, edited by A. Klamer. Amsterdam: Amsterdam University Press.

Costonis, John J. 1997. "The Redefinition of Property Rights as a Tool for Historic Preservation." Pp. 81–99 in *Preserving the Built Heritage: Tools for Implementation*, edited by J. M. Schuster, J. D. Moncheaux, and C. A. E. Riley. Hanover: University Press of New England.

Cowen, Tyler. 1998. *In Praise of Commercial Culture*. Cambridge: Harvard University Press.

Creigh-Tyte, Stephen. 1997. "The Development of British Policy on Built Heritage." Pp. 133–154 in *Economic Perspectives on Cultural Heritage*, edited by M. Hutter and I. E. Rizzo. London: Macmillan.

Diamond, Peter A. and Jerry A. Hausman. 1992. "Contingent Valuation of Nonuse Values." Pp. 3–38 in *Contingent Valuation: A Critical Assessment*, edited by J. A. Hausman. Amsterdam: Elsevier.

Droogenbroeck, Nathalie van. 1994. "The Economic Dimension of the Cultural Built Heritage." MSc. Thesis, Faculté des Sciences Economiques, Université Catholique de Louvain, Louvain.

Eagleton, Terry. 2000. *The Idea of Culture*. Oxford: Basil Blackwell.

Forte, Fransesco. 1997. "Towards a European Market for Arts and Culture Goods: Some Proposals." Pp. 211–224 in *Economic Perspectives on Cultural Heritage*, edited by M. Hutter and I. E. Rizzo. London: Macmillan.

Frey, Bruno S. 1997a. "The Evaluation of Cultural Heritage: Some Critical Issues." Pp. 31–49 in *Economic Perspectives on Cultural Heritage*, edited by M. Hutter and I. E. Rizzo. London: Macmillan.

Frey, Bruno S. 1997b. *Not Just for the Money: An Economic Theory of Personal Motivation*. Brookfield, Vt.: Edward Elgar Publishers.

Frey, Bruno S. 2000. *Arts and Economics: Analysis and Cultural Policy*. New York: Springer.

Frey, Bruno S. and Werner W. Pommerehne. 1989. *Muses and Markets: Explorations in the economics of the arts*. Cambridge, Mass., USA: B. Blackwell.

Getty Art History Information Program. 1996. *Research Agenda for Networked Cultural Heritage*. Santa Monica, Calif.: Getty Art History Information Program.

Grampp, William. 1989. *Pricing the Priceless: Art, Artists and Economics*. New York: Basic Books.

Granovetter, Mark. 1985. "Economic Action and Social Structure, the Problem of Embeddedness." *American Journal of Sociology*, 91: 481–510.

Greenfield, Jeanette. 1989. *The Return of Cultural Treasures*. Cambridge [England] and New York: Cambridge University Press.

270 *Arjo Klamer*

Hampshire, Stuart. 1983. *Morality and Conflict.* Cambridge: Harvard University Press.

Hannerz, Ulf. 1980. *Exploring the City: Inquiries Towards an Urban Anthropology,* New York: Columbia University.

Harrison, Lawrence E. and Samuel P. Huntington (eds). 2000. *Culture Matters: How Values Shape Human Progress.* New York: Basic Books.

Hausman, Jerry A. 1993. *Contingent Valuation: A Critical Assessment.* Amsterdam and New York: North-Holland.

Heilbrun, John and William Gray. 2000. *The Economics of the Arts.* Cambridge: Cambridge University Press.

Hunter, Michael. 1996. *Preserving the Past: The Rise of Heritage in Modern Britain.* Stroud: Alan Sutton.

Hutter, Michael. 1996. "The Value of Play." Pp. 122–137 in *The Value of Culture: On the Relationship between Economics and Art,* edited by A. Klamer. Amsterdam: Amsterdam University Press.

Hutter, Michael and Ilde Rizzo (eds), 1997. *Economic Perspectives on Cultural Heritage.* New York: Macmillan Press.

Klamer, Arjo. 1996. *The Value of Culture: On the Relationship between Economics and Arts.* Amsterdam: Amsterdam University Press.

Klamer, Arjo. 1997. "Towards the Native Point of View." In Don Lavoie (ed.), *Hermeneutics and Economics.* London: Routledge.

Klamer, Arjo. 1997. "The Value of Cultural Heritage." Pp. 74–87 in *Economic Perspectives on Cultural Heritage,* edited by M. Hutter and I. E. Rizzo. London: Macmillan.

Klamer, Arjo and D. N. McCloskey. 1992. "Accounting as the Master Metaphor of Economics." *The European Accounting Review,* 1–1, May: 145–160.

Klamer, Arjo and David Throsby. 2000. "Paying for the Past: The Economics of Cultural Heritage." In *World Culture Report, 2000.* Paris: UNESCO Publishing, pp. 130–145.

Klamer, Arjo and P.W. Zuidhof. 1999. "The Values of Cultural Heritage: Merging Economic and Cultural Appraisal." *Economics and Heritage Conversation,* Los Angeles: Getty Conservation Institute.

Kopytoff, Igor. 1986. "The Cultural Biography of Things: Commodization as Process." In Arjun Appadurai, *The Social Life of Things: Commodities in Cultural Perspective.* Cambridge: Cambridge University Press, 64–94.

MacCannell, Dean. 1976. *The Tourist: A New Theory of the Leisure Class.* New York: Schocken Books.

Mauss, Marcel. 1990. *The Gift: The Form and Reason for Exchange in Archaic Societies.* London and New York: Routledge.

McCloskey, Deirdre N. 1996. *The Vices of Economists, the Virtues of the Bourgeoisie.* Amsterdam: Amsterdam University Press.

McCloskey, Deirdre N. 2006. *The Bourgeois Virtues: Ethics for an Age of Commerce.* Chicago: University of Chicago Press.

McCloskey, Deirdre N. and Arjo Klamer. 1995. "One Quarter of GDP is Persuasion." *American Economic Review,* May 2: 191–195.

McCracken, Grant. 1988. *Culture and Consumption. New Approaches to the Symbolic Character of Consumer Goods and Activities.* Bloomington and Indianapolis: Indiana University Press.

Meyer, Birgit. 1999. "Commodities and the Power of Prayer: Pentecostalist Attitudes Towards Consumption in Contemporary Ghana." In Birgit Meyer and Peter Geschiere (eds), *Globalization and Identity: Dialectics of Flow and Closure.* Oxford and London: Blackwell Publishers, 151–175.

The lives of cultural goods 271

Miller, Daniel. 1987. *Material Culture and Mass Consumption*. Oxford: Backwell.

Miller, Daniel. 1994. "Artefacts and the Meaning of Things." In Tim Ingold (ed.), *Companion Encyclopedia of Anthropology: Humanity, Culture and Social Life*. London: Routledge, 396–419.

Mohr, E. and J. Schmnidt. 1997. "Aspects of Economic Valuation of Cultural Heritage." *Saving Our Architectural Heritage*: 333–348.

Mossetto, Gianfranco. 1994. "The Economic Dilemma of Heritage Preservation." Pp. 81–96 in *Cultural Economics and Cultural Policies. With Contributions by Giorgio Brosio et al*, edited by A. Peacock and I. E. Rizzo. Dordrecht and Boston: Kluwer Academic.

Myerscough, John. 1988. *The Economic Importance of the Arts in Britain*. London: Policy Studies Institute.

Palmer, Norman. 1995. "Recovering Stolen Art," pp. 1–37 In *Antiquities Trade or Betrayed: Legal, Ethical and Conservation Issues*. edited by Kathryn Walker Tubb. London: Archetype.

Peacock, Alan. 1994. *A Future for the Past: The Political Economy of Heritage*. Edinburgh: David Hume Institute.

Peacock, Alan. 1997. "Towards a Workable Heritage Policy." Pp. 225–235 in *Economic Perspectives on Cultural Heritage*, edited by M. Hutter and I. E. Rizzo. London: Macmillan.

Peacock, Alan T. 1978. "Preserving the Past: An International Economic Dilemma." *Journal of Cultural Economics*, 2(2): 1–11.

Peacock, Alan., ed. 1998. Does the Past have a Future: The Political Economy of Heritage. London: Institute of Economic Affairs.

Pignataro, Giacomo and Ilde Rizzo. 1997. "The Political Economy of Rehabilitation: The Case of the Benedettini Monastery." Pp. 91–106 in *Economic Perspectives on Cultural Heritage*, edited by M. Hutter and I. E. Rizzo. London: Macmillan.

Polanyi, Karl and Harry W. Pearson. 1977. *The Livelihood of Man*. New York: Academic Press.

Portes, Alejandro. 1998. "Social Capital: Its Origins and Applications in Modern Sociology." *Annual Review of Sociology*, 24, 1–24.

Prentice, Richard. 1993. *Tourism and Heritage Attractions*. London and New York: Routledge.

Price, Nicholas Stanley, Mansfield Kirby Talley, and Alessandra Melucco Vaccaro. 1996. *Historical and Philosophical Issues in the Conservation of Cultural Heritage*. Los Angeles: Getty Conservation Institute.

Puffelen, Frank van. 1987. *The Economic Impact of the Arts in Amsterdam*. Amsterdam: Stichting voor Economisch Onderzoek.

Puffelen, Frank van. 1992. *De Betekenis van Impact Studies*. Amsterdam: Stichting voor Economisch Onderzoek.

Putnam, Robert, Robert Leonardi, and Rafaella Y. Nanetti. 1994. *Making Democracy Work*. Princeton: Princeton University Press.

Reddy, William M. 1984. *The Rise of Market Culture: The Textile Trade and French Society, 1750–1900*. Cambridge. Cambridge University Press.

Robb, John. 1998. "Tourism and Legends." *Annals of Tourism Research*, 25(3): 579–596.

Schuster, J., Mark Davidson, John De Monchaux, Charles A. Riley, and Salzburg Seminar. 1997. *Preserving the Built Heritage: Tools for Implementation*. Hanover, NH [Salzburg]: University Press of New England; Salzburg Seminar.

Sen, Amartya. 1993. "Capability and Well-Being." In Martha Nussbaum and Amartya Sen (eds), *The Quality of Life*. Oxford: Oxford University Press. pp. 30–53.

272   *Arjo Klamer*

Snow, C. P. 1959. *The Two Cultures and the Scientific Revolution*. New York: Cambridge University Press.

Staveren, Irene van. 2001. *The Values of Economics*. London: Routledge.

Steiner, Christopher B. 1994. *African Art in Transit*. Cambridge: Cambridge University Press.

Throsby, David. 1994. "The Production and Consumption of the Arts: A View of Cultural Economics." *Journal of Economic Literature*, 32: 1–29.

Throsby, David. 1995. "Culture, Economics and Sustainability." *Journal of Cultural Economics*, 19(3): 199–206.

Throsby, David. 1997a. "Making Preservation Happen: The Pros and Cons of Regulation." Pp. 32–48 in *Preserving the Built Heritage: Tools for Implementation*, edited by J. M. Schuster, J. D. Moncheaux, and C. A. E. Riley. Hanover: University Press of New England.

Throsby, David. 1997b. "Seven Questions in the Economics of Cultural Heritage." Pp. 13–30 in *Economic Perspectives on Cultural Heritage*, edited by M. Hutter and I. E. Rizzo. London: Macmillan.

Throsby, David. 1998. "Cultural Capital." Lecture presented at *The Biannual Conference of International Association for Cultural Economics*. Barcelona.

Throsby, David. 2000. *Economics and Culture*. Cambridge: University of Cambridge Press.

Tunbridge, J. E. and G. J. Ashworth. 1996. *Dissonant Heritage: The Management of the Past as a Resource in Conflict*. Chichester and New York: J. Wiley.

UNESCO. 2000. *World Culture Report 2000*. Paris: UNESCO.

Urry, John. 1990. *The Tourist Gaze: Leisure and Travel in Contemporary Societies*. London and Newbury Park: Sage Publications.

Vaughan, D. R. 1984. "The Cultural Heritage: An Approach to Analyzing Income and Employment Effects." *Journal of Cultural Economics*, 8(2): 1–36.

Velthuis, Olav. 2005. *Talking Prices: Symbolic Meanings of Prices on the Market for Contemporary Art*. Princeton, NJ: Princeton University Press.

Waltzer, Michael. 1983. *Spheres of Justice: A Defense of Pluralism and Equality*. Oxford: Basil Blackwell.

World Commission on Culture and Development. 1996. *Our Creative Diversity: Report of the World Commission on Culture and Development* (2nd rev. edn). Paris: UNESCO Pub.

Zelizer, Viviana. 1985. *Pricing the Priceless Child: The Changing Social Value of Children*. New York: Basic Books.

Zelizer, Viviana A. 1997. "How Do We Know Whether a Monetary Transaction Is a Gift, an Entitlement, or Compensation?" In Avner Ben-Ner and Louis Putterman (eds), *Economics, Values and Organization*. Cambridge: Cambridge University Press, pp. 329–336.

Part IV

Moral economies and the romance of money

13 The rhetoric of prostitution

Jennifer Doyle

> He pressed her hand gently and she tried to withdraw it. At first he held it fast, and she no longer protested. Then he slipped the greenbacks he had into her palm, and when she began to protest, he whispered: "I'll loan it to you—that's all right. I'll loan it to you."
>
> He made her take it. She felt bound to him by a strange tie of affection now …. Carrie left him, feeling as though a great arm had slipped out before her to draw off trouble. The money she had accepted was two soft, green, handsome ten-dollar bills. Theodore Dreiser, *Sister Carrie*.
>
> (Dreiser, 1991)

Introduction

Figures of prostitution, sexual abjection, and illicit forms of economic exchange dominate the paintings, novels, and poems associated with the advent of realism and modernism. In the attempt to adequately capture the upheavals of the Haussmanization of Paris, the industrialization of England, or the development of a mass culture in the US, writers as diverse as Elizabeth Gaskell, Theodore Dreiser and Émile Zola were drawn to the fallen woman and, as John Berger puts it, "the realism of the prostitute" (Berger, 1977). Where we do not find prostitutes, we find overlapping figures for sexual abjection and economic perversion in, for example, the recurrence of the actress (another kind of "painted woman"), the celebrity (a living commodity), or the sodomite (who engages in a prohibited form of reproduction). We have a myriad of brothel scenes in French art (by Manet, Degas and Toulouse Lautrec, for instance), Zola's infamous (and influential) *Nana*, the web of debt and scandal in William Dean Howells's *The Rise of Silas Lapham*, and the spectacularly magnetic title character of Dreiser's *Sister Carrie*. The latter's rise to theatrical celebrity is explicitly figured as a descent in character, and is initiated by her acceptance of money from a suitor. As she fingers the dollar bills, feeling how soft they've become from having passed through so many hands, Carrie trembles not with fear, but with an almost sexual excitement. Once she puts the money in her pocket, there is no going back. The change that comes over her is as permanent as it is mysterious. Every step she takes away from domesticity and honest work seems both inexplicable and inevitable.

276   *Jennifer Doyle*

The money Drouet puts into her hand merely seals a deal which had long been in the works.

Characters like Carrie bridge the sexual and the economic and seem to allegorize a modernization of both realms. When Berger uses the phrase "the realism of the prostitute," he refers to the way that the figure of the prostitute appears in modern art as a stand-in for "the real." A few feminists have made note of the strength of this theme: Griselda Pollock touches on it when she asks "Why [is modernism so frequently] installed upon the territory of a commodified female body?" (Pollock, 1988). In her study of realism in painting, Linda Nochlin also observes that figures of prostitution were a privileged subject. She speculates that "the overwhelming attention accorded by both writers and artists to a social category [that of the prostitute or demimondaine] previously neglected or treated with less than seriousness" was not only "consistent with the Realist concern to get at the truth" but may have been realism's defining preoccupation (Nochlin, 1971).

In criticism, the observation of the link between the prostitute and modernity is almost *de rigeur*, as if pointing out the simple preponderance of figures of prostitution in modern art is all the critic need do—as if the connection between the prostitute and modernity were obvious (see Berger, 1977; Nochlin, 1971; Pollock, 1988).[1] As is the case with Berger, Pollock, and Nochlin, the prostitute is invoked in an attempt to identify the specific concerns of modernism and realism, but with little reflection on what this association between prostitution and art means, where it comes from, or what its legacy might be.

Two scholars have ventured into this terrain. Sander Gilman has periodically explored the connections between ideologies of racial and sexual difference in medical, legal, and artistic representations of the prostitute (see Gilman, 1986). Charles Bernheimer's book-length study of figures of prostitution in French art and literature, *Figures of Ill Repute*, goes a long way toward giving the allegorical use of prostitutes in modern art a context and a history (Bernheimer, 1989). As useful as both of those projects are, neither pays much attention to the textual flavor of the works they explicate, nor do they explain the staying power of such narratives in critical discourse today. Where other critics have made passing comment on the prostitute's presence in so much modern art, I propose to unpack and examine the dense collection of anxieties about art that the figure of the prostitute embodies. The prostitute works in art and criticism as an index of the truth about the work of art. It is not the sociality of sex that she represents in these texts, but the aesthetic.[2]

In his preface to *The American*, Henry James tells us that, for him, "The real represents ... the things we cannot possibly not know, sooner or later, in one way or another ..." (James, 1984). From this perspective, a novel may seem most "real" when it describes, as Eric Auerbach argued, familiar things. Checking the syntax of James's sentence against his own writing, we might assume that, for James, these familiar things are the somewhat buried, closeted, haunting bits of knowledge that lurk everywhere in ordinary life—ordinary life being, however, possible only when these things are absorbed by the mental trick of disavowal. James's novels and stories describe a practice of realism as an articulation of the impossible contortions that define the ordinary bourgeois subject (see Gilman, 1986).[3]

The rhetoric of prostitution   277

I am interested in a somewhat different configuration of desire and the "real"—the puzzle that grows out of trying to imagine, characterize, or inhabit the space between people and the art objects they consume. The double negative in the assertion that "The real represents … the things we cannot possibly not know, sooner or later, in one way or another …" gets at what is most true, and yet most difficult to describe, about art. The thing that "we cannot possibly not know" about a novel, a painting, a sculpture is that they are art objects. And the thing "we cannot possibly not know" about the work of art is that is a commodity. We nevertheless habitually disavow our awareness of the economic (and libidinal) relationships which structure the enjoyment of aesthetic objects, as if our ability to take pleasure from the artwork were contingent upon maintaining this particular state of unknowing.

In the late nineteenth century the work of art was increasingly seen as at risk of becoming a kind of sex work. The autonomy of art emerges during this period against the negative example of prostitution. Figures of prostitution (figures which describe an extremely alienated relationship to their work, to their own bodies) operate for some writers and artists (Walter Benjamin, Émile Zola, Edouard Manet) as productive (if sometimes melancholic) allegories for the work of the artist. In much criticism of the period, however, figures of prostitution rise up like demons—fallen angels who warn the would-be artist by negative example.

I have developed the phrase "rhetoric of prostitution" to describe the ways that the artist, art object, and reader/spectator are represented in criticism as participating in an illicit sexual exchange.[4] In the rhetoric of prostitution, the critic routes anxiety about the category of art through discourse about women and sex, using the pejorative energies of moral panic to reinstate the virtue of aesthetic experience (as, for example, not licentious). The emphasis on sex within this rhetoric may be thought of as an effect of what Michel Foucault described as the "repressive hypothesis" which ascribes to sexuality the value of "a fundamental secret." The unveiling of this secret, or truth, promises to describe the mechanisms of, Foucault writes, "not only an economy of pleasure but an ordered system of knowledge. Thus sex gradually became [in the nineteenth century] an object of great suspicion; the general and disquieting meaning that pervades our conduct and our existence … the point of weakness where evil portends to reach us" (Foucault, 1978). The rhetoric of prostitution in criticism is an extension of this overdetermination of sex into how we understand art as a category because it inevitably suggests (if often only by suggestion) sexual deviancy as the generative source of "bad" art.

In what follows, I will examine the use of rhetoric of prostitution by authors linked to American realism (William Dean Howells, Frank Norris), and I will suggest a historical context for this fusion of discourse on art and sex: The vocabulary and mood of the moral panics about prostitution and "white slavery" animated the warnings issued in criticism against the effects of mingling art and money. A larger aim of this project is to make visible some of the bonds which tie discourse on aesthetics and discourse on sex together. In order to understand the aesthetic ideology of this period, it is crucial that we examine the appropriation

278   *Jennifer Doyle*

of a specifically *feminine* figure as an emblem for so wide a range of concerns in art. At the very least, the appropriation of figures who are commodified in this particularly sexual way marks an intersection between the history of art and literature, and the history of sexuality.

The rhetoric of prostitution: art and money

In the rhetoric of prostitution, money and sex move along a Möbius strip. We have the impression that they exist on separate planes, but as we chase these terms we find that these separate planes are one and the same. The whore or the act of prostitution appears in criticism as a condensation of not only art's relation to the market, but as a mixture of money's stigma of the abject, as well as the aura of the sexual that clings to scenes of exchange. Simmel describes the circulation of these qualities around both money and the prostitute in *The Philosophy of Money*: "We experience in the nature of money itself something of the essence of prostitution. The indifference as to its use, the lack of attachment to any individual because it is unrelated to any of them, the objectivity inherent in money as a mere means which excludes any emotional relationship—all this produces an ominous analogy between money and prostitution" (Simmel, 1990). When Simmel writes that we find "the essence of prostitution" in "the nature of money itself," it is, really, another way of saying that "money itself" has no essence, no ontological ground. He uses a set of assumptions about prostitution (as devoid of love or feeling, as non-procreative, the prostitute imagined as diseased and sterile) to describe the devastating effects of money and economic relations expressed through its circulation.

The rhetoric of prostitution manages the same anxiety in the work of art—that it has no inherent value. It works rhetorically to contain the fear; furthermore, that this lack is contagious, routing the lack at the heart of the art object through discourses which would appear to be external to aesthetics. In reaching for some standard according to which he can judge the text at hand, the critic borrows from a language of sex and desire to represent its value to the reader, or from a language of money and investment. Or he uses these same words and images to prove the artist's corruption and the art's worthlessness.[5]

In the moment when the critic tries to discern an origin of aesthetic value, discourse on money, art, and sex propel each other towards judgment. By the late nineteenth century it was utterly commonplace for writers and artists to describe themselves as prostitutes. The French painter Bougereau complained, for instance, that the market forced painters to "prostitute themselves" and that the intrusion of the market into the art world forces artists to abandon their "dedication to the 'high' goals of art" in favor of their "professional survival."[6] The novelist Frank Norris similarly asserts that the authors of popular fiction are "copyists … fakirs— They are not novelists at all, though they write novels that sell by the hundreds of thousands." He continues, "if they are content to prostitute the good name of American literature for a sliding scale of royalties—let's have done with them."[7] The erosion of the aristocratic system of patronage which underwrote the

The rhetoric of prostitution 279

production of art and literature and its replacement with a marketplace, whose rules are determined more by popular taste than by an ethical imperative (always already underwritten by class interest), set one system of value (aesthetic) against the other (economic). Or, to rephrase the problem somewhat differently, the development of an art market—in substitution for a system of explicit patronage—set into motion a nostalgic longing for a time when the artist's relationship to his work was less mediated.

The prostitute's appearance in complaints about the state of the arts exploits her significance as a living commodity. She dramatizes anxieties about the struggle to reconcile the need for an audience and for money with an aesthetic standard of value that measures artistic worth in terms of its distance from the pecuniary. In short, artists and authors feel that, like a prostitute, they were being forced to attach a price to something that is not supposed to have a price at all: Art in the case of the artist, sex in the case of the prostitute. We therefore find that prostitution, the practice of mixing things that are supposed to be kept separate (sex and money), emerges as the negative ground against which critics might assert the autonomy of art, the independence of aesthetic value from the economic, the political, or the sexual.

I would like to make clear, however, that the rhetoric of prostitution is not simply criticism which explicitly represents the artist as a prostitute or as a sexual degenerate. I use the phrase to mark a shift in discourse on art, in which the *most* important aspect in determining an artwork's aesthetic worth is the attitude it appears to take toward the act of being sold. The prostitute plays a crucial function in critical writing about the state of the arts, even when she is only a shadowy presence: Even—or especially—when she is unnamed, standing on the periphery, she serves as a powerful negative example. Take, for example, a different passage from Norris's essay. He offers the following advice to the would-be writer: "... the man must be above the work or the work is worthless, and the man better off at some other work than producing fiction. The eyes never once should wander to the gallery, but be always and with single purpose turned *inward* upon the work, testing and retesting it that it rings true" (Norris, 1986). This is the kind of prescription that I am most interested in. Norris imagines the writer as an actor on the stage, and also, implicitly, as a body up for sale. He argues, however, that the "true novelist" will maintain for his audience (and presumably for himself) a suspension of the knowledge that his "work" is a paid performance. Here, Norris advocates for a literary version of what Michael Fried described as "the primacy of absorption" (Fried, 1988). In order to produce "good" fiction, the writer must visibly perform the disavowal of the audience's presence.

In the rhetoric of prostitution, the artwork's aesthetic value is denounced for having the "wrong" relationship to the market. For Norris, the difference between a popular novelist (whom he hardly considers a novelist at all) and a good novelist is that the former appears to play to its audience's desires. The former's self-presentation is too solicitous. The latter appears absorbed in the world of his own work and ignorant of the gallery of eyes watching him. He works for the same crowd as the "fakir," but, like Bougereau's demure traditional female nude, at once

280   *Jennifer Doyle*

demure and utterly content in her nudity, Norris's writer wears his modesty as a shield.

In his 1908 essay, "The Man of Letters as a Man of Business," William Dean Howells (editor of *The Atlantic Monthly*) reveals a similar understanding of the artist's dilemma: "I do not think any man ought to live by an art ... There is an instinctive sense of this, even in the midst of the grotesque confusion of our economic being; people feel there is something profane, something impious, in taking money for a picture, or a poem, or a statue. Most of all, the artist himself feels this. He puts on a bold front with the world, to be sure, and brazens it out as a business; but he knows very well that there is something false and vulgar in it; and that the *work* which cannot be truly priced in money cannot be truly paid in money. ... The artist can say that ... unless he sells his art he cannot live ... and ... this is bitterly true. ... All the same, the sin and shame remain, and the averted eye sees them still, with its inward vision" (Howells, 1959). The artist finds himself longing to convert aesthetic value into a pecuniary form to ensure not only his own survival, but the survival of the work, as a precious object, into the future. But once the artist turns his time as an artist into money, the artwork becomes "false," "vulgar," and "profane." Note the recurrence of the posture Norris prescribes (eyes "always and with single purpose turned *inward* upon the work") in Howells's words: the "averted eye" which sees "the sin and shame" of his situation "with its inward vision." Howells acknowledges that the scene of art production is so saturated with the market that there is no sanctuary: the artist's turn "*inward* upon the work," to ensure that "it rings true," is ultimately, for Howells, an act of bad faith. "The sin and the shame remain" no matter how deep into the work of art the artist attempts to retreat. The only decent position available to him—and this is the posture that Howells suggests the artist adopt—is as a reluctant participant in the art market.

Like other writers of his generation, Howells imagines the artist as caught in the same double-bind as women—in which her worth is ultimately derived from an equation that requires she sacrifice her integrity. He writes: "It does not change the nature of the case to say that Tennyson and Longfellow and Emerson sold the poems in which they couched the most mystical messages their genius was charged to bear mankind. They submitted to the conditions which none could escape; but that does not justify the conditions, which are none the less the conditions of hucksters because they are imposed upon poets" (Howells, 1959: 299).

The sale of a novel offends Howells because literature is, in his eyes, "the most intimate ... of the arts." Writing, he continues, "cannot impart its effect through the senses or the nerves as the other arts can; it is beautiful only through the intelligence; it is the mind speaking to the mind" (299). It would be easy to mistake this as a statement in favor of writing as the most intellectual (and least impassioned) of the arts. (Extending the same assumption also tends to set up writing as the medium most suited to getting at the "real" because it is least handicapped by the appeal to the senses.) The quality of writing's abstraction, as Howells describes it here, might appear to make it a most hospitable environment for the cultivation of something like Kant's disinterested pleasure. But for Howells and others working toward

The rhetoric of prostitution   281

the end of the nineteenth century, the mind is first and last an organ inside the body. The peculiar property of writing (which never belongs exclusively to the page) is such that reading, as Howells imagines it, is a bit like an encounter with a succubus. The attraction of reading is not intellectual and abstract, but physical and dangerously hypnotic. The intimacy that Howells associates with reading, this meeting of minds, makes the act of selling one's writing all the more unsavory, as if the difference between selling your writing and selling yourself were all the narrower for the apparent lack of mediation: "[Writing] cannot awaken this emotion in one, and that in another; if it fails to express precisely the meaning of the author ... it says nothing, and is nothing. So when a poet has put his heart, much or little, into a poem, and sold it to a magazine, the scandal is greater than when a painter has sold a picture to a patron, or a sculptor has modeled a statue to order. These artists are less articulate and intimate than the poet; they are more exterior to their work; they are less personally in it; they part with less of themselves in the dicker" (299).[8] According to this model, the writer's body does not disappear in writing: It, on the contrary, is contiguous with it.

Throughout his criticism, Howells struggles with the implications of his position: To imagine the artist in this relationship to the market is to imagine his work as deeply feminized. For example, he worried that the writer's dependence on a market would inevitably lead to the feminization of American literature, not only because the act of selling one's art amounts to a kind of prostitution, but because the primary consumers for literature are women: "The man of letters must make up his mind that in the United States the fate of a book is in the hands of women. It is the women with us who have the most leisure, and they read the most books. ... If they do not always know what is good, they do know what pleases them, and it is useless to quarrel with their decisions, for there is no appeal from them" (Howells, 1959). His concern, furthermore, is not only that it is women who read, but that women read differently. Women engage in the voracious, addictive reading of popular novels and sentimental fiction, a kind of reading practice Howells sees as "the emptiest dissipation, hardly more related to thought or the wholesome exercise of the mental faculties than opium eating" (Howell, 1971: 46). Such characterizations of women's reading habits are hardly unusual.[9] Howells famously reproduced the standard debate about popular literature and women's reading habits in his novel *The Rise of Silas Lapham*, in which dinner party guests discuss a popular novel called "Tears, Idle Tears"—the title alone stands as an implicit critique of the sentimental novel (Howells, 1971).

Against something like "Tears, Idle Tears," Howells recommends a fiction "of real usefulness" to combat the denigration of writing by its association with women and money. His description of useful or productive literature is deeply structured by a reactionary need to re-assert the artist's masculinity, because at every turn the artist's work begins to look like women's work. Howells offers, as an antidote, a masculinized version of writing, in which it is imagined as a form of production, and positioned as far from the world of consumption as possible. He writes: "A man's art should be his privilege, when he has proven his fitness to exercise it, and has otherwise earned his daily bread ..." He recommends manual

282 *Jennifer Doyle*

labor to the artist, as necessary to building his strength and self-reliance.[10] This kind of work experience steels the writer against the luscious exchange between author and audience. With manual labor the artist will develop a worker's calluses—this thickening of his skin will, he imagines, work as a buffer against the overwhelming sensuality of market culture—a marvelous confusion, as if the one thing (the toughness one develops in response to regular encounters with physical difficulty) ever necessarily translates into the other (an indifference to the sensuousness of advertisement, of popular culture, of celebrity, fame, and wealth). For Howells, aesthetic integrity is synonymous with physical vigor—it is the product of the well-conditioned body.[11]

While casting the artist's work in terms of manual labor, Howells carefully explains that he does not mean the sort of work that women do. The "the art of fiction" is not related to "the rudest crafts that feed and house and clothe." This is a striking contradiction: Howells borrows from ideas of privilege, fitness, and natural right to secure the value of cultural production as a kind of production, as a kind of work, but nevertheless defines art against domestic labor. The association of women with the work of reproduction is strong enough for Howells to avoid placing his artist in relation to it, and to force Howells to look to the factory as his haven.

One might say that recommending the labor of the worker over the labor of the wife as a suitable model for the artist goes against all that Howells has argued. The laborer sells the product of his hands just as the artist does—How could such an experience function as a refuge from the pressures of the market, from the experience of money, as the thing that gives your work value? And whence the disdain for the "rudest crafts" of the home, if not from a deeply anchored disdain for the work of women: After all, what sort of work eludes the market more effectively than the continually unpaid labor of the wife? Howells's acrobatic negotiation of the interface of art and work brings the following problem to our attention: Underneath narratives about "good" and "bad" relations to the literary market are deeply gendered narratives about the value of women's work.

Implicit in Howells's concern with the seduction of the artist by the romance of money is the equation of an artist's integrity with a woman's virtue.[12] The rhetoric of prostitution holds out the possibility of a pure, innocent relation to art as an ideal which one must work toward. The commodification of the art object is represented as, at best, a regrettable process, a necessary evil which the artist must somehow transcend. The rhetoric of prostitution is a post-lapsarian lament— restoring authenticity to aesthetic experience by decrying its loss. As such, it is a distinctly modern (and bourgeois) jeremiad. The value of a work of art is, within this model, supposed to be intrinsic—it is supposed to transcend popular taste into a realm of classic, timeless, universal value.[13] A balance of formal harmony and ethical purpose is supposed to be the source for an aesthetic value which precedes any price one might attach to a work of art. The prostitute offers herself as the embodiment of all of the things drained from the work of art—sexual interest, money, and the public's demand that its desires be met at any cost to the people whose time and labor are invested in the objects they consume.

The rhetoric of prostitution: sex and money

When a critic describes an artist as engaging in a form of prostitution, and asserts this in a lament about the decline of culture, he draws the pejorative energy of his rhetoric from a pathology of prostitution in order to negotiate the question of what art is and is not, and of what art ought to do.[14] Thus when the French naturalist writers, the Goncourt brothers, for instance, deride popular novels as "spicy little works, memoirs of street-walkers, bedroom confessions, erotic smuttiness, scandals that hitch up their skirts in pictures in bookshop windows" they not only align the writing of sensation novel with prostitution, they confuse the sensation novel itself with a prostitute—as if to pick up such a book is to answer to a whore's solicitous display of her body.[15] Such confusions of figures of speech—in which a book becomes a picture, which becomes a woman's body—indicate how overdetermined the figure of the prostitute is. Without missing a beat, she can be symptom and then disease, agent and then victim.

These kinds of assumptions about the whore's sexuality underwrite Simmel's discussion of prostitution in *The Philosophy of Money*. He offers the following insight into the modern public's discomfort with prostitution: In selling sex, the prostitute interferes with the social negotiation of the difference between "personal value," or the degree to which each person is seen as a unique individual, and monetary value, which erases all difference by rendering all things fungible. The bourgeoisie, in Simmel's argument, is disturbed by prostitution because of the sex industry's reversion to a pre-capitalist, pre-modern economy which did not place a premium on the individual at all, and could therefore, for instance, practice slavery. Prostitution exposes the worst elements of a money economy because in prostitution both parties disregard the enlightenment imperative "never to use human beings as a mere means." The "mutual degradation" of the sex-for-cash exchange grows, for Simmel, not only from the debasement of the sex act (in the disassociation of sex from the expression of love or the reproduction of the family), but from the shameful insight it brings to all relations of exchange—the whore exposes as an empty promise the prohibition against treating people as things. The prostitute "degrades" both the sanctity of a woman's sex and the value of each individual subject by asserting that a woman's virtue is worth less than the money she might earn by selling it.

We might take this to mean that the figure of the prostitute is useful for launching a critique of the hypocrisy of the enlightenment imperative not to "use human beings as a mere means." But, for Simmel and other social theorists of this era (like, for instance, Thorstein Veblen), the ability for the figure of the prostitute to throw the difference between personal and economic value into such extreme relief is based as much on assumptions about women's relationship to sex as it is on an ideology that manages the subject's relationship to money. Simmel extracts a moral imperative against prostitution—as the practice which is the *most* exploitative (more exploitative than, for instance, child-labor)—from naturalized assumptions about the difference between men and women. He writes: "the purely sexual act that is at issue in prostitution employs only a minimum of the man's ego

284   *Jennifer Doyle*

but a maximum of the woman's" (Simmel, 1990: 378–9). Simmel's discussion of prostitution is in fact deeply informed by an understanding of the woman who sells herself as an always already corrupted subject. He writes that the "prostitute has to endure a terrible void and lack of satisfaction in her relations with men," hence "the frequently reported cases of lesbianism among prostitutes" (Simmel, 1990: 378–9). The whore's problem, in Simmel's view, is that she has abandoned all will—she no longer chooses who she sleeps with because, on some level, she no longer cares (and is lesbian by default).

My point here is that the rhetoric of prostitution in art rests on a misogynist discourse about women. Not only is this rhetoric misogynist. It is also tautological. The critic needs to check the loss of an epistemological ground for determining the art object's aesthetic value—a loss set into motion by the assignation of a monetary value to it. He shores up the category of art with the prostitute—a figure *against* whom he can define the work of the artist. As I've argued in my work on the reception of Andy Warhol, when a critic mobilizes a rhetoric of prostitution to evaluate an artist's work, he or she maps anxieties about prostitution "onto the vicissitudes of the category of art itself. The end product is a profoundly tautological rhetoric which backs up the assertion 'I know art when I see it' with the accusation 'I know a whore when I see one'" (Doyle, 1996: 194–5).[16]

When a critic uses the rhetoric of prostitution he applies the moral outrage that the public might be expected to have concerning the corruption of a woman, of womanhood itself, to something the public might not be very concerned with at all (the commodification of the art object). The depiction of the artist as in danger of being romanced by the promise of wealth and fame can be thought of as an extension of the seduction narratives that structured novels of the eighteenth and early nineteenth centuries. "The female was the figure, above all else," Nancy Armstrong observes, "on whom depended the outcome of the struggle among competing ideologies. For no other reason than this could Samuel Richardson's novel *Pamela* represent a landowner's assault upon the chastity of an otherwise undistinguished servant girl as a major threat to our world as well as hers" (Armstrong, 1987). In those romances, a woman's survival appears to hinge on the surrender of her virtue/virginity, which she manages to preserve by proving her self (if not her body) impervious to the base demands of her seducer. Her struggle, contrived as it is, manifests itself as an elastic coupling and uncoupling of self and body. The heroine at some point disassociates her "true worth" from the condition of her body, and in doing so discovers a power over herself that no master can claim.[17] Howells describes the same basic seduction detailed in Stephen Crane's "Maggie, Girl of the Streets," or Dreiser's novels *Sister Carrie* and *Jennie Gerhardt*. The honor at risk belongs not to a woman but an artist. Here, the starry eyed naiveté of Gerhardt or Maggie (modern versions of the irresistably virginal domestic servants of *Pamela* or *Jane Eyre*) is replaced with the writer who would prefer to keep his honor but can't.

Norris's and Howells's rhetoric taps popular sentiment of the time. Both of their essays resonate with the moral outrage circulating at that moment around urban prostitution and sensational reports of sex trafficking or, as it was then known, "white slavery." During the decades in the nineteenth century when the

The rhetoric of prostitution   285

use of the prostitute as an allegorical stand-in for the modern artist was gaining momentum, American and British reading publics were perpetually whipped into frenzies over "the social disease" of urban prostitution—which some American journalists and public health officials represented as "the greatest crime in world history."

Until the mid-nineteenth century, the sex industry was understood as a necessary evil not unlike sewers, and the only answer to the question of why women engaged in prostitution was that these women who sold themselves did so in expression of an inherited depravity. In fact, the first serious chronicler of the modern urban sex industry, the French health official Alexandre Parent-Duchâtelet, was himself an expert on the link between sewage treatment and urban hygiene. His 1836 encyclopedic study of prostitution (the first modern analysis of the subject) is an extension of this work on the treatment of waste. Prostitutes, Parent-Duchâtelet argues, are an inevitable product of the city. Their activities must be scrutinized at every level because they pose "the most dangerous [public health threat] in society," more dangerous than open sewers and improper disposal of offal (Parent-Duchâtelet, 1836).[18] Commensurate with this view on prostitution was the enforcement of, for example, in England, the Contagious Disease Acts—which generated lists of suspected prostitutes whom the state could track, and supported the forced examination of these women identified as prostitutes as a way to curb the spread of venereal diseases.

Towards the end of the nineteenth century, the figure of the inherently diseased, internally corrupt prostitute was re-invented by the British journalist W. T. Stead, when he rewrote the subject of urban prostitution as a form of "white slavery." In 1885 the London newspaper *Pall Mall Gazette* published Stead's infamous series, "The Maiden Tribute of Modern Babylon." The product of a "secret commission" (Stead's own undercover reporting) these stories describe in lurid detail the traffic in women—especially young white women and girls sold into prostitution by dissolute and abusive working class families. "Maiden Tribute" sold countless copies in England and created a huge sensation in the United States as well (Stead, 1885).[19]

"The Maiden Tribute" is not about corrupt women who turn to prostitution from a congenital flaw. For Stead and his contemporaries, "the characteristic which distinguishes the white slave traffic from immorality in general [meaning from women who engage in prostitution out of their own dissolution or lassitude] is that the women who are the victims of the traffic are *forced unwillingly* to live an immoral life" (Sims, 1910). The women in these stories are "innocent victims"— they are "snared, trapped, [and] outraged, either when under the influence of drugs or after a prolonged struggle in a locked room"—they are sold or seduced without an understanding of the nature of the exchange. These reports sparked major reform movements in England and in the US—which, interestingly, resulted in the eventual repeal of the Contagious Disease Acts, and the passing of age of consent laws, as well as the articulation of late nineteenth-century feminism. These reports were, furthermore, so sensational that they were themselves targeted by an outraged public as inflammatory in their descriptions of the sexual violation of girls as to be obscene.

286 *Jennifer Doyle*

To return to Howells's essay, by the time the editor of the *Atlantic* writes "The Man of Letters as a Man of Business" (in 1898) the congenitally diseased whore who had so preoccupied early and mid nineteenth-century city health officials and sexologists had been upstaged in the public imagination by the "white slave"—the woman abused by circumstance. This revision of the character of the prostitute makes it possible—even desirable—to look to her condition as analogous to that of the writer or painter who must make a living. Like the woman "drafted" by the white slave market, the artist that Howells describes is a reluctant whore.

Howells in particular takes the moral outrage at the subject of "white slavery" as an unquestioned assumption, and uses it to fuel the rhetorical strategy by which he announces the intrusion of money into the mise-en-scene of the artist or writer's studio as a problem. Ultimately, a misogynist discourse founded on the unquestioned assumption that a woman's value is reducible to her sexual virtue (and that the very worst thing that could possibly happen to a woman is that she would be forced to sell sex) supports the rhetoric of prostitution in art, which assumes that aesthetic value is always compromised in the exchange of money for an artist's work.

The rhetoric of prostitution is a permanent shadow of the ideology that imagines the aesthetic as removed from the concerns of the everyday, the personal, the libidinous, and the political. It works in the neighborhood of the high modernist slogan, "art for art's sake," in the attempt to ward off its antithesis ("art for profit").[20]

The rhetoric of prostitution plays out a crisis in the determination of the value of art as a crisis in economic and sexual relations between people. The exchange of money for art is allegorized by a woman who takes money for sexual favors, and soon enough we find the collapse of two different kinds of seduction in discourse about the corruption of art by things feminine, by mass culture, by the seductive appeal to a mass audience's basest desires. Figures of prostitution embody the always already overdetermined association of women and money with negativity, lack, and nothingness. The image of the prostitute, furthermore, holds together the contradictions that are inherent to the art market. The whore is, Walter Benjamin writes, "commodity and seller in one" (cited in Buck-Morss, 1988: 186). In the prostitute, "both moments [of production and consumption] remain visible" in contrast with the display of the object for sale, in which "every trace of [the] wage labor who produced the commodity is extinguished" (Buck-Morss, 1988: 184–5).

For William Dean Howells—or, more fairly, for the traditions of aesthetic judgment in American criticism that he now represents—aesthetic value is derived from the transcendence of processes of objectification. The category of "art" is, however, only recognizable against the negative ground of the market, personified as the sexually debased woman. The fantasy of the art object that exists independently from economic relations is itself a product of that market.

Notes

1 See also Buchloh (1989). In that essay Buchloh compares the effect of Warhol's Marilyn Monroe portraits on audiences with that of *Olympia*. He writes: "By responding to

The rhetoric of prostitution 287

paintings such as [Jasper] Johns's *Flag on Orange Field, II*, 1958 with his emblematic *Gold Marilyn Monroe*, 1962, Warhol made Johns's work seem to be safely entrenched in a zone of unchallenged high-art hegemony. By contrast, his own new mass-cultural iconography of consumption and *the portraits of collective scopic prostitution* looked suddenly more specific, more concretely American than the American flag itself, perhaps in the way that Manet's *Olympia* had appeared more concretely Parisian to the French bourgeois in 1863 than Eugène Delacroix's *Liberté*." This double-comparison (which feels right) is connected by the phrase "collective scopic prostitution," which Buchloh does not explain. In many ways, my own project is an extended meditation on Buchloh's term.

2 This is also to say that although a number of artists ground their major works in portraits of women who sell themselves (in one way or another), if we find them performing some form of ideology critique, it is not usually a critique of the organization of sex or gender. There are, of course, nineteenth-century novels about women who "sell themselves" which do make some intervention in sex politics: Harriet Jacob's *Incidents in the Life of a Slave Girl* manages to launch a critique of sex/gender exploitation in slavery, while also raising serious questions about the sex/gender/race exploitation embedded in abolitionist rhetoric. Her novel is almost never placed in a genealogical relationship with either realism or modernism. In England, Elizabeth Gaskell's realist novel *Ruth* uses a story about a "fallen woman" to make the exploitation of women within homosocial exchanges visible. These are, however, exceptions which prove the rule—that high modernism and the ethos of a generative male creativity is frequently installed, as Griselda Pollock once put it, on the "commodified female body"—resulting in a near inverse relation between the popularity of male artists representing women as sexual subjects in art (think: Picasso, Gaugin), and the admission of women as active participants in the art world.

3 See, for example, Eve Kosofsky Sedgwick (1990).

4 In developing the term, I settled on the word "rhetoric" (rather than discourse) as a more precise name for a critical turn, a strategy of argument, particular to the description of the difference between "good" and "bad" art. The term "discourse of prostitution" has, furthermore, been used to refer to discourse about prostitutes and sex-for-money exchanges. The rhetoric of prostitution in criticism is *shaped* by discourse about prostitution—and my discussion of the former will require some explication of the latter. The rhetoric of prostitution is not, however, explicitly concerned with prostitutes or the sex industry. I borrow my understanding of the discursive shape of "moral panic" from Simon Watney's (1987) discussion of theories of moral panic. There he glosses several takes on moral panic theory from within gender studies—most notably from Gayle Rubin and Jeffrey Weeks. Watney distinguishes his work on the phobic rhetoric surrounding AIDS by asserting that, in general, moral panic theory describes nearly "*all* conflicts in the public domain where scapegoating takes place" and therefore seems an inadequate framework for addressing "the overall ideological policing of sexuality."

5 I trace the characteristics of this practice in some detail in my survey of the reception of Andy Warhol's work (Doyle, 1996).

6 See Robert Jensen's gloss of the impact of market tastes on the choices Bougereau made as a painter. (Jensen, 1994).

7 Norris is referring to the boom in the production of historical novels modeled after Sir Walter Scott. See Norris (1986).

8 Also interesting in the passage is Howells's counterintuitive dismissal of the intimacy of painting and sculpting. The intimacy of writing is related to the immateriality of writing—in that it is not localizable to a single art object. The apparent "exteriority" of the plastic arts, however, is, in other settings, what makes painting and sculpting so problematic in the inevitability of their appeal to the senses. The modern

288 *Jennifer Doyle*

    painter's struggle would be to, as Frank Stella once put it, make art that "resists interest."

9 See, for example, Janice Radway's (1986) survey of the rhetorical equation of reading with other modes of consumption.

10 See Mark Seltzer (1992) in which he contextualizes the works of Jack London and Stephen Crane with national anxiety about the masculinity of the bourgeois man and of the factory worker.

11 Dreiser more than Howells examined his own hopes for the curative powers of "hard work" in his autobiographies *An Amateur Laborer* and *The Genius*. Dreiser described his bout with neurasthenia as the experience of being broken open to the world: "It seemed as if my mind had been laid bare as if by a scalpel to the mysteries of the universe, and that I was compelled to suffer, blood-raw, the agonies of its weight." Earning an "honest living" offered at best a limited refuge for Dreiser. His attempts in this area were pitiful at best.

12 See two texts on the connection between the rise of the novel and fascination with the nature of women's bodies and subjectivity: Armstrong (1987) and Gallagher (1994).

13 For the definitive perspective on modern articulations of aesthetic value, see Hernnstein-Smith (1988).

14 In the criminalization, regulation, and policing of prostitution a common theme emerges: The intervention of the state in the sex industry to criminalize or legalize prostitution has historically served to prevent women from asserting economic autonomy through their bodies. See Pheterson (1996), McClintock (1993), and Delacoste and Alexander (1987).

15 Quotes by Huyssen in *After the Great Divide*, p. 50.

16 For an analysis of legal discourse on prostitution, see McClintock (1992).

17 This is the same kind of disassociation which makes thinkable the possibility that a woman could be sold into prostitution, and yet remain innocent.

18 Charles Bernheimer discusses Parent-Duchâtelet's interest in prostitution and the abject at length in *Figures of Ill Repute: Representing Prostitution in Nineteenth-Century France* (1989).

19 In both countries, readers raised serious questions about the difference between its "undercover" reporting and simple pornography. Competing London journalists described the sensational detail of Stead's reports as "the vilest parcel of obscenity." British politicians also demanded that "Maiden Tribute" be labeled as an obscenity even as throngs demonstrated in Hyde Park against the abuse of young women's virtue. The "Maiden Tribute" spawned a series of lawsuits and charges of obscenity and fraud— many insisted the story inappropriately capitalized on the sensationalism of its subject, and several of the participants in the exchange of women described by the story charged Stead himself (who bought virgins from parents undercover) with fraud and engaging in prostitution. The controversy sparked by Stead's report led to the passage of age-of-consent laws in the UK—raising the age of consent to 16 (from 13) for girls, and, interestingly, forbidding consensual sex between men. Age of consent laws were raised in several states in the US in response to the public outrage provoked by Stead's report (Terrot, 1959).

20 The model of authorship which emerges at this moment ties the artist and his work more and more tightly together. In a meditation on modernity and the art world, the feminist artist and critic Mary Kelly (1996) writes that the category of "art," and the artist (and, we might add, literature and the author), are products of bourgeois models of self-possession: "... the work of art, filtered through the institutions and discourses that determine its specific conditions of existence, produces artistic authorship in the fundamental form of the bourgeois subject: creative, autonomous, self-possessed. In a sense there is no 'alternative' to that passage; for the very moment that the work of art enters into circulation, it is sanctioned by law as the property of a creative subject

The rhetoric of prostitution   289

(but not to enter into such a contract would be to forfeit even the possibility that the artistic text ... could indeed interrogate [art as such])." In other words, an artwork that challenges the link between self and expression, or the way that a work belongs to its author, is often not recognizable (at least not at first) as "art."

References

Armstrong, Nancy. 1987. *Desire and Domestic Fiction: A Political History of the Novel* (New York: Oxford University Press).

Berger, John. 1977. *Ways of Seeing* (New York: Penguin Books).

Bernheimer, Charles. 1989. *Figures of Ill Repute: Representing Prostitution in Nineteenth-Century France* (Cambridge, Massachusetts: Harvard University Press).

Buck-Morss, Susan. 1989. *The Dialectics of Seeing: Walter Benjamin and the Arcades Project* (Cambridge, Massachusetts: the MIT Press).

Buchloh, Benjamin. 1989. "Andy Warhol's One-Dimensional Art," in *Andy Warhol: A Retrospective*, Kynaston McShine, ed. (New York: Museum of Modern Art).

Delacoste, Frédérique, and Piscilla Alexander. 1987. *Sex Work: Writings by Women In the Sex Industry* (Pittsburgh: Cleis Press).

Doyle, Jennifer. 1996. "Tricks of the Trade: Pop Art/Pop Sex," in *Pop Out: Queer Warhol*, Jennifer Doyle, Jonathan Flatley, and José Muñoz, eds. (Durham, North Carolina: Duke University Press), pp. 191–209.

Dreiser, Theodore. 1991. *Sister Carrie* (New York: Oxford University Press).

Foucault, Michel. 1978. *The History of Sexuality Volume I: An Introduction* (New York: Vintage Press).

Fried, Michel. 1988. *Absorption and Theatricality: Painting and Beholder in the Age of Diderot* (Chicago: University of Chicago Press).

Gallagher, Catherine. 1994. *Nobody's Story: The Vanishing Acts of Women Writers in the Market Place, 1670–1820* (Berkeley: University of California Press).

Gilman, Sander. 1986. "Black Bodies, White Bodies: Toward an Iconography of Female Sexuality in Late Nineteenth-Century Art, Medicine, and Literature," in *Race, Writing, and Difference*, Henry Louis Gates, ed. (Chicago: University of Chicago Press) pp. 223–61.

Hernnstein-Smith, Barbara. 1988. *Contingencies of Value* (Cambridge, Massachusetts: Harvard University Press).

Howells, William Dean. 1959. "The Man of Letters as a Man of Business," in *Criticism and Fiction*, Carla Marburg Kirk and Rudolf Kirk, eds. (New York: New York University Press).

Howells, William Dean. 1971. *The Rise of Silas Lapham* (New York: Bantham).

James, Henry. 1984. *The Art of the Novel* (Boston: Northeastern University Press).

Jensen, Robert. 1994. *The Marketing of Modernism in Fin-de-Siècle Europe* (Princeton: Princeton University Press).

Kelly, Mary. 1996. "Re-Viewing Modernism," *Imaging Desire* (Cambridge, Massachusetts: The M.I.T. Press), pp. 80–106.

McClintock, Anne. 1992. "Screwing the System: Sex Work, Race, and the Law," in *Feminism and Postmodernism*, a special issue of *Boundary 2*. Margaret Ferguson and Jennifer Wicke, eds. (Durham: Duke University Press).

McClintock, Anne. (Ed.). 1993. *Social Text 37*, Special Issue on the Sex Trade (Winter).

Nochlin, Linda. 1971. *Realism* (New York: Penguin Books).

290 *Jennifer Doyle*

Norris, Frank. 1986. "The True Reward of the Novelist," in *Frank Norris: Novels and Essays* (New York: Library of America): 1147–51.

Parent-Duchâtelet, Alexandre. 1836. *De la prostitution dans la ville de Paris*, 2 vols. (Paris, Baillière).

Pheterson, Gail. 1996. *The Prostitution Prism* (Amsterdam: Amsterdam University Press).

Pollock, Griselda. 1988. "Screening the Seventies: Sexuality and Representation," in *Vision and Difference* (New York: Routledge).

Radway, Janice. 1986. "Reading is Not Eating: Mass Produced Literature and the Theoretical, Methodological and Political Consequences of a Metaphor," in *Book Research Quarterly* 2: pp. 7–29.

Sedgwick, Eve Kosofsky. 1990. "The Beast in the Closet," in *The Epistemology of the Closet* (Berkeley: University of California Press).

Seltzer, Mark. 1992. "The Love-Master," in *Bodies and Machines*, (New York: Routledge).

Simmel, Georg. 1990. *The Philosophy of Money*, Tom Bottomore and David Frisby trans. (New York: Routledge).

Sims, Edwin W. 1910. "Introduction," in Ernest A. Bell, *Fighting the Traffic in Young Girls or War on the White Slave Trade* (Chicago: Ball), pp. 13–17.

Stead, W. T. 1885. *Maiden Tribute of Modern Babylon (The Report of the Pall Mall Gazette's Secret Commission)* (London: Pall Mall Gazette).

Terrot, Charles. 1959. *The Maiden Tribute: A Study of the White Slave Traffic of the Nineteenth Century* (London: Frederick Muller Limited).

Watney, Simon. 1987. *Policing Desire: Pornography, AIDS, and the Media* (Minneapolis: University of Minnesota Press): pp. 38–57.

14 A heap of worthless fragments

The nineteenth-century literary revaluation of the classical statue

Yota Batsaki

By the beginning of the nineteenth century, the anthropomorphic, free-standing classical statue had been raised to the pinnacle of aesthetic and cultural value. As the heyday of archeological discovery, this period saw a significant increase in the circulation of authentic Greek sculpture, while the growth of tourism to Italy and Greece, and the multiplication of casts, engravings, and photographs, made the antique statue accessible to a growing number of nineteenth-century travelers and writers. At the same time, early modern art theory found its chief representatives in Johann Joachim Winckelmann, Gotthold Ephraim Lessing, and G. W. F. Hegel, who formulated a hierarchical and evaluative system of the arts that rendered Greek sculpture a synecdoche for classical excellence. Due to this privileged aesthetic and cultural character, acquisition of ancient works and collections became the object of considerable international competition among the English, French, and Bavarian sovereigns.[1] A rare 1813 Sèvres vase depicts Napoleon's Parisian parade of his antique spoils from the Vatican as a Roman triumph, with the statues in the role of war captives (Figure 1). The parade exemplifies the sculptural canon constructed by Winckelmann and his followers: the Apollo Belvedere, the Medici Venus, and of course the Laocoön all are present. The contrast of the gleaming nudes to the clothed and animated figures of the soldiers and bystanders, the simultaneously elevated and subdued position of the statues, and the overtones of display and defeat suggested by the procession all reflect the complex hold of the classical statue on the nineteenth-century imagination.

The vase is a rare visual manifestation of a trope that appears with uncanny insistence in several nineteenth-century literary texts. The implied capture of the Vatican collection, soon to be reversed following Napoleon's fall from power, mirrors the surprisingly contested and precarious status of the statue in literature of the period. Surprisingly, because although since the eighteenth century the classical statue had been set up as a privileged object of disinterested aesthetic contemplation, nineteenth-century texts repeatedly place it in competition with other kinds of value, economic, religious, sexual, and moral. In this competition the statue's own value is shown to be contingent, multiple, and unstable. Understanding the way in which classical sculpture was theorized by earlier

Figure 1 Etruscan-shaped vase. Antoine Béranger (1785–1867), "Entry into Paris of the artworks destined for the Napoleon Museum." 1813. Sèvres, National Museum of Ceramics. Photo RMN/© Christian Jean/Jacques L'hoir.

critics will shed light on the statue's role in the representational economy of literary modernity: its *economimesis*, to use Jacques Derrida's coinage for the interrelation between a particular political economy and a representational mode (Derrida, 1981). Engaging with three nineteenth-century texts, Prosper Mérimée's "The Venus of Ille" (1837), Nathaniel Hawthorne's *The Marble Faun* (1860), and Henry James' "The Last of the Valerii" (1874), this paper develops a model for reading the classical statue as a literary and economic trope.

The work of Winckelmann, Lessing, and Hegel shaped the way in which classical sculpture was – and still is to an extent – received and evaluated. Winckelmann's early *Thoughts on the Imitation of Greek Works* (1755) somewhat paradoxically presented classical art as an unsurpassable aesthetic ideal, yet also as a model for imitation by the modern artist. His seminal *History of Ancient Art* (1764) is perhaps the first work of aesthetics to offer a periodization of artistic styles along the lines of "archaic," "classical," and "late" or "decadent."

A heap of worthless fragments 293

The classical statue is, for Winckelmann, the supreme artwork; self-sufficient in its "noble simplicity and quiet grandeur," devoid of extremes of emotion, like the finest spring water is devoid of taste, its ideal beauty is founded in the absence of individuality. In his *Thoughts on Imitation* Winckelmann tries to place Greek sculpture in its historical context, albeit a highly fanciful one, and celebrates it as the product of a culture free from political oppression and bodily inhibitions. Subsequent commentators have seen in Winckelmann's idealization a longing for "shameless and childlike" sensuousness and wholeness, untainted by postlapsarian, post-Christian guilt (Pater, 1948). This trope of childhood will assume a different cast as it mutates into the savage and the primitive.

In contrast to Winckelmann's seamless comparison of various artistic media, Lessing's *Laocoön* (1769) emphasized instead the limits and limitations of the "sister arts." Differences in medium posed material constraints that entailed a different representational decorum: in the famous *Laocoön* example, Virgil's literary creation may cry out in pain, but the sculptor's figure should only emit a noble sigh. Lessing is working in the tradition of the *paragone* or competition among the arts, and his comparison of the visual (or spatial) and the verbal (or temporal) reveals an underlying evaluative and hierarchical scheme that privileges poetry over painting and sculpture. Sculpture should restrict itself to the "pregnant moment" rather than the climax of an action, as it lacks the ability to represent progression. Lessing's division of the arts argues that the more material art forms are paradoxically more wedded to, and constrained by, abstraction. Poetry as an art of temporal succession is better equipped to represent relationships of cause and effect, motive, transformation, and therefore interiority; it is a more self-conscious art, and one better suited to modernity.

Hegel's lectures on aesthetics, given between 1820 and 1830 and reconstructed from his own and students' notes, apply the concept of periodization not only to artistic styles, in the manner of Winckelmann, but to the historical progression of the arts themselves. Hegel distinguishes between "symbolic," "classical," and "romantic" periods and singles out a particular art as the best expression of each. The "symbolic" is associated with oriental art and especially architecture; sculpture is, of course, "the art proper to the classical ideal" (Hegel, 1999, 708); while "romantic" art is associated with poetry and music—its defining characteristics are Christianity, individuality, the separation of spirit from the material, and modernity (Barasch, 1990, 216). Hegel agrees with Winckelmann's placement of Greek sculpture at the pinnacle of aesthetic achievement, yet he assigns it to an earlier phase of the historical development of the spirit. The ideal human figure represents a perfect fusion of body and spirit, but remains abstract; it cannot strive to contain an individual "soul" that might give itself away in facial expression or, as we will see, in the eye: "The work of sculpture has no inwardness which would manifest itself explicitly as this ideal glance" (Hegel, 1999, 732). Hegel's consignment of sculpture to a pre-Christian, preindividual phase of art history also makes it an anachronistic mode unsuitable for representing modernity. It continues Lessing's extraction of interiority from sculpture and will find its

294   *Yota Batsaki*

more extreme expression in Baudelaire's statement, in his 1846 Salon review, that sculpture, wedded to the material and being all too close to nature, is the art form that appeals to "the peasant, the savage, or the primitive man" (Barasch, 1990, 216). Lack of inwardness or interiority, a self-sufficiency void of emotion, and an earlier position in the development of the arts and, by implication, of the human spirit are the characteristics ascribed to classical sculpture; it is thus given the somewhat paradoxical status of an ideal that has been overcome or left behind.

Given that in the modern *paragone* sculpture has been thus subtly demoted, its recurrent adoption by the narrative art associated with modernity signals a strategic intent. The theoretical framework constructed by Winckelmann, Lessing, and Hegel enables sculpture to function discursively as both ideal and anachronism. Indeed, literary representations of classical sculpture in the century that follows show the astonishing cultural currency of these theories and their influence in shaping the reception and use of the statue. They offer an evaluative and hierarchical system that makes the statue particularly useful to the literary text's *economimesis*, as shorthand for the political and moral economy that lurks behind the text's representational strategies. In addition to the theoretical definitions that will emerge again and again in literary discourse, there are consistent patterns that accompany the statue's textual discovery and function, and enable us to construct a model for reading it as a trope.

The three texts that follow all enact the discovery of a classical statue of the highest period. Yet, against the Kantian postulate of aesthetic disinterestedness, the found statue immediately enters into relations of evaluation and exchange. It is simultaneously pronounced incomparable, used as a measure of value, and measured against other kinds of value. Indeed, situations where the statue is prized for its use value (religious, sexual, etc.), as opposed to its exchange value, are judged vaguely criminal and lead to its destruction or disposal. Two other characteristics persist: the found statue is often initially pronounced a Roman copy, but is always ultimately hailed as a Greek original. This move reenacts Winckelmann's shift of attention from Roman to Greek antiquity, as well as the novel availability of Greek originals for comparison with Roman or Hellenistic copies in the period. Concomitantly, a human being hailing from Italy or Greece is pronounced to resemble a statue and simultaneously endowed with dangerously atavistic characteristics (pagan, savage, or primitive).[2] In the repeated transition from Roman copy to Greek original, the statue exemplifies the trope of infinite regress. However, nostalgia is ultimately less crucial to the narrative politics than the overcoming of the past, represented both by the classical statue and the atavistic human being. Moreover, the conflict between past and modern values triggered by the discovery of the statue is consistently moralized: the past is associated with pagan, sensuous, unself conscious, and at times criminal pleasure; the modern is associated with moral rigor, responsibility, toil, and self-consciousness. In contrast to the endurance of the classical statue as aesthetic object, the function of the literary statue is to be ultimately and unsympathetically dismissed by modernity.

The statue in bronze: "there's enough of it to make hundreds of coins"

Unlike the majority of nineteenth-century literary treatments of the statue, Mérimée's "The Venus of Ille" is situated outside Italy, and features a statue made of bronze rather than marble. These very differences, however, highlight several economic aspects of the literary statue. Contrary to the aesthetic autonomy formulated by Kant and anticipated by Winckelmann—"Beauty is an autonomous value, its cause cannot be found outside itself" (Barasch, 1990, 217)—the bronze of Mérimée's Venus accentuates the statue's convertibility and exchangeability. The narrator, with his antiquarian interests and metropolitan condescension, is ironically modeled on Mérimée's own experience as Inspector General of Historical Monuments. He arrives at Ille, in the Pyrenees, soon after a magnificent bronze Venus, wearing a strangely malicious expression, is discovered under an olive tree by the village mayor, Peyrehorade. Unearthed on the eve of Peyrehorade's son's wedding to a rich and beautiful girl, the statue signals a moment of intense erotic financial, and later cultural exchange, a crux of things and people changing hands.

Peyrehorade's workers are uprooting an olive tree killed by the frost, when "a black hand appeared, which looked like the hand of a dead man coming out of the ground" (Mérimée, 1966, 2). Peyrehorade is so excited that he digs with his own hands; upon discovering the bronze statue he reacts as if "he'd found buried treasure" (2). This treasure takes the form of "a huge black woman, more than half naked … all in copper" (2–3). A pattern of equivalences and substitutions is immediately set into motion. The bronze Venus is described in terms of monetary equivalents: not just its price on the art market, but also its material convertibility into money: "It's made of copper, and there's enough of it to make hundreds of coins. It weighs as much as a church bell" (2). (The reference to "bell metal" prefigures the statue's fate at the end of the story.) Indeed, recycling of bronze into coin or other metallic objects accounts for the scarcity of surviving antique bronzes. At times of war or need, the art object has been frequently destroyed to retrieve what is presumably most alien to its aesthetic value: the material from which it is made. Nevertheless, the possible translation into copper coins also evokes a less antagonistic relationship between statues and coins. Ancient coins have contributed significantly to the history of sculpture as they often feature miniature reproductions of ancient masterpieces, especially works mentioned in ancient texts (Pliny, Pausanias, and Strabo), but subsequently lost or surviving only in later copies (Imhoof-Blumer, 1964, 3–5). Moreover, the term "money" derives from the temple of Juno Moneta (*monere*, to warn, to remind) on the Capitoline where the first Roman mint was established.

The literary statue consistently exceeds the spectator's expectations by proving to belong to the highest period, identified by Winckelmann as the fifth century BC: "I had expected some work of the Later Empire, and I was confronted with a masterpiece of the most perfect period of sculpture" (10). Yet the ascription is somewhat confused by the fact that the statue is called "a Roman."

296   *Yota Batsaki*

Moreover, despite its superb workmanship, it does not display the "calm and severe beauty" that Winckelmann identifies as the high Greek style. Instead, "[d]isdain, irony, cruelty could be read [*se lisaient*] in that face which was, notwithstanding, of incredible beauty" Krieger (1992). The Venus's expression is troubling not only because it is malicious, but also because as a Greek work it should not have any expression at all. According to Winckelmann, "[e]xpression ... changes the features of the face, and the posture, and consequently alters those forms which constitute beauty" (Winckelmann, 1856, 113). For Hegel, expression "is only something accidental and fortuitous which sculpture must keep at arm's length"; it individualizes the work in an accidental manner, thus undermining the universality of sculpture (Hegel, 1999, 735). And for Lessing, expression makes a statue unrecognizable because it destroys the formal abstraction associated with a particular deity. Thus the Venus's oblique eyes, upturned corners of the mouth, and slightly inflated nostrils all offend against the systematic description of the Greek ideal. In a sly instance of intersemiotic translation, it is only her presence in a literary text, with its recourse to the proper name, that enables her recognition. Such intersemiotic translation or *ekphrasis* mediates the uneasy relationship between the visual and the verbal. In *Laocoön*, Lessing argues that a statue should immediately convey its meaning without recourse to a servile inscription, but the Venus is literally written over: aside from the inscription on her pedestal, she also bears some cryptic words "engraved on the arm" (13). Her nasty expression irresistibly triggers the story or *istoria* full of passions that Winckelmann sought to exclude from sculpture (Barasch, 1990, 117). Lessing uses the self-same example of an enraged Venus to argue that, to the visual artist, the gods "are personified abstractions, which must always retain the same characteristics if they are to be recognized. To the poet, on the other hand, they are real acting beings who, in addition to their general character, have other qualities and feelings" (Lessing, 1984, 52).

If the Venus has too much expression, the bridegroom has too little. The narrator describes Alphonse as "lacking in expression" (5) and rigid as a herm. The sexual jealousy of the narrator, who admires the young bride, vents itself in a description of the groom as an inferior kind of statue: not the free-standing ideal work, but the utilitarian, only half-anthropomorphic herm, a marker of limits or boundaries. Alphonse's hands, "the hands of a ploughman poking out of the sleeves of dandy" (5), represent an incongruous conflation of the economic with the aesthetic, labor with leisure. A moral dimension is added to this aesthetic condemnation when Alphonse subsumes his bride's beauty to her wealth: "The best of it is she's very rich. Her aunt ... left her all her money" (16). The narrator adduces Alphonse's wedding ring as further proof of vulgarity, which once again adulterates aesthetic value by means of a financial admixture: "a large ring blazing with diamonds, and formed with two clasped hands: a most poetic conceit, I thought. It was of ancient workmanship, but I guessed that it had been retouched when the diamonds were set" (16). At a time when the restoration of sculpture had fallen out of fashion, the narrator reminds the reader that "retouching" an antique diminishes its aesthetic value. The hyper-symbolic ring enacts in its very form the function

A heap of worthless fragments   297

of bringing two hands together in marriage. Yet the ring never finds its way to the bride, waylaid as it is by the Venus's own ring finger. Instead, Alphonse gives to his bride another, simpler ring that he had received as a gift from a Parisian *grisette*. Due to this careless exchange of the rings, which presumably invites the angry Venus to the wedding bed, Alphonse ends up dead. After the unsolved murder of Alphonse the narrator learns that the statue has been melted down to make a bell.[3]

The destruction of statues incited Mérimée's own appointment as Inspector of Historical Monuments, provoked by the iconoclastic momentum of the French Revolution and its aftermath. In "The Venus of Ille," however, the effect is not one of conflict between merciless innovation and the spirit of conservation, but between Christian and pagan. Mme Peyrehorade had wanted to recycle the Venus from the beginning, in the hope of becoming the godmother of the bell. Yet this forced conversion does not exorcise the statue's evil influence: "it would seem that an evil fate pursues those who possess that piece of bronze. Since that bell began to ring in Ille, the vines have twice been frost-bitten" (32).[4] The pagan statue that brings bad luck to its Christian possessors is an old superstition; Kenneth Clark recounts the story of the inhabitants of Siena who exhumed and then disposed of a magnificent statue of Venus in enemy (Florentine) territory (Clark, 1990, 94). The association of sculpture with idolatry plays itself out here in a clash of pagan with Christian, but the provocation of the image can be transposed onto the tension between Protestant and Catholic forms of worship. The nineteenth-century American visitors to Italy that we will go on to encounter expressed reactions ranging from amusement to shock at the "idolatrous" worship of "popish" ritual (Vance, 1989, 3–17). In the subsequent treatment of the statue by James and Hawthorne, Christian is to Pagan as Protestant to Catholic.

The statue in marble: "a perfect fragment"

Mérimée's bronze Venus highlights the convertibility of the statue within a textual economy of equivalence and exchange. The marble statue lends itself less easily to material recycling but is more amenable to recomposition. Despite its fragility, indeed because of it, the statue is somehow more whole in fragmentation, which attests to its antiquity and therefore added value. In addition, like the vacuum created by aesthetic disinterestedness and immediately filled by an array of competing economic and sexual interests, the missing part invites substitution and re-appropriation. Before the nineteenth century, it was usually restored in suggestive ways: in the case of the Medici Venus the arms were arranged in a modest gesture that both covered and drew attention to her nakedness. In the nineteenth century, the broken hand is free to become an autonomous artistic object. This detachability of the statue's hand is one way of marking the difference between a statue and a human being. (In Mérimée's story, Venus announces her malicious intentions by breaking the leg of one of the workers involved in her discovery, Jean Coll; the leg never heals properly.) Yet, if physical harm to a human being can never be adequately compensated, resulting in a net loss, in a

298   *Yota Batsaki*

statue mutilation or fragmentation can actually increase its value and multiply it into several art objects.[5]

The American narrator of James' "The Last of the Valerii" is a painter and the godfather of an American heiress who has recently married the Italian Count Valerio, heir to an illustrious but impoverished line. The bride, Martha, is enthusiastic about Valerio's ancestry and undertakes costly excavations at Valerio's villa; next to her lover's smile, "it was the rusty complexion of his patrimonial marbles that she most prized" (James, 1962, 91). Martha conceives of archeological excavation as money-laundering: "she was not without a fancy that this liberal process would help to disinfect her Yankee dollars of the impertinent odor of trade" (98). The Count is initially unwilling to disturb the statues' repose, but he soon becomes so excited that the narrator wonders "whether he had an eye to the past or to the future—to the beauty of possible Minervas and Apollos or to their market value" (99). The excavations produce first the hand, and then the rest of a magnificent marble Juno.

As with the Venus of Ille, the found statue is irresistibly assigned the highest possible aesthetic value by being ascribed to the high Greek period. "The workmanship was of the rarest finish; and though perhaps there was a sort of vaguely modern attempt at character in her expression, she was wrought, as a whole, in the large and simple manner of the great Greek period" (101). But James does not give his Juno enough expression to make her, like Mérimée's Venus, a character in the story. Instead, with James' Juno we move from the statue as potential subject to the statue as object. On the level of narrative relations, we move from the supernatural to the psychological.

The statue's discovery is announced by a proliferation and substitution of hands: in particular, of a severed marble hand ominously placed in the hollow of a human arm. The explorer in charge of the excavations in Valerio's villa appears "cap *in hand*…," in a playful reversal of the *handicap* caused by the Venus of Ille. "Resting *in the hollow of his arm* was an earth-stained fragment of marble. In answer to my questioning glance he *held it up to me*, and I saw it was *a woman's shapely hand*" (100, my emphases). As a human hand it would be worthless, but in marble it is "a perfect fragment," just as the Juno is "of perfect human proportions" (100). The severed hand resurfaces in the Count's dream, where the Juno "laid her marble hand" (101) on his. The statue's affective hold on the Count is announced by means of this gesture, which reenacts in reverse Alphonse's placing of the ring on the Venus's hand. From that moment the Juno competes with Valerio's American wife for his attention; the Count "gave no response as his wife caressingly clasped his arm" (102). The Count's seduction is also evinced in his attitude to the severed hand left lying on the grass like a serpent. "Such a fragment as that would bring more *scudi* that most of them had ever looked at" (105), but Valerio refuses to restrict his appreciation to its monetary value: "He values it so much that he himself purloined it … the less we say about it the better." The act is judged vaguely criminal and ethically unsavory by the American narrator, and the Italian responsible for the excavations hints that the Count has moved from sexual frustration to religious sublimation: "When a

A heap of worthless fragments 299

beautiful woman is in stone, all he can do is to look at her. And what does he do with that precious hand? He keeps it in a silver box; he has made a relic of it!" (105). The Count's worship of the Juno is represented by the narrator as an atavistic characteristic indicative of the pagan tendencies previously identified in Valerio by his Catholic confessor.

Even more disturbing than the accusation of paganism in a Christian age, however, is the rearrangement of the affective hierarchies and allegiances caused by the superior appeal of the statue. As the pinnacle of anthropomorphic beauty, it marks a division between human and non-human, and triggers competition: "That he should admire a marble goddess was no reason for despising mankind; yet he really seemed to be making invidious comparisons between us" (106). The American narrator and his niece are wealthy, but they cannot rival the sculptural magnificence of the Juno. Even more ominously, the statue's rise in the affective hierarchy seems to threaten human beings with marmorization: "Her beauty be blasted! Can you tell me what has become of the Contessa's? To rival the Juno, she's turning to marble herself!" (106).

By bringing matters to a point between the impoverished but aristocratic Italian and his upstart but wealthy American wife, the statue enables a polarization of the narrative politics along the lines of past and present. Filtered through the perspective of the American narrator, this opposition is not only understood in economic terms, but is also endowed with moral significance. As long as the Count is devoted to his bride, the narrator tolerates his distance from the "modern work-a-day world" (96), but after the Juno's discovery he becomes in the narrator's imagination "a dark efflorescence of the evil germs which history had implanted in his line. No wonder he was foredoomed to be cruel. Was not cruelty a tradition in his race, and crime an example? ... back through all the darkness of history it seemed to stretch, *losing every feeblest claim on my sympathies* as it went" (107, my emphasis). Not only does Valerio's connection to the past confirm his moral liability, it also enables his imaginary transposition beyond the sympathy of his contemporaries. His cultural and moral makeup is understood as radically alien, and potentially criminal. His midnight sacrifice to the Juno then comes as something of a relief. The Protestant narrator is on familiar territory again, able to pathologize the Count's idolatry: "The Count took the form of a precious psychological study ... with an unwholesome mental twist which should be smoothed away as speedily as possible" (112–114).

The supposed cure is represented through the narrator's appropriation of the trope of the hand; satisfied that "[the Count] had a conscience we could take hold of," the narrator prides himself on his psychological *tact*; he decides to "lay a healing hand" after having "touch[ed] the source of [the Count's] trouble" (111). He proceeds to reassure his goddaughter in language that links modernity with financial metaphors of redemption as payment: "The modern man is shut out in the darkness with his incomparable wife. ... He pays you the compliment of believing you an inconvertible modern. He has crossed the Acheron, but he has left you behind, as a pledge to the present. We'll bring him back to redeem it" (117). Valerio will be obliged to return to the present to discharge his financial responsibilities,

300 *Yota Batsaki*

yet her godfather's rhetoric does not appear to reassure Martha. In its mixture of religious and financial motifs, pagan and Christian elements, the metaphor is even spatially confusing since, if Valerio has crossed the Acheron on a trip to Hades, his modern potential is also shut out with Martha. With the fate of both in suspense, Martha's pragmatic solution is to reassign the Juno to Hades instead: "we must smother her beauty in the dreadful earth" (120). The "hand of improvement" (93) was allowed to touch Valerio's villa only lightly, but the statue is accorded a more heavy-handed treatment. Yet the Juno's purloined hand remains as an uncanny residue, shut up in the dark recesses of an Italian cabinet, while the Count "never became a thoroughly modern man" (122). His relationship both to the classical statue and to the classical past, invested with moral and economic meaning, serves to place the Count, albeit in the ironic narrative politics of James' story, outside the sphere of modernity.

"And what does he do with that precious hand?" A digression

There are specific reasons for the obsessive recurrence of the trope of the hand in nineteenth-century statue narratives. The actual discovery of the statue is usually announced by a hand, which, like the disembodied hand in the margins of old books, calls attention to the statue's entry into a system of exchange; to the ethical and economic questions surrounding its handling; and to the affective problems created by the imperative to relate to the statue as representation of a human being.

The hand is also a locus for gauging authenticity. The extremities of statues were identified by Winckelmann as tell-tale sites of modern intervention, and he criticized the tendency to supply missing hands holding on to naïve symbols (like the apple of Paris) in an effort to make statues more readable. But fundamental changes in the attitude to restoration during the late eighteenth and early nineteenth centuries proclaimed the untouchability of antique masterpieces. Before this time, a well-restored statue was generally deemed superior to a mutilated one; indeed, "antique" statues were often manufactured by *bricolage* of various found body parts.[6] The arrival in England of the Parthenon sculptures was a significant turning point. The sculptor Canova was called upon to restore them, but decided that "it would be sacrilege in him or any man to presume to touch them with a chisel" (Rothenberg, 1977, 185). This shift in attitude toward restoration had important financial implications for English collections acquired at great cost and expensively restored. Hegel interprets the depreciation of the Venus Medici and the Apollo Belvedere as the result of progress in art history and refinement of modern taste: "At the time of Lessing and Winckelmann boundless admiration was paid to these statues as the supreme ideals of art; nowadays, when we have come to know works deeper in expression and more vital and more mature in form, these have become depressed in value, and they are ascribed to a later period" (Hegel, 1999, 766).

We have also seen that the statue's hand can become detached and prized as a precious artwork on its own. Sculpted hands were a popular and highly symbolic product of the nineteenth-century workshop: the clasped hands of the Brownings

A heap of worthless fragments 301

wrought by Harriet Hosmer are mentioned in *The Marble Faun*. Valerio keeps the Juno's hand in a casket; the sculptor Kenyon in *The Marble Faun* keeps a marble copy of Hilda's hand, modeled from memory, unbeknownst to its proprietor. Not only are hands valuable works of art in themselves; they are also an acceptable euphemism for sexual desire and a way of legitimizing this desire through the exchange of hands and the wearing of rings in marriage. The hand, we may assume, is the one body part that is acceptable as fetish.

Finally, the trope of the hand may also suggest a moment of self-reflexivity on the part of the text at its purloining the modes of meaning of the *plastic* (OED "formed, moulded") arts. This borrowing is mutual, and provides a nineteenth-century version of the *paragone*. American neoclassical sculptors like Hiram Powers have been dubbed "the literary sculptors," both because they often found inspiration in literary works, and because they accompanied their statues with literary glosses, frequently in justification of their nudity (Farrand, 1965). The literariness of such sculpture might be seen as a sign of its neoclassical derivativeness; a failure to succeed within the parameters—or limitations—of its own medium. In contrast, the literary texts that so often represent sculptors and their work make several sly references to the anonymous "mechanical" hands, often those of Italian stonecutters, behind the ideal productions of the "literary sculptors." When, in *The Marble Faun*, Miriam visits Kenyon's studio, the elusive narrator draws attention to the copyists that are responsible for the immortalization of the sculptor's idea in marble:

> The sculptor has but to present these men with a plaster-cast of his design … and, in due time, without the necessity of his touching the work with his own finger, he will see before him the statue that is to make him renowned. His creative power has wrought it with a word. In no other art, surely, does genius find such effective instruments, and so happily relieve itself of the drudgery of actual performance; doing wonderfully nice things, by the hands of other people, when, it may be suspected, they could not always be done by the sculptor's own. … They are not his work, but that of some nameless machine in human shape.
>
> Hawthorne (1990, 115).

The "literary sculptor" is deemed to create verbally ("with a word") rather than mechanically ("by the hands of other people"), but the ironic coloring of the passage ("surely," "relieve itself of the drudgery") implies that this is not a process of genius but rather of mechanical reproduction. The denigration of sculpture as a "mechanical" art goes back to Leonardo's comments on the difference between painting and sculpture, in a famous Renaissance statement on the *paragone* (Farago, 1991). Although the literary texts repeatedly "purloin" the works of sculpture, as Hawthorne admits in the preface to *The Marble Faun*, the writer resents the appropriation of literary media by the sculptor. And although Hawthorne borrows from his compatriot sculptors in Rome, his novel continues a tradition of texts that, at least since Lessing's *Laocoön*, subtly uphold the superior

302 *Yota Batsaki*

resources of literary narrative to describe human action and motivation, and by implication the modernity of literature vis-à-vis the art of sculpture.

The statue in the flesh: "past human sympathy"

In *The Marble Faun* we encounter a full-blown case study of the implications of the sculptural and literary preoccupation with the art object as a human likeness. The narrative use of the statue enables an exploration of the very boundaries of the human not only in the aesthetic, but also in the moral, realm. The handsome Italian characters in James' "The Last of the Valerii" and Hawthorne's *The Marble Faun* (as well as Tito in George Eliot's near-contemporary *Romola*—another Italian who turns out to be Greek) are compared to statues. Unlike the discovered statues of Greek goddesses, however, the statues resembling Italians are ascribed to the period of excessive refinement and mannerism that marks the decay of Greek art. Count Valerio is explicitly likened to a portrait "statue of the Decadence" (Hawthorne, 1990, 93), while Donatello resembles the faun of Praxiteles, a sculptor whose work is already veering into the "beautiful" phase characterized by "a morbid delicacy of execution" (Clark, 1990, 45). The fluid and sensual contours of the faun, "somewhat voluptuously developed," contain all that is pleasing, but exclude the serene and heroic qualities of the highest Greek ideal. Indeed, for Hegel the faun is not so much a hybrid of the human and the animal, as an injection of humanity into the divine principles embodied in sculpture: "there is introduced into their sphere what remains excluded from the lofty ideal figures of the gods, namely human need, delight in life, sensuous enjoyment, satisfaction of desire" (Hegel, 1999, 760).

The novel opens in the Capitol's sculpture gallery, where three artists—two Americans and a European of unknown origin—are debating Donatello's resemblance to the faun. Their gentle bantering makes the young Italian distinctly uncomfortable. The faun's nudity may be part of the problem. While the Greek nude, according to Clark, expresses the "Greek idea of wholeness; physical beauty is one with strength, grace, gentleness, and benevolence" (Clark, 1990, 46), in Hawthorne this prelapsarian delight in the naked body constitutes a seductive but outdated foil to the modern, "fallen," and self-conscious world. More importantly, resemblance to a statue, especially to the problematic hybrid that is a faun, undermines a character's full humanity. Donatello is said to be descended from a race "not altogether human" and "never quite restrainable within the trammels of social law" (Hawthorne, 1990, 233); as a result, he displays "deficiencies ... in the development of the higher portion of man's nature" (235). Similarly, James' narrator doubts whether Valerio has "anything that could properly be termed a soul" and muses on "the strange ineffaceability of race characteristics" (James, 1962, 111) that may taint the Count with the cruelty of his ancestors. Donatello senses the threat posed to his humanity: when asked to prove that his ears are not the furry, pointed ears of a faun, he anxiously entreats his friends "to take the tips of [his] ears for granted" (Hawthorne, 1990, 12).

The danger in the conflation of human being with statue stems from the identification of sculpture in late-Enlightenment and Romantic art criticism with

A heap of worthless fragments 303

an outdated version of the human: the child, primitive, or savage. Association with the statue thus stumbles upon the particular position and limitations of sculpture in the historical progression of the arts. Lessing argues that only poetry, not sculpture, can depict interiority, and Hegel puts it more convolutedly: "into this mould [of sculpture] the spirit is poured, yet without coming out of this externality to appear in its withdrawal into itself as something inward" (Hegel, 1999, 705). Donatello is represented by two different statues that depict his states before and after his "fall": the statue of the faun, suspended between humanity and animality, and an unfinished portrait bust in Kenyon's studio. The bust depicts a frozen moment in Donatello's struggle for self-consciousness, suspended in "the riddle of the Soul's growth, taking its first impulse amid remorse and pain, and struggling through the incrustations of the senses" (381). More subtly than the transformation of the Venus of Ille into a Christian bell, or the reburial of the Juno worshipped by Valerio, the enfolding of Donatello in a narrative of fall and redemption is yet another attempt to Christianize the classical statue. The bust of Donatello, representing a transitional rather than "pregnant" moment in his individuation, is, therefore, attempting to capture the impossible in sculpture. For sculpture "lacks the point where the person appears as person, i.e. the concentrated expression of soul as soul" (Hegel, 1999, 706).

This limitation does not involve only the mechanics of sculptural representation, but also fundamental questions of sculptural decorum. Descriptions of the privileged eighteenth-century example or problem of sculptural propriety, the Laocoön group, are paradigmatic of the art historical limitations placed on sculptural representation. Lessing's discussion of the Laocoön expresses discomfort in the arrested representation of extreme states and a horror of the orifice in sculpture. The spectator's interest in such painfully prolonged extremes cannot be adequately maintained for any length of time, and such representations thus result in a failure of the aesthetic experience. In order to fit the theory, Laocoön must be interpreted to emit a noble sigh, not an anguished cry. In the *Marble Faun*, the sculptor Kenyon voices a similar objection to the Dying Gladiator, who refuses either to sink down in death or to experience relief; Kenyon compares the statue's effect to that of a piece of marble thrown into the air and suspended there in defiance of the laws of gravity (16).

The extent to which the decorous limitations on the representational possibilities of sculpture throw into relief a certain distancing or outright rejection of the human can be seen on one occasion where the void created by real human beings of the past was filled in to create sculpture. Giuseppe Fiorelli, during his excavation of Pompeii in 1863–1875, developed a technique for casting the void left by the inhabitants killed by the volcano's eruption. The plastercast gallery of these empty human spaces constitutes a veritable anticanon to the postures prescribed by Lessing and Hegel as appropriate to sculptural decorum: "crouching and squatting are not to be found on the soil of freedom because they indicate something subordinate, dependent, and slavish"; (see Hegel, 1999, 739). An anticanon, at least, as far as art theory is concerned; though the crouching or sinking attitudes of the plaster-casts do evoke actual works of sculpture like the Crouching Venus or the Dying Gaul (or gladiator) (Figures 2 and 3).

Figure 2 Fiorelli plastercast, Pompeii. By permission of the Italian Ministry for Cultural Heritage and Activities, Archeological Surintendance of Pompeii.

Literature exploits the classical statue's putative status as supreme object of disinterested aesthetic value (antique, unique, anthropomorphic) in order to stage a modern contest of values: aesthetic, economic, sexual. But if sculpture is, in addition, unable to embody interiority, suffering, and the soul, the likening of a person to a statue also determines negatively the exchange of affect. The resemblance of a human being to a statue is thus employed by the literary text to effect the strategic withdrawal of a specific kind of human interest.[7] The ethics of this process, which we might call "marmorization" or "statufication," can be located in the nature of the interest that the reader is encouraged to invest in the statue or person. This ethical reading of "statufication" draws on two models of the role of interest in aesthetic and moral judgments: Kant's postulate of aesthetic disinterestedness, and Adam Smith's postulate of the imaginative investment of self-interest in another as the fundamental mechanism of sympathy.

Figure 3 The Dying Gaul, Capitoline Museum, Rome. Photographic Archive of the Capitoline Museum.

A person resembling a statue invites a primarily aesthetic appreciation, whose ethical implications can be pursued further. Kant's *Critique of Judgment* is sparse in its treatment of actual works of art, preferring to draw its examples of aesthetic judgment from the natural world. To the developmental model of art history proposed by Winckelmann and Lessing, leading up to a "high" period and then descending to decadence, Kant juxtaposes a formalist model of the aesthetic experience that pivots on the observer's disinterestedness in the aesthetic object. Kant's subtraction of personal interest from the moment of aesthetic contemplation can be related tellingly to the human being regarded as a statue. According to Kant, "the judgment of Taste is contemplative, is indifferent to the existence of the object, and merely compares the representation of the object with the feeling of pleasure or pain" (Kant, 1964, 23). By aestheticizing a person, one is no longer invested in that person's presence in the world, but remains content with their function as representation.[8]

Herein lies the ethical importance of the resemblance of a person—an Italian, a woman, etc.—to a statue. The objectified and aestheticized individual is, therefore, excluded from the exchange of human sympathy, defined by Smith as the investment of personal interest in another's predicament. In his moral as well as economic theory, Smith is using an empiricist model of the individual educated through feelings of pleasure and pain; a model with a sculptural history, of a different kind, in Étienne Bonnot de Condillac's *Treatise of Sensations* (1754). In that empiricist work, Condillac posits a "statue-man" as a developmental case

306   *Yota Batsaki*

study of a being brought to experience the world through his senses (*aistheseis*). According to Condillac's statue model, pleasure and pain are the primary stimulants of the senses; they form the rudimentary basis of the human being's interest in the world, and of self-interest in general. This empiricist association of pleasure and pain to self-interest may account for their lingering presence in the quote from Kant ("merely compares the representation of the object with the feeling of pleasure or pain"); their absence as direct sources of motivation confirms the disinterested attitude to the aesthetic object. Smith is also preoccupied with representation and comparison, but in contrasting ways. Since, for Smith, it is impossible to experience another's pain or joy directly, one must substitute, by comparison, one's own feelings: "The compassion of the spectator must arise altogether from the consideration of what he himself would feel if he was reduced to the same unhappy situation."[9] Sympathy thus depends on an exchange that brings the case home to oneself, and it is founded on an "imaginary change of situations" (19) that also involves the activation of self-interest on behalf of another.

Due proportion—decorum—is everything in this exchange. Smith notes the economic asymmetry in the exchange of sympathy: the spectator's investment always falls short of the sufferer's need. Since the demand for sympathy exceeds the supply, the person who demands sympathy must "flatten ... the sharpness of [his] natural tone, in order to reduce it to harmony and concord with the emotions of those who are about him [from] the secret consciousness that the change of situations, from which the sympathetic sentiment arises, is but imaginary" (22). Although Smith naturalizes the economic inequality of sympathy, he nevertheless also insists on the moral necessity of participating in these imaginary exchanges and argues that we should be troubled by instances of failure: "it is always disagreeable to feel that we cannot sympathize with him, and instead of being pleased with this exemption from sympathetic pain, it hurts us to find that we cannot share his uneasiness" (16). In Hawthorne a dividing line interrupts the exchange of sympathy, but what is now naturalized is the failure of sympathy, not its necessity.

If statufication serves a modern politics of exclusion, it can be brought into interesting relation with alternative ways of placing a person outside the sphere of humanity. If Donatello is tainted by animality, the European painter Miriam is tainted by moral disrespectability; the same reservations and qualifiers that applied to Donatello's relation to the human race are now employed to compromise Miriam's moral status. Several commonplace scenarios are spun around her origins: Miriam may be "the daughter and heiress of a great Jewish banker"— where the general association of the Jew with usury is intensified by the explicit allusion to banking—"an idea perhaps suggested by a rich oriental character in her face"; or perhaps the daughter of a Southern planter with "one burning drop of African blood" in her veins (22–23). Imagined as a member of a power-hungry aristocratic family, she may have entered unwillingly into a mercenary marriage that led to crime. Later she is associated with a portrait of Beatrice Cenci that evokes the specter of incest (67). The overdetermined construction of Miriam's otherness strikingly enumerates several favorite subjects of neoclassical sculpture produced by Americans in nineteenth-century Italy: American Indians, Christian women sold into Muslim slavery, black Africans, and "richly oriental" figures such as Cleopatra and Zenobia.[10]

Even before becoming murder accomplices, Miriam and Donatello are surrounded by hedging and doubts, but after the crime they are firmly placed outside the sphere of humanity. The narrative voice generalizes their predicament into a moral fact of human experience: "This perception of an infinite, shivering solitude, amid which we cannot come close enough to human beings to be warmed by them ... is one of the most forlorn results of any accident, misfortune, crime, or peculiarity of character, that puts an individual ajar with the world" (113). The predicament of the solitary individual who cannot be *warmed* by the human evokes the coldness and aloofness of the statue. The narrative voice goes on to speculate that "possibly ... the nice action of the mind is set ajar by any violent shock. ... For it is one of the chief earthly incommodities of some species of misfortune, of a great crime, that it makes the actor in the one, or the sufferer in the other, an alien in the world, by interposing a wholly unsympathetic medium betwixt himself and those whom he yearns to meet" (92). The reiterated notion of *ajarness* is useful in considering the role of the statue in the narrative politics; the statue's discovery opens a door into the past that ushers in competing values, and it also offers an oblique perspective on the normative human predicament that represents modernity. "Your very look," says Miriam to Hilda, "seems to put me beyond the limits of humankind" (208).

Exclusion from humanity also entails a prohibition of touch. After the crime Donatello and Miriam are pronounced untouchable to others as well as to each other; Hilda literally refuses to touch Miriam. The prohibition is formally pronounced by Kenyon in Perugia under the bronze statue of the Pope, whose outstretched hand seemed to bless Miriam and Donatello as they clasped hands, before Kenyon reinterprets the gesture: "Take heed; for you love one another, and yet your bond is twined with such black threads, that you must never look upon it as ... for earthly happiness! If such be your motive, believe me, friends, it were better to relinquish each other's hands, at this sad moment. There would be no holy sanction on your wedded life" (322). Whereas the statue is refused a "life" above ground by modernity, the human couple aligned with the statue is refused *futurity* in the form of sexual fulfillment and offspring.

Refusing to reconstitute the statue: "a heap of worthless fragments"

For the statue to be put together a certain amount of sympathy is required. Hawthorne's text self-consciously ironizes its appropriation of tropes surrounding the classical statue, thus partly undermining the moral polarity between past and present that it worked so hard to set up. As if to signal their awareness of the trope of statufication operative in the novel, Miriam and Donatello stage the discovery and recomposition of a statue by Kenyon. The result is ultraconventional: "It was earth-stained, as well it might be, and had a slightly

308   *Yota Batsaki*

corroded surface, but at once impressed the sculptor as a Greek production, and wonderfully delicate and beautiful" (423). The missing pieces are conveniently at hand; Kenyon locates the arms, and places them "in the manner that nature prompts, as the antique artist knew, and as all the world has seen, in the Venus de' Medici" (423). Since Winckelmann had already cast doubt on the restoration of the Venus's hands, the bad faith of the ascription of prudery to the pagan goddess infects both the narratorial and Kenyon's perspectives.

Kenyon proceeds to restore the head in a move that completes the puzzle and brings together the salient attributes of the literary statue: "The beautiful Idea at once asserted its immortality and converted that heap of forlorn fragments into a whole, as perfect to the mind, if not to the eye, as when the new marble gleamed with snowy luster. ... It was either the prototype or a better repetition of the Venus of the Tribune. ... Why were not the tidings of its discovery already noised abroad? The world was richer than yesterday, by something far more precious than gold. ... Another cabinet in the Vatican was destined to shine as lustrously as that of the Apollo Belvedere; or, if the aged Pope should resign his claim, an Emperour would woo this tender marble, and win her as proudly as an imperial bride!" (423–424). The description manages to refer to two canonical works and compresses several stock elements of the literary statue: the comparison to precious metal; the reactivation of pagan powers; ancient beauty as an addition to the world's "riches." The competition to obtain the statue is not only politicized but also sexualized, and described through metaphors of courtship and marriage. Yet this half-hearted attempt to conjure the economic, aesthetic, and erotic attraction of the statue is immediately undermined.

Kenyon quickly subordinates the marble goddess to a mortal woman; he "strove to feel at least a portion of the interest which this event would have inspired in him, a little while before. But ... by the greater strength of a human affection, the divine statue seemed to fall asunder again, and become only a heap of worthless fragments" (424). Interest in his American counterpart overcomes the interest in the aesthetic object. And this withdrawal of interest in the statue explicitly provokes fragmentation, and empties it of value: the pathetic fallacy of "forlorn fragments," with its faint promise of personification, is reduced to a dismissal. Kenyon understands the force of his own implicit comparison: "I seek for Hilda, and find a marble woman! Is the omen good or ill?" (423). This dismissal of the ancient statue, however, also reveals the impoverishment of Kenyon, as an artist and as subject capable of aesthetic—and, by implication, of moral—appreciation and distinction. As Miriam playfully though somewhat maliciously hints, Kenyon does indeed find in Hilda a woman of stone, while the sculptor is dubiously called "a man of marble" (411).

While the Juno's hand was shut away in a cabinet, Donatello is shut away in prison; yet again the process leaves a residue that may return to haunt the present. The novel's conclusion takes the time to look back nostalgically on Donatello's original presence, and to describe modernity as a lamentable process of mechanical reproduction. "The growth of a soul, which the sculptor half imagined that he had witnessed in his friend, seemed hardly worth the heavy price that it had cost. ... A creature of antique healthfulness had vanished from the earth; and, in his stead, there was only one other morbid and remorseful man, among millions that were cast in the same indistinguishable mould" (393). Modernity dismisses the classical statue, only to expend itself in a proliferation of inferior, mass-produced replicas. The economic metaphors of the text suggest that this is hardly a good bargain.

Postscript: "the terrible and desolating hand of Rome, who grasped every body and thing"[11]

The nineteenth-century text appropriates the classical statue and makes of it the center of interest, only to finally dismiss it as an aesthetic, economic, and moral anachronism. This dismissal often assumes a violently hostile form. The villagers throw stones at the Venus of Ille, James' narrator itches to break off the noses of the antique statues that distract Valerio, and his goddaughter "smothers" the Juno. In a similar mood, the narrative voice in *The Marble Faun* indulges in a fantasy of immolation that would destroy Rome and all towns older than fifty years: "All towns should be made capable of purification by fire, or of decay within each half-century. Otherwise, they become the hereditary haunts of vermin and noisomeness, besides standing apart from the possibility of such improvements as are constantly introduced into the rest of man's contrivances and accommodations" (301–302). Modernity deplores the grievous boon of "interminable ancestry" shared by antique statue, Italian, and eternal city. Lack of inheritance is instead recast as freedom from the burden of a criminal and violent past. As representatives of the present, the upright, commonsensical Americans are not a fit subject for the sculptor. According to Hawthorne, "[i]t is particularly singular that Americans should care about perpetuating themselves in this mode," which puts to the test the "very little time ... during which our lineaments are likely to be of interest to any human being"; such a bust promises no enduring interest and is destined to be "auctioned off" by a forgetful progeny. Worse, this progeny might succumb to the irreverent impulse to mutilate the bust by "firmly taking hold of the nose between their fingers and thumb" (118–119).[12] The fantasy of mutilation of the antique is reversed into a castration anxiety: what modernity most fears may not be the terrible and desolating hand of the past, but the unsympathetic touch of the future.

Notes

1 On the first, large-scale rediscovery of ancient sculpture in the Renaissance see Barkan (1999). The Parthenon sculptures were acquired by Lord Elgin and purchased by the British Parliament in 1816; the Aegina sculptures, discovered in 1811, were bought by the Crown Prince of Bavaria; and during his conquest of Italy Napoleon temporarily transferred the Pope's collection of antique marbles to the Louvre (Haskell and Penny, 1981).
2 The trope of human resemblance to a statue appears, for example, in George Eliot's *Romola* (1863), Leopold von Sacher-Masoch's *Venus in Furs* (1870), Henry James' *Roderick Hudson* (1875), Villiers de l'Isle Adam's *L'Eve Future* (1886), and Wilhelm Jensen's *Gradiva* (1903).

310   *Yota Batsaki*

3 A bell can also be a statue, as in Melville (1987).

4 Sacher-Masoch's Venus, obliged to dress in furs, charges the modern world with hostile coldness: "Stay in your northern mists and Christian incense and leave our pagan world to rest under the lava and the rubble. ... You do not need the gods—they would freeze to death in your climate!" See (Sacher-Masoch, 1971, 145).

5 However, if a human being is defined as a body to which mutilation is an outrage, the slave is excluded. In works like Aphra Behn's *Oroonoko* (1688) and Mérimée's *Tamango* (1829), a slave is likened to an antique statue and subsequently mutilated as if he were a statue.

6 On these "antique Frankensteins" see Rothenberg (1977, 63–68, 185, 215). On the marbles' transferral to Britain see St Clair (1967).

7 Walter Pater concludes his essay "Winckelmann" (1867), a text steeped in Hegelian art theory, with the remark that sculpture as synecdoche of Greece cannot embody the modern-day interesting: "Certainly, for us of the modern world, with its conflicting claims, its entangled interests, distracted by so many sorrows, with many preoccupations, so bewildering an experience, the problem of unity with ourselves, in blitheness and repose, is far harder than it was for the Greek within the simple terms of antique life" (Pater, 1948, 122).

8 The politics of aestheticization may also account for the general absence of interest in contemporary Italian politics during the *Risorgimento* (Salomone, 1968).

9 See Adam Smith (1984). Subsequent references in the text. On the moral dimension of Smith's political economy see Emma Rothschild (2001).

10 See, for example, William Wetmore Story's *Cleopatra* (1858); Edmonia Lewis' *Death of Cleopatra* (1876), *Old Arrowmaker and His Daughter* (1866), and *Forever Free* (1867); Hiram Powers, *Greek Slave* (1846); Thomas Crawford's *Dying Indian Chief Contemplating the Progress of Civilization* (1856) from the US Senate pediment; Harriet Hosmer's *Zenobia in Chains* (mid-nineteenth century); as well as John Rogers' popular small-scale plaster groups *Is It So Nominated In the Bond?* (1880) and *Slave Auction* (1859).

11 Sophia Hawthorne, from her 1869 *Notes in England and Italy*, quoted in Vance 31(1989).

12 In contrast, Pliny complains about his contemporaries' neglect to secure their enduring representation in sculpture. "And yet, at the same time, we tapestry the walls of our galleries with old pictures, and we prize the portraits of strangers; while as to those made in honor of ourselves, we esteem them only for the value of material, for some heir to break up and melt, and so forestall the noose and slip-knot of the thief. Thus it is that we possess the portraits of no living individuals, and leave behind the pictures of our wealth, not our persons ... and these, too, people who wish to live without being known!" See (Pliny, 1857, 224). For Pliny, the measure of success is the desire of one's successors to know what one's features had been.

References

Barasch, M. 1990. *Modern Theories of Art: From Winckelmann to Baudelaire*, vol. 1. New York: New York University Press.

Barkan, L. 1999. *Unearthing the Past: Archaeology and Aesthetics in the Making of Renaissance Culture.* New Haven: Yale University Press.

Behn, A. 1688. *Oroonoko; or, the Royal Slave. A true history*. London: Will Canning.

Clark, K. 1990. *The Nude: A Study in Ideal Form*. Princeton, N.J.: Princeton University Press.

Condillac, Ètienne Bonnot de. 1754. *Traitè des sensations*, Paris: de Bure.

Derrida, J. 1981. "Economimesis," *Diacritics*, 11: 3–25.

Eliot, G. 1863. *Romola*. London: Smith, Elder & Co.

A heap of worthless fragments   311

Farago, C. J. (ed.) 1991. *Leonardo da Vinci's "Paragone."* Brill Studies in Intellectual History, vol. 25. New York: E.J. Brill.

Haskell, F. and Penny, N. 1981. *Taste and the Antique: The Lure of Classical Sculpture 1500–1900.* New Haven: Yale University Press.

Hawthorne, N. 1990. *The Marble Faun.* Harmondsworth: Penguin.

Hegel, G. W. H. 1999. *Aesthetics: Lectures on Fine Art*, vol. 2, tr. T. M. Knox. Oxford: Clarendon.

Imhoof-Blumer, F. 1964. *Ancient Coins Illustrating Lost Masterpieces of Greek Art: A Numismatic Commentary on Pausanias.* Chicago: Argonaut.

James, H. 1962. "The Last of the Valerii," in *The Complete Tales of Henry James.* Philadelphia: J. B. Lippincott. 89–122.

James, H. 1876. *Roderick Hudson.* Boston: James R. Osgood.

Jensen, W. and Freud, S. 1993. *Gradiva and Delusion and Dream in Wilhelm Jensen's Gradiva*, tr. Helen M. Downey. Los Angeles: Sun & Moon Press.

Kant, I. 1964. *The Critique of Judgement*, tr. James Meredith. Oxford: Clarendon Press.

Krieger, M. 1992. *Ekphrasis: The Illusion of the Natural Sign.* Baltimore: Johns Hopkins University Press.

Lessing, G. E. 1984. Laocoön. *An Essay on the Limits of Painting and Poetry*, tr. E. A. McCormick. Baltimore: Johns Hopkins University Press.

Melville, H. 1987. "Bell-Tower," in *The Piazza Tales and Other Prose Pieces, 1839–1860, The Writings of Herman Melville*, vol. 9, ed. Harrison Hayford. Evanston: Northwestern University Press. 174–187.

Mérimée, P. 1966. "The Venus of Ille" in *The Venus of Ille and Other Stories*, tr. Jean Kimber. London: Oxford University Press.

Mérimée, P. 1967. *Tamango.* In *Romans et Nouvelles.* vol. 1. Ed. M. Paturier. Paris: Garnier. 285–307.

Pater, W. 1948. "Winckelmann," in *Selected Works*, ed. R. Aldington. New York: Duell.

Pliny the Elder. 1857. *Natural History*, vol. 6, tr. John Bostock and H. T. Riley. London: Herny G. Bohn. 32: 2.

Rothenberg, J. 1977. *Descensus ad terram: The Acquisition and Reception of the Elgin Marbles.* New York: Garland.

Rothschild, E. 2001. *Economic Sentiments: Adam Smith, Condorcet, and the Enlightenment.* Cambridge, Mass: Harvard University Press.

Salomone, W. 1968. "The Nineteenth-Century Discovery of Italy: An Essay in American Cultural History," *The American Historical Review*, 73(5): 1359–1391.

Sacher Masoch, L. 1971. *Venus in Furs*, in Deleuze, G. *Sacher-Masoch: An Interpretation*, tr. Jean McNeil. London: Faber and Faber. 117–229.

Shell, M. 1978. *The Economy of Literature.* Baltimore: Johns Hopkins University Press.

Smith, A. 1984. *The Theory of Moral Sentiments.* Indianapolis: Liberty Fund.

St Clair, W. 1967. *Lord Elgin and the Marbles.* London: Oxford University Press.

Thorp, M. F. 1965. *Literary Sculptors.* Durham: Duke University Press.

Vance, W. 1989. *America's Rome*, vol. 2. New Haven: Yale University Press.

Villiers de l'Isle Adam, J. 1886. *L' Eve Future.* Paris: M. de Brunhoff.

Winckelmann, J. J. 1856. *The History of Ancient Art*, vol. 2, tr. Henry Lodge. Boston: Little, Brown, and Co.

Winckelmann, J. J. 1987. *Reflections on the Imitation of Greek Works in Painting and Sculpture*, tr. Elfriede Heyer and Roger C. Norton. La Salle, Ill.: Open Court.

Woodmansee, M. and Osteen, M. (ed.) 1999. *The New Economic Criticism. Studies at the Intersection of Literature and Economics.* London: Routledge.

Index

abstract art 45–7; multiplicity of meanings 47; representation of production 45–7

Adams, Robert 242–3

aesthetic and market value 1708–871, 95–111; analysis 97; assessment of excellence 98–101; color 103; comparison between aesthetic and economic ranking 102–3; de Piles 98–101; form 103; imitation 104; ingenuity 104; intrinsic and economic values 95–8; intrinsic value of paintings 96; measuring performance on numerical scale 96–7; pleasure in consumption 109; pleasure-yielding properties of subjects 101; rarity 103; Richardson 98–101; Smith on pleasure-giving properties of goods and services 101–5; Smithian movement 97–8; variety 103; weighting 96; William Stanley Jevons 105–8

Arnold, Matthew 160–161

Biology 161–165

Biotechnology 165–169

Bloomsbury Group 137–51; aesthetics, and 137–51; arts education 148–9; characteristics of works of art 140; "classicists", and 145–6; criticisms 149; E. M. Forster 141–2; economics 137–51; ideal art market 144; imaginative life 139; impact of 150; lack of reliable information 148; members 137; modern manufacturing corporations, and 146; "path dependency" 139; peculiarities of markets, and 147–8; "plutocrats", and 145–6; policy directions 146–7; potential market failures 143–4; private demand 147; products of imaginative life 144; rent seeking in art markets 149; Roger Fry 137–8; "snobbists", and 145; success of market system for arts 143; Thorstein Veblen, and 138–9; Tolstoy, and 139, 140; utilitarian stimuli, and 141; valuation in imaginative life 139–40; valuation in the arts 142–3; vision of perfect art market 145

Boggs, J.S.G. 212–213

Brener, Alexsandr 203

capitalism *see also* fleeing from capitalism; anti-capitalist texts 176–7; art and money 278–82; capitalist modernism 34; consumer citizen 166–7; Kunst = Kapital 214; modern market 5; resistance to 5; rise of 4

Career Education movement 126–7

Chelsea, Manhattan 220–49; art gallery areas 1978–2008, 221; Barbara Gladstone 229; commercialism/the market 224–34; concentration of commercial galleries 220; content of art displayed in 237–41; data 224; debate over the commercial market and its dominance 220–4; free art show 246; Gagosian Gallery 225, 226; galleries versus museums 236; gallery system 224; gallery system as opportunity for artist 236–7; growth of galleries 1997–2008, 221; High Line railroad 231; international galleries 224–7; Manhattan real estate estate market 227–34; Mary Ellen Mark 243–6; Matthew Marks Gallery 225; multiplicities of small galleries 237; non-commercial forces 234–46; persistence of small galleries 237; proposed zoning 232; real estate market, and 22; Robert Adams 242–3; *Silva Morosa* 240; sociology of new art

Index 313

gallery scene 220–49; Sotto 228; subject matter of art shows 239; "the best free show in town" 234–6; trends in direct asking rents and new construction completions 227; triumph of commercial gallery system 222; what audience see in works 241–2; zoning 230

Clark, T.J.: Impressionism, on 38–9; Malevich, on 50

classical statues 291–311; "a heap of worthless fragments" 307–9; bronze 295–7; danger in conflation with human being 302–3; decorum 303; destruction of 296–7; due proportion 306; economimesis 292; ethical importance of resemblance 305–6; evaluation 292–3; exclusion from humanity 307; Hegel on 293–4; hostility to 309; Lessing on 293; "literary sculptor" 301; marble 297–300; marmorization 304; nineteenth-century literary revaluation 291–311; *paragone* 301; "past human sympathy" 302–7; refusing to reconstitute 307–9; restoration 297–8, 307–9; statue in the flesh 302–7; statufication 304; *The Dying Gaul* 305; trope of the hand 300–2; Winckelmann on 292–3

classicists: Bloomsbury Group, and 145–6

collectivism 197

cosmetology 124–5; aesthetics of 130

culture: cultural turn 75; economic practice, and 67, 71–2; economy, relationship with 215; meaning 73–7; modern usage 74; objects of economic discourse, and 76; social-scientific use of term 74; sociological discourse 75; traditional usage 74

de Piles 98–101

Denki, Maywa 214

Derrida, Jacques: imaginary currencies, on 206–7

Duchamp, Marcel: *Tzank Check* 44–5

economic practice 65–81; cultural factors 71–2; culture, and 67; mathematical logic 65–6; neoclassical paradigm 69–70; presentational features 65; supplement 77–8; value, and 68

education: arts 148–9; vocational *see* vocational education

eToy 213–14

eugenics 167

Fascism 164, 185

flatness 38–41; Impressionism, and 38–9; representation of not representing, and 38–41

fleeing from capitalism 172–200; abolition of art 175–6; American black music 200; anti-capitalist texts 176–7; "aristocracy" 196; artistic practice 185; *Buddenbrooks* 191; codes 181; collectivism 197; commodification 193–4; "connection" 184–5; counterdiscourse 183–4; displacement 189; Dutch Jews 188–9; enoblement 195; established religion 194–5; fascism 185; Impressionists 184; Italian Futurism 178; Marxist view 186–7; modernism 177–8; moral economy 199; Nazis 187; new economic criticism 181–2; politics of representation 182; postmodernism 189; psychoanalytic literature 182; realistic films 192–3; representation through act 174–5; rural ethic and image 178–9; social realism 175; socialism 190; *The Grapes of Wrath* 187; "trace" 186; unfair representation of bourgeoisie 173–4; Van Gogh 180; Vermeer 179–80; "virtue ethicists" 198

Forster, E. M. 141–2

Freud 161–4

Fry, Roger 137–8

Fryer, John 210

Futurism 178

Gagosian Gallery 225, 226

gallery system 224; international galleries 224–7; opportunity for artist, as 236–7; triumph of commercial 222

gift theory 43–5

Gladstone, Barbara 229

globalization 7–8

Hauser, Arnold: capitalist modernism, on 34

Hegel: classical statues, on 293–4

Hicks, John R.: *Graph* 42

High Line railroad 231

Holzer, Jenny: *Protect Me From What I Want* 37–8

Howells, William Dean 280–2

314 *Index*

imaginary currencies 203–19; affirmative type 208–9; appropriation art 207–8; *Capital Affair* 209–10; contemporary art on the market 203–19; dematerialization of art object 204; eToy 213–14; from criticism to complicity 207–9; *Invite yourself* 210; J.S.G. Boggs 212–13; Jacques Derrida on 206–7; John Fryer 210; Kunst = Kapital 214; Louise Lawler 207; market deployed as provocation 210–11; market is medium 209–11; Matthieu Laurette 213; Maywa Denki 214; modern art as structural critique on capitalism 204; non-commodifiable work 207; playful economy 211–14; postmodern economy, and 215; readings 206; relationship between economy and culture 215; revered imperialism 211; *Tzank Check* 212; variety of knowledge produced by 206
imperialism 7–8, 211
impressionism 38–9; flatness, and 38–9

James, Henry 161
Jevons, William Stanley 105–8; experiment no.2 107; experimental data 105–6; graph of diminishing intensity of effect 107; initial axiom 108; law of utility 106; physical "necessities" 108; turn away from pleasures of the mind 105–8; utility 106–8;

Klamer, Arjo: modernism, on 43

Laurette, Matthieu 213
Lawler, Louise 207
lessing: classical statues, on 293
lives of cultural goods 250–72; conversation as heuristic 250–2; cultural economic perspective 265–6; cultural goods 260–2; different valuations possible 263–5; economic, social and cultural values 257–60; economists versus culturalists 252–3; evaluation 256–7; goods in general 260–2; mode of financing matters 263–5; moral ownership 253–5; realization of values 262–3; valorization 256–7; valuation 256–7; values 253–5;
Lombardi, Mark; global economy, on 205
Lyotard, Jean-Francois 6–7

Malevich, Kazimir 29–30; *Black Square* 49–50; economic valkue of art, and

41–2; hybridization 30; polemicist, as 30; *Red Square* 29–30; supremacism 29–30
manufacturing corporations: Bloomsbury Group, and 146
Mark, Mary Ellen 243–6
market democracies 152–71; anxiety, and 156; autonomy and independence 154–8; biology and the masses 161–5; biotechnology and the consumer-citizen 165–9; civilization, and 152–71; competitive market individualism 154; consumer-citizen 166–7; cost of female autonomy 157; cultural super-ego 161–3; enchainment 165–6; eugenics 167; Fascism, and 164; fear of mass society 152; female autonomy, and 153–4; fraternal autonomy 159–60; Freikorps 167–9; Freud, and 161–4; Henry James 161; individualism, and 152–71; leisured class 160; "male fantasies" 168; Marxism 163; Masterman, and 152–3; Matthew Arnold 160–1; national character, and 152–71; New Woman writing 155–6; Philistinism, resistance to 159; politicizing the psychological 164–5; psychological individualism 158–61; psychological poverty of groups 161; self-regulating individual 156; service industries 166; sexual selection, and 154–5; stereotypes of individualism 169; Victoria Cross 157–8
marmorization 304
Marxism 82–4, 163, 186–7
mathematical logic: economic practice, and 65–6
Matthew Marks Gallery 225
Mattick, Paul: sublime economy, on 2
McCloskey, Deirdre 172–200
Merz collages 48–9
modern art and economics 30–2; ersatz economics 31
modernism 43, 177–8
Morris, William 33–4; competitive commerce, on 33–4
Mosquera, Gerardo; non-figurative art, as 40
Mouffe, Chantal 88
music: American black 200

Nazis 187; Freikorps 167–9
new woman writing 155–6

Index 315

Newman, Barnett: *Vir Heroicus Sublimis* 45
non-representational art: recognition of 39–40

Parergon 66–79
philistinism 159
pleasure: consumption, in 109; pleasure-yielding properties of subjects 101
plutocrats: Bloomsbury Group, and 145–6
political economy of art: Ruskin on 31
Pompeii: Fiorelli plastercast 304
postmodernism 189; postmodern economy 215
Poussin 112
production of knowledge 204–7; imaginary economics, and 204–7
psychoanalytic literature 182

rarity: market value, and 103
reading modern art for economic value 41–3
religion: capitalism, and 194–5
rent seeking: art markets, in 149
rhetoric of prostitution 275–90; art and money 278–82; artists, and 278–9; determination of value of art 286; discourse on art 279–80; hypocrisy of enlightenment imperative 283; meaning 277; misogynist discourse about women 284; moral outrage 284; moral panic, and 277; necessary evil, as 285; popular sentiment, and 284–5; sex and money 283–6; sexuality 283; strength of theme 276; *The Maiden Tribute* 285; white slavery 286; William Dean Howells 280–2
Roger de Piles 112–23; art philosophy, and 116; *Balance des Peintres* 112–23; estimation results 118; genius, on 112; interpretation of coefficients 117; length of entry in Turner's *Dictionary of Art* 119–20; number of paintings sold at auction 1977–93, 119–20; Poussin, and 112; prices as indicators of values 116; quantitative methods 117; regression analysis 113; score of property 114; score on property 114; scores attributed by 119–20; statistical quality of adjustments 117; value, and 113
Ruskin, John 31, 32–3; political economy of art 31–3

Schwitters, Kurt 47–9; 7.Slagen 47; bridging representational gap of economic value 48–9; Merz collages 48–9; *The Big-I Painting* 48–9
service industries 166
Shapiro, Mayer: oppositional Marxist voice, as 40–1
Shell, Marc: economic context of works of art, on 41
slavery: white 286
Smith, Adam 2–3; pleasure-giving properties of goods and services, on 101–5
Smithian movement 97–8
snobbists 145
socialism 190
state censorship 126
sublime economy: Adam Smith 2–3; "aesthetics of value" 8–9; analysis of cultural productions 9; economics meets aesthetics 12–14; encounters between economics and cultural theories 9–10; "everywhereness" of economics 8–9; *Germinal* 5; globalization, and 7–8; hallucinatory splendor 7; imperialism, and 7–8; intersection of art and economics 1–25; Jean-Francois Lyotard 6–7; Kent 4–5; modern market capitalism 3–4; moral economies and the romance of money 15–16; "name your price" 14–15; Paul Mattick on 2; resistance to capitalism 5; rise of capitalism, and 4; sublime intercourse 12–14; tokens of eccentricity 10–12; value and the aesthetic representation of economy 10–12; Wonder 2–3

Tolstoy 139, 140
tracing the economic 29–64; modern art's construction of economic value 29–64

Universitizing 134
use, value, aesthetics 82–91; Chantal Mouffe 88; destabilization 90; expansion of the textuality of value 85; exploitation 89; gambling with difference 82–91; marginality 86–7; Marxist analysis 82–4; sector becoming endlessly variable 89; speculating with value 82–91; strategic essentialism 87; value, meaning 83
utilitarian stimuli 141
utility and desire 36–8; problematic representation of 36–8

316 *Index*

Van Gogh 180

valuation: arts, in 142–3; imaginative life, in 139–40; intrinsic value of paintings 96; lives of cultural goods, and 256–7

Veblen, Thorstein 138–9

Vermeer 179–180

vocational education 124–36; aesthetic value and integrity 131; aesthetics, and 124–36; aesthetics of cosmetology 130; aesthetics of self 132; allegorical interpretation 125; beauty becoming a class process 135; best students 131; Career Education movement 126–7; career advice and motivation 127–8; collective political action, and 134–5; consumption of work, and 128; cosmetology 124–5; cultural images of beauty, and 128–9; consumption as work 129; current labor conditions 131–2; economics, and 124–36; educational self-formation 133–4; higher education, and 134; individual motivations and desires 129–30; job mobility 128; self-management 130; state censorship 126; state funding of the arts 126; state instituted examination 132–3; tracking system 126; universitizing 134

Wallis, Henry: *The Stonebreaker* 32–3

Willink, Carel: *The Bank of Philadelphia* 35–6

Winckelmann: classical statues, on 292–3

Zoning 230